A
LINGUISTIC
INTRODUCTION
TO THE
HISTORY OF
ENGLISH

Map of Great Britain

A
LINGUISTIC
INTRODUCTION
TO THE
HISTORY OF
ENGLISH

Morton W. Bloomfield

HARVARD UNIVERSITY

&

Leonard Newmark

UNIVERSITY OF CALIFORNIA AT SAN DIEGO

New York   Alfred A. Knopf

1 9 6 5

L. C. catalog card number: 63-13125

THIS IS A BORZOI BOOK,
PUBLISHED BY ALFRED A. KNOPF, INC.

PUBLISHED 1963
REPRINTED 1964, 1965[2]

FOR

Caroline and Ruth

Preface

Throughout history, but especially in this century, we have seen again and again particular "facts" and particular scientific systems once held to be certain and unquestionable severely cast into doubt by new scientific developments, but the unflinching integrity of the scientific mode of thinking has been consistently maintained. Even recently, within the decade 1950–60 the basic organization of the linguistic description of English has been subverted three times by three major publications: once by C. C. Fries, *The Structure of English,* again by George L. Trager and Henry Lee Smith, Jr., *Outline of English Structure,* and most recently by Noam Chomsky, *Syntactic Structures.* In each case, it was the honest searching into the principles of linguistics as a science that created the changes in our thinking, much more than discovery of previously unknown linguistic phenomena.

Recognizing, then, the evanescence of particular orthodoxies in linguistics, we have avoided in this book any one orthodox position in respect to the linguistic description of the history of English, and have assumed different positions in presenting different chapters of the history of English. We have also resisted the attractive temptation merely to summarize our apparently certain present knowledge of the history of the English language, although we recognize the great value that such a summary could have. Nor have we felt ourselves competent to revise and synthesize older works in order to bring their great contribution to our subject up to date, important as such a synthesis would be. Of course, we have learned and borrowed much of what we include here from both present and past scholars; but we have had to sacrifice the quantity of factual material in the interests of our main qualitative goal: to introduce the student to sophisticated linguistic attitudes towards English and its history. If we have succeeded in attaining our goal, the student will learn from this book something both of the history of our language and of a variety of linguistic approaches to that history.

An implicit, basic contention of this book is that the richness of our object of study—language—can be fully exploited only by a catholicity of approaches to it. All points of view in linguistic study, whether historical or contemporary, diachronic or synchronic, semantic or grammatical, comparative or descriptive, have important values to add to our understanding of the nature of language. Arguments for the exclusive right of various particular points of view to be deemed "scientific linguistics" have been persuasive at various times in the past, and have served the function of exhilarating their adherents and driving them harder in the service of their cause; but as humans and humanists we must take a broader historical, more tolerant view of the goals of scientific endeavor, and must grant all serious attempts to understand the how's and what's and even the why's of language the honorific title of linguistics.

In the specifically historical chapters of this book, after short summaries of the striking general characteristics of a period of English and a summary of historical changes which led to that period, we have selected single aspects to be treated. In all, we have tried to emphasize the significance of terms used in studying language rather than the particular results of that study. Although in the field of linguistics it is often difficult to separate textbook from original investigation, this book is fundamentally a textbook.

Being neither a reference history of English nor an introduction to general linguistics, but rather a specific application of several types of linguistic study to the history of English, this book cannot hope to take the place of the valuable works that already exist (for a number of these, see the Bibliography on pp. 369-375). It is intended to serve as an *introduction* to the study of English linguistics, not as a substitute for that study itself. We have thus been more interested in exposing the student to ways of looking at the language than in presenting him with the results that previous studies have achieved. Such a goal will invite the criticism of teachers, who will miss the treatment in depth of particular subjects in English linguistics, and there are several places in the book (e.g., our treatment of the Great Vowel Shift or our presentation of ENE grammar) where our decision not to examine various alternative lines of thought may lend support to the imputation of one-sidedness. We must in such cases take the blame for having decided to sacrifice normal scholarly completeness to the special pedagogical interests of our own approach.

In keeping with our pedagogical intentions, we have tried to define carefully our terms and concepts and have given considerable thought to our questions at the end of each chapter. One of the difficulties in teaching the history of English in universities is that it is aimed at students on different levels of advancement. This diversity creates difficulties in planning such a book as this. Some parts, notably the section on generative grammar in Chapter VI, may be rather difficult for undergraduates; although we have been as clear as we can be, these parts require careful reading and attention. It may be that a teacher of undergraduates will want to omit the detailed exposition of generative grammar and merely use our summarizing sections. Chapter III assumes at times some knowledge of grammatical terminology not fully given until Chapter IV. But this knowledge is not of an advanced nature.

The book is so arranged that after Chapter II, the remaining chapters can with little loss be taken in almost any order. Some teachers may wish to reverse the order of chapters completely after Chapter II.

We should like to acknowledge the help of George N. Soppelsa in preparing many of the figures used in the book. We are particularly grateful to Noam Chomsky, James Sledd, David Reibel, Francis Lee Utley, Randolph Quirk, William S-Y. Wang, John F. Leyerle, and H. M. Smyser for their many helpful criticisms and suggestions. We are heavily in debt to the many linguistic scholars, living and dead, in this country and Europe, who have contributed to the development of linguistics and to whom its present high eminence is due. We have endeavored to acknowledge what we owe to them in our text and its notes, but many indebtednesses will undoubtedly have escaped us. Finally, we must admit that without the encouragement and understanding of Robert M. Estrich this book could not have been written.

Cambridge, Massachusetts
La Jolla, California

Contents

Figures

DRAWN BY WILLIAM METZIG

Maps

DRAWN BY WILLIAM METZIG

Symbols

For English phonetic and phonemic symbols, see charts on pp 46, 50, and 67. For generative grammar symbols, see chart on pp. 254-256.

~	Indicates alternate forms
´	Accent mark
(above) ˈ	Phrase stress
(below) ˌ	Syllabic phone
ʔ	Glottal catch
ł	Dark *l* (closure made by touching uvula against extreme back of tongue)
[ ]	Enclosures for phonetic symbols. In Chapter VI they enclose a symbol which designates a special restriction on the preceding symbol
/ /	Enclosures for phonemic symbols
˥	Unaspirated sound
≠	Contrasts with.
#	Linguistic pause between sentences
1, 2, 3, 4	Degrees of pitch from low to high
→	Suspensory terminal pitch level
↓	Fading terminal pitch level
↑	Rising terminal pitch level

between phonemic clauses

Space between letters	Disjuncture between phonemic word groups
-	Juncture within phonemic word groups
(above vowels) ~	Nasalized quality
(below) ˰	A more forward tongue position
(below) .	A tongue position further back

→ Has as constituents or generates or is or may be rewritten as

ɱ Labio-dental nasal consonant

ʰ Aspirated sound

> Becomes or became

< Derived or coming from

⁕ Hypothetical form unattested in documents. In Chapter VI non-grammatical form

: IPA symbol of length of preceding phone

{ } Enclosures for morphemes. In Chapter VI enclosures for joining two source sentences

⇒ Is transformed into

x̄ Vocoid indicated below macron is long

x̥ Sound indicated above circle is voiceless.

ʻ Release of closure

ʼ Formation of closure

ˇ A lower tongue position

ˆ A higher tongue position

Abbreviations

ACD—*American College Dictionary*
DAE—*Dictionary of American English*
ENE—Early Modern English (1500-1700)
Gmc—Germanic or Teutonic
  IE—Indo-European
IJAL—*International Journal of American Linguistics*
 IPA—International Phonetic Alphabet
  LE—Language event
LNE—Late New English (after 1700)
 ME—Middle English
MED—*Middle English Dictionary*
 NE—Modern (New) English or North-Eastern
NED—*New English Dictionary* (Same as OED)
NW—North-Western
NWD—*Webster's New World Dictionary*
 OE—Old English
OED—*Oxford English Dictionary* (Same as NED)
 ON—Old Norse
 PLE—Participant(s) in the language event
PMLA—*Publications of the Modern Language Association*
 PRE—Participant(s) in the reported event
 RE—Reported event
 SE—South-Eastern
SPE—Society for Pure English
SW—South-Western

A
LINGUISTIC
INTRODUCTION
TO THE
HISTORY OF
ENGLISH

CHAPTER

I

LANGUAGE AND THE
HISTORY OF LANGUAGE

Language is fundamentally the means by which men communicate with each other and with themselves, and by which they express themselves. All societies of human beings use language; there are no known exceptions. A person's linguistic destiny is determined by his birth and early circumstances, and the individual conforms and becomes a speaker and hearer of the language or languages thrust on him. The existence of a usable language gives human beings a potential social, historical, and intellectual dimension, linking them to each other, to the past, and to the world.

Language is a product of human culture, and speech is an aspect, a very important aspect, of human behavior. In all cultures, "there occur, among others, certain events known as utterances, or single instances of speech produced at given times and places by individual speakers."[1] In order to perform their social function, the noises people make must somehow be grouped into shared samenesses, or what are taken to be samenesses in the

---

[1] Ralph L. Beals and Harry Hoijer: *An Introduction to Anthropology* (New York: The Macmillan Co.; 1953), 507.

conventions of the language, so that recognition of meaning in each other's speech may take place. Without this recognition, any speech utterance would be a mere jumble of noise.

We are deeply attuned to the samenesses we hear or see in the use of language, so much so that when we unexpectedly hear a foreign language, whose rules are different from those which operate in our own language, we try to force it into our own language pattern. Everyone has had this experience, an experience which testifies to the strong hold our own language has on us. When we speak a foreign language, if we are not complete masters of it, we also tend to force the language into the pattern and rules with which we are familiar. We find it difficult to hear distinctions which are of importance in the foreign language but are not in our own, and to ignore distinctions which are of significance only in our own. We find it difficult to pronounce sounds of a foreign language with which we are not familiar.

A Frenchman trying to speak English will have difficulty with our *th* in *the*, because that sound does not occur in his language. He may say *ze* instead of *the* because *z* is familiar to him. An American speaking French will have much difficulty with the French word *rue* 'street,' because in English we have neither a uvular *r* nor a front rounded vowel, as in *ue*. In English we do not use *thou* except in prayers; when we speak French, German, or Italian we find it difficult to remember that some of our *you*'s should be *thou*'s in the acceptable forms of the language being used.

All this proves how important the rules of language are in practice. Rules are the fundamental principles by which we can both use and understand our noise signs; without them we should not be understood nor should we understand others. When we know a language we know its rules thoroughly, though obviously not consciously, and indeed try to impose them, even without knowingly intending to do so, on other languages.

The samenesses of speech must lie in some kind of regularity in the sounds or combinations of sounds, in the orderly pattern of utterances. The existence of meaningful utterances, utterances with samenesses that can be interpreted, presupposes orderliness and pattern—in short, a *system* that we call a language. A language in this sense is that interpretative system which enables its users to make understandable utterances and to interpret properly utterances made by other speakers. The utterances we call speech; the interpretative system, language.

The importance of the distinction between language and speech was first insisted on by the great Swiss linguist Ferdinand de Saussure. In the field of linguistic activity, he distinguished between what he called *parole* (the speech utterance) and *langue* (the system by which *parole* is carried on). In this sense, the proper subject of linguistics is not speech as such, but language, although we may investigate a language only through its individual speech acts or utterances.

We may, of course, study a language purely as a system operating at a given time, thus disregarding the ways in which the system has changed through time and continues to change through use. In doing so, we abstract the language from its history and life and study it as a system of correspondences, arrangements, and potentialities. We call this kind of study **synchronic** linguistics. If, on the other hand, we concentrate on change and development in language, we call the study **diachronic** linguistics. To achieve a total understanding of a language, we must consider not only its anatomy and physiology, its form and function, but also its phylogeny and ontogeny, its history and development.

The utterances by which language lives (or, if the language is dead, the documents of the language which survive) are the physical means through which we arrive at the language system. Utterances as such are ephemeral unless they are recorded in some way, and these records of whatever sort are speech utterances at one remove. Until recently visual representation (writing) was the only available method of making these records, but today, of course, we have additional ways at our disposal—phonograph records, for example, and magnetic tapes—which are certain to play important roles in future speech and language study.

Language is a subject of great complexity. It is a connecting medium: it connects men with other men, men with the world, men with themselves, parts of the world with other parts of it, and, in terms of time, the present with the past and the future. It forms a complex series of intricate relationships. We must even use language in our analysis of language. In order for us to see it as a whole satisfactorily, we must regard a language from a variety of perspectives. In both its oral and written forms, it is an aspect of human behavior; a biological and sociological phenomenon with a survival role in evolution; the basis for all education in the broadest sense of the word; a consistent structure with dynamic possibilities; a key to the intellectual structure of various cultures; an esthetic and magical phenomenon. It is a process, a structure, and a preserving medium all at once. It is no wonder that the word "language" is full of ambiguities and that scholars attempt to resolve them by distinguishing terms such as speech, language, tongue, discourse, utterance, and so forth.

Language is not only a creature of society, but like other social institutions, it is also a creator of society: sharing a language is a necessary result and a necessary condition of people living together. But a language is also of the most intimate importance for individuality as such. The acquisition of language in the life of an individual is closely bound up with his mental development and growth. His sense of the world, for example, depends to a great extent on the language he uses. Language enables man both to express himself and to orient himself to the world and society. Because the structure of an individual's personality is so intimately bound up both genetically and systematically with the language he speaks, it is very difficult for people to be objective about their own language. We are so conditioned to these conventionally accepted noises that it is hard for us even to think of them as noises. Thus, to become linguistically aware requires a special concentration on language as an object, which, for humans, who tend to regard the vagaries and accidents of their own language as having an inherent universal and permanent validity, is difficult and perhaps even shocking. We should remind ourselves that linguistics, the objective study of language, can serve not only its own proper function of adding to our general knowledge about language, but can also serve to liberate us from the tyranny, in its subtlest form, of the word. In the course of his life each human being discovers his language, and comes to think of it as a given natural object, rather than as the product of human behavior that it is. One of the reasons we find it difficult to look at our own language objectively arises from the way by which we come to know it. A horse is really a "horse" because our experience tells us it is a "horse."

As Julian Marias writes, "Language is something which each of us encounters; we have not made it ourselves; no one in particular has made it; it is 'there,' with its precise phonetic laws, with a phonemic system, with a vocabulary and a syntax; it is a *social* reality and it serves us precisely for that reason: a language is understood because it is apart from the individuality of each one of its speakers, because it is valid for all, and therefore recourse to it is automatically effective. . . . There is, then, a linguistic ambit which is prior to individuals, in which the latter find themselves immersed, just as they do in the physical world or in the system of beliefs and customs."[2]

The great contribution of modern linguistics has been its stress on the structural aspect of language—the synchronic "systematicness" of language design. Language has a structure in its own right; it is not merely a formless, changing phenomenon. Although the development of English as seen at different periods and from different perspectives is to be the main subject of this book, much attention will be paid to its internal organization. In the nineteenth century, before the recent revolution in linguistic studies, language was studied largely in terms of individual psychology and historical development. The nine-

---

[2] *Reason and Life, The Introduction to Philosophy.* Trans. from the Spanish by K. S. Reid and E. Sarmiento (New Haven: Yale University Press; 1956), 267.

teenth century liberated linguistics from too close a dependence on logic, but came to depend, in its study of language, too much on psychology and history.

In this century, new developments in linguistics, especially in America, have been chiefly concerned with structure, and all over the world we find an increasing interest in the structural rather than the historical analysis of language. Today this interest is beginning to lead us once again into some aspects of logic. But we shall probably not fall again into the logical trap. The greater danger today is that we may neglect the importance of the history and psychology of language.

Modern linguistics has developed new concepts which enable us to analyze a language at any given stage of its history in a more systematic and exact way than was previously possible. We have discovered kinds of contrasting and complementary elements (differences and samenesses) within a language that were only suspected before, and kinds of patterning in languages that can now be more precisely identified and specified. A language is not a static structure; it is a structure with potentialities for change. The changes that will occur in languages cannot be exactly predicted, but they can be explained in terms of the development of potentialities within the language structure under particular historical circumstances.

In the past, the problem of the origin of language was of great concern to linguists. Modern linguists, however, have generally ignored the subject.[3] The range of speculation had been so great that most present-day linguists have thrown up their hands in despair and abandoned it as an unsolved, if fascinating question. There can be no serious doubt that the origin of language is bound up with the rise of social organization itself; a society of any but the crudest sort is inconceivable without some means of communication. But the exact form or forms of that communication from which language developed will prob-

---

[3] For a recent résumé and exposition of a new theory, see G. Révész: *The Origins and Pre-history of Language.* Trans. J. Butler (New York: Philosophical Library; 1956).

ably never be known: gestures with the tongue while the hands were occupied, forms of ritual and play, expressions of emotional release, imitations of natural sounds have all been suggested as the ancestral forms of language. The theories are interesting to contemplate but, based as they are on speculative evidence, they cannot be accepted as part of the realm of solid knowledge.

A **language,** in a broad sense, is a system in terms of which something can be presented by one user and understood by another: that is, it is a system of communication. This sense of the term, which includes so-called languages of science, of animals, of gesture, of music and art, as well as "natural" languages, is of little use to us here, since the problems specific to the study of historical languages (that is, *languages* in the ordinary sense of the word), such as English, would get lost in the investigation of "language" in general terms. Instead, we may limit our discussion to languages taken as historically developed, socially learned, orally transmitted systems of communication— that is, to natural languages, of which English is only one example out of something like three thousand.

It is with the historical development of a language that we shall be most concerned in this book. It is characteristic of artificial languages that historical mutability is precluded by their very nature. Artificial languages are devised to exclude or to control mutability; the rules which establish and fix an artificial language are constructed before the fact, so to speak, of the use of that language. The rules define the language, and it is inconceivable that the use of the language could force a change in the rules. In contrast, the "rules" of a natural language are constructed after the fact of language use, so that changes in the use of the language determine changes in the rules themselves. Only to a limited extent does the very formulation of a rule influence the use of a natural language and thus create new regularities. (Consider the general but not complete ineffectiveness of English teachers in modifying the common regularities of the language.) It is obvious here that we are using "rules" in a special sense in reference to natural languages; a brief discussion of this use may be helpful here.

As applied to natural languages, "rules" are simply formulations of the observed regularities of language use. In English, for example, we observe that *I laughed, I heard him, he laughed, he heard me* are all regular occurrences, but that *me laughed, me heard he, him laughed, him heard I* are not used and, as a matter of fact, are rejected by English speakers as occurrences in English. We may now formulate a rule to account for such regularity: *I* and *he* may appear in constructions followed by verbs like *heard* and *laughed,* while *me* and *him* may appear in constructions following such verbs. Note that the regularities of the language exist independently of whether the formulation of a rule happens to have been made or not. The rule—i.e., the formulation of the rule—may even be false or incomplete; our rule does not, for example, provide for the fact that in some dialects of English *Me and him laughed* occurs. Or the language usage may change, as it did when *me thinks,* a standard form in Shakespeare's English, disappeared from English in favor of *I think.* In both cases, it is the formulation of the rule that is to be considered inaccurate according to the facts of the language, not the facts of the language that are to be considered improper because of their clash with previously formulated rules. We may even say that originally artificial languages, such as Esperanto and Modern Hebrew, have become natural languages exactly to the extent that users of those languages have made the language usage primary over the formulations of the rules that originally established them.

We may use the term "grammatical rule" to mean an actual regularity observable in a language, rather than a formulation of an actual or alleged regularity. If we do so, there is no harm in saying that all languages must and do obey grammatical rules. It will follow that the grammatical rules of a language change as the use of that language changes; by definition, however, the rules of an artificial language as such remain constant. It is with real justification that we can say of an inaccurate grammatical description of a natural language: it is bad because it describes an artificial language.

The fact that natural languages are socially learned, not genetically inherited and not privately acquired, accounts for the special kind of arbitrariness that characterizes them. For any particular social group, the relation of what is said to how it is said is arbitrary. For example, there is nothing other than social convention that dictates that *Donnez-moi le crayon* will be the way that a member of a French social group will say what we say as *Give me the pencil.* To say *da*, as Russian speakers do, or *ja*, as German speakers do, or *po*, as Albanian speakers do, seems neither more nor less reasonable than to say *yes*, as we do. On the other hand, as users of a given language, we are not free to say what we want in any way we like: we cannot, as English users, say *po* if we expect our listeners to understand *yes*, and cannot say *Me heard he*, if we want our listeners to understand *He heard me.* The language we use arbitrarily holds us to strict limits in communicating with others, and as individuals we may not arbitrarily extend those limits.

That natural languages are orally transmitted will seem less than obvious to literate users of a language. And indeed it would be foolish to ignore the fact that a great deal of linguistic communication is carried on by graphic devices—writing, printing, Braille dots, and the like. But we would be confusing the picture with the depicted if we were to identify directly these devices as language, rather than as reflections, representations, or records of speech or potential speech. Just as the arts of painting and photography have introduced immense new possibilities of presentation in what they depict, so writing, the visual representation of language, introduces immense potentialities of expression and communication in language. You may learn much about nature by studying pictures and photographs and much about languages by studying written records, but no serious student of nature should be satisfied until he has studied nature directly, and no serious student of language should be content until he has studied language in its oral form, if it is at all possible. Otherwise, one's insights into language would be dimmed; one's grasp on reality would be unreliable; one's confusion of the representation with what was represented would be inevitable.

Let us now take up some of these points in greater detail.

In the common, though perhaps incorrect, interpretation of the *Cratylus*, it is said that Plato argued that there was some logical connection between the sounds used to symbolize events or objects and what is symbolized by them. Today no serious linguist or linguistic philosopher would maintain this proposition, except perhaps in the case of a few onomatopoeic words. The sounds used for linguistic symbolism are logically arbitrary, although if we have enough material and can start at a certain point in the past, we can explain how it came to be that we pronounce a word as we do or how it came to mean what it does mean. It is perfectly easy to explain, if we start at a certain point in history—say the Old English period—how it comes about that we pronounce *knight* as *nite* or even how it came to have its present meaning. But there is no explanation as to why this combination of sounds should designate what it does designate. It is not more natural to say it this way than to use the corresponding words *Ritter, chevalier,* or *caballero,* in German, French, and Spanish.

It used to be thought, however, that the structure or grammar of language (its system), as opposed to its vocabulary, was based on logic, the permanent and universal categories of the human mind. The great growth of our knowledge, in the past hundred years, of languages other than those classified as Indo-European and Semitic (the only families of languages well known in the West before) has cast considerable doubt on this belief. Newly studied languages have revealed linguistic categories and structures so different from those with which we had been familiar that many linguists have given up trying to establish any categories that would be general to all languages. Certain linguistic categories, such as *adjective* and *tense,* for instance, which seemed completely natural and logical to earlier students of language, are simply irrelevant in some languages.

However, it is possible that some general statements can be made about linguistic categories and that some relations between language and the world are not so completely arbitrary as the relations between things and the sounds that designate them. As John Carroll puts it, "Language universals, phenomena found in all languages, would be of as much interest psychologically as language differences. Is it true that all languages have subject-predicate construction in sentences? Do all languages have some type of noun-verb contrast? What features of verb-tense system are common to all languages? Answers to such questions would assist in the development of a generalized psychology of cognitive functions."[4] It will take some time before such answers can be given, if indeed they ever can be.

The patterning that a language imposes on thought is a fascinating subject; in recent years it has been the subject of considerable discussion in the United States, as a result of the work of Benjamin Lee Whorf, following the lead of the great American anthropological linguist Edward Sapir. If language is ultimately responsible, as some philosophers think, for many if not all of our philosophical confusions, it may also be responsible for all our thinking in a much more fundamental sense. It may occupy a very special place in the determination of culture, fundamental not only in being the *sine qua non* of all culture but in the sense of creating the very preoccupations and mode of thinking characteristic of any culture. Whorf has made just this claim. He argues that the very language we use, and especially its over-all grammatical categories, controls the way in which we see the world and influences the basic concepts of our culture.

Speakers of English organize their utterances in the form of subjects and predicates. We say, to take an example from

---

[4] In his introduction to Benjamin Lee Whorf: *Language, Thought and Reality, Selected Writings* (New York and London: Technology Press of Massachusetts; 1956), 30–31.

Whorf's writings, "*a light flashes*," with a division of the "thing" from the "action," although the light and the flashing are obviously the same. In Hopi, a North American Indian language, the same point is made by a simple word equivalent to *flash*. Hopi does not typically put its utterances into an agent-action pattern as we typically do. Our agent-action pattern determines, in some measure, how we think about and look at the world.

The differences in fundamental world view between the various languages of western civilization—what Whorf calls SAE (Standard Average European)—are not, he claims, very significant. The grammatical categories of these languages correspond very closely, and the chief differences lie in vocabulary and idiosyncratic idiom; but when we come to some of the more exotic—the so-called primitive—languages, we have to do with a very different matter. In these languages we often find radically different grammatical concepts from those current in SAE. In them we can recognize a completely different way of looking at the world, of dividing it up into categories. No longer do we find the classification of matters which speakers of SAE automatically take for granted—singularity and plurality of substances, even substances themselves, measurable time, certain spatial relations, and so forth; but matters which we think to be of secondary or occasional importance—such as the degree of validity of the statement made, the shape of the object handled, the extent of persistence of the event—may in these languages have to be designated in almost every sentence.

If, as he has sometimes been interpreted, Whorf would claim the complete sovereignty of his principle, that is, that intellectual activity within a culture is linguistically determined, it would be easy enough to refute it. If there were no area of intercultural truth, then the principle itself would be impugned. Also if it were true, translation would be impossible, and we would not be able to follow his argument when Whorf tells us what it is like to think in Hopi. As Hockett says, "An effective

speaker—for example, Whorf—will have the skill to force his
native language to express meanings for which he may believe
some other language (say Hopi) is better adapted."[5] We are
forced then to the conclusion that "intercultural communication,
however wide the difference between cultures may be, is not
impossible. It is simply more or less difficult, depending on
the degree of difference between the cultures concerned."[6]

Whorf probably overemphasized his insight and underestimated the fact that a language can express matters of any sort
in some way, as he himself demonstrated by describing Hopi.
One can get out of one's language pattern, though sometimes only
with difficulty, and this fact alone refutes the complete relativity
of language categories. But there is now good evidence that the
language one speaks, especially the vocabulary it offers to its
speakers—the kinds of things, events, sensations, for which there
are unitary, individual words—has a definite influence on the
thinking one does.

Let us turn to another aspect of historical languages: the
relation between the oral and written aspects of language.

Historically and ontogenetically speaking, it is clear that the
spoken aspect of language is prior to its written aspect.
Probably from the beginnings of human society (estimates run
from 250,000 to 1,000,000 years ago) language has existed in
its oral form. Then, in the Near East about 5000 years ago, it
was discovered that a more enduring set of visual symbols,
carved in stone or made on papyrus, could be used to symbolize
the existing sound signs. The speech utterance could be
preserved and made into an object, an artifact, by writing or
carving. Anthropologists and archaeologists attribute the rise
of civilization to two factors—the creation of cities and the invention of writing. The latter, for the first time, made possible
the preservation of records and ritual in a form more objective

---

[5] In a review in *Language* XXXII (1956), 467.

[6] J. Greenberg in *Language in Culture; Conference on the Interrelations
of Language and Other Aspects of Culture.* Ed. Harry Hoijer (Chicago:
University of Chicago Press; 1954), 94.

and reliable than human memory could give them. The invention of writing took a great burden off the human memory and transformed the evanescent sounds of human speech into artifacts which could be moved about and preserved at will.[7]

Languages constantly change, but there are certain conservative forces which obscure the process. Among them the influence of writing is perhaps the most important; written forms remain stable long after the spoken forms they represent have changed. If one considers the great gap between English speech and English spelling, for example, one can get a good idea of the conservatism of writing. In spite of the historical priority of speech, educated people who speak a language with a written form tend to think of the written form as prior to and more fundamental than their speech. Instead of reforming spelling to conform with speech, men have occasionally done the opposite and made pronunciation conform to spelling. From this attitude we get phenomena which linguists call **spelling pronunciations.** The "w" in *Greenwich* used to be pronounced in a way reflected by the spelling. After a time the pronunciation changed so that a more accurate spelling would have been *Grennitch*. Now, hundreds of years later, many people influenced by the traditional spelling pronounce the name as if it were a combination of *green* and *witch*.

Although there is actually a very long history of interest in language of a general or descriptive sort, in the early days of linguistics, beginning in the late eighteenth century, the emphasis was put on languages with a literary tradition. This study had to be based on documents and led perhaps to an

---

[7] For recent studies of the history of writing, see David Diringer: *Writing, Its Origins and Early History* (London: Thames and Hudson; 1962), I. Gelb: *A Study of Writing, The Foundations of Grammatology* (Chicago: The University of Chicago Press; 1952), and David Diringer: *The Alphabet, A Key to the History of Mankind.* Second Edition (New York: Philosophical Library; 1951). For a good popular study of the history of the decipherment of many ancient scripts, see Ernst Doblhofer: *Voices in Stone, The Decipherment of Ancient Scripts and Writings.* Trans. M. Saville (New York: The Viking Press; 1961).

undervaluation of the oral aspect of language. With the rise of the science of phonetics in the late nineteenth century and the coeval development of anthropology with its interest in preliterate societies, the oral aspects of language began to be emphasized. The influence of anthropology on modern linguistics has been great, and this may have led to an unjustifiable neglect of the written aspect of language. Both speech and writing may be used for the study of languages, and neither one nor the other should be condemned or neglected. We may admit a kind of fundamental priority to speech without at the same time minimizing the importance and role of writing.

This book, because it is a book, presents language by means of fixed printed marks on pieces of paper. But we should try to remember that these marks reflect some actual speech reality. The marks on paper or parchment are conventional signs of the conventional sound forms which compose numerous speech acts or possible speech acts. Once writing has been invented, it is of course possible to use language, yet bypass the oral aspect of speech. In writing this chapter we pass from thought to writing and do not have to speak out the lines we write. When you read these words you understand them without converting them into speech, unless you are such a poor reader that you must frame the words aloud to understand them. Writing becomes a system in itself, and it introduces a new factor into language behavior, a factor of great complexity and importance.

It is widely recognized that communication is a fundamental function of language. When language exists, people may communicate with each other in carrying on the work and amusements of society. Without any form of communication, no social effort would be possible; in deaf-mute societies, artificial gesture systems based on natural languages perform the necessary functions of language. If all the papers and records—all language surrogates—were destroyed, things would get seriously entangled, but without speech, organized life as we know it would be impossible.

The role that expression plays in language is less widely recognized, but is certainly no less important, than the role of substantive communication. Much speech is not uttered for the purpose of communication in an ordinary sense at all. It reassures people, affords emotional release, and gives ego satisfaction. When a man stubs his toe and says "damn it!" he is not communicating at all. It is true that such a remark does tell bystanders what the injured man feels, but his purpose is not communication. We all know people who cannot help talking, and much of their talk, although in the form of communication, is not seriously meant to convey information but is merely intended to be friendly or to externalize internal tensions. Of course, much of the value of language as expression does depend on the fact that it also exists to communicate. Human beings are not, however, completely rational beings who talk only to convey wishes and information to other human beings.

In many of the uses of language the information which seems to be conveyed is of no great importance in itself. Language may be used to exercise power over other human beings. It may satisfy a need to dominate or control others. Language can serve ritualistically to solemnize and even legalize occasions, as when the preacher says, "I pronounce you man and wife." This sentence is not merely a communication of a fact, but is also the establishment of that fact. John Austin has called these types of sentences performatives.[8] And language may also be used to comfort other human beings.

Thinking and language are intimately connected. We think to ourselves in language. During the course of a day most people think in words more than they utter them. This internal dialogue with oneself is an extremely important function of language. It enables one to communicate with oneself. Much, if not all, thinking is the internal use of words: if we had no language, we could not really think, although we might well have mental or emotional experiences of other sorts. Thus,

---

[8] See his *Philosophical Papers*. Ed. Urmson and Warnock (Oxford: Clarendon Press; 1961), Chapters 3 and 10.

although communication with others is the essential characteristic of language, it is not its only function.

Language is not an innate characteristic as, for example, walking or one's blood group is. If such a concept as race has any validity, it certainly has none with respect to language. Now it is true that part of what makes Frenchmen French is the French language and part of what makes Americans American is American English, but there is no innate connection between a language and a people; there is merely an historical one. We can say that no known historical or natural language is more advanced *per se* than any other; this fact is irrelevant in an argument as to whether certain peoples are more advanced than other peoples. Hottentot has no vocabulary to deal with physics whereas English has. This does not mean that Hottentot is less advanced as a language than English, but merely that speakers of Hottentot have not used their language for physics whereas English speakers have.

These comments would perhaps not be necessary if it were not for the fact that in the past century and even in this one, crude racial and evolutionary concepts were applied to language development, largely, though not always consciously, for the purpose of supporting certain prejudices in social thinking. Superior races implied superior languages. This idea dies hard, in spite of its having been totally discredited in linguistics, especially since linguists have become aware of the variety and complexity of languages.

Leaving our general discussion of language, let us turn to the question of why we should study the history of a language.

First of all, we should study the history of our language for the same reason that we should study the history of our country and of Europe. The man who does not know some history is a man who loses one of the major dimensions of his humanity. History has made man what he is today, and to understand him one must know something of his past.

A person is not born with his language; as we have already said, he learns it. And he learns it from other people who in turn learned it from others, and so on back in time, and back into unrecorded history. Thus the language of a given person is in some sense the creation, or at least the product, of the whole society and of that society's historical antecedents. Since historical events and conditions have a way of being reflected in language—for instance, in the names of technical achievements (such as the telephone), in words borrowed from societies with superiority in a given area (Italian musical terms in English), even in individual sounds which are influenced by sounds in a language felt to belong to a superior culture (the final sound in some people's pronunciations of the words *garage* and *rouge*, which English has adopted under the influence of French)—there is a very valid sense in which we can say that a person's language contains within itself the history of the societies in which that language was developed. A man who has no knowledge of the history of his language lacks a sure foundation for the study of the history of his nation or people.

A second reason is that in order to read properly—in the original—the great written monuments of his civilization, a man must know something about the history of his language. To know Shakespeare, one must know something about Elizabethan English; to read the Declaration of Independence intelligently one must know something about eighteenth-century English. Not everyone can be a specialist in Old English or Middle English, but anyone can increase his appreciation of the great written achievements of the past by increasing his knowledge of the language in which they were written.

Third, one studies the history of the language to be liberated from a narrow view of his present language. One learns that language changes and that the "rules" of grammar are not fixed like the "laws" of nature or the rules of artificial languages. One learns that what is now often considered a heinous solecism was not considered such a long time ago. Although one must follow certain grammatical norms in order to be considered educated, one should realize that much that has gone into the making of English is due to the replacing of some norms by others. The "errors" of the past have made present-day English for us. A language which is alive will change its rules and what is considered correct at one time may only be a current fad. This, of course, is not to say that "anything goes," but it should suggest tolerance and understanding in linguistic matters.

Fourth, we study the history of a language to understand many of its apparent irrationalities. Why do we, for instance, say *men* rather than *mans* for the plural of *man?* The history of English will give us a very satisfying explanation of this irregularity. Although we do not know why *book* has a plural *books* when from OE we would expect *beech*, we can easily show many historical parallels for the change and for the resultant analogical construction. We cannot explain a language by laws of logic, but we can account for much of what seems illogical in a language by referring to historical periods in which the present anomaly fitted into a regular, systematic structure.

Fifth, the study of language at various stages in its past can provide us with an opportunity for studying language objectively and can introduce us to linguistic methods through materials which are important in their own right and fascinating to boot. It is this last goal which this book stresses—to introduce the student to the elementary history of his own language and to some of the methods of modern linguistics.

The purpose of this book is to apply some of these new methods to the history of the English language at various stages in its development. It does not pretend to be anything like a complete description of the history of English; but it does hope to present little insights into that history at various points in its development. We hope that the student who conscientiously reads and studies this book may become enriched in his understanding of the history of his language and of some of the techniques in the study of language—enriched both in linguistic method and linguistic history. If he wishes to pursue these matters further, however, he will be just at the beginning of his work, for this book can be at most only an introduction to the two subjects.

The following chapter introduces us to modern or new English (NE) through a study of its sound elements—the phonemes, as they are called. The phonological—that is, the oral—aspect of language is a particularly useful subject to begin with. The student will not only be given a view of modern English phonemics and phonology; he will be presented with a way of approaching language to help him appreciate other aspects of linguistics and linguistic history to which he will then be introduced.

In Chapter III, he will learn something about the comparative and genetic method by being introduced to the Indo-European family of languages, to which English belongs. The purpose of the chapter is to help him understand what is meant by a family of languages, and how a family is established. The morphology of Old English (OE) will be the subject of the following chapter. There he will learn one set of terms by which the grammatical structure of a language can be analyzed. He will also be introduced to an important aspect of the earliest written form of his own language.

Chapter V introduces the student to the important concept of dialect through the study of the dialects of Middle English (ME). From this study we hope he will learn what a dialect is and how the standard form of English developed. Chapter VI is devoted to an exposition of Elizabethan English, especially in regard to its syntactic structure. What principles may we use to expound the syntax of a language?

The seventh chapter will be devoted to the problem of usage and the rise of the idea of correct English. We will discuss something of what a standardization of a language means and how our modern English grammars arose. The principal materials for this chapter will be drawn from eighteenth- and nineteenth-century English.

Chapter VIII will give us a picture of the English vocabulary and how we go about building or creating new words. It will tell the student something about the interaction of history and culture on vocabulary and how we can discern a great deal of our cultural history in our words.

This book, then, is a series of studies of English from selected perspectives and at different stages in its past and present; our purpose is, first, to introduce the student to various aspects of linguistic science, and, second, to give an introductory knowledge of aspects of our language in the past, in the belief that the aspects chosen are especially appropriate for study in the periods chosen. The authors of this book feel that an introduction to English phonology can best be obtained through a study of the language of today, and that an introduction to the question of usage can best be attained through a study of eighteenth- and nineteenth-century English, and its grammarians, rhetoricians, dictionary-makers, and so on. We expect the student to learn something of morphemics and OE morphology when he studies Chapter IV, and something of dialect study and ME dialects in particular when he studies Chapter V, and so forth. He will *not* be offered a complete history of the English language, but rather an introduction to selected parts of it and to certain linguistic methods. To some extent, introductory parts of the chapters will fill in some of the gaps in treatment we have left by not considering every aspect for every period, but only further study of the many good books and articles by the great scholars in the field can give the interested student an adequate idea of the richness of our knowledge of the history of our language.

It should be noted that certain topics are taken up more than once, although in every case there is one part of the book where a subject is treated in greater detail than elsewhere. The relation between writing and speech, for instance, is discussed in this chapter and the next, and dialects are treated in both Chapter II and Chapter V. All of these repeated subjects are of great importance in the understanding of language and in the opinion of the authors deserve repeated emphasis and discussion in various contexts.

QUESTIONS

1. Can you think of any further examples of spelling pronunciations in English besides the one example given above on p. 16? If so, list them.

2. Can you think of any analogies to the distinction between language and speech? De Saussure contrasts the timetable of a railroad line with the actual train trips. Give another analogy.

3. What is a logogram? How do the numerals 1, 2, 3, 4, etc. differ in function from the letters of the alphabet?

4. Relate the following quotation from Sapir to the Whorfian hypothesis discussed in this chapter. "Human beings do not live in the objective world alone, nor alone in the world of social activity as ordinarily understood but are very much at the mercy of the particular language which has become the medium of expression for their society. It is quite an illusion to imagine that one adjusts to reality essentially without the use of language and that language is merely an incidental means of solving specific problems of communication or reflection. The fact of the matter is that the 'real world' is to a large extent unconsciously built up on the language habits of the group." "The Status of Linguistics as a Science." *Language* V (1929), 209.

5. Can you think of any further reasons besides those given in this chapter for studying the history of English?

6. Give some further examples of how the rules and pattern of a foreign language influence English when spoken by a speaker of the foreign language.

7. In what senses can it be said that the oral aspect of a language is more fundamental than its written aspect?

8. Give an example of an artificial language other than mathematics and Esperanto. How does an artificial language differ from a natural language?

9. Smoke is a natural sign of fire. Give some further examples of natural signs. Is a STOP sign on a highway a natural sign? Is red a natural sign to indicate that a stop is called for?

10. Why is writing called an artifact? Look up the meaning of this word in a good dictionary and discuss its applicability to writing. Why is speech not an artifact?

11. What is the runic alphabet? Are smoke signals as used by

Indians an alphabet? If not, what are they? If they are, then in what sense?

12. On p. 13 it is said that language is the *sine qua non* of all culture. How would you explain and defend this statement?

II

PHONOLOGY AND
MODERN ENGLISH

LANGUAGE AND SOCIETY

Every human society uses language. To the extent that members of a society understand each other in communication, they may be said to share the same language. But just as no two physical objects in the world can be identical in respect to every possible criterion of judgment, so no two acts of language can be identical. Of course, communication would be impossible if there were no sense in which "sames" could appear; fortunately, communication is not impossible. The sense in which sames do appear in language is this: Acts of language which are interpreted by users of the same language as the same *are* the same in respect to the criterion of judgment used.

We, as observers of language-use, can often detect differences between items which users of the language treat as the same. If those differences are connected with nonlinguistic but societally important distinctions, we say that the differences are **dialectal** and that the two acts of language belong to different **dialects.**[1] Thus, if users of English interpret a Southern American

---

[1] The terms *dialect* and *dialectal* are thus used in a special sense here;

pronunciation of *I* as the same as a Northern pronunciation of *I*, we can assign the easily detectable differences to a difference in two **regional dialects**; if users of English interpret an uneducated man's *he don't know* to be the same as an educated *he doesn't know*, we ascribe the difference to two different **educational dialects** (sometimes called "levels of usage"); if users of English tell us that a stockbroker's term *board* means stock exchange, that a dope addict's *H* means heroin, that a miner's *power* means explosives, that a sportswriter's *apple* is a baseball, and that a *padre* is an army chaplain, we realize that we are dealing with different **specialized dialects**. Dictionaries, basing themselves on the opinions of their editors or on the opinions of people respected by their editors, use labels like "slang," "colloquial," "dialectal," or "vulgar" to advise dictionary-users that a particular item is appropriate only to a limited dialect. But in the sense we are employing here, everyone uses a dialect—as a matter of fact, most people make use of many different dialects, employing at a given time that dialect which is most appropriate to the particular purpose of the user.

LANGUAGE AND WRITING

Every human society uses language, but only a small minority of these societies make use of visual representations of their languages; that is, only some societies use a written or printed record of the language they speak. The distinction between societies which are literate and those which are not is important enough to be used by anthropologists as the basis for a primary division of human societies, corresponding to the somewhat outdated division between "civilized" and "primitive" societies.

Visual representation of language (which we may call "writing" for short) is so important in civilized societies that many people mistakenly equate language with writing. An implicit example of this mistaken equation occurs every time someone says something

---

the more popular term "accent" corresponds partially to what we mean here, but unfortunately is too narrow and too ambiguous for our purpose.

like, "You should pronounce words fully, giving all letters their full value; in *sophomore* be sure to pronounce the second *o* roundly." The mistake here is in thinking that the pronunciation of words is determined somehow by the writing; actually the spelling of words is essentially an attempt to represent their pronunciation. The conservatism of writing systems that led present English writing to fail in this attempt has already been briefly referred to and will be discussed again later.

Now suppose you were a member of one of the societies that does not use writing. You would, of course, have a language which you could use every day—for communicating your wants, expressing your feelings, getting people to admire you, teaching others what you knew, and talking about the weather. As a matter of fact, your language, like all known languages in the world, would be adequate for the expression of everything you wanted to say, in one way or another. The trouble is that you could not say anything to anyone who couldn't hear you, such as your great-grandchildren in the year 2075 or the milkman who was to deliver your milk at 5:00 the next morning while you were fast asleep. In such circumstances you could buy or invent a tape recorder, record your voice at leisure, and rest confident that a future listener would hear exactly what you had to say. Such a device would have the advantage of great faithfulness to your original message. But a tape recorder is heavy to carry around, and tapes are expensive, inconvenient to revise, and cumbersome to duplicate in large quantities.

A better solution might suggest itself to you: you could try to make a visual record of what you wanted to say. But how?

Well, you might try to represent every different whole message in your language by a different symbol. Thus you might use ▭ to stand for: "Leave two quarts of milk and a pound of butter," and △ for "Don't leave any milk until a week from Wednesday." We do something similar in some states when we paint a yellow line to the right of the center line on a road to mean something like, "It is too dangerous here for you to pass a vehicle in front of you." The difficulties of such a system for any but the most restricted kinds of communication are apparent: to represent all the different things you might want to say, you would need an indefinitely large number of symbols, and these would be so troublesome to learn that no one could ever use the system for most practical purposes of communication.

On the other hand, you might try to devise a set of symbols in such a way that each symbol would represent a meaningful element capable of entering into combinations with other symbols in some flexible way, so that very many different combinations would be possible, using a limited number of symbols. For example, you could write 〖bottle〗〖bottle〗 〖box〗 for "Leave two quarts of milk and a pound of butter." The meaning of 〖bottle〗〖box〗〖box〗 and 〖bottle〗〖bottle〗〖bottle〗〖box〗 and an indefinitely large number of similar messages would immediately be clear. You might even expand the system by introducing new symbols—e.g., 〖box〗 for cottage cheese—or refine it by introducing modifications of the old ones—e.g., you could let a yellow 〖bottle〗 designate cream, in contrast to a white one for milk. An advantage of such a system is that speakers of entirely different languages could learn the same system of writing without having to learn each other's language. Such systems of **pictorial representation** have been developed many times and in many places, from modern Australia to ancient Crete, from recent central Africa to prehistoric France. However, of the forty-odd languages in which extensive literatures developed, not one retained this direct system. Even in systems which most evidently reveal their pictorial origins, e.g., Egyptian hieroglyphics and Chinese character writing, the "pictures" were so conventionalized, both in form and designation, by the time they were employed for extensive writing that they cannot be considered examples of direct pictorial representation. Although most of the writing systems in present use may be ultimately derivable from pictorial systems, no significant work of literature, science, or what have you was ever written in pictorial script.

Reasons for the replacement of pictorial representation by linguistic representation are easy to find: in the pictorial system, the number of different symbols needed increases enormously as the writer wants to represent more and more different thoughts. The apparent advantage of pictorial representation—the physical resemblance of the sign to what it designates—is lost as soon as the system must be used (as all adequate systems must) to refer to non-visible ideas; think of the difficulties in devising little pictures to suggest notions like *don't* or *until* or *a week from Wednesday* or *Existence presupposes self-cognition.* In practice the symbols in originally pictographic systems acquire values as arbitrarily related to what they represent as the symbols used in linguistic systems.

By **linguistic representation** is meant the use of visual symbols to represent elements of language. In the history of writing, there have been systems (such as Chinese character writing and Egyptian hieroglyphics) in which individual symbols have represented whole words; systems (such as Sanskrit *devanagari* or Japanese *kana*) in which they have represented whole syllables; and some (including our own) in which they have represented segments of syllables, that is, individual "sounds." As a matter of fact, over periods of extended use, none of the systems has employed symbols of only one kind: all the systems have become "mixed" to some extent. In English, for example, there is a direct symbol-to-sound relationship in the spelling *pet*, a symbol-to-syllable relationship in *O.K.* (where both *O* and *K* represent whole syllables rather than single sounds), and a symbol-to-word relationship in numerals (e.g., 7 stands for the whole word), names of letters of the alphabet (e.g., *W* as the name of the letter itself), and miscellaneous other symbols like +, −, &, ¢, $.

Writing systems which are **logographic**, that is, in which a large number of individual symbols represent words, are very laborious to learn; this perhaps accounts for much of the difficulty people claim to find in learning Chinese—actually a difficulty in learning the system traditionally used to write it, rather than one in the language itself. Even native speakers of a language have difficulty in learning to write logographically. In contrast, writing systems employing a **syllabary**, in which individual symbols represent syllables, or an **alphabet**, in which individual symbols represent individual sounds, are very easy for native speakers to learn; historically, the introduction of such writing systems has had enormous effects on the development of the cultures that have adopted them. Finnish children, whose language is written in a very consistent alphabetic system, need spend only a few months learning to read and write the language they speak, while Chinese children spend many years learning to read and write their language. English-speaking children suffer from the fact that their basically alphabetic system is used so inconsistently that they must spend years memorizing what are actually largely logographic conventions for writing words like *rough, through, though, cough, hiccough, ought, ghost, women, lead, led, read, phantom.*

For most of our ordinary purposes in writing English, our traditional orthography, once it has been learned, is rather adequate. We can write *caught* as the past tense of *catch* without confusing anyone who has learned that this is the way to write it. But for the special purpose of indicating specific pronunciations, our traditional orthography is hopelessly cumbersome and inadequate. If we want to trace the changes in pronunciation of *caught* in various parts of the United States, we shall find that the inconsistent spelling fails to provide a system of visual representation of English sounds that will make it possible for us to communicate accurately the pronunciations under discussion.

What is needed for the scientific study of language is some kind of **phonetic transcription**, a system of writing a language such that there is a consistent representation of segments of speech by visual symbols. During the rather short history (only a little more than a century) of scientific **phonetics**—the systematic study of speech-sounds as sounds—many systems of transcription have been developed, but the very development of greater and greater accuracy in the description of speech-sounds has paradoxically made a completely phonetic transcription impossible of attainment. As phoneticians became more and more skillful in hearing differences between sounds; as they came to realize that during a stretch of speech, sound is being produced in a continuously varying stream, rather than proceeding from one point of rest to another; and as they saw that in case after case, when a previously undescribed language was described, phonetic differences thought to be insignificant were found to be significant for the new language—the search for a universal system of direct representation of the continuum of sound in speech by a finite set of discrete visual symbols was seen to be naïve and futile.

But if a direct symbol-to-sound representation of speech is impossible, how can we devise a system of transcription that will be any more consistent and any more accurate than our traditional orthographies? To answer this question, let us consider more closely the general requirements we want to impose on an ideal writing system.

It will be apparent to everyone who knows a language—and this means almost every member of the species *homo sapiens* over the age of four—that a language contains meaningful units, units which have characteristic forms (in speech, the material of these forms is sound) and characteristic meanings (values in contributing to the understanding of what is said). Communication in speech requires that one user of the language recognize the meaningful units that another user intends. In recognizing the units, he hears, or at least thinks he hears, the characteristic **phonological** forms of those units. He listens to the sounds of *parole*—of speech—but he hears the forms of the *langue*—the system.

Now if the phonological forms of all meaningful units bore no physical resemblance to one another, a language could not exist; human beings are incapable of making as many totally different auditory discriminations as there are meaningful units. But languages do exist, and they provide the necessarily enormous number of distinct phonological forms by synthesizing an indefinitely large number of higher units out of a very small and restricted number of elements. To understand the nature of this synthesis, we may look at an analogy in music. Consider a person singing a particular song or musical phrase several times. Now every one of his renditions will be physically different somehow from every other: no person could sing a song in *exactly* the same way twice. And yet we want to say that in some sense these are various performances of the same song. In what sense *can* we say that the same song is being sung each time? In the sense that the song has a certain characterizing form, a form that remains constant throughout the variations present in the actual performances. And in what terms can we state what that characterizing form is? In terms of notes of a scale, notes that are combined together differently to form different characteristic forms for different pieces of music.

In a language, **linguistic units** (such as sentences and words) correspond to songs and recognizable phrases in music. Corresponding to musical notes are the **phonemes** of a language and corresponding to a musical scale is the **phoneme inventory** of a language. Just as the form of every song can be thought of as composed of a particular, characteristic sequence of notes, so the form of every linguistic unit can be thought of as composed of a particular, characteristic sequence of phonemes. Notice that just as a musical note is not the same as the visual mark used to write down the song, so a phoneme is not the same as the visual mark used to transcribe it; that is, phonemes are not letters, any more than musical notes are black dots on a piece of paper. Just as different cultures employ different musical scales—for example, Japanese, Indonesian, and Comanche music all have scales radically different from ours—so different cultures have different inventories of phonemes in their languages. For example, Japanese has a phoneme inventory which does not make an *l* vs. *r* distinction, Hindi has a phoneme inventory that includes four different *t* phonemes (as contrasted with our one *t* phoneme), and the phoneme inventory of Comanche includes a set of "whispered" vowels as well as the kind we have. With a relatively small phoneme inventory (the number of phonemes in historical languages seems to range somewhere between fifteen and ninety) an indefinitely large number of different linguistic units can be composed, just as an indefinitely large number of different songs and musical phrases can be made using a scale with only a small number of notes. The inexhaustible variety of phonological forms depends not on the number of phonemes in the inventory, but on the way in which these phonemes can combine into units of no maximum size: in English there is no upper limit on the number of phonemes in a word, and in no historical language is there an upper limit to the number of words in a sentence.

In writing, the phonemes of speech are paralleled by **graphemes** —roughly what are ordinarily called *letters*. Just as phonemes are the constituents of the characteristic spoken forms of linguistic units, so graphemes are the constituents of the characteristic written forms of linguistic units. Since the writing system we have agreed to use is one which is a representation of speech, it becomes evident that the most reliable writing system will be one in which the meaningful units of speech are what are represented in writing: this can most economically be accomplished if the letters in writing have a consistent correspondence to the phonemes of speech. A piece of writing that satisfies this criterion is called a phonemic transcription. A **phonemic transcription**, then, is a written representation of a stretch of speech, such that the letters of the transcription have a consistent correspondence to the phonemes in that stretch.

The inadequacy of the traditional spellings for discussions involving the sounds of English can be explained chiefly by the fact that most of our traditional spellings were at one time accurate phonemic transcriptions, but—as has been true in all writing systems employed over long periods of time—the transcriptions of particular units have been preserved as the characteristic written forms of those units even when the spoken forms themselves have changed. For example, the differences between the traditional spellings of pairs like *knight* and *night, beat* and *beet, through* and *threw,* preserve differences in phonemic transcriptions of the spoken forms of units at a time long since past.

The fascinating and intricate history of our writing system has been well studied (see Chapter I, footnote 7, page 16). Without going into detail, we may briefly summarize the Middle Eastern origin of our alphabet. Starting from what were probably picto-

graphic and then logographic symbols, Mesopotamian and Egyptian peoples developed a rebus technique by which signs for whole words (logograms) could be put together to form longer words—as if, for example, we were to use logograms for *boy, stir,* and *us,* to indicate the word *boisterous.* Perhaps from just such a technique, or perhaps from an incompletely developed syllabary derived from it, certain Semitic peoples—notably Canaanites, Hebrews, and Phoenicians—adapted and used a system of writing, probably earlier than 3500 years ago, that represented consistently the consonant, but not vowel, distinctions of their languages by distinct figured symbols. It was not until the Greeks borrowed the Semitic alphabet from the Phoenicians in the eighth or ninth century B.C. and adapted it for Greek, that the writing system was able to represent vowel distinctions. The Semitic alphabet gradually spread, in a number of other forms, over the whole world, so that most writing systems in use today (with the notable exception of the Chinese and Japanese systems) originate from some form of this alphabet, modified almost beyond recognition but preserving some traces of the great original invention. Our own alphabet is derived from a Latin form which was adapted indirectly from one of the Greek forms of the Phoenician alphabet.

PHONEMES OF MODERN ENGLISH

Phonetic Description and Labeling

What are the phonemes of English and how shall we represent them visually? To the second part of the question the answer is fairly easy: we shall find it simplest to represent each distinct phoneme by one distinct letter, and since any particular visual mark would have only an arbitrarily assigned relation to any particular phoneme, we might as well use the letters which have a strong tradition of use. The actual letters chosen by most American linguists are adapted from the International Phonetic Alphabet (IPA), which in turn was adapted from the Latin alphabet as used in the more consistently written European languages—such as Spanish, Czech, and Finnish—by a group of scholars around the turn of this century.

However we decide to represent phonemes by letters, we will still need to describe the phonemes as sounds, that is, phonetically. This phonetic description can be made in three complementary ways: **articulatory**, **acoustic**, or **auditory**, according to whether we specify the mechanism which generates the sound, the physical nature of the sound itself, or the impression the sound makes on a human hearer.

The most precise specifications of a sound available to us can be given in acoustic terms: our machinery for measuring the components of speech sounds as physical events can be calibrated to as high a degree of exactness as the measuring instruments used in any of the other exact sciences. Acoustic measurement is in a sense *too* exact for the purposes of most linguistic study. We discover from acoustical study that no two language events occurring naturally are ever physically the same, and yet we must say that there are constant repetitions, in some sense, of linguistic units, if we are to make use of the notion of linguistic unit at all. The precision that acoustic measurement affords, then, is not needed for the kinds of linguistic study we undertake in this book. We would hasten to add that there are interesting and important things to be learned about language in acoustic study, and the field of experimental phonetics, which more and more includes techniques and results from acoustic phonetics, has made and will continue to make valuable contributions to our general understanding of the way languages work and the way they change. Acoustic phonetics is a highly technical field, which requires a rather elaborate presentation of basic notions in physics in order to be properly meaningful. However, such notions do not have enough relevance to other current problems in English linguistics to warrant much discussion in this short treatment of phonetics.

The most widespread kind of identification of phonemes as sounds is the auditory one: statements such as "Pronounce

Cholmondeley to rhyme with *comely*," or "The German *ch* in *ach* sounds like someone gargling without water," or "Use a soft *th* in *lathe*," depend on a speaker's ability to match sounds to a model, to identify one occurrence of a sound (or sequence of sounds) with another occurrence. The auditory identifications of sounds used in dictionary guides to pronunciation are well known. For all their practical usefulness, such descriptions of sounds unfortunately lack the rigor and constancy required in scientific discussions of language, particularly in discussions of languages or dialects other than one's own; furthermore, many of the generalizations that we can make about the phonetic nature of phonemes are unstatable in auditory terms of the sort used in most dictionaries. We must recognize that in the oral use of language, i.e., speech, it is exactly the auditory identification of phonemes that is operative, and so auditory descriptions can never be totally dispensed with. However, since the methods of auditory description are as yet insufficiently developed to provide the rigor and generalization we need to describe phoneme systems, we must complement auditory identifications by articulatory descriptions.

Articulatory descriptions—essentially recipes for making sounds—take advantage of the fact that a human language uses a limited mechanism to produce speech. The vocal apparatus, no part of which has specially evolved for the production of speech, consists of relatively few parts, which can be brought together, held apart, and otherwise modified to take on various shapes, providing a flexible system capable of producing an indefinitely large number of different sounds. Fortunately, in any one language, the number of significant (i.e., phonemic) sound discriminations is quite small and the descriptive system for analyzing them is fairly simple.

In order to identify and describe phonetically the phonemes of the English of today (which we will refer to as NE—for *New English*), we need to examine the mechanism of speech. The discussion that follows is only an outline of a very complex and interesting subject. In this discussion, when sounds are represented as sounds—that is, when we make a phonetic transcription—the transcription is enclosed between square brackets: e.g., [pʰ], [ɛˆ], [tʔ], [pʰɛˆtʔ]. When sounds are represented as components of significant linguistic wholes—that is, when we make a phonemic transcription—the transcription is enclosed between slants: e.g., /p/, /e/, /t/, /pet/.

English **phones** (segments of speech sound, considered without regard for their distinctive value) are all produced by modifying air as it is exhaled from the lungs under pressure from the contraction of abdominal and intercostal (between-the-rib) muscles. As the air is driven towards the outside opening of the mouth or nose, it passes through a cavity—called the **vocal tract**—which can be changed in shape and size, and within which obstacles can be created in various ways during emission of air.

The first place at which an obstacle can be created in the path of the air on its way out is the **larynx** (the "voice-box," which forms the bump we call the Adam's apple). In the larynx the air passes through a slit, called the **glottis**, whose size and shape is controlled by two bands of muscles called the **vocal bands** (also called "vocal cords"). These bands can be pressed tightly together to close off the passage through the glottis completely; the sound made by the closure and subsequent explosion caused by relaxing the bands to allow air through the glottis is called the **glottal catch** (also called "glottal stop") and can be represented by the letter [ʔ]. We make such a sound when we begin to cough, or between sobs, or in the middle of saying "No" by going *unh-unh,* or at the beginning of a word like *oh* or *angry* or *early* (words that otherwise begin with vowels) when we try to say them distinctly.

While the vocal bands are held closed together, the cartilages to which they are attached may be held apart so that the air may pass through, and the turbulence which is thus produced is called **whispering.**

The vocal bands can be held wide apart to allow the air to pass freely and noiselessly through the open glottis. This happens in normal breathing as well as with certain phones—which are audible only because of obstructions placed in the path of the air in the tract above the larynx. Phones made with the bands thus held apart are called **voiceless.**

Finally, and most important for speech, the vocal bands can be tightened to just such a degree that air passing through the glottis will cause them to open and close rapidly and periodically. The periodic pulsation of the air stream thus produced is called **voice** or **voicing,** and is responsible for the audibility of a large part of our speech. Voicing provides a basic, complex sound wave that can be modified with great variety in the vocal tract above the larynx. The rate of opening and closing of the glottis (approximately 110–170 times per second in the normal speech of men, and 220–330 times per second in the normal speech of women) is determined by the tenseness of the vocal bands and in turn largely determines the **pitch** of the voice.

From the larynx, the air under pressure enters a cavity, the **pharynx,** which opens into the oral (mouth) and nasal cavities. At the opening into the nasal cavity is a flexible flap, the **velum,** which can be raised to keep air from flowing into the nasal cavity, or can be lowered to allow the air to pass through it. In breathing through the nose, the velum is in its relaxed, lower position, but for most speaking in English it is raised so that air is forced out through the mouth. At the back end of the velum is a muscular pendant, the **uvula.**

Given the elaborate musculature which constitutes and controls the tongue, lower jaw, and pharynx, the shapes and relative sizes of the oral and pharyngeal cavities can be modified continuously during speech. The characteristic quality of the sound emanating as speech from the vocal tract depends on two kinds of modification in the vocal tract: **resonance** and **obstruence.** The first depends on the fact that the rapid opening and closing of the glottis that produces voicing causes the moving air stream to pulsate in a complex way. As the vocal tract above the larynx is modified in size and shape, the character of these pulsations is modified—modified by a phenomenon called **resonance.** Sounds characterized by their resonance, by the special way in which the vocal tract "shapes" the voiced air stream (and consequently the sound wave), are called **resonants.**

The second kind of modification, **obstruence,** is created by

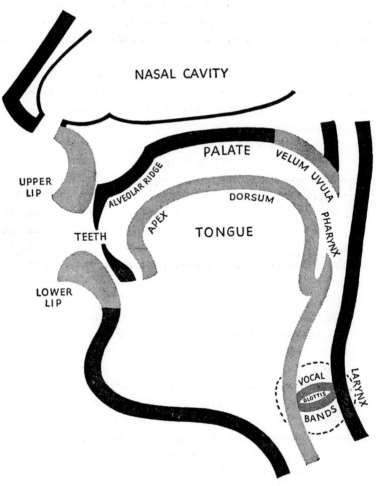

FIGURE 1. Drawing of vocal tract. Parts whose movements may be specified in phonetic description are in grey. Other parts are in black.

obstructions in the way of the air stream on its way out. Interference with air moving under pressure will produce noise (technically, non-periodic sound), and thus **obstruents** differ from resonants in being noisy rather than resonant.

In order to describe the different kinds of speech sounds, it will be convenient to make use of simplified schematic drawings to represent the vocal tract. Figure 1 shows a side view of the vocal tract with the relevant parts labeled. Figure 2 shows an even simpler schematic drawing, with only the relative positions of the parts of the tract indicated. Such drawings can make clearer the general features of the various classes of sounds and may make it easier to visualize how continuous speech proceeds.

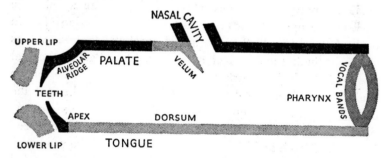

FIGURE 2.   Schematic representation of vocal tract. Like Figure 1, but simplified to indicate only features relevant for phonetic description.

Resonants

The particular quality of a resonant[2] depends on the relative shapes and sizes of the parts of the vocal tract that are separately movable: namely, the walls of the pharynx, the velum, the tongue, and the lips. Resonants can be classified into groups depending on whether the air stream is maximally, partially, or minimally impeded in the mouth. Maximal oral impedance

---

[2] As opposed to the general quality of the voice, characteristic of the individual speaking. General quality varies with the absolute size of the cavity, condition of the teeth, palate, mucous membranes, etc.

produces **nasals**, partial impedance produces **liquids**, minimal impedance produces **vocoids**. A subclass of vocoids, the semivocoid resonants, is distinguished from the others by timing or pressure differences.

Nasals

With the air stream being voiced in the larynx and with the velum in a relaxed, lowered position, the nasal passage will be added as a resonating cavity. If at the same time the air stream is prevented from escaping through the mouth a **nasal** resonant will be produced. If the oral closure is made by closing the lips together, the **bilabial** (two-lip) **nasal** [m] is produced, as at the beginning of *mill* or the end of *limb*. If the oral closure is made by pressing the **apex** (tip) of the tongue against the back of the upper teeth or against the **alveolar ridge** (just in back of the upper teeth), the **apical nasal** [n] is produced, as at the beginning and end of *nine*. (See Figure 3.) If the oral closure is made by pressing the **dorsum** (back) of the tongue against the velum, the **dorsal nasal** [ŋ] is produced, as at the end of *sing*. If the oral opening is not closed off at the same time that the velum is relaxed, **nasalized** phones, such as the nasalized vowels in French and in some dialects of English, are produced. We may mark the latter by placing a tilde (~) over the symbol for the corresponding oral sound, e.g., [ɛ̃].

APEX

FIGURE 3. Schematic representation of [n]. Note the vibration of the vocal bands, the opening into the nasal cavity, and the closing off of the oral passage by the apex of the tongue.

With voicing, but with the velum raised to close off the nasal passage, there are two sets of possibilities for resonants: the oral passage may be shaped so as to force the air stream to take a non-direct route to the outside, giving us **liquid** resonants, or it may be shaped so as to allow the air stream a direct route to the outside, giving us **vocoids.**

Liquids

If the center line of the oral passage is closed off by touching a middle part of the tongue against the top of the mouth, but allowing the air free passage around one or both sides, a liquid called a **lateral** [l] is produced. For a "light" [l], as at the beginning of *late*, the central closure is made only with the apex (see Figure 4), but for a "dark" [ł] there is also a closure made by touching the uvula against the extreme back of the tongue, as at the end of *swell*. If the air stream is partially impeded by an obstacle placed in the central line of the oral cavity, but not so as to create a non-periodic interruption, an

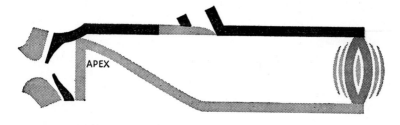

APEX

FRONT
VIEW

FIGURE 4. Schematic representation of [l]. Note the vibration of the vocal bands, the closing off of the nasal cavity, the central closing of the oral cavity by the apex (for a dark [ł] the closure would employ the dorsum in contact with the uvula). In the front view, an [l] would also result if only one of the side openings was present.

[r] phone is produced, as at the beginning of *rate*, the middle of *berry*, or the end of *fear* (absent in some dialects of English). Such impedance for [r] may be created by allowing the tip of the tongue to vibrate (or merely tap) rapidly against the alveolar ridge, by allowing the uvula to vibrate (or tap) rapidly against the back of the tongue, or by raising the tongue tip, center, or back, into close proximity to the roof of the mouth without touching it. (See Figure 5.) Phoneticians use a variety of symbols to distinguish these various kinds of **central liquids,** but for our purposes, the general symbol [r] for the whole class will suffice.

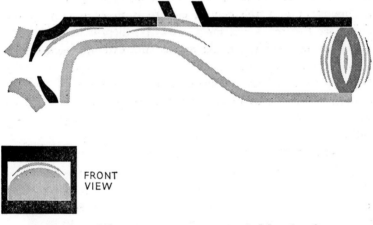

FRONT
VIEW

FIGURE 5. Schematic representation of [r]. The figure attempts to show that the oral closure must be only partial, either with the tongue (apex or dorsum) approaching but not touching the roof of the mouth, or with intermittent tapping (at the alveolar ridge or the uvula).

Vocoids

The traditional way of describing vocoids (loosely called "vowels") is in terms of the positions of the tongue, lips, and velum. Since the quality of any resonant does depend on the shape of the resonating cavity above the larynx, and the variation in the shape of that cavity is in turn dependent on its movable parts, it is natural that this traditional method of description should have worked as well as it has. However, it is well established that the acoustic and hence auditory quality of a vocoid depends, not on the position of any one or two of the "articulators," as the movable parts are called, but on the total configuration of the entire vocal tract. And recently, the part played by the mobility of the walls of the pharynx itself has been realized to have an importance not recognized by the traditional articulatory recipes. Unfortunately, the body of basic research that might establish more accurate descriptions of the shapes of the resonating cavity has not yet been completed.[3] Fortunately, however, even the incomplete characterization of resonants by an account of only the oral articulators suffices to distinguish each of the categories relevant for English from one another.

Vocoids are resonants in which the air stream has unimpeded egress to the mouth opening. (See Figure 7 on page 47.) Our classification of vocoids in this book will consider three factors: 1) the position of the tongue in determining the shape of the oral-pharyngeal cavity; 2) the relative size of the aperture at the lips; and 3) the width of the air stream as determined by pharyngeal and lingual shaping.

1) The musculature that comprises and controls the tongue is extremely flexible, and the tongue can be moved into an endless variety of positions. The crucial movements in determining the quality of vocoids, however, are those which affect the shape of the oral-pharyngeal cavity. In describing this shape, the critical factor seems to be the location and size of the "neck" of the resonating cavity,[4] the point at which the tongue is nearest the roof of the mouth. It is traditional to state the location and size of this "neck" as the height—**high, mid,** or **low**—and forward position—**front, central,** or **back**—of the tongue with respect to the roof of

---

[3] Although a giant step forward has been taken recently by C. Gunnar M. Fant: *Acoustic Theory of Speech Production* (The Hague: Mouton; 1960).

[4] R-M. S. Heffner: *General Phonetics* (Madison: The University of Wisconsin Press; 1960), Plate 22, p. 89.

	FRONT				CENTRAL		BACK			
Air stream Width	Narrow		Wide		Wide		Wide		Narrow	
Lip Aperture	Un-rounded	Rounded	Un-rounded	Rounded	Rounded	Un-rounded	Un-rounded	Rounded	Un-rounded	Rounded
Tongue Position										
High	i *beet*	ü French *but*	ɪ *bit, kiss*	ü German *mündlich*		ɨ *but* (unaccented)	ï Russian *byt'*	ʊ *book, put*		u *boot*
Mid	e *bait*	ö French *boeufs*	ɛ *bet*	œ French *boeuf*		ə *butt, put*		ɔ *balk*		o *boat*
Low			æ *bat*			a French *patte*	ɑ *bar*	ɒ *box* (with a British accent)		

FIGURE 6. VOCOIDS. The examples given as illustrations are meant to be suggestive, not definitive. For the speech of a given individual, other examples might be better. For instance, [ɨ] is more familiar to many people as the vocoid in *just* and in *'im* in the casual, rapid pronunciation of *I just saw 'im*; for some people, [ɒ] appears in words like *fog* or *sorry*; and [a] is used by some people, especially in the eastern United States, in *aunt* or *pass*, and by many in the southern United States for *I*.

This chart indicates only a small sample of the different vocoids discriminable by the human ear; each symbol stands for any vocoid in the general area indicated by its position in the chart.

the mouth. For the sake of making this kind of description meaningful to the student, the same procedure will be followed here, but for a more accurate statement the student should look into a detailed, modern handbook of phonetics.[5]

2) The lip aperture may be relatively open or closed. If it is relatively closed, we speak of the vocoid as being **rounded**; if it is relatively open, we say that it is **unrounded**.

3) The air stream may be emitted in a relatively narrow or wide band. A relatively **narrow** vocoid is also called "tense" or "close"; a relatively **wide** vocoid is also called "lax" or "open."

Figure 6 presents symbols for a number of vocoids; Figure 7 gives a general schematic for any vocoid; and Figure 8 gives schematics for nine of the principal vocoids.

FIGURE 7.   Schematic representation of any vocoid. Significant here is the vibration of vocal bands, the closure of the nasal passage, and the unimpeded egress to the outside through the oral cavity.

The Semivocoid Resonants [h], [y], [w]

The phones [h], [y], and [w] all have some of the characteristics of vocoids, but differ in significant ways from the vocoids proper.

The phone [h] has the interesting property of being identical with a vocoid, except that it is forced through the larynx with more pressure than for ordinary voicing. It can thus be thought

---

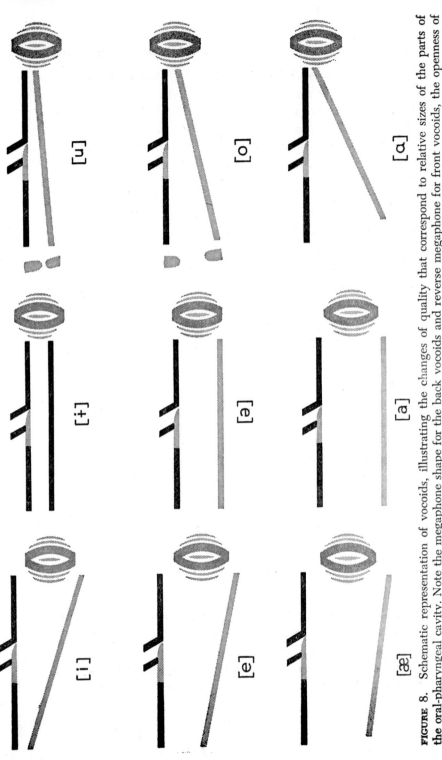

FIGURE 8. Schematic representation of vocoids, illustrating the changes of quality that correspond to relative sizes of the parts of the oral-pharyngeal cavity. Note the megaphone shape for the back vocoids and reverse megaphone for front vocoids, the openness of the channel for low vocoids in contrast to closedness for the high ones, and the use of the lips for the "rounded" vocoids [u] and [o].

of as a super-pressured vocoid. As a result of the extra pressure, there may actually be some friction created in the larynx or pharynx, leading some phoneticians to talk about [h] as a "whispered" vocoid, others to say that it is a voiceless vocoid, still others to describe it as a laryngeal or pharyngeal fricative. (See p. 52 for the meaning of "fricative.")

The phone [y] is a resonant produced as the tongue moves to or from a high front position. It is the relative rapidity of this movement that distinguishes [y] from the high front vocoids [ɪ] and [i] (as you can determine for yourself by pronouncing the initial sound of *yolk* at an exaggeratedly slow rate of speed). In the International Phonetic Alphabet (IPA), the symbol [j] is used for this semivowel; we have preferred to use [y] here because of the possible confusion of [j] with the symbol [ǰ] (see p. 54).

Exactly parallel to the relationship between [y] and [i] or [ɪ] is the relationship between [w] and [u] or [ʊ]; [w] is a resonant produced with the tongue in relatively rapid movement to or from a high back position, with the lips in movement to or from a rounded aperture.

Obstruents

The non-periodic interruption of the air stream that characterizes obstruents is also of three degrees: maximal, minimal, or partial. During the obstruction in the oral cavity, voicing—the periodic opening and closing of the glottis—may or may not be going on in the larynx, producing a whole series of voiced *vs.* voiceless obstruents. You may want to refer to Figure 9 during the following discussion.

Stops

Maximally interrupted phones are called **stops**. For a stop, the air stream, blocked from coming out through the nose by the raised velum, is forced under pressure toward the mouth opening, but before it can reach the outer air it is stopped completely by an obstruction placed in its path at various **points of articulation.**

Obstruents			
Articulation	*Labial*	*Apical*	*Dorsal*
Impedance			
Stops (Maximal)			
voiceless	p *pill*	t *till*	k *kill*
voiced	b *bill*	d *dill*	g *gill*
Affricates (Partial)			
voiceless			č *chill*
voiced			ǰ *Jill*
Fricatives (Minimal)		θ *thigh*	š *Aleutian* x *Bach*
voiceless	f *fail*	s *race*	
voiced	v *vail*	ð *thy*	ž *allusion* γ *raggedy* (in rapid
		z *rays*	speech pronounced with only slight obstruction of its air stream)

FIGURE 9.   Chart of selected obstruents. [p] and [b] are bilabial, while [f] and [v] are labio-dental. [č], [ǰ], [š], and [ž] are all apico-dorsal, that is, they employ both the apex and dorsum of the tongue in their articulations. For [f], [v], [θ], [ð], [x], and [γ], the air stream is forced through a *slit* opening, while for [s], [z], [š], [ž], [č], and [ǰ] the air stream is forced through a *slot* opening. The term **sibilant** is sometimes used to refer to any of these "slot" phones.

The stoppage may be made by placing the two lips together, yielding a **bilabial** stop, designated as [p] if voiceless, [b] if voiced. (See Figure 10.) Or it may be made by placing the apex of the tongue against some part of the roof of the mouth, some-where between the back of the teeth and the back of the hard palate, yielding an **apical** stop, designated as [t] if voiceless, [d] if voiced. (See Figure 11.) Or it may be made by placing the dorsum of the tongue against the roof of the mouth, somewhere

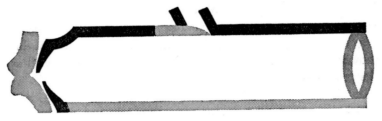

FIGURE 10.   Schematic representation of the voiceless
bilabial stop [p]. Notice the open glottis, the closure of
the nasal passage, and the oral closure at the lips.

on the **hard palate** (or simply **palate**), or the **velum** (**soft palate**),
yielding a **dorsal** stop, designated as [k] if voiceless, [g] if voiced.
(See Figure 12.) Note that the points of articulation for stops correspond exactly to those for nasal resonants.

The descriptions and symbols given in the previous paragraph
are of a very general kind; we can be much more specific in our

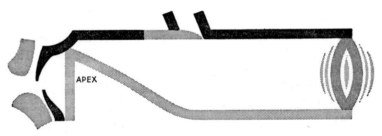

FIGURE 11.   Schematic representation of the voiced apical
stop [d]. Notice the vibrating vocal bands and the oral
closure with the apex of the tongue. Compare with Figure
3, to see the position of the velum in closing off the nasal
passage.

designation of phones if we like. For example, we can distinguish
a whole set of **voiceless aspirated** stops, which are made by
building up relatively more pressure behind the obstruction and
releasing it in an audible puff; these can be designated by modifications of the general symbols with **diacritic** marks thus: [pʰ],

[tʰ], [kʰ]. There are many other distinctions we can make if we have occasion to. We can attach dots, arrows, or similar marks to the symbols we have already discussed, in order to represent differences in the exact point of articulation of a sound, as well as the precise manner of articulation.[6]

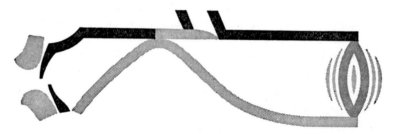

FIGURE 12. Schematic representation of the voiced dorsal stop [g]. Compare the tongue position with that in Figure 11.

Fricatives

Obstruents with a minimal interruption of the air stream are called **fricatives** (some phoneticians call them **spirants**). The audibility of fricatives (so called because of the friction that produces them) is due to the turbulence set up when air under pres-

---

[6] For example, we can distinguish between apical stops by the point of articulation at the roof of the mouth. If the apex touches the back of the teeth, we speak of an **apico-dental**, or more simply a **dental** stop. If the apex touches the gums behind the teeth, we speak of a **gingival** stop. If it touches the bony **alveolar ridge** behind the gums, we speak of an **alveolar** stop. If it touches still further back, we speak of a **retroflex** (also called **domal** or **cacuminal**) stop. Again, we can designate these by modification of the general symbols [t] and [d], placing a small arc below a symbol to indicate one of the more forward pronunciations ([ṭ] [ḍ] for a dental or gingival stop), or a dot below a symbol to indicate a pronunciation further back in articulation ([ṭ] [ḍ] for retroflex stop). We can use similar devices for distinguishing between dorsal phones made by placing the back of the tongue relatively forward in the mouth, against the back of the hard palate, yielding **palatal** stops [ḳ] and [g], or further back in the mouth, against the velum or even the uvula, yielding **velar** or **uvular** stops [ḳ] and [g].

sure is forced through a small opening. The opening may be between the lower lip and the upper teeth, yielding the **labiodental** fricatives, voiceless [f] and voiced [v]. (See Figure 13.) Or the opening may be between the apex of the tongue and edges of the teeth, yielding the **interdental** voiceless [θ] and voiced [ð] (as in *ether* and *either* respectively). Or a very narrow, short opening may be made between the apex of the tongue and the base of the upper teeth (or the area behind them), yielding the **sibilants** voiceless [s] and voiced [z]. Or a wider, longer opening may be made between a larger portion of the front of the tongue and the palate, and the consequent air stream is directed against the lower teeth, yielding the **sibilants** voiceless [š] (the IPA symbol is [ʃ]) and voiced [ž] (IPA [ʒ]). The opening can also be made between the dorsum and the palate or velum, yielding the dorsal fricatives voiceless [x] and voiced [ɣ]. (See Figure 14.) These latter phones do not occur in modern English, but they are common in many other languages, including modern German and Old English.

FIGURE 13. Schematic representation of the voiced labiodental fricative [v]. Notice the narrow slit between the lower lip and upper teeth through which the air stream is forced.

Affricates

Obstruents with a partial interruption of the air stream are called **affricates**. Affricates are made by stopping the air stream momentarily (not so long as for a stop obstruent) and quickly releasing it as a fricative. In English the only affricates are those formed by stopping the air as for [t] and [d] and releasing it as for [š] and [ž], yielding voiceless [č] and voiced [ǰ] respectively. Some phoneticians prefer to consider the affricates as simply clusters of the phones [tš] (IPA [tʃ]) and [dž] (IPA [dʒ]), but for English it will be simpler to consider them unit phones.

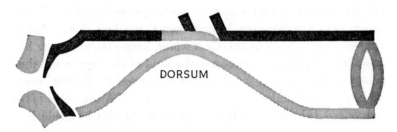

DORSUM

FIGURE 14. Schematic representation of the voiceless dorsal fricative [x].

THE CONTINUUM OF SPEECH

During an act of speech, the parts of the vocal apparatus are in almost continual movement. In pronouncing an apparently simple sequence *kink* [kʰɪŋk], a very complex set of individual actions—only a small number of which are listed here—take place. First, the back of the tongue is raised against the roof of the mouth to shut off the air stream and build up pressure to be released with the explosion of the [kʰ]. Even as the back of the tongue is rising, the whole tongue is moving forward into position for the following [ɪ], so that the closure of the air stream is actually made at a position on the velum considerably further forward than it would be for a [kʰ] followed by an [u] (as in *cool* [kʰul]). The explosion, itself voiceless, of the [kʰ] has something of the quality of the following [ɪ] (again contrast the [kʰ] of *cool*) and, with the addition of voicing from the larynx, changes into a resonant [ɪ]. After the front of the tongue has begun to move forward and up for [ɪ], the back of the tongue begins to rise to make the oral blockage required for the following [ŋ], and this movement

has the effect of producing a variety of [ɪ] that is higher than varieties produced in other phonetic contexts. (Compare the [ɪ] of
kink with that of *kin*; but also notice that this [ɪ] is not as narrow
as the [i] of *keen*.) During the later part of the [ɪ], the velum,
which has been closing off the nasal cavity until now, relaxes to
open that cavity, allows the air stream to pass through the nasal
passage, and thus adds a quality of nasalization to the [ɪ]. When
the back of the tongue has reached the velum, completely closing
off the oral passage, an [ŋ] is produced. For the following [k]
now, the larynx must stop producing voicing and the velum must
again close off the nasal passage. Depending on which of these
events begin first (perfect simultaneity would rarely occur), between the [ŋ] and [k] will come either a brief voiceless [ŋ̥] or a
voiced [k]. Finally, the pressure that has built up behind the
closure for [k] is released, drawing the back of the tongue away
from the velum to let the air out through the lip opening. We
could attempt to represent these details of movement by a more
detailed phonetic transcription—for example, by something like
[ˈkkʼ ɪ̯ʳɪ ɪ̃ŋŋˈkkʼ]. But we would be forced to recognize that such
transcription is always doomed to be imperfect, as judged against
the greater and greater precision and detailing that our ever developing instruments of acoustic measurement allow us to achieve.
We would be forced to recognize that the continuity of speech
can theoretically never be accurately represented by a finite number of discrete symbols. We would, indeed, eventually be led to
recognize that a phonetic transcription, like a musicologist's
transcription of a performance of a piece of music, must always
represent a continuum of sound as a set of discrete elements in
terms of which the continuum can be reconstructed.

A phonemic transcription, as we have already explained, goes a
step further and attempts to represent not the continuous speech
itself, but the linguistic units by which that speech is interpreted.
In a phonemic transcription, we record only enough elements—
i.e., phonemes—to represent the distinctive phonetic forms of the
linguistic units of the particular language in question—in this
case, English. Compare the "narrow" phonetic transcription

of *kink* in the paragraph above with the "broader" phonetic transcription [kʰɪ̂ŋk] and with a phonemic transcription /kɪŋk/.

For most purposes of linguistic description (e.g., citing forms in a grammar, indicating pronunciation of lexical items in a dictionary), phonemic transcription serves perfectly well. However, in order to record the way in which phonetic change takes place in language, so that the "same" linguistic unit will have different phonetic forms from one individual speaker to another, from one speech community to another, and from speakers at one period of time to another, we must also be able to describe and represent the detailed phonetic characteristics of utterances.

For example, we should not be surprised to discover that in the history of English, word-final sequences of /mb/—e.g., in the ME words *lamb, climb, comb*—changed to simply /m/ and have remained such in modern English. We will note that the only articulatory difference between [m] and [b] is in the position of the velum: relaxed and down for [m], contracted and up for [b] (thus shutting off the nasal passage). A single articulatory change was all that was needed for the simplification of /mb/ to /m/ to take place. Similarly, the difference between pronunciations of *once* as [wəns] and [wənst] in some dialects is accounted for by a single articulatory change: the tip of the tongue, close to the alveolar ridge but not touching it for [s], does touch it for [t].

In general, in tracing the history or the geographical or social distribution of complex phonetic changes, we try to reconstruct these changes as series of single, simple component changes. For example, to understand how an early OE *ic* [ɪk] might have developed into NE *I* [ay], we could reconstruct a series of steps as on page 57 (although this does not pretend to be an account of the actual historical details).

Phonological changes of a similar type can be seen operating in the English of today (NE). For example, we know that in NE the pronunciation of unstressed *and* in fast speech may be [əm] if the next word begins with a bilabial consonant (e.g., *Joe 'n Bill*), [əŋ] if it begins with a dorsal consonant (*tennis 'n*

Single change represented

Old English

1. [ɪk] > [ɪk̬]

For [ɪ] the highest position of the tongue is forward in the mouth; for [k] it is in the back. For [ɪk̬] the hump of the tongue never gets to the position for [k], but touches the roof of the mouth further forward. (Compare the [k] of NE *poke* with the [k̬] of NE *peak*.)

2. [ɪk̬] > [ɪx̬]

The hump of the tongue, instead of touching the roof of the mouth for [k̬], merely comes close to it for the fricative [x̬]. (Compare Modern German *ich* "I".)

Middle English

3. [ɪx̬] > [ɪγ]

For [ɪ] the larynx produces voicing; for [x̬] it stops producing voicing. In the change voiceless [x̬] > [γ] the voicing of the sequence [ɪγ] is continuous.

Early Modern English

4. [ɪγ] > [ɪy]

The hump of the tongue is in close proximity to the palate for the fricative [γ]. For [y] it is far enough away not to create friction.

Present-day English

5. [ɪy] > [əy]

The hump of the tongue, forward for [ɪ], moves to a central position for [ə].

6. [əy] > [ay]

The hump of the tongue, relatively high for [ə], moves to a low position for [a].

Modern English

golf), [əɱ][7] if it begins with a labio-dental consonant (*back 'n forth*), [ən] if it begins with an apical consonant or with almost anything else (*give 'n take, ham 'n eggs*). This kind of phonetic change, in which the sound comes to resemble a neighboring sound, is labeled **assimilation,** and can be found in many cases in English as well as other languages. Terms like "assimilation"

---

[7] [ɱ] stands for a labio-dental nasal consonant, while, of course, [m], [ŋ], [n] stand for bilabial, dorsal, and apical nasal consonants respectively.

are indeed useful as descriptive labels for phenomena of very general distribution among languages of the world.[8] However, it is misleading to think of them as expressing inexorable laws of change. If, for instance, we were to posit assimilation as the sufficient *cause* of the various forms of *and* just mentioned, we would be unable to account for its failure to operate universally in English as well as in other languages.

Similarly, if we were to try to explain the simplification of word-final sequences of /mb/ to /m/ in *lamb, comb, climb*, etc., and the word-final sequences of /ŋg/ to /ŋ/ in *song, hang, going*, etc., by the famous "Principle of Least Effort"[9] (which has been advanced as the explanation of all assimilation), we could not escape circularity of argument when we came to account for the fact that the similar word-final sequence /nd/ in *land, hand, wind*, etc., did not simplify to /n/. And although we may find the label "The Great Vowel Shift" (see Chapter VI) a great help in classifying the series of English vowel changes that have resulted in our modern pronunciations of *stone, house, I, green*, and thousands of other words, we should not be so foolish as to think that the Great Vowel Shift is a *causal* explanation of these pronunciations.

PHONEMES OF PRESENT-DAY ENGLISH

Now that we have provided the means for describing the phonetic characteristics of phonemes, we can turn our attention back to the question of *what* the phonemes of English are. We want to know what the phoneme inventory of NE is; that is, what are the elements by which the forms of the linguistic units in NE can best be represented?[1] We must consider our

---

[8] See Stuart Robertson and Frederick G. Cassidy: *The Development of Modern English* (New York: Prentice-Hall; 1954), 79–85 for other such labels.

[9] Which attempts to account for linguistic change by positing a universal process in language working towards ever greater efficiency.

[1] Actually, we will present here only the phonemes required to represent the speech of the two authors of this book. This set of phonemes will suffice

answer carefully. As the constituents of the characteristic forms of meaningful units, there must be just enough phonemes to distinguish each of those meaningful units from every other, and we thus need only as many different symbols as there are different sound contrasts between meaningful units. Since these symbols are to represent all the elements of sound that have the power to make meaningful distinctions in English, the correctness of the inventory of phonemic symbols is to be judged by the adequacy with which they represent the forms of all meaningful units and combinations of meaningful units.

What we are presenting here is not *the* inventory of *the* phonemes of English, but rather a *theory* of the phonemes of English, a theory that is subject to modification, adoption, or rejection. Like other scientific theories, the validity of any given system of transcription of a language can be tested by the generality and efficiency with which it handles data, although no absolutely rigorous procedure can be defined which will enable one to discover the best theory. If we keep in mind what tests a phonemic theory of a language will have to face, however, the task of arriving at an acceptable theory can be greatly facilitated.

In accordance with what we have said above (p. 34) about the nature of a phonemic transcription, any statement of the inventory of phonemes in a language must satisfy two requirements: first, it must provide sufficient elements to distinguish all the different phonological forms (though not all the various manifestations of those forms in speech) in that language from one another, and second, the elements provided must consistently represent segments of sound, that is, each phoneme must have a definable and consistent relation to speech phones. These conditions do not require that each distinct phone be represented

---

for many other varieties of English, spoken by many millions of speakers, but there are certainly some varieties for which additional phonemes are needed. The reader is referred to George L. Trager and Henry Lee Smith, Jr.: *An Outline of English Structure* (*Studies in Linguistics,* Occasional Papers, 1951), for a rather different analysis of the phonemes of this and other varieties of English.

as a distinct phoneme. They do require that each phoneme have a consistent phonetic value and that every distinct phonological form (the sound form of a linguistic unit) have a distinct representation as a sequence of phonemes.

The first requirement leads to the most direct test of whether a particular system of phonemic transcription (including its inventory of phonemes) is adequate for a language: the "minimal pair" test. In this test we take two actual meaningful utterances (the shorter they are, the easier it is to apply the test) which are phonetically similar to each other. If ordinary native speakers of the language interpret the two utterances as "different," the phonological forms of the linguistic units manifested in those utterances must differ, and our phonemic transcription must differ for the two utterances by at least one element, i.e., one phoneme. For example, native speakers of English have no difficulty in distinguishing spoken *ether* and *either* or between a *bow* (bending from the waist) and a *bow* (that shoots arrows), but they cannot tell which is which in pronunciations of *weigh* and *way* or a *bank* (for money) and a *bank* (along a river); in the former, there are phonemic differences between the forms with different meanings, while in the latter there are no phonemic differences. (Notice that the traditional orthography, i.e., conventional spelling, of the forms is undependable as a guide to phonemic distinctions.) It would be an inadequate phonemic transcription that failed to indicate the differences between the members of the pairs *ether-either* and *bow-bow*, but it would also be an inadequate transcription that indicated nonexistent differences between the members of the *weigh-way* and *bank-bank* pairs. Whatever our phonemic transcription for *ether* is, it must differ somehow from that of *either*; similarly, the transcriptions for *bow* (bending from the waist) and *bow* (for shooting arrows) must differ. Whatever our transcription of *weigh* is, it must be the same for *way*, just as the two *banks* must be represented by the same phonemic transcription.

The second requirement demanded of a system of phonemic transcription for a language derives from our desire to make descriptive statements of maximal generality and simplicity. For example, let us see what would happen if we tried to assert that the initial sound segment of *pin* and the final sound segment of *ham* belonged to the same phoneme /X/, and that the initial sound segment of *mat* and the final sound segment of *tap* both belonged to another single phoneme /Y/. If we did this, we would need separate statements in order to describe the phonetic character of each phoneme for each position:

/X/ is a bilabial voiceless stop [p'], opening orally in initial position.

/Y/ is a bilabial voiceless stop [p'], closing orally in final position.

/X/ is a bilabial nasal [m'], closing orally in final position.

/Y/ is a bilabial nasal [m'], opening orally in initial position.

It is obvious that each of these statements is more limited in scope and more complex than the statements that can follow if we assign the initial sound segment of *pin* and the final one of *tap* to a phoneme /X/, and the initial sound segment of *mat* and the final one of *ham* to another phoneme /Y/. Then our descriptive statements may be made without limitation on position:

/X/ is a bilabial voiceless stop [p] in all positions.

/Y/ is a bilabial voiced nasal [m] in all positions.

This argument leads to a second test of the adequacy of a system of phonemic transcription: Sound segments should be assigned to phonemes in such a way that the simplest, most consistent, and most general statements of phonetic description can be made for each of the phonemes. We may call this the principle of **phonetic consistency**. (Many linguists call it the principle of **phonetic similarity**.)

A special terminology has become established for talking about the relationship between phonemes and segments of sound. A **phoneme** (= element in a characteristic sound form of a linguistic unit) is said to have **allophones** (= the various actual sound segments manifesting a phoneme [e.g., the initial sound segment of *pin* and the final one of *tap* are allophones of the same phoneme]). When the phonemic status of sounds is not determined or not relevant to our discussion, we may use the term **phone** for a sound segment.

As a requirement that is important in the practical business of describing languages, although it is of no theoretical importance, we should choose symbols to represent the phonemes of a given language in accordance with some convention general for all languages. As has been suggested previously, the most convenient convention is one which assigns a simple letter suggested by the International Phonetic Alphabet (IPA), or one of the current modifications of the IPA. Thus, in the example above, instead of using an arbitrary letter /X/ for the phoneme some of whose allophones are represented by IPA [p], we use the letter /p/. Note that we use brackets [   ] to enclose phonetic symbols, but slants /   / to enclose phonemic symbols.

A more indirect test of the adequacy of a system of phonemic transcription and the inventory of phonemes it entails is also based on our desire for simplicity and generality in descriptions of phenomena. Consider the pair *pill-spill* in English. Now, any phonetician can tell you that the initial phone of *pill* and the second phone of *spill* are different. You can prove this to yourself by holding a lighted match in front of your mouth and saying *spill* and *pill* in that order; when you say *spill,* the match will probably flicker a little but stay lit, but for *pill* it will probably go out. The phonetician calls the puff of air that blows out the match in *pill* "aspiration" and represents the initial phone in *pill* as [pʰ]; the second phone of *spill* is called "unaspirated" and may be represented by [p˥]. The phonetician will be able to tell you that aspiration is regularly missing in English voiceless stops after [s], but is regularly present in voiceless stops in initial positions. Must a phonemic transcription indicate this difference in aspiration? The answer is no, and the reasoning for not indicating it goes like this: We can easily establish a phoneme /s/ that marks the difference between *sin* and *in*, *Sam* and *am, law* and *loss,* etc. If, following the principle of phonetic consistency, we indicate a phoneme /s/ in *spill,* we will have enough to distinguish that word from *pill.* Since the phonetic difference between [pʰ] and [p˺] is thus superfluous in distinguishing these words (and all other minimal pairs with [sp˺] versus [pʰ]), our desire for simplicity dictates that we not indicate it; *spill* and *pill* and all other like pairs are sufficiently distinguished in English as /sp/ versus /p/. We can put the matter in a kind of formula like this:

/p/ = /s/ [p˺]∼[pʰ] (To be read: The phoneme /p/ has the allophone [p˺] after /s/, in alternation with the allophone [pʰ]).

Whenever the occurrences of two phones (in this case, the two allophones of /p/) can be so stated that one phone never occurs in the same phonemic environment as the other, the two phones are said to be in **complementary distribution** and their occurrence is said to be *determined* or *conditioned* by the presence of some other phoneme or sequence of phonemes (in this case, by the preceding phoneme /s/).

Now, when is it not superfluous to indicate the difference between two phones; or, to put it positively, when *are* two different phones phonemically distinct? Exactly when we do *not* have a constant conditioning factor (like /s/ in the case of *spill, spell, spin, spit,* etc.) that will account for the phonetic difference. For instance, suppose that we are trying to decide whether the phones [š] (as in sh*in*) and [ž] (as in *measure*) are phonemically distinct in English, and suppose further that we have not hit upon a minimal pair (such as *Aleutian-allusion*) for them. How could we apply our indirect test to find out whether the two phones are allophones of one phoneme or are allophones of two distinct phonemes? Well, we would try to find a constant conditioning factor to which the difference between the two could be assigned. Consider the pair *fission* and *vision*. In *fission* we find [š] and in *vision* [ž]. Now we might try to say that the difference between the two is that *fission* begins with [f] and *vision* with [v], so that the phonemic distinction /f/-/v/ (established already for minimal pairs like *fail-veil*) is sufficient to account for the difference between [š] and [ž]—[š] occurring medially in words beginning with /f/, [ž] in words beginning with /v/. But this hypothesis would immediately fail as soon as we discovered *vicious,* with initial /v/ but medial [š]. Since the only constant difference besides [š] and [ž] between *fission* and *vision* is in the /f/ and /v/, which we now see is not a constant conditioning factor for [š] and [ž], the difference between the phones [š] and [ž] is proved to be phonemic, and we establish them as allophones of the phonemes /š/ and /ž/ respectively. The three words *fission, vision,* and *vicious* thus establish the contrast /š/ ≠ /ž/ (to be read: the phoneme /š/ contrasts with the phoneme /ž/).

PROMINENCE

Not accounted for in our description of phones so far are the different degrees of prominence in utterances. That is, not every part of an utterance is equally prominent phonetically—equally loud, if you like. Just what the acoustic and articulatory characteristics of all these prominences are has not yet been firmly established, but auditorily we can readily detect several different degrees of prominence: the cues seem to be duration (indicated in a phonetic transcription in one of several ways: by a colon [:] placed after a symbol, by a macron [‾] placed over a symbol for a vocoid, or by a tick [ˌ] placed under a symbol for other resonants or for fricatives); rate of change of pitch; and amount of energy in the phones. The linguistic representation of the different degrees of prominence is of two kinds: phonetically dependent (sub-phonemic), and phonetically independent (phonemic).

Dependent Prominence

In a given utterance it will be evident that a small number of resonants have in general relatively more prominent allophones —allophones that may be called **syllabic**—than the other phonemes: we call these more prominent phonemes **vowels,** and all other resonants and obstruents **consonants.** Thus, we have already sufficiently represented many of the differences in promi-

nence between phones in an utterance when we have assigned
some of the phones to vowel phonemes and others to consonant
phonemes. In English the vowels are all vocoids, or rather, they
would be were it not for sequences with prominent nasals and
liquids (marked with a [ˌ]) like *cotton* [katn̩], *bird* [br̩d], *fiddle*
[fidl̩], *rubber* [rəbr̩], *rope 'em* [ropm̩], *they c'n go* [ðe kŋgo].
Possible contrasts such as *polite* [pl̩ayt] ≠ *plight* [playt]; *light-
ening* (making a load lighter) [laytn̩iŋ] ≠ *lightning* (electrical
flash in the sky [laytniŋ]; *caressed* [kr̩est] ≠ *crest* [krest], demand that a phonemic distinction be posited between the syllabic
(i.e., longer, more prominent) phones [r̩], [l̩], [m̩], [n̩], [ŋ̩],
and the nonsyllabic (i.e., shorter, less prominent) ones [r], [l],
[m], [n], [ŋ]. We might posit ten individual phonemes to account
for such contrasts, but a simpler solution is available. Starting
from the almost true statement that all vowels in English are
vocoids, we can make it completely true by postulating a special
phone whose phonetic value is the prominence of a following
resonant, and which may be identified phonemically as an allophone of the phoneme /ə/. Thus [r̩], [l̩], [m̩], [n̩], [ŋ̩]
(the so-called syllabic resonants) may be represented phonemically as /ər/, /əl/, /əm/, /ən/, /əŋ/, respectively.

Following a parallel line of reasoning, in many languages it
proves best to consider [y] and [i] (nonsyllabic and syllabic
respectively) as allophones of a single phoneme, but the description of English is simplified by assigning the two phones
to different phonemes. Thus if [y] is considered to belong to a
consonant phoneme /y/, it is possible to state the general rule
that the article *a* has the form /ə/ or /e/ before consonants, but
the form /ən/ or /æn/ before vowels—e.g., *a yolk* /əyók/ and
a ewe /əyú/, but *an evil* /ənívəl/ and *an itch* /əníč/. If [y] were
considered an allophone of /i/, the general rule would have to
be abandoned in favor of one with a special exception for some
occurrences of the vowel /i/. The same argument against considering [y] an allophone of /i/ or /ɪ/ applies against considering
[w] an allophone of /ʊ/ or /u/. That is, we say *a will* /əwíl/
and *a one* /əwə́n/, but *an ooze* /ənúz/.

From examples like these we can see that the question of what the phonemes of a language are cannot be answered by a mere inspection of the phonetic data, but must be decided by considering the over-all simplicity and generality of the total description of the language. Of the possible alternative phonemic descriptions of English resonants, we have chosen those—/ə/ + resonant for syllabic resonants, /y/ and /w/ for nonsyllabic [y] and [w]—that satisfy this criterion most effectively.[2]

An utterance can now be said to have as many **syllables** as it has vowels, with each vowel the center of prominence of its syllable. The degree of relative prominence of the whole syllable is given by the prominence of the vowel. A **diphthong** is a sequence of two vocoids in a single syllable, that is, with a single center of prominence. In NE, the diphthongs /ay/ as in *bite*, /aw/ as in *bout*, and /ɔy/ as in *boil* are particularly important.

Besides the dependent prominence of vowels over consonants, within the vowel and consonant classes some types of phones are inherently more prominent than others. Although it is difficult to know just what measurement is involved in such statements of comparison, we may say that in English, other factors being equal, narrow vowels are more prominent than wide ones—the vowel [ə] being the weakest of all vowels; resonants are more prominent than obstruents; and voiceless obstruents are more prominent than voiced ones.

Degree of Oral Impedance	*Type of Modification of Air Stream*		
	RESONANTS	*OBSTRUENTS*	
Maximal	NASALS	STOPS	
Partial	LIQUIDS	AFFRICATES	
Minimal	VOWELS	SEMIVOWELS	FRICATIVES

FIGURE 15. Chart of classes of phonemes in English, according to the phonetic characteristics of their allophones.

---

[2] A phoneme whose allophones are semivocoids is **called** a semivowel.

CONSONANTS				
OBSTRUENTS				

	Bilabial	*Apical*	*Dorsal*	EXAMPLES
STOPS				
Voiced	b	d	g	ta*b* ta*d* ta*g*
Voiceless	p	t	k	ta*p* ta*t* ta*ck*

AFFRICATES		
Voiced	ǰ	ri*dge*
Voiceless	č	ri*ch*

FRICATIVES		
Voiced	v ð z ž	*v*eal ei*th*er *z*eal allu*s*ion
Voiceless	f θ s š	*f*eel e*th*er *s*eal Aleu*t*ian

RESONANTS				
	Bilabial	*Apical*	*Dorsal*	
NASALS	m	n	ŋ	ta*m* ta*n* ta*ng*

	Central	*Lateral*	
LIQUIDS	r	l	*r*aid *l*aid

	For-ward	*Back-ward*	*Vari-able*	
SEMIVOWELS	y	w	h	*y*ell *w*ell *h*ell

VOWELS					

	Front		*Central*	*Back*	
	Narrow	*Wide*	*Wide*	*Narrow*	*Wide*
High	i p*ea*t	ɪ p*i*t	ə b*u*t / p*u*tt	u b*oo*t	ʊ p*u*t
Mid	e p*a*te	ɛ p*e*t		o b*oa*t	ɔ b*ou*ght
Low	æ p*a*t			a f*a*ther	

FIGURE 16. Chart of the phonemes of one widespread dialect of American English. Deviation from this inventory for vowels and their combinations with semivowels is substantial in other dialects. Other interpretations of the English phonemic system result, of course, in rather different inventories of phonemes, particularly for affricates and vowels.

The quantitative differences in degrees of prominence we have just discussed are all sub-phonemic—phonetically dependent—since they are already implicit in the qualitative differences between the phonemes involved. There are, however, other differences in prominence that *are* phonemic—i.e. phonetically independent—that must be represented in a phonemic transcription, that may occur contrastively. These phonemes involving prominence, labeled stress and accent, are discussed below (pp. 79ff.).

The accompanying charts (Figures 15 and 16) group the phonemes of NE into classes, according to the phonetic characteristics that distinguish them from one another. The charts should be studied, and the illustrative examples should be pronounced aloud to establish firmly in mind the auditory and articulatory characteristics of each phoneme.

TRANSCRIPTION EXERCISES

Use the symbols in the charts to transcribe the following items (The first six have been done for you as illustration.):[3]

A.
1. speech /spič/	16. breathe
2. characteristic /kɛrɪktərɪstɪk/	17. of
3. refer /rifər/	18. off
4. extricate /ɛkstrɪket/	19. W
5. examination /ɛgzæmmešən/	20. B
6. measurement /mɛžərmənt/	21. fraction
7. judge	22. scheming
8. H	23. fortunate
9. ache	24. careful
10. swords	25. tanker
11. bullets	26. vision
12. watches	27. fission
13. thy	28. vicious
14. thigh	29. think
15. breath	30. thing

[3] There will be a certain amount of variation in the transcriptions, especially of vowels, from one person to another, depending on the speed at

B. Make a list of twenty words. Transcribe them phonemically like those in the exercise above.

LINGUISTIC UNITS

Suppose you received the following two telegrams:
1) REFER CELLERS TO BYRNE STOP MAIL ORDERS NOW
2) REEFER SELLERS TO BURN STOP MAIL ORDERS NOW?

Suppose further that you understood telegram 1) to concern two people named Cellers and Byrne and to order the stoppage of some mail orders, and telegram 2) to report the electrocution of marijuana pushers and to ask whether some new orders should be mailed. Now assume that you want to read these telegrams aloud to another person and that you want to make a phonemic transcription of what you say. Given the phonemes we have discussed so far, both transcriptions would read the same:

/rifərsɛlərztubərnstapmelɔrdərznaw/[4]

Clearly, such a transcription is inadequate, since it fails to provide sufficient elements to distinguish utterances which do have different phonological forms. It is the purpose of the following sections to provide the missing elements. In these sections several terms will be used that will already be familiar to you; the terms have been deliberately chosen to be suggestive. But please note: the terms *word, phrase, clause,* and *sentence* are all used in technical senses; they all refer to *phonologically* (that is, *phonemically*) defined units, and such units only partially correspond to units defined differently in other treatments of English. Remember that these units are elements in a system of analysis of the language, in contrast to the physical events of

which the words are pronounced, the meticulousness of the pronunciation, and the dialect of English spoken. The teacher should allow some leeway in the transcription, at least until the section dealing with stress has been discussed in class. For example, reasonable alternative transcriptions of item number 5, *examination*, might be /ɪgzæmənešʊn/, /ɛksæmənešm/, etc.

[4] Many speakers of English say /rəfər/ rather than /rifər/ for *refer*. For the purposes of this discussion, assume that the transcription here is correct.

actual speech. In rapid speech the divisions between the units, as defined here, may be and often are absent. For all linguistic units the characterizing features discussed in this chapter are to be taken as potentially distinguishing rather than as present in every occurrence of the units to which they apply. That is, the characterizing features are available to mark the occurrence of the linguistic units, but the units may be present even though not all the characterizing features are present. For example, what we call word accents in a given utterance are attributed and assigned to words, although it may be that not every word in that utterance will be manifested with a word accent.

The Discourse

Telegram 1) and telegram 2) above each comprise a distinct message, a message whose parts are connected together to form a whole. The connection between the largest constituents of each telegram—namely, sentences—is not phonological, and the unity established by each message thus plays only a limiting role in phonemic transcription. A discourse—in this case a telegram, but in other cases a single sentence, a paragraph, a chapter, a book, a telephone call, an exchange of greetings, or a conversation—is the only linguistic unit occurring as an independent whole.

Discourses, the largest linguistic units, seem also to be units of connected thought. Within a long discourse, progression and connection in thought, however tenuous, hold the discourse together. For example, no English speaker would doubt that passage #1 below made sense and was a possible English utterance, but passage #2 would seem to belong to no one English utterance, but perhaps to four or five different ones.

#1 Yesterday I was in this bar. The funniest thing happened. A lady walked in and asked for the manager in a loud voice. Well, he came over and asked what the trouble was. All she said was, "You Satan," and then she hit him over the head with her wet umbrella.

#2 All she said was, "You Satan," and then she hit him over the head with her wet umbrella. Well, he came over and asked what the trouble was. A lady walked in and asked for the manager in a loud voice. The funniest thing happened. Yesterday I was in this bar.

Passage #1, a discourse, makes good linguistic sense, though perhaps not much intellectual sense. The reader or listener follows it from one part to the next, and even though he has no idea of the significance of the events described, he is willing to accept that the writer or speaker means to describe these events as a whole. In contrast, passage #2, a mere collection of sentences and no discourse, makes no linguistic sense; the reader or listener can make nothing out of the strange sequence. It could not stand on its own as a discourse to be interpreted in its own right, as passage #1 could.

A discourse can, under appropriate extralinguistic circumstances, be as short as a single sentence or even a single word: for example, "The walls are caving in!" or "Water!" in the proper desperate situations. As a matter of fact, linguists have at various times tried to define both sentences and words as the minimal discourses of a language. Attractive as such definitions seem, they do not provide much help in deciding that, "The funniest thing happened," is a sentence or that "said" is a word.

The Sentence

If we take our transcription of the two telegrams and introduce pauses, symbolized by /#/ in appropriate places, we will discover that some of the ambiguity of our transcription disappears:

Telegram 1) /rifərsɛlərztubərn#stapmelɔrdərznaw#/

Telegram 2) /rifərsɛlərztubərnstap#melɔrdərznaw#/

What we have done is to divide each discourse into **sentences**, linguistic units which terminate in linguistic pauses /#/. Note that there might also be other kinds of pauses—internally engendered (as when you hesitate while thinking) or externally imposed (as when a train whistle forces a break in the flow of speech)—that do not mark off sentences. This characterization of sentence by linguistic pause is circular: a *linguistic* pause is exactly one which terminates a sentence. However, such circularity is not necessarily bad. We are postulating a phoneme /#/ to account for the grammatical pauses in actual utterances; the other pauses are to be accounted for in terms of physiological or physical mechanisms like uncertainty and train whistles. It is not necessary to account for everything that occurs in utterances, in an exposition of the linguistic systems operating in a language. Some linguistic behavior—such as stuttering, laughing, hesitating—can better be approached in terms of other kinds of description, e.g., psychological. But sentences *are* linguistic units, and the pause that separates them from one another is thus linguistically relevant.

The Phonemic Clause

Not represented by the phonemes described so far are the linguistically relevant **intonation contours** (created mainly by variations in pitch) of our two telegrams. Intonation contours, the characterizing features of phonemic **clauses** (note, not of grammatical clauses), are represented in terms of **pitch patterns** and **terminals.** Every sentence contains at least one phonemic clause and hence at least one intonation contour, which in turn is composed of one terminal phoneme and at least two phonemes of pitch.

When the air stream passing through the larynx pulsates, it must pulsate at a certain frequency, a frequency that can be varied continuously by various laryngeal adjustments. This frequency of pulsation largely determines what we hear as the pitch of the voice. In singing, the exact pitch of a voice at a given moment is crucial for the acceptability and appreciation of the song; in speech, however, what is crucial for accurate communication and understanding are the relative differences in pitch within the speech of each individual. For example, in singing, a bass's A must bear a certain absolute physical relation to a soprano's A, if we are to accept the bass's and soprano's rendition of a piece of music. But in English speech, the physical value of a bass speaker's low pitch has no direct physical relation to a soprano speaker's low pitch: all that is relevant is that each individual's low pitch be lower than all his other pitches; that his highest pitch be higher than all his other pitches; and that his two intermediate pitches fall between his highest and lowest, with one intermediate pitch being relatively higher than the other.

For example, look at the musical transcription of a pronunciation of *It's raining* in Figure 17. Such a transcription is misleading linguistically; it is much too precise in one sense and much too imprecise in another sense, for linguistic transcription. In the first sense, it is too explicit about the number of syllables involved, and fixes the pitch intervals and durations of those syllables in terms of absolute measures of pitch and time; in a language, a given intonation contour may stretch over any number—from one on up—of syllables, and the pitch and time ratios obtaining between syllables have very flexible limits. In the second sense, a transcription of intonation as if it were music fails to distinguish the significant from the insignificant; what is crucial for making *linguistic* distinctions gets lost among all the *musical* distinctions. Notice, for example, that musical transcriptions for *It's raining, It's raining hard, It's raining harder now than it was yesterday* must be quite different (see Figure 17). But linguistically they may all have the same intonation contour, stretching over a longer or shorter sequence of syllables, a contour consisting of a pattern that may be represented in a generalized graphic form as ‾‾‾‾┌‾‾‾┐___﹨. This contour contrasts with many others in English. For example, there is one that you could use if you were not sure you had understood what someone had just said, and you were asking to make sure: _____┌‾‾‾‾‾. And there is another one you could use if you were adding doubt to your question about what he had said: ‾‾‾‾┌‾‾‾└___﹍. In asking a question with two alternative answers, you would probably use a combination of two clauses, the first of which had the contour ____┌‾‾‾ and the

UTTERANCE Written Expression	Approximate Musical Transcription	Graphic Representation	Phonemic Representation	Intonation Contour Involved
NEUTRAL TONE:				
It's raining.			²It's ³raining. ¹↓	2 3 1 ↓
It's raining hard.			²It's raining ³hard. ¹↓	
It's raining harder now than it was yesterday.			²It's raining harder now than it was yesterday. ³↓¹	
UNCOMPREHENDING TONE:				
It's raining?			²It's ³raining? ↑	2 3 3 ↑
It's raining harder?			²It's raining ³hard? ↑	
It's raining harder now than it was yesterday?			²It's raining harder now ³than it was yesterday? ↑	
DISBELIEVING TONE:				
It's raining?			³It's ⁴raining? ²↑	3 4 2 ↑
It's raining hard?			³It's raining ⁴hard? ²↑	
It's raining harder now than it was yesterday?			³It's raining harder now ⁴than it was yesterday? ²↑	
Would you like tea or coffee? (CHOOSE ONE)			²Would you like ³tea ³or ²coffee? ¹↓	2 3 3→2 3 1 ↓
Would you like tea or coffee? (SOMETHING TO DRINK?)			²Would you like ³tea or coffee? ³↑	2 3 3 ↑

second ⌐‾‾‾‾‾⌐   ⌐___; as in *Would you like tea or coffee?*
(Take your choice), while *Would you like tea or coffee?* (Answer
yes or no, do you want something to drink?) would have a single
contour ___⌐‾‾‾‾⁄.

For the representation of English clauses, only four distinct
pitch levels have been discovered to be significantly different:

> highest: represented by the number /⁴/
> high: represented by the number /³/
> mid: represented by the number /²/
> low: represented by the number /¹/

To represent the pitch pattern of a clause, at least two pitch level
phonemes must be marked: one to indicate the initial pitch and
one the final pitch of the clause. In addition a pitch phoneme
must be marked for each **phrase stress** (see following section)
and one for any significant change in the pitch at any other point
within the clause.

To complete the representation of intonation contours we
must supplement the pitch level phonemes with three **terminal**
phonemes, which we may symbolize as /→/, /↓/, and /↑/—for
the sake of convenience, we may call them **suspensory, fading,**
and **rising** terminals, respectively. Allophones of the last resonant
before a terminal, and of any obstruent between that resonant
and the terminal, are relatively longer in duration than allophones
of the same phonemes in other positions, other factors being
equal. At a suspensory terminal /→/, the final pitch of the clause
is maintained over these long allophones. At a fading terminal
/↓/, the final pitch of the clause is lowered over the long allophones. At a rising terminal /↑/, the final pitch of the clause is
raised over the long allophones.

FIGURE 17. Comparison of representation of intonation
by musical, graphic, and phonemic transcriptions. Note
the simplicity of the phonemic transcription, which allows
one to abstract the significant aspects of intonation out
of the phonetic continuum (as in the right-hand column)
for purposes of comparison of utterances.

Examination of the phonemic transcription of the intonation contours in Figure 17 will make clearer how the pitch patterns and terminal phonemes are represented in actual phonemic clauses.

Our two telegrams may now be represented as follows (other oral renditions would also be possible and would of course require different representation):

1) /²rifər³sɛlərztu³bərn¹↓#²stap³melɔrdərz³naw¹↓#/

2) /³rifərsɛlərztu³bərn³→³stap¹↓#²mel³ɔrdərz³naw³↑#/

As you can now see, the first discourse (Telegram 1) is composed of two sentences, each of which consists of a single phonemic clause with an identical intonation contour 2331↓. The second discourse (Telegram 2) consists of two sentences, the first of which contains two clauses—with the intonation contours 333→ and 31↓ respectively—and the second of which contains a single clause with the intonation contour 2333↑.

Disjuncture and the Word-group

To represent the separation between phonemic sentences, we have postulated a phoneme of linguistic pause /#/. To represent the separation between phonemic clauses, we have postulated terminal phonemes /↑/, /→/, and /↓/. Now, to represent the separation between phonemic word-groups, we shall need to postulate a phoneme of disjuncture, symbolized by a space between letters /xyz abcd/.[5] This disjuncture is marked phonetically by 1) lengthening of phonemes preceding the disjuncture

---

[5] Many linguists use the symbol /+/, "plus juncture," to represent both our disjuncture / / and our juncture /-/. Such a solution is a reasonable alternative to ours, but it necessitates a representation of phonemic degrees of stress in a way that seems to introduce as many difficulties as it solves.

When no other word-group immediately precedes, the space before a given word-group is conventionally omitted; when no other follows, the space after is conventionally omitted.

and 2) a strengthening of phonemes following the disjuncture.[6] The effect of the presence of disjuncture can be heard in pairs like: *new deal* /nu dil/ ≠ *nude eel* /nud il/; *changed over* /čenjd ovər/ ≠ *change Dover* /čenj dovər/; *kiss Ted* /kis tɛd/ ≠ *kissed Ed* /kist ɛd/; *bandana* /bændænə/ ≠ *banned Anna* /bænd ænə/.

Our two telegrams can now be transcribed more accurately by indicating the separation between phonemic word-groups:

1)   /²rifər ³sɛlərz tu³bərn¹↓#²stap ³melɔrdərz ³naw¹↓#/

2)   /³rifərsɛlərz tu³bərn³→³stap¹↓#²mel ³ɔrdərz ³naw³↑#/

JUNCTURE

There is one kind of separation that we have not yet provided for. Within a phonemic word-group there may be a separation that has the same qualitative effect—namely, lengthening of preceding phonemes and strengthening of following ones—as disjuncture, but less quantitative effect. We may call this phoneme **juncture** and symbolize it by a hyphen /-/. The classic example of contrast between the presence and absence of juncture is *night-rate* /nayt-ret/ ≠ *nitrate* /naytret/. Other examples are: *uneasy* /ən-izi/ ≠ *an easy* (job) /ənizi/, *re-seed* /ri-sid/ ≠ *recede* /risid/, *ray-burn* /re-bərn/ ≠ *Rayburn* /rebərn/. Contrasts between juncture and disjuncture may be heard in *Long Island* /lɔŋ-aylənd/ ≠ *long island* /lɔŋ aylənd/, *White House* /wayt-haws/ ≠ *white house* (not the black one) /wayt haws/, *blackbird* (the species of bird) /blæk-bərd/ ≠ *bláck bírd* (not the white one) /blæk bərd/.

---

[6] The "lengthening," that is, prolongation in time, applies to the last resonant to precede the disjuncture, and to any obstruent between that resonant and the disjuncture. A voiceless stop immediately preceding the disjuncture is usually pronounced with a simultaneous glottal catch [ʔ]. The "strengthening" applies to the next resonant to follow the disjuncture, and to any obstruent between the disjuncture and that resonant. A vocoid immediately following disjuncture may be "strengthened" by being preceded by a non-phonemic glottal catch [ʔ]. A voiceless stop immediately following disjuncture may be "strengthened" by being released with aspiration [ʰ].

It is characteristic of careful, deliberate speech to maintain the three-way contrast. But in rapid, casual speech the three-way contrast of no separation, juncture, and disjuncture is often not present. Juncture either merges with disjuncture or is lost completely. In some cases both juncture and disjuncture may disappear. In many cases this loss of separation is accompanied by other changes at the point of separation. For example, when the separation between /t/ and /y/ is lost, /č/ commonly occurs to replace both phonemes at the former point of separation (as when *don't you* /dont-yu/ becomes /donču/). Similarly /d/ plus /y/ becomes /ǰ/, /s/ plus /y/ becomes /š/, and /z/ plus /y/ becomes /ž/, if there is no separation. Without an intervening separation the nasal resonant /n/ is replaced by bilabial /m/ before bilabial stops /p/ and /b/, by dorsal /ŋ/ before dorsal stops /k/ and /g/, and has special allophones such as labiodental [ɱ] before labiodental fricatives /f/ and /v/, and retroflex (tongue-tip back) [ɳ] before retroflex /r/. Such assimilation (see p. 57) is very common in American English, with the loss of phonemic separation. For example:

	In deliberate speech	In casual speech
Why don't you place your bet?	/way dont yu ples yur bɛt/	/waydončə plešərbɛt/
Why did you raise your hand?	/way dɪd yu rez yur hænd/	/wayǰə režər hænd/
in Paris	/ɪn perəs/	/ɪmperəs/
in case	/ɪn kes/	/ɪŋkes/
in fact	/ɪn fækt/	/ɪnfækt/=[ɪɱfækt]

The Phonemic Phrase

Within a phonemic clause, the phonemes in English—unlike those in many other languages, such as French and Spanish—cluster into phonemic **phrases:** phonological stretches which occupy roughly the same amount of time, though they may consist of very different numbers of syllables.[7] Each phrase

---

[7] See Kenneth L. Pike: *The Intonation of American English* (Ann Arbor: University of Michigan Press; 1945), 34–36. It should be noted that

has one clearly most-prominent syllable, sometimes called the **center** or **focus**. The boundaries of a phonemic phrase always coincide with boundaries of phonemic word-groups, and sometimes coincide with boundaries of phonemic clauses, but are not otherwise specially marked by any phonetic feature. We may represent the phrase center by marking a phrase-stress /'/ over the symbol for the vowel at the center of prominence:

Telegram 1): /²rifər ³sɛ́lərz tu³bə́rn¹↓#²stap ³mɛ́l-ɔrdərz ³nàw¹↓#/

Telegram 2): /³rifər-sɛlərz tu³bə́rn³→³stàp¹↓#²mel ³ɔ́rdərz ³nàw³↑#/

The Phonemic Word and Word-Accent

The characterizing feature of a phonemic **word** unit is **accent**. The accent of a given word is the part of a word which is most prominent under phrase-stress. In addition, when a given word does not have phrase-stress, the accented part has a degree of prominence greater than nonaccented parts that occur or may occur in that same phrase. We may indicate the position of the accent phoneme by /'/, written over the symbol for the vowel at the center of prominence in the word. Every occurrence of /'/, then, marks the occurrence of a word.

Telegram 1): /²rifɔ́r ³sɛ́lərz tu³bə́rn¹↓#²stáp ³mɛ́l-ɔ́rdərz ³nǎw¹↓#/

Telegram 2): /rǐfər-sɛ́lərz tu³bə́rn³→³stǎp¹↓#²mél ³ɔ́rdərz ³nǎw³↑#/

Thus Telegram 1) contains seven phonemic words: /rifɔ́r/, /sɛ́lərz/, /tubə́rn/, /stáp/, /mél/, /ɔ́rdərz/, and /náw/, Telegram 2) contains the same words, except for /rǐfər/ instead of /rifɔ́r/. Note that what traditional orthography writes as separate words —e.g., *to burn*—does not necessarily correspond with what we consider phonemically separate words to be.

---

some linguists dispute the facts underlying this characterization of phonemic phrases. See Yao Shen and Giles G. Peterson: "Isochronism in English," *Studies in Linguistics,* Occasional Papers 9, 1962.

Notice that there are minimal pairs of words in standard English distinguished only by differences in the position of accent. For example: *refer* /rifɔr/ ≠ *reefer* /rífɔr/, *depose* /dipóz/ ≠ *depots* /dípoz/, (an) *increase* /ínkris/ ≠ (to) *increase* /ɪnkrís/. When they appear in phrases with other words, but do not bear phrase-stress, words may lose their accent. An unaccented word is called a **clitic—proclitic** or **enclitic,** depending on whether it regularly appears without stress only before or after (respectively) another word in the same phrase. In normal, rapid speech, many clitics have special forms (often with the vowel of the accented form "reduced" to /ə/ or to nothing). While a proclitic form is usually separated from a following form by a juncture or disjuncture, an enclitic form is usually not so separated from a preceding word. For example, the word *it* /ít/ has the proclitic form /ɪt/ in phrases such as *it might rain* /ɪt máyt rĕn/ and the enclitic form /ət/ in phrases such as *take it* /tĕkət/.

Several classes of words in English—prepositions, pronouns, modals, conjunctions—are especially rich in clitic forms. The following list is representative:[8]

	Accented	*Proclitic*	*Enclitic*
Preposition			
to	/tú/	/tu/~/tə/	
in	/ín/	/ɪn/	
for	/fɔ́r/	/fɔr/~/fər/	
by	/báy/	/bay/	

---

[8] The symbol ~ appears between alternate forms. For all words with initial /h/, the clitic forms which retain the /h/ appear in deliberate speech and otherwise only at the beginning of a phrase. The standard modern pronoun *it* is descended from an older pronoun *hit* whose initial /h/ was lost in just this way. Some dialects of NE reflect the older form with /hɪt/ instead of /ɪt/. The standard, colloquial form *'em* /əm/ is similarly a descendant of the OE pronoun *hem* /hɛm/—not, as is commonly thought, a corruption of NE *them* /ðɛm/, which has its own enclitic form /ðəm/.

Accented		*Proclitic*	*Enclitic*

Pronouns

he	/hí/	/hi/	/hi/~/i/
him	/hím/		/hɪm/~/ɪm/~/əm**/**
her	/hɔ́r/		/hər/~/ər/
I	/áy/	/ay/	/ay/
you	/yú/	/yu/~/yə/	/yu/~/yə/

Modals

can	/kǽn/	/kæn/~/kən/	/kən/
will	/wíl/	/wɪl/~/wəl/	/əl/~/l/
shall	/šǽl/	/šæl/~/šəl/	/šəl/
am	/ǽm/	/æm/	/əm/~/m/(only directly after *I* /ay/)
have	/hǽv/	/hæv/	/əv/~/v/(only directly after pronouns)

Conjunctions

and	/ǽnd/	/ænd/~/æn/~/æŋ/ (only before dorsal stops)~/æm/, (only before labials)~/ənd/~/ən/~/əŋ/~/əm/
but	/bɔ́t/	/bət/
if	/íf/	/ɪf/~/əf/
when	/hwɛ́n/~/wɛ́n/	/wɛn/~/wən/

The selection of the variant forms of the clitics depends primarily on the style of speech used by the speaker. In deliberate speech the clitic forms which are like the corresponding accented ones, but without accent, prevail; in casual speech more and more departure from the accented forms is evident. At the beginning of phrases, clitics with initial /h/ forms appear for words like *he*, *have*, *has*, *had*, and *when*.

On p. 64 we suggested that the prominence of a phone (its heard loudness) corresponds approximately to its duration in time. In various later sections of this chapter our discussion has implied that a number of factors determine the duration—and hence the prominence—of phones. We may summarize these factors as follows:

1) Phoneme class
    More prominent ⟵————————⟶ Less prominent

Vowel			Consonant		
Narrow	Wide		Resonant	Obstruent	
	Other wide vowels	/ə/		Voiceless	Voiced

2) Separation (position in respect to disjuncture or juncture /-/)
    More prominent ⟵————————⟶ Less prominent

After separation	Before separation	Not at separation

3) Stress and accent
    More prominent ⟵————————⟶ Less prominent

Stressed	Accented	Unaccented

4) Terminal position (position in respect to /→/, /↓/, /↑/)
    More prominent ⟵————————⟶ Less prominent

Before terminal	After terminal	Not at terminal

PARALANGUAGE

There still remain a number of phonetic features of speech that we have not described. Obviously, a great part of our intention in speaking is conveyed by phonetic signals not described in this chapter. For example, the total meaning of a discourse or part of a discourse would depend very heavily on whether it was delivered with a laughing, sobbing, yelling, placating, whispering, singing, gruff, hollow (as for a certain kind of melodramatic delivery), breathy, clipped, or drawled voice. There are two reasons for our omission of these aspects of speech in the system of phonemic transcription employed in this chapter. First, the whole area of fascinating investigation into these phenomena of **paralanguage**[9] is not yet well enough established for us to give anything like an approximate inventory of paralinguistic "phonemes"; for example, while laughing seems clearly enough to contrast with sobbing, does it also contrast with chuckling? Is there a distinct number of kinds of laughter during speech? Second, we stated early in this treatment that a phonemic transcription was a representation of *linguistic* units. It is not at all clear that paralinguistic phenomena should be treated as parts of linguistic units (although they might conceivably be treated as characteristic features of discourses, in the same way that silences are treated as characteristic of sentences) or as linguistic units themselves; indeed, there is good reason to think that they should *not* be so treated.

The system of phonemic transcription provided in this chapter, then, does not provide for the representation of all features of what is popularly called "tone of voice." However, in representing silence, pitch, stress, accent, juncture, disjuncture, and terminals, it does provide for many of the components of this vital aspect of oral communication.

CONCLUSION

A description of a language, like other descriptions in science, is a testable theory about that language—a theory that accounts economically for the observed linguistic phenomena. Comprising such a theory are statements about linguistic units and their relations to one another. **Linguistic units** are the terms in a linguistic theory which allow for the most general, i.e., most

---

[9] This name has been given to the phenomena by George L. Trager, who, together with Henry Lee Smith, Jr., has made the most systematic and most elaborate contributions in this area. For presentation and bibliography see George L. Trager: "Paralanguage: a first approximation," *Studies in Linguistics*, XIII, Nos. 1–2 (1958), 1–12.

economical, statements that will account for the observed phenomena. Also, if the theory is a good one, the linguistic units which it employs as terms will often correspond to the units which we need to account for the language behavior of people, that is, to **psycholinguistic units** (which in turn may be thought of as terms in a theory about the behavior of people using language) of speakers, listeners, writers, and readers of the language. Thus the terms *phoneme, word, word-group, phrase, clause, sentence,* and *discourse,* used in this chapter, have been chosen not only as hooks on which to hang our descriptive phonological statements, so to speak, but also as terms useful for designating units at different levels in the production and understanding of language acts.

Phonemes, in terms of which the characteristic sound forms of all linguistic units are stated, seem also to correspond to the smallest discriminated units of sound used by speakers and listeners of the language. For example, an English speaker will tend to distinguish the same sounds when he is speaking or listening to French, Russian, or Chinese as he does when he is speaking or listening to English. One important part in the learning of a new language is the acquisition of the same habits of discrimination between phonemes that speakers of that language have. An English speaker feels it natural to discriminate between an /l/ and an /r/ phoneme, but a Chinese speaker finds this a very difficult and unnecessary distinction, while a Russian finds it easy but insufficient (there are two different *l* phonemes and two different *r* phonemes in Russian). Every teacher of a foreign language knows how difficult it is for speakers of one language to learn the phonemic distinctions of another language.

Phonemic **words,** in terms of which phrases are stated, seem also to correspond to the smallest units which users of a language will be willing to produce and interpret in isolation. That is, an English speaker will say the words *hog* and *hog-caller* by themselves, and will even try to tell you what they mean, but he will hardly produce and explain the *-er* of *hog-caller* by itself.

Phonemic **phrases,** in terms of which clauses are stated, seem also to correspond to the units of focused attention for English speakers. That is, within a phrase, one and only one center of attention appears. For example, in the phrase *Géorge léft* the focus is on George—the phrase might occur in answer to *Who left?*—while in the phrase *Géorge léft* the focus is on the leaving, perhaps answering the question *What did George do?*

Phonemic **clauses**, in terms of which sentences are stated, seem also to correspond to the minimal units of "expression of attitude" for the speaker. For example, ²*Géorge* ³*léft*¹↓ may be a neutral statement of fact, while ²*Géorge* ³*léft*³↑? may be a question of a preceding statement by another speaker, and ²*Géorge* ²*léft*²→ may indicate that the speaker intends to continue discussing the subject.

Phonemic **sentences**, in terms of which discourses are stated, seem to be the minimal units which speakers of a language will treat as complete. For example, note that with ²*Géorge* ³*léft*¹↓ ³*yésterday*¹↓#., it would be considered an interruption for a second speaker to start talking after *left*, but with ²*Géorge* ³*léft*¹↓#. ³*Yésterday*¹↓#. (with a linguistic pause between *left* and *yesterday*), it would be quite usual for a second person to start talking after *left*.

The term **discourse** designates a unit consisting of a sentence or sequence of sentences with a given order between them. Communication in a language proceeds not by placing one random sentence after another, but by relating and connecting sentences in groups. Within a given discourse, e.g., a conversation or a chapter of a book, there may be sub-discourse groups—marked by "changes of subject" or by paragraph breaks, for instance. The nature of the ordering of sentences that holds discourses and sub-discourses together has not yet been satisfactorily described. However, that the discourse is a linguistic unit, that the lower linguistic units can be said to be determined only in respect to the discourses in which they are embedded, and that discourses are themselves elements in the total communicative behavior of human beings, cannot be seriously doubted. It is only within a given discourse that we can know whether a

particular sentence is to be taken seriously or as a joke, as a
figurative or literal statement, as a question or a statement; it is
only in respect to a total discourse in a total "communication
situation" that we can know whether particular words and
sentences are appropriate or inappropriate, polite or impolite,
literary or every-day.

Every discourse in English contains at least one sentence; every
sentence at least one clause; every clause at least one phrase;
every phrase at least one word; every word at least one phoneme.
The possible complete discourse *Hey!* /³hĕ¹↓#/ contains one
sentence (marked by /#/), one clause (marked by the intonation
pattern ³¹↓), one phrase (marked by the phrase-stress /'/), one
word (marked by the accent /'/ and the sequence of phonemes
/he/), and the phonemes /#/, /³/, /¹/, /↓/, /'/, /'/, /h/, and
/e/. This chapter, in oral rendition, is also a discourse—though
one of considerably greater length—and is analyzable into units
of exactly the same type as *Hey!*

The hierarchical, boxes-within-boxes structure of discourses is
what makes infinite variety possible within a language. It has
been the purpose of this chapter to make possible the representation of some of that structure in visual form.

QUESTIONS

1. On p. 26 we indicated that by "sameness" of linguistic items
   is meant sameness of interpretation by users of a language, but
   on pp. 32-33 and 59 we intimate that sameness is to be accounted
   for as sameness of characteristic form. Are these mutually contradictory notions? Can you think of some way to reconcile them?

2. It has been frequently suggested that some of the methodology
   of linguistics, especially its nonstatistical treatment of variation
   and its approach to the determination of significant units, might
   be extended to subjects other than language. Can you give an
   example of how this might work out? For example, you might
   expand the analogy between linguistic and musical analysis
   mentioned on p. 32. Or you might show how the social organi-

zation of a community or the structure of a literary form (like a sonnet) can be analyzed in terms of a hierarchy of units of ever increasing generality.

3. Consult at least five of the books in the Bibliography on pp. 369-375 for definitions of *sentence*.

   a) Sort the definitions according to whether they are based on grammatical, semantic, or phonological criteria.

   b) Compile a list of English utterances which would be included as sentences by at least one definition but excluded by another.

   c) Discuss the relative merits of the various definitions.

4. Transcribe phonemically the following discourses:

   a) "Your slip's showing."
      "So's yours."

   b) "Early to bed and early to rise
      Makes a man healthy, wealthy and wise."

   c) "Has anyone seen my basketball?"
      "No, where did you put it?"
      "In the living room, under the coffee table."

   d) "Our sun's rays meet in a common pool."
      "*Our* sons raise wheat individually."
      "You have no poetic appreciation."

5. Take an eight-to-ten-line paragraph at random from a book or magazine. Read it aloud at a normally fast rate of speed. Transcribe the resultant discourse.

6. Are the phones [r]—the voiced liquid that appears in *ray, arouse, brim, grime*—and [r̥]—the voiceless fricative that appears in *tray, attract, prim, crime*—phonemically distinct in English? Defend your answer.

7. Compile a list of five pairs (or triplets) of words pronounced the same by you but spelled differently; five pairs spelled the same but pronounced differently; and five words whose spellings are misleading in peculiar ways. What would happen to these with spelling reform? How strong an argument against spelling reform do you consider this, and why?

8. For discussion:
   It is often said that "English is an unphonetic language." What is meant by this remark? How is this notion of "phonetic" inconsistent with our analysis of the relationship between language and writing as presented in this chapter? Restate the original remark in a more proper form. Now give evidence to support this properly stated assertion.

9. Find five words that are considered hard to spell (you may consult an elementary spelling-book or a dictionary listing commonly misspelled words). Transcribe each of them phonemically. Explain briefly why each word is hard to spell, citing as evidence other words in which the same phonemes are represented by different spellings.

CHAPTER

III

——

COMPARATIVE LINGUISTICS
AND THE INDO-EUROPEAN
FAMILY OF LANGUAGES

Because the possible number of combinations and permutations which can be created from a relatively small number of elements is very great, most if not all languages could theoretically build up the many different units they need from a relatively small number of simple units. In all known languages, however, many combinations are excluded by rules of syllable structure. Even allowing for these restrictions, we can get many differences by various combinations of a few units. With only some forty different units of significant sound elements (phonemes), well over 400,000 different words in English have been created and can be used without any serious ambiguities. New and different words can always be and are continually being created, without exhausting the number of permissible combinations of English sounds.

It is true that most languages contain a certain number of **homonyms**—words that have different meanings but the same sounds—but in comparison with the total number of words these are very few. The homonyms that do exist in English have arisen for various historical and phonological reasons and not at all for lack of possible alternatives, the phonological forms of which would not conflict with those of words already in the language. Nothing illustrates better the historical nature of language than the existence of homonyms. If we had free choice in the matter, we would probably choose different phonological forms for *son* and *sun* rather than use these historical homonyms. Except in deliberate punning contexts, there is rarely any ambiguity in their use because the context almost always determines the desired meaning. Even if two languages had the same phonemes and the same sequences of phonemes, grammatical and semantic differences would easily be sufficient to make these languages entirely different.

In observing any two languages, one will find certain similarities. Many kinds of similarities are of limited interest. For example, the fact that two or more languages both have p-phonemes, a-phonemes and k-phonemes, or even the same phoneme sequences, as /pak/ in the English *pock,* the Albanian word for *slightly,* the French word for *Easter,* the Dutch word for *suit of clothes,* seems completely fortuitous. Much more significant are those items in different languages which exhibit similarities in both form *and* meaning—for example, the similarity between OE (Old English) *hlaf* (NE 'bread') and Czech *chléb* 'bread', and that between the *s* that indicates the genitive case in both English and German. These latter similarities suggest a more than casual relationship, and argue for some sort of historical relationship between the languages involved. This historical relationship must be due either to borrowing or to descent from a common ancestor language. In the past, the principal interest of **comparative linguistics** has been to study those relationships which are due to common descent, that is, **genetic** relationships.

This family view of languages has often been a useful way of accounting for linguistic similarities. For example, to explain the many similarities exhibited by English and German in spite of geographic and cultural separations, it has been valuable to regard them as having descended from a common ancestor, called proto-West Germanic. The purpose of this chapter is to look at English from the point of view of such genetic relationships and to point out what methods are used to determine them.

Now it is clear that not all resemblances or similarities between languages are evidence of their descent from a common origin. How can we determine what kinds of similarities are important in determining genetic relationships?

It has been the experience of comparative linguists, as we have seen, that in two languages congruencies of form with meaning carry more weight than mere similarities of form or meaning alone. For example, the fact that there is an English word /hænd/ meaning 'hand', and a German word /hant/ meaning 'hand' is a more compelling reason to assume a common genetic origin than the fact that English has a form /lip/ meaning 'leap' and German /lip/ meaning quite another thing, 'dear'. The probability that both form and meaning will coincide by accident in two languages is much less than the probability of coincidences in one aspect alone. To take another example, the fact that English and German both use apical stops /t/ or /d/ in forming the past tense form of verbs, as in *hoped* and *hoffte*, has far greater significance than that both have grammatical ways of expressing the object of a verb. If, contrary to chance expectation, there is a significant number of similarities of this type between two different languages, we may assume some historical factor as the cause. As L. R. Palmer puts it: "The more arbitrary the connexion between sound and meaning and the more far-reaching the similarities of the systems compared, the greater is the degree of improbability that the resemblances may be accidental."[1]

Even for form and meaning similarities, of course, chance does operate, and certain resemblances in these elements are more significant than others. When, for instance, corresponding paradigms in two languages are similar in form, as in the English

---

[1] *The Latin Language* (London: Faber and Faber, Ltd.; 1954), 4.

comparison *good, better, best* corresponding to German *gut, besser, best,* we may rate this similarity very high in arguing against chance.[2] Or, if language A has the following words: *tep, kes, fesh,* corresponding in meaning to the words in language B *dab, gaz, važ,* even though no sounds are the same, we can suspect a common ancestor for the words. Our evidence here is the consistent correspondence between voiceless and voiced consonants and the regular correspondence between *e* in language A and *a* in language B. It is just such patterns of correspondence that are most revealing of historical relationship. Not a single sound need be the same in both languages to prove some kind of historical connection. Consistency of parallels is all that is necessary.

All this leads us to the next question. What historical explanations can we offer for a correspondence in significant form-meaning congruences between two or more languages? In general, there are only two possible explanations: descent from a common source, and borrowing. In either case, some historical connection between the users of the language has been responsible for the similarity. But how do we decide between the alternate explanations? Although in individual cases some doubt may remain, the question can usually be decided satisfactorily. French and English have many resemblances to each other, and we know that they have descended from a common origin, but most of their resemblances are actually due to borrowing by English from French or to borrowing by both languages from Latin, and not to their common descent. How, then, *do* we identify the sources of such resemblances?

METHODS IN COMPARATIVE LINGUISTICS

Since the purpose of the comparative method, as commonly understood, is to discover what languages are related to each other by descent, i.e., genetically, the first task of a comparative

---

[2] See Joseph H. Greenberg: *Essays in Linguistics* (Chicago: The University of Chicago Press; 1957).

investigation is to eliminate, if possible, those similarities between languages being investigated which are the result of chance and borrowing. Borrowing is, of course, an important and significant study in its own right, but in determining the familial relations of languages, the effects of borrowing must be dealt with only to be laid aside.

A useful first step is to classify the areas of vocabulary in which the similarities occur. Are the similar words concentrated in special fields or are they in the basic general vocabulary of the language? In the former case, the more probable explanation is borrowing; in the latter, the more probable explanation is common descent. Languages commonly borrow words from other languages in fields which are new for the borrowing culture. The bulk of French words borrowed into English, for example, will be found in special vocabularies such as those pertaining to military, legal, administrative, fashion, cuisine, and political matters. Only a few words have been borrowed for parts of the body, common actions, numbers, and so forth.

A second test can be derived from the general principle that words related by borrowing are closer in form to each other than the older resemblances stemming from their common origin. Most of the words in English that were borrowed from French resemble closely in form the French originals. In contrast, those resemblances between French and English which are due to descent from a common ancestor will often not be immediately recognizable—for example, words like *père* and *father*, *nid* and *nest*, *un* and *one*; or, if they are recognizable, they can be immediately distinguished from the borrowings by other methods, as we shall see shortly.

A third test, which can be applied only when the history of the peoples speaking the languages we are studying is to some extent already known, is that of historical plausibility. When a nation borrows customs, institutions, and cultural objects, it frequently takes over their names as well. We know from our study of French and English history that the two peoples have been in fairly continuous contact for over a thousand years, and that

French-speaking Normans, after overthrowing the Anglo-Saxon dynasty, settled and ruled in England. French-speaking kings governed England for some three hundred years. Some evidence of this contact can be expected to appear in both languages, and particularly in English. Since the Normans provided a new upper class and introduced new governmental machinery into England, it is not surprising to find vocabulary borrowings concentrated in cultural areas connected with the upper class. Furthermore, we know that in the past three hundred years or so, French culture has been admired by speakers of English, and admiration frequently leads through imitation to cultural borrowing. It is another historical fact that the Latin language had great influence on French and English cultures, since for many centuries Latin dominated the religious and learned communications of Western civilization, of which these cultures formed a part. Latin was thus a natural source for many words in English and French, and common borrowing from Latin easily accounts for a number of the form-meaning congruencies we find in the modern languages.

Our knowledge of history may help us negatively also. We know that until very recently—until the late eighteenth century—there were no extensive contacts between speakers of English and speakers of Chinese. We would, therefore, on historical grounds alone suspect *a priori* that any similarities between these two languages would be due to chance or to recent borrowings.

A fourth test rests on our knowledge of the history of word forms in the individual languages involved. Knowledge of historical sound changes can tell us whether it is likely that a word is borrowed, whether it shares a common origin with a similar word in another language, or in some cases from what language it may have been borrowed. We know a good deal about the phonemic and phonological history of many individual languages. *Gut* 'good' in German (*guot* in the oldest recorded form of the language) and *good* in English are similar enough in form and meaning to make us suspect some historical relationship. Now,

on the basis of our knowledge of the sound changes in the
history of English, we can say that a form *guot* in OE or ME
could not have become *good* in NE, and so the English word
could not have been borrowed from the German one. The similarity between the words *gut* and *good* must antedate the development of both English and German as separate languages; thus,
a common origin for the words is strongly indicated.

Another example of how we can use our knowledge of the
history of the languages involved may be seen in the case of
English *vow*, which exhibits obvious similarities of form and
meaning with the French *voeu* 'vow'. The Latin source of *voeu*
was *vōtum*. In French, word-medial Latin *t*'s disappeared, as we
may see by comparing the Latin *vīta* with Modern French *vie*
meaning 'life'. Now if we had borrowed the word *vōtum* from
Latin, or if our two words in English and French derived from
a common origin, we should have a *t* in the middle of the English word, since original medial *t*'s did not disappear in English
(cf. OE *bītan*>NE *bite*). Thus, the explanation of the English
word as a borrowing from French is strongly indicated.

The form of the word can often show, if not exactly when it was
taken into the language, at least a limiting date for its appearance
in the language. For example, if the form of the word has not
undergone a certain general phonological change, then it must
have been taken into that language after that change ceased to
be operative. Inasmuch as all accented long /ī/'s had become
/ai/'s in NE by, say, 1650, the different pronunciations of the
second vowel in *delight* and *caprice* tell us that the latter came into
English after 1650. Or if we know that a certain change had taken
place in the donor language before a certain date, and we see
that that change appears in the word in the recipient language,
then the word must have been borrowed after that date. Both
chief and *chef* are borrowed from French (in fact they are the
same word borrowed at different dates), but the initial consonant
variation shows that *chef* is the later borrowing, reflecting a sound
change in French from [č] to [š] in the later Middle Ages. In
general, if the form of the word in one language shows signs of

having been affected by general phonetic changes operative only in the other language, we may reasonably assume that the first is the recipient and the second the donor language in a borrowing. However, later "normalizations" must often be taken into account before all these chronological tests can be safely applied.

A fifth test relies on our dating of the earliest appearance of words in our records. We do not find the words *measure* and *pleasure* in OE, but we do find them in ME, after English has been exposed to French influence. We know these words were in Old French before the Norman Conquest. It is therefore a reasonable surmise that they were borrowed from French. We should be careful here, however, for the absence of a word from our records may reflect a deficiency of the records and not of the language itself. Still, this test can be of value if cautiously applied, especially as a secondary test to back up one of the others here listed.

A final check on our accuracy in explaining correspondences between languages is the evidence of the power of the explanation itself. If a number of the similarities between two languages can be explained by assuming a simple set of elemental correspondences, and if this assumption will also uncover further unsuspected similarities, we may have some confidence in the validity of our hypotheses.

Discovery of non-borrowed and pervasive phonological correspondences between two languages has since the nineteenth century been the cornerstone for the establishment of the common descent of those languages. To take the case of German and English, in which we know that borrowing is slight and very recent, we find correspondences like OE *bān* and modern German *Bein*, and OE *stān* and modern German *Stein* ('bone' and 'stone', respectively); and we shall find the assumption that OE *ā* corresponds to modern German *ei* [ai] a simple and fruitful one to make. The number of such correspondences is quite large and provides an argument in its own right for common descent. The fact that OE *f* corresponds to Latin *p* in a number of cases is a similar argument for common origin of the languages: e.g., English *father* corresponds to Latin *pater*, and OE *nefa* 'nephew' to Latin *nepos*. A knowledge of correspondences enables us to appreciate the genetic relation even between the English noun *tear* (OE *tēar*<*tēagor*)—read, "OE *tēar*, derived from an older form *tēagor*"—and Latin *lacrima* (older form *dacruma*) 'tear', since English *t* corresponds to Latin *d* and English *g* to Latin *c*/k/. Our phonological correspondences enable us to see relationships where none seemed to exist before. The correspondences which we can establish on the assumption of common origin enable us to bring together disparate forms and to account for them in a simple way. The neatness of the explanation and the number of forms accounted for by such correspondences give us evidence for common descent.

In speaking of the relations between languages in this chapter, we have used the word "similarities" rather than "samenesses." The distinction here is an important one, for the resemblances between corresponding words in related languages are usually not exact but only approximate. If these similarities are to be genetically significant, they must fall into patterns. The patterns into which phonological changes fall are commonly called **sound laws**.

If we look at the following words for 'house,' we see obvious similarities: English [haws], Dutch [həüs], German [haus], and Danish [hu:s]. We suspect, once we have eliminated borrowing as a cause, that these words all go back to a common ancestor. They are similar in their initial and final sounds but vary in their medial ones. If we take a similar group—the words in these languages for 'mouse,' for instance—we find that they fall into a similar pattern: English [maws], Dutch [məüs], German [maus], and Danish [mu:s]. Now if we look back to the oldest forms of these words in the languages in question, we shall find even more similarity. If we look at the Old English and Old German documents, we find evidence that the forms were [hu:s] in both of these languages, and we have good reason to think the Old Dutch vowel was also [u:]. From all this we hypothesize a proto-Germanic[3] form **hu:s*. We place an asterisk before it to indicate

---

[3] The languages themselves are designated by the term *Germanic* or *Teutonic*.

that it is a hypothetical reconstruction. It is the form from which we choose to explain the observed similarities. Although we employ common phonetic symbols in the reconstruction, we do not thereby assert that this formula indicates an actual phonological form in proto-Germanic; we use this method of representation only to reflect the correspondences of phonemes in the descendant (commonly called "daughter") languages. However, it is not unlikely that there was an actual word whose form was close to that represented by this formula.

We occasionally have some evidence for the living reality of our formulas. By comparisons parallel to that just discussed we can reconstruct the proto-Germanic formula for 'king' as *kuningaz. Then we find, to our pleasure, that the Finns borrowed this word from the Germanic peoples before either had any writing. The Finnish form is still *kuningas,* nearly the same as our reconstructed form. Finnish is not a Germanic language, as intensive investigation has already shown. What we have here is a Finnish borrowing from the Germanic tribes before *kuningaz* developed into its various forms in the modern Germanic languages—*king* in English, *König* in German, etc. It is not, of course, always possible to find such convincing confirmations of our reconstructions, but when we do, it gives us confidence in our method. With this method, we have gradually built up a whole series of proto-Germanic formulas, perhaps representing actual words in an ancestor language. It is thus that we can most elegantly explain the similarities between the various Germanic languages.

In carrying out linguistic reconstruction, we are helped by getting the earliest possible forms of the word to be studied, since these are less likely to have diverged greatly from the original. In the case of the Germanic languages, almost all of our knowledge of the common tongue must be arrived at by reconstruction, since writing came after the break-up of proto-Germanic. In the case of the Romance languages (French, Spanish, Italian, Provençal, Roumanian, Catalan, Sardinian, Portuguese), however, we have much information about their common ancestor—popular, spoken Latin (usually called *Vulgar Latin*). Of course, most of our knowledge of Latin is based on literary dialects; but we do have some texts in Vulgar Latin, and in general, Vulgar Latin was not greatly different from its literary counterpart. It is not unreasonable to say that Modern French is Vulgar Latin spoken by modern Frenchmen.

Our best guess about the character of *proto*-Germanic "is thus the sum of all the inferences which can be drawn from"[4] the oldest forms preserved of the individual Germanic languages, with whatever help we can get from borrowings (as in the case of *kuningas* above), or from comments on the early stage of the language gleaned from those Latin and Greek writers who spoke of early Germanic speech habits. This help is, however, slight; and inference is the characteristic mode of reconstructing an ancestor language.

We are in effect using inference to work back to the earlier forms of the language; to go backwards in history by our reasoning powers; to reconstruct what seems to have happened. We may suppose that the earliest Germanic speakers said [hu:s], or something close to it, for 'house'; and that after groups had separated themselves from the main body, several varieties of the word developed among them, resulting ultimately in different standard forms in the various literary languages. But since no written evidence exists, we cannot go back in time and check this supposition. We must therefore regard it as an unattested, but nevertheless legitimate, inference.

Let us again be careful to qualify what we intend by these reconstructions. They are what we have chosen to call, following Holger Pedersen, "formulas." They are not necessarily the actual word as pronounced by the prehistoric speakers of the language. To quote Pedersen: "The formula *ekwo-s* tells us at a glance, for instance, a great many things about the forms of the word for *horse* in the various Indo-European [the language family to which English, French, Persian, Latin, Sanskrit, etc. belong] languages: it tells us that there is virtually nothing in the form of the Indian

---

[4] W. J. Entwistle and W. A. Morison: *Russian and the Slavonic Languages* (London: Faber and Faber, Ltd.; 1949), 52 (referring to common Slavic).

aśva-s which we can regard as wholly primitive . . . [Pedersen gives us further examples of what this formula tells us about the Indian word for *horse.*] In the same way the formula with its five characters tells us many things about the presumable development of the other languages that it would take much longer to express in words. But if we are asked whether *ek̑wo-s* is identical with the pronunciation of the noun which the linguistic ancestors of our race used thousands of years ago in their original home, we must reply only that we cannot be sure."[5]

The description of what seems to have happened in proto-Germanic raises the question of what is to be considered a separate language. What we have been suggesting by the reconstructions above is that what are now separate languages were at one time dialects of proto-Germanic, and that all members of the same language family were at one time varieties, or dialects, of the ancestor of the family. Old English is proto-Germanic as spoken by the Anglo-Saxons; Old High German is proto-Germanic as spoken in the eighth to eleventh centuries by the Germanic inhabitants of what is now central and southern Germany, Switzerland, and Austria. The normal process of linguistic change tends to splinter language into various forms. Today, however, with writing, widespread education, nationalism, and excellent means of communication, strong forces are operating to establish and maintain the predominance of standard forms in a language. These forces were absent in early times, so that speakers of proto-Germanic who were isolated from other proto-Germanic speakers for, say, 50 or 100 years, would exhibit differences from the main group, either because of changes arising within the separated group itself, or because of changes which were affecting only the main body of proto-Germanic speakers from which they had separated, or, more probably, for both reasons.

Dialects will be discussed in some detail in Chapter V, but we may state briefly here that dialects can be said to become separate

---

[5] *Linguistic Science in the Nineteenth Century, Methods and Results.* Trans. John Webster Spargo (Cambridge, Mass.: Harvard University Press; 1931), 268. (Reprinted as paperback MB40, Indiana University Press; 1962.)

languages when their speakers can no longer understand the other varieties of their original language. This generalization needs qualification, as we shall see later.

We have briefly discussed patterns of phonological change, sometimes called sound laws, above. We must look into this subject a little more closely now, for we shall soon be examining the most famous of all the numerous sound laws ever discovered, "Grimm's Law."

The term "law" is no longer in favor to describe the particular sound changes which affect a language at a given time, for the reason that the term implies the operation of a sustained force to yield constant effects, and the changes we observe in languages simply do not exhibit such general consistency. However, we do still use the word to refer to certain formulations of important phonological changes, for the most part discovered in the nineteenth century—that great period in the historical investigation of languages. When we use the term in historical linguistics, we must understand that it is not the kind of law formulated in physics. Phonological changes are historical, not natural, events. They may be summed up in a neat statement after they occur; they may not as yet be successfully predicted. If we call a particular sound change a law, we do not mean to be describing changes in every language at every time, but rather a particular set of changes. The pattern of sound changes in which every OE [a:] became an [ɔ:] in most ME dialects is the concern of phonological laws as we understand them. This particular law does not imply that every [a:] in English will always become an [ɔ:], but merely that at one period this change was quite general within certain English dialects.

In the later nineteenth century, a dispute arose over whether there were any exceptions to sound laws. This dispute, which involved a school of linguists known as the *Junggrammatiker* (Neo-grammarians), had interesting implications. If we know that a certain sound change occurred in a language, and we find one or two cases in which the change did not occur, what is to be our explanation? For instance, we know that proto-Germanic

*h (probably [x]) corresponds to Latin /k/ (spelled c) in instance after instance. We assume that the common ancestor of this sound (since Latin and Germanic are genetically related) was *k, for reasons that we hope to explain shortly, and that in Germanic this *k became *h but in Latin it remained k. We thus have such parallels between English /h/ and Latin /k/ (c) as in English *horn*: Latin *cornu*; English *hund(red)*: Latin *centum*; English *head* (OE *hēafod*): Latin *caput*. However, we find the English *have*, which seems to correspond to the Latin *habēre* 'to have.' What are we to do? Are we to say that this case is an exception to the rule of the correspondence of OE *h* with Latin *k*, or are we to say that in spite of appearances these words are not descendants of a common ancestor and are not related, or are we to say that some other factor as yet unknown is operating here to obscure or prevent the change?

The *Junggrammatiker* maintained that there were no exceptions to sound changes, but that what seemed to be exceptions had some kind of explanation which we did not as yet know. In other words, they said that if we reject the second alternative above we must accept the third; in the face of an apparent exception we must assume some other factor not yet known. This attitude proved to be one of the most fruitful and exciting in the history of linguistics. By assuming the absolute regularity of sound laws, linguists were driven to discover new factors which explained hitherto mysterious irregularities.[6]

The reason sound changes seem to have an absolute validity is that the phonological structure of a language constitutes a kind of general, pervasive system, inaccessible to human willfulness because the speakers of the language are unaware of it. The connection between synchronic phonological systems and the diachronic regularity of sound change has recently been subjected to intensive study.[7] Just what instigates a sound change in

---

[6] As an example, see the discussion of Grimm's and Verner's Laws below, pp. 105 ff.

[7] See for instance, A. Martinet: *Economie des changements phonétiques: Traité de phonologie diachronique* (Berne: Francke Verlag; 1955); "Func-

various cases is not clear; and conditions that seem to give rise
to a sound change in one situation will not do so in another. It has
been argued by some linguists that one of the major reasons that
phonological changes are uniform when they do occur is that
there is a tendency for a set of contrasts in a language to be maintained. Phonemes have more stability than phones. That is, the
system of contrasts between phonemes may remain, even though
the constituent phones change. For example, if we suddenly
started to pronounce the [h] in *hire* as [x] without at the same
time changing the [h] of *hide* also to [x], a new phonemic contrast would be established: /h/ ≠ /x/. However, if all the English [h]'s were changed to [x]'s there would be no phonemic
change, for the set of contrastive differences would have remained constant.

PRINCIPLES OF GERMANIC LINGUISTICS

Until the latter part of the eighteenth century, the family relationship of European and West Asiatic languages had not been
properly worked out.[8] Some matters were understood: it was
known for instance that French, Spanish, and Italian were
descended in some way from Latin; that there were fundamental
differences of some sort between Welsh and English, and fundamental agreements between English, Dutch, and German; and
that there was a relationship between Hebrew and Arabic. Ever
since the Renaissance, and in some cases even earlier, scholars
had made comparisons of words from different languages and

---

tion, Structure and Sound Change," *Word* VIII (1952), 1–32; and "Concerning the Preservation of Useful Features," *ibid.*, IX (1953), 1–11. See
also Henry M. Hoenigswald: *Language Change and Linguistic Reconstruction* (Chicago: University of Chicago Press; 1960).

[8] See G. Bonfante, "Ideas on the Kinship of the European Languages
from 1200 to 1800," *Journal of World History* I (1953–54), 677–99. Bonfante finds a number of earlier thinkers and scholars who had suggested
the solution later adopted. Marcus Zuerius Boxhorn, a Dutchman, had in
1647, for instance, suggested a common ancestor for most European languages which he called *Scythian*.

formulated theories of genetic relationships, some of which were sound; but the concept of the Indo-European family of languages, which we now believe properly accounts for the differences and similarities in well-known Western languages, had not yet been grasped. Standing in the way were certain notions of language relationships based on a too literal reading of the Bible, or on eccentric theories of language origin and development.

What precipitated the solution to this somewhat confused situation was the discovery of Sanskrit by Western scholars as a by-product of imperialist—mainly English—ambitions in India. The Jesuit Gaston Laurent Coeurdoux in 1767 sent a memoir from India to the Institut de France on the similarities of Sanskrit to Latin and Greek, and concluded that only a common ancestor could explain them. Sir William Jones (1746–94), an Orientalist of renown, learned Sanskrit and was struck by the resemblances between it and Latin and Greek. In 1786 he put forth the theory that these languages were all descended from a common ancestor language and that probably the Germanic and Celtic languages sprang from the same source. He wrote:

> The *Sanscrit* language, whatever be its antiquity, is of a wonderful structure; more perfect than the Greek, more copious than the Latin, and more exquisitely refined than either; yet bearing to both of them a stronger affinity, both in the roots of verbs and in the forms of grammar, than could possibly have been produced by accident; so strong, indeed, that no philologer could examine all three without believing them to have sprung from some common source which, per-haps, no longer exists. There is a similar reason, though not quite so forcible, for supposing that both the Gothick and the Celtick, though blended with a very different idiom, had the same origin with the Sanscrit; and the Old Persian might be added to the same family, if this were the place for discus-sing any question concerning the antiquities of Persia.[9]

---

[9] Quoted in Louis H. Gray: *Foundations of Language* (New York: The Macmillan Co.; 1939), 435–36.

At the same time, thinkers such as Herder and Vico were putting much emphasis on language as revealing the soul of a people, and Europeans in general became fascinated with the question of origins. Europe was entering into a historicist period when history was rediscovered, and men hoped to find answers to the meaning of life and man through history, especially early history. The hope of Western mankind was shifting from pure reason to historical reason. Widespread disillusionment with the Enlightenment, which had dominated Western thinking for over a century, led to a reaction and a movement towards historicism. It was felt that an understanding of origins, beginnings, and development would lead to a surer foundation for all knowledge than abstract reason itself.

These two circumstances made possible a science of linguistics, which came into being in the first half of the nineteenth century and which was developed with special assiduity by German scholars. "The real beginning of a systematic comparison of the Indo-European languages"[1] came in a work published in 1816 by Franz Bopp (1791–1867). He was shortly followed by others. Linguistic studies were now given a historical cast which still persists, although in our own century there has been a reaction against the excesses of the historical approach.

In making comparisons of various languages which showed striking similarities, Rasmus Rask, a Dane, and Jacob Grimm, a German, discovered in the early nineteenth century the set of phonological correspondences now known as **Grimm's Law.** As Voltaire said of the Holy Roman Empire that it was neither Holy, nor Roman, nor empire, so we say of Grimm's Law that it is neither Grimm's nor a law. Actually it was Rask who discovered the pattern of the sound changes first, and as we have seen, such patterns hardly constitute laws in the sense in which the term was used in the other sciences of the time.

What Rask and Grimm saw was that there was a regular system of parallel sound changes which set off the Germanic

---

[1] Leonard Bloomfield: *Language* (New York: Henry Holt and Co.; 1933), 14.

languages from all the other European and Asiatic languages which in general resembled them.[2] In other words, when Indo-European became Germanic in the mouths of its Germanic speakers, a characteristic patterned series of phonological changes occurred. The discovery of the pattern was made by Rask and Grimm through the close examination of a number of words in the basic vocabularies of the IE languages. The family of languages which Jones had postulated and for which Grimm and Rask provided the first systematic evidence came to be known as Indo-European.[3]

What were these phonological patterns? They can best be seen by examining a list of **cognate words,** as words from a common ancestor are called. Once languages or dialects are separated geographically or socially they undergo the normal processes of change and chance; words may change in meaning and phonological shape in the different languages, and some words disappear altogether. Thus, cognate words do not necessarily retain their historical meaning (although we can usually see the semantic plausibility of the change), and not all cognate words appear in every cognate language. In the list of cognates on page 107 note that we are comparing the Germanic word not with its hypothetical IE original, but with attested words in documented IE languages which give evidence for the form of the original word.

It was from examples like these that Grimm's Law was deduced. In general and somewhat simplified terms, it showed that IE voiceless stops *p, *t, *k> (became) Germanic voiceless aspirated (with a strong puff of breath) stops *ph, *th,

---

[2] There were some troublesome exceptions which Rask and Grimm either did not see or ignored. Most of these were cleared up, by a further principle of explanation, by K. Verner in 1876. See below, pp. 108 ff. Armenian also shows some of these same changes, which are hence not unique to Germanic, but at the time when Rask and Grimm lived it was not known that Armenian was an Indo-European language.

[3] The terms *Aryan* and *Indo-Germanic* are sometimes used for this family. In English, however, *Aryan* is now used primarily to indicate one branch of IE—the Indo-Iranian branch. Many Germans use the term *Indo-Germanic* (*Indogermanisch*) for IE.

IE		Gmc		

*p   corresponds to   f :   Latin *pēs* :ʹ English *foot;* Latin *piscis* : English *fish;* Latin *plēnus* : English *full*

*t   „   θ :   Latin *trēs* : English *three;* Latin *tenuis* : English *thin*

*k   „   h :   See examples above on p. 102

*b   „   p :   Lithuanian *dubùs* : English *deep*

*d   „   t :   Latin *dens* : English *tooth;* Latin *duo* : English *two;* Old Latin *dacruma* : English *tear* (in the eye)

*g   „   k :   Latin *grānum* : English *corn;* Latin *genu* : English *knee*

*bh   „   b :   Sanskrit *bhárati* : English *bear* (carry); Sanskrit *bhrå̃tr* : English *brother*[4]

*dh   „   d :   Sanskrit *mádhu* : English *mead*

*gh   „   g :   Latin *hostis* : English *guest;* Latin *hortus* : English *garden*[5]

*kh (later English f, th, and h); IE voiced stops *b, *d, *g> Germanic voiceless stops *p, *t, *k; and IE voiced aspirated stops *bh, *dh, *gh> Germanic voiced stops *b, *d, *g.

Looking at the list above, the student may well wonder how certain words are discovered to be related. He will see that in words of similar meaning, as in *pēs* and *foot*, nothing in the forms seems the same. How could both have descended from a common ancestor? In the case of *piscis* : *fish*, the resemblance seems greater, but is still not exact. The answer is that the correspondences for each sound in these words has been worked out by scholars in possession of detailed knowledge of the history of various IE languages, including insights gained

---

[4] Sanskrit *bh* preserves the IE *bh* which became *f* in Latin; hence the Latin cognates for these two words are *fero* and *frater*. *bh* stands for an aspirated *b*.

[5] IE *gh* (a heavily aspirated *g*) became *h* in Latin. The developments bh>b, dh>d, gh>g are only exact in some positions.

from earlier or fuller forms of the words listed here. For instance, the genitive of *pēs* is *pedis;* here we have a Latin *d* which would correspond to the English *t* of *foot,* according to the patterned correspondences we have pointed out above. Historians of the Latin language postulate an older nominative form **peds,* which developed into the classical *pēs.* Even with this knowledge, however, there are several matters unaccounted for. Why does the Latin *e* seem to correspond to the English *oo?* This correspondence is certainly not the usual one, as we may see by looking at Latin *trēs* and English *three* and other words above. And what happened to the final *s* in English?

As for the *ē* in *pēs,* if we look at the genitive form of the Greek word for 'foot', ποδός (podos), we find the *o* reflected by the *oo* in English *foot.* This suggests that the IE original had an *o* rather than *e.* Actually, linguists have been led to assume, from many examples of a similar vowel vacillation, an IE alternation e/o (called **ablaut**) and to reconstruct the root in IE in the formula $*p^e_o d$. The Hellenic and Germanic words here stem from the **o* form; the Italic (that branch of IE that has Latin as its principal member) form descends from the **e* form. As for the bothersome *s* of *pēs,* consider the Gothic word *fōtus.* Now, Gothic is the Germanic language of which we have the oldest extensive written records. Here is our *s,* and so is it recognized by linguists in their formula for the proto-Germanic word for 'foot' in the nominative singular: **fōts.*[6] Like every such *s* (nominative singular suffix) it disappeared in English.

We pointed out above (p. 102) that exceptions to a sound law should not be immediately accepted as such but that some other factor which may have obscured its effects should be sought. Karl Verner in 1876 discovered a factor which accounted for many of the most disturbing exceptions to Grimm's Law, as well as for the otherwise inexplicable cases of a Germanic *r* from IE **s,* which usually turns up in Germanic as an /s/. Verner's notable discovery deserves some attention here, espe-

---

[6] Actually the story is more complicated than this: proto-Germanic **fots* became **foss;* the *t* was reintroduced in English from the other inflected forms of the noun by analogy.

cially because it underlines the important principle that seeking satisfactory explanations for apparent exceptions often "pays off," and that a sound law justifies itself by bringing what otherwise seems inexplicable under some rational, general explanation.

Let us consider the example of OE *fæder*. We have pointed out that a Germanic /f/ corresponds to an IE *p, as preserved in the initial phoneme of the Latin *pater* 'father,' its demonstrated cognate. But IE *t, as preserved in Latin *pater* and Sanskrit *pitár* 'father,' according to Grimm's Law, should correspond to a Germanic /θ/. Whence and why the /d/ in the OE word? We find a number of these apparent exceptions in Germanic languages, where we discover a medial /d/ instead of the expected medial /θ/ or a medial /r/ instead of the expected /s/ (as we have pointed out above, /s/ usually remains in Germanic), and a few other such patterned exceptions, all affecting medial consonants.

In all these cases, Verner noted that the accent in proto-IE, as conjectured from other IE languages like Vedic Sanskrit, Lithuanian, and Greek, fell on the word-medial syllable which the phoneme in question began. By assuming that all these Germanic voiceless consonants (f, θ, x, s <[coming from] IE *p, *t, *k, *s) became voiced in such positions, the apparent irregularities could be explained in the Germanic languages. That is, in these cases, Germanic f, θ, x, s>(became) v, ð, γ, z. The accent in Germanic later became generally fixed on the root—usually the first—syllable of the word. The developments in the separate Germanic languages explain the rest. In English, ð>d and z>r, to take the two examples we are mainly concerned with, and the /d/ of OE *fæder* and of NE *sodden,* and the /r/ of NE *were* were thus explained. We may visualize this process in a simplified scheme:

IE	PG			OE	NE
*patér	*faθér	>	*faðér	>	*fáðer	fæder	*father*
*wes-́	*wāsún	>	*wāzún	>	*wázun	wǽron	*were*
*sut-́	*suθán	>	*soðán	>	*sóðen	sóden	*sodden*

Similarly, other apparent irregularities affecting proto-Germanic *f, *θ, *x, and *s can be explained by Verner's Law, which thus provided striking confirmation of the value of assuming the regularity of sound laws.

Unfortunately for our purposes, the operation of **analogy**, that is, the regularization of a previous irregularity—as when older *help, holp, holpen* became *help, helped, helped* on the analogy of verbs like *walk, walked, walked*—has obscured the effects of Verner's Law in NE. Only in a few instances, such as in the alternation between /z/ and /r/ in *was* and *were*, and between /ð/ and /d/ as in *seethe* and *sodden* (formerly a past participle of *seethe*), can the effects of Verner's Law still be seen in NE. More frequently the differential effects of the law have been levelled out. NE *father*, from OE *fæder* and Chaucerian *fader*, has replaced a medial /d/ with a medial /ð/, as happened with other similar words like ME *hider* (NE *hither*). OE shows clearly the effects of Verner's Law; NE does so only occasionally.

The discovery that sound changes were not haphazard, but followed rigorously formulable patterns, was to have great importance in diachronic linguistics. It made it possible for the first time to put the study of **etymology**—the study of the history of words—on a systematic basis for IE languages. No longer were subjective opinions alone possible; there was now an objective basis for judging the validity of theories as to the origin of many words. The particular regularities noted in Grimm's and Verner's laws could cover only a limited number of words, but once the idea was grasped that sound changes could be systematized, other patterned sound changes were soon discovered and the IE etymologist had a series of reliable tests to go by. The secrets of many IE words were unlocked, and their histories were outlined with some confidence. The same methods were applied to other language families, and the history of languages was at last given a scientific method. No one could put forward wild guesses as to the origin of words and expect linguistic scholars to take them seriously. This has not caused wild etymological theorizing to cease—humans learn slowly—but it has made possible a firm basis upon which to criticize spurious etymologies. The assignment of languages to language families, and the discovery that phonological change was systematically patterned, changed the whole subject of etymology from fanciful theorizing to respectable science.

Finally, the discovery of Grimm's Law and other patterned phonological changes invited students to recognize that individual languages are highly systematic. One aspect of human behavior, at least, was not so arbitrary and haphazard as it had seemed, even though the causes of many sound changes were still, and are still, unknown.

Once a sound law has been established for a language by a convincing number of examples, and the apparent exceptions—or most of them—have been accounted for, we may use the "law" to discover whether certain words which contain the relevant sounds were in the language before the law operated. In other words, we may use it as a criterion for dating borrowing, or even for determining borrowing itself. Now Grimm's Law is especially valuable for determining borrowing in English and the other Germanic languages, for it is the earliest set of phonetic changes affecting Germanic that we know—indeed, together with a few other elements, it can be used to determine which English words are Germanic. If an English word containing a relevant sound occurs in a Germanic language, without its form having been affected by the patterned change described in Grimm's Law, then we conclude it must have been borrowed into the language and is not part of the original stock.

For example, if we are trying to determine which of the pair *fatherly* and *paternal*, both cognate in the root with the Latin *pater*, was borrowed into English, we can tell from Grimm's Law that *fatherly* may well contain an old Germanic root, whereas we know that *paternal* is certainly borrowed, given its initial *p*. If English had received the word directly from IE through proto-Germanic, its initial phoneme would have been /f/ as in *father*, which did get into English this way. Therefore the word *paternal* must have come into English as a later borrowing. *Paternal,* we discover, is indeed borrowed from the Latin adjective made from the noun *pater.* The evidence we have concerning the first appearance of this word—as recorded in the OED (*The Oxford English Dictionary,* which attempts to give the dates of the first appearance of words and their various usages in English by quotations from documents)—substantiates this fact, for the earliest record of the word is dated 1605. (There is an earlier adverbial use recorded in 1603.) *Fatherly* (OE *fæderlic*), on the other hand, already occurs in OE documents.

If a word in a Germanic language contains any of the sounds affected by Grimm's Law and if it has cognates in non-Germanic IE languages, we thus have a test to tell whether it could have belonged to the original Germanic word stock. The condition, "if it has cognates in non-Germanic IE languages," is an important qualification, for some words in the Germanic languages seem to have no cognates in non-Germanic IE languages. In such a case, they may have had cognates which disappeared without leaving a trace in any surviving document; or they may have been newly created, or have been borrowed from an unknown language after Grimm's Law ceased to be operative. The vocabulary items that seem to be unique to Germanic probably are to be accounted for in both these ways, although we can no longer tell which applies in a particular case. The Germanic languages have in common some words, such as the ancestors of the modern English words *horse, drink, heaven, rope, swear, world,* which do not appear in any other IE language group. Each individual language also has certain words which seem to be unique to it. There seem to be no cognates at all outside English for a significant, although not great, number of old words like *bird, ever,* and *heifer.* We cannot tell whether these words were borrowed at an early time from unknown sources or perhaps made up in English itself, or whether they are IE words not preserved in any other IE language.

It is not only sound correspondences which indicate the relationships of IE languages to each other, but also various particular grammatical features. IE languages have certain characteristic features which set them apart from non-IE languages, and within the IE family certain features are shared by several branches. We will discuss some of these features very shortly (p. 124).

Let us examine those elements which distinguish Germanic languages from the other IE languages: 1) Germanic languages show the signs of the operation of Grimm's Law. 2) Germanic languages have a set of vocabulary items, small but unique to them. 3) Germanic languages have a special kind of verb inflection,[7] seen in NE in the distinction between regular verbs (*play, played, played*) and irregular verbs (*eat, ate, eaten*). 4) Germanic languages have or have had two sets of declined adjective forms, best seen in Modern German, where adjectives are declined in either of two patterns, depending on whether they do or do not appear after one of a set of "particularizing" adjectives. In German we find such contrasts as *ein guter Mann* 'a good man' and *der gute Mann* 'the good man.' After a non-particularizing word like *ein* 'a,' the adjective *gut* takes an *-er* ending in the nominative masculine; after a particularizing word like *der* 'the' in the nominative masculine, the adjective *gut* takes an *-e* ending. English in its OE period had a similar system, which had disappeared by NE times. 5) Finally, Germanic languages have a characteristic fixed accent on the root, usually the first, syllable of a word. Other individual IE languages, such as Old Irish, also have this feature, but of no IE branch besides Germanic is this accentual principle general throughout the branch.

As we may see, of these five criteria two are phonological; the others are inflectional or lexical. These criteria can be used in various ways to determine whether elements in Germanic languages are of native origin or not. For example, one way of telling whether a word is borrowed into English is to see whether its accentual pattern is Germanic. If it is, it does not

---

[7] That of the "weak" conjugation, discussed in the next chapter as it appears in OE.

tell us much, since the accent may have been shifted to conform to the English pattern, as for instance the older *balcóny*
has become *bálcony* (this word is borrowed from Italian, where
it is still accented on *có*), or the borrowed word may have had
the same accented syllable in the original language. But if it
is not, the word is probably borrowed. The word *photógraphy*,
for instance, has a non-Germanic accent pattern (otherwise it
would be accented *phótography*). Even if we did not know
Greek, from which the elements of this word come, we would
know from the accent alone that this word was borrowed into
English.[8]

As far as we can tell, the parent IE language had phonemic
accent (probably marked by the same kind of pitch movements that were preserved in classical Greek and Vedic Sanskrit
and Lithuanian as so-called pitch accent). By phonemic accent, we mean that in any particular word the choice of what
syllable is accented, is not determined by a general phonological
rule. Each word form has a non-predictable characteristic accentual pattern.

THE INDO-EUROPEAN LANGUAGE FAMILY

We are now prepared to look at the IE family as a whole.[9] We
have discussed briefly or referred to some of its branches; now

---

[8] Since there are certain special rules that counteract the general rule
that the first syllable is accented, we must be careful in using this rule as
a test. For example, *forbéar* is accented on the second syllable, but is
Germanic. A special accent rule applies to verbs with prefixes.

[9] It should be pointed out here that some linguists reject the whole concept
of an ancestor language for the IE languages, and attempt to explain the
many similarities as the result of extensive borrowing between the various
language groups usually subsumed under the title of IE. However, the
assumption of common ancestry can be defended at least on the grounds of
its heuristic value. It has not only provided a graphic scheme for thinking
about language relationships, but it has stimulated many important works
of scholarship and speculation. For a recent study of the branches of IE
and their justification, see Walter Porzig: *Die Gliederung des indogerman-
ischen Sprachgebiets,* Indogermanische Bibliothek, Dritte Reihe (Heidelberg: Carl Winter Universitätsverlag; 1954).

we will consider them systematically. Using the comparative method as we have shown it above in the discussion of Grimm's Law, comparative linguists have listed characteristics which seem to distinguish and group the various IE languages into units and branches. The authorities are not all in agreement on some questions, but by 1900 it had been recognized that there were at least eight branches of IE, that is, over a period of time IE had become split into eight different significant dialects from which modern IE languages developed. None of the early dialects is still extant as such, of course, but some descendants of each are extant, and from them we can deduce the existence and early forms of the ancestor dialect as we have done in the case of proto-Germanic. Each branch has enough characteristics—in phonology, grammar, or vocabulary—to warrant our considering it as a separate dialect of IE. What we find in related languages and dialects are regular correspondences—similarities in sounds and grammatical features. The terms used to characterize each branch may be used either of the earliest form of that branch or of the later dialects (or languages) which developed from that earliest form. For the sake of clarity the prefix *proto-* (some linguists also use the adjective *primitive*) is used to designate the earliest form.

The branch for which we have the oldest documentary evidence is Indo-Iranian, sometimes called Aryan.[1] As the name implies, this term is used to characterize a large number of languages spoken in India and Persia, as well as in Afghanistan, Pakistan, and southern Russia. The two main language families of the Indian subcontinent are Indo-Iranian and the non-IE Dravidian, the former comprising most of the languages spoken in Pakistan, northern and central India, the latter most of those spoken in the south.

The two main divisions of this branch are Indian and Iranian. The speakers of proto-Indo-Iranian apparently broke into two groups, that which invaded the Iranian (Persian) plateau and

---

[1] With the possible exceptions of Hittite and Mycenaean Greek (Linear B). See below, p. 119.

that which crossed the Himalayas (or bypassed them in what is modern Afghanistan) into India. The oldest form of this latter division is preserved in the Vedas, the oldest religious texts of India, composed in the second millennium B.C. This language, known as Vedic Sanskrit, or Vedic, preserves many features of the parent IE language, especially the pitch accent. Classical Sanskrit, described in a brilliant grammar by Pāṇini in the fourth century B.C., was a standard literary and probably spoken Indian dialect in which a great many works were written. It still remains an important learned language for many Hindus. Modern Indian IE languages, such as Bengali, Gujerati, Hindi, and so forth are descended from certain popular and sister languages of Classical Sanskrit known as the *Prakrits*. Two of them in older form—Pali and Jaina—provided the languages for the Buddhist and Jainist scriptures, both of which are of great religious importance.

Iranian is preserved today mainly in modern Persian, which also has, however, a large borrowed Arabic[2] vocabulary. In its oldest forms it appears in Old Persian, which is preserved in inscriptions, and in Avestan, which is the language of the sacred books of the Zoroastrian religion.

A second branch is Armenian. The modern descendants are divided into Eastern and Western Armenian. The classical form of the language is preserved mainly in a Biblical translation of the fifth century and in a number of theological and historical works. This branch shows a consonant shift from IE somewhat similar to that summed up in Grimm's Law. Its syntax has been much influenced by the non-IE languages of the Southern Caucasians and by Turkish. Its vocabulary also shows much Persian influence.

A third branch is Balto-Slavic, although some authorities treat the Baltic languages (Old Prussian, Lithuanian, and Lettish) as a separate branch. Old Prussian became extinct at the end of the sixteenth century, but some earlier documents in

---

[2] Arabic is a Semitic, rather than an IE, language.

this tongue are extant. Lithuanian is the most interesting of the three languages to the comparative linguist, because of its preservation of certain important IE features. Of all present-day IE languages, it is the most like proto-IE in its declensions and phonology. Compare the following sentences which all have the same meaning:

> *Latin:* Deus dedit dentes; Deus dabit et panem. (God has
>   given teeth; God will give bread.)
> *Lithuanian:* Dievas dawe dantis; Dievas duos ir duonos.
> IE (reconstructed): *Deivos ededòt dntns; Deivos dedōt
>   (*or* dōt) dhonas.[3]

Lettish (or Latvian) is an offshoot of Lithuanian influenced by Estonian, a language that belongs, together with Finnish and Hungarian, to the Finno-Ugric family.

The Slavonic or Slavic group of the Balto-Slavic branch comprises an important group of languages today. Slavic is divided into Southern, Northern, and Western subgroups. Bulgarian, Serbo-Croatian, and Slovenian are the main modern representatives of Southern Slavic. Bulgarian in its oldest written form, known as Old Bulgarian or Old Church Slavonic, became the theological and liturgical language of the Russian and Bulgarian Orthodox Churches, where it is still used, no doubt because the first Slavic translation of the Bible, in the later ninth century, was in this dialect. Part of the struggle to develop a Russian literary language was directed in the eighteenth century against the dominance of Old Church Slavonic and against those who felt that serious literature in high style could not be written in the common language of Russia. Russian, or Great Russian, because of its literary and political importance, is the main language of the Northern group. It preserves from IE a fairly elaborate declension of the noun, and has, along with other Slavic languages, a characteristic way

---

[3] From Paul Thieme, "The Indo-European Language," *Scientific American* CXC No. 4, October, 1958, 74. This article may be recommended as a good general article on proto-Indo-European and its speakers.

of distinguishing in the verb between perfective and imperfective aspects, i.e., roughly, the difference between discrete and continuous action. The chief modern languages of the Western Slavic group are Polish and Czech. All the Slavonic languages preserve many features and much vocabulary in common and seem not to have diverged from each other as much as the other IE branches.

Albanian is a fourth branch of IE, whose earliest extant document goes back to 1462. Albanian today exists in two main dialects—Geg and Tosk, corresponding originally to location in northern or southern Albania. It has borrowed so extensively from other languages that its native vocabulary is today quite small. This has made its classification difficult, but most authorities make it a separate branch of IE. Certain extinct IE languages, such as Illyrian, have been mentioned inconclusively as possible earlier forms of modern Albanian.

The four branches above have been classified as **satem** languages. Indo-European languages can be divided on the basis of what happened in them to the IE *k, which in some branches has sibilants as its reflex. (**Reflex** is the term used for the descendant of an earlier form.) Those which have the sibilant reflex are known as *satem* languages; those which do not are known as **centum** languages. The words *centum* and *satem* are themselves the reflexes of the same IE root *kmt '100' in Latin and Avestan respectively. In Germanic *kmt became *xund> hund, as would be expected according to Grimm's Law, and is still detectable in the first part of our word hundred. In Avestan (and Sanskrit) the nasal of *kmt disappeared. The division into centum and satem languages, roughly Western and Eastern IE respectively, was long supposed to be the major dialectal distinction in IE, but today less significance is assigned to it. We shall treat this matter in more detail below when we discuss the proto-IE breakup.

The main *centum* branches are four. The one for which we have the oldest documentary evidence is Hellenic. Classical and modern Greek are its most important exemplars. Classical Greek preserves with remarkable fidelity what was probably the old IE verbal system. Its dialect diversity is quite complicated, and has been further complicated recently by the decipherment of Linear B, a type of writing discovered on the Greek mainland in the late nineteenth century, which gives us a glimpse of Greek as it was spoken in Mycenae about 1500 B.C. Up to this discovery, the oldest Greek documents went back only to about 750 B.C. The full implications of this view of a very early stage of the Greek language have not yet been assimilated. Greek was the chief language of Byzantium until its fall to the Turks in 1453. Modern Greek is still spoken in Greece and parts of Asia Minor; but there is a considerable gap between the spoken and literary languages, the latter having been much influenced by classical models. Modern demotic Greek contains many Slavic and Turkish elements, especially in its vocabulary.

Italic is a second branch of the *centum* languages. Its most important ancient exemplar is Latin, which in its popular form is the ancestor of all the modern Romance languages—among which are French, Italian, Spanish, Portuguese, and Roumanian. This branch has been extremely important in the linguistic history of Europe in many ways.[4]

A third *centum* branch is Celtic, which seems to have diverged more than most of the other branches from their common ancestor, and it was some time before its phonological correspondences with the other IE branches were worked out.

The Celtic languages were once widespread over Europe but now are mainly preserved around the western fringes of northern Europe—in the Irish (or Erse), Welsh, Gaelic (still spoken to some extent in Scotland and Nova Scotia), and Breton languages. All these languages are still preserved by small but loyal groups of speakers, Welsh being the most successfully maintained. One Celtic language, now dead, was

---

[4] For a good introduction to the development of Romance comparative studies and their general importance, see Iorgu Iordan: *An Introduction to Romance Linguistics, Its Schools and Scholars.* Revised, translated and recast by John Orr (London: Methuen & Co., Ltd.; 1937).

Gaulish, spoken in ancient Gaul (modern France). Its speakers adopted a form of Latin which became modern French. Gaulish itself is not very well known, since little epigraphical material has been preserved in it. The Gauls, after the Roman conquest, apparently carved their inscriptions in the language of their conquerors. Modern Breton is not a descendant of the Gaulish spoken in the extreme northwest of France, but of Welsh, brought to France by fleeing Welshmen or Cornishmen in the fifth and sixth centuries. Both Irish and Welsh have a rich medieval literature.

A fourth *centum* branch of IE is Germanic, which we have already discussed in some detail. It has been traditionally subdivided into North, East, and West Germanic. North Germanic is that subgroup spoken today in Iceland, Denmark, and the greater part of the Scandinavian peninsula. As with all groups in language classifications, Icelandic, Danish, Norwegian (in two important varieties), and Swedish have features in common which allow us to posit a common ancestor. The usual genealogical tree in simplified form is as follows:

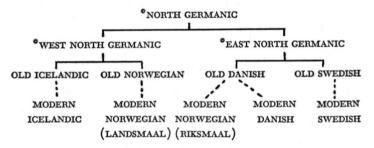

The East Germanic subgroup was spoken by a large number of Germanic tribes, notably the several varieties of Goths who were such a trouble to the Roman Empire. Its main document is a translation of part of the Bible by a Bishop Ulfilas (or Wulfila) in the fourth century, into what appears to be a kind of standard Gothic of the period. Ulfilas was himself a Visigoth.

Present-day major West Germanic languages are Frisian (spoken in northern Holland and in adjacent islands), English,

Dutch-Flemish, Afrikaans (spoken by the descendants of the Dutch settlers of South Africa), German, Swiss, and Yiddish (a Germanic language spoken by Eastern European Jews who migrated from Germany during the fourteenth, fifteenth, and sixteenth centuries). The first four are descendants of low Germanic dialects, and the latter three of high Germanic dialects. They are classified this way because of an important dialect division between the coastal (low) and interior (high) areas of the Germanic area. Their hypothetical ancestor is called proto-West Germanic. This subgroup may be visualized roughly as follows:

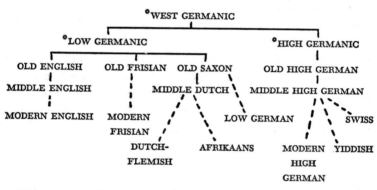

This group of eight IE branches comprises the major divisions as understood around 1900. We now know, however, of at least two other languages related to IE: Tokharian and Hittite, in addition to Illyrian and Thraco-Phrygian, of which only a few inscriptions are preserved. Tokharian is firmly established now as a ninth branch, although it does not fit neatly into the *centum-satem* division formerly thought to be of such great significance. For one thing, there are certain phonological difficulties, and for another, it was spoken far to the east of any known *centum* language. Tokharian records were discovered by expeditions into Central Asia between 1902 and 1914; it is no longer spoken, being preserved only in a group of medical and Buddhist writings, dating from 600 A.D.

During the First World War, inscriptions which had been

dug up earlier near Ankara, Turkey, were finally deciphered by the great Czech scholar Hrozny. One result of his work was the revelation of a group of languages used by peoples of the Hittite Empire, which flourished in the second millenium B.C. There are still many problems connected with the decipherment of some of these inscriptions and the relations and interrelations of the languages uncovered, but it is clear that some languages of this group, especially the major one known as Hittite, are Indo-European. The value of classification of languages by family or supposed descent comes out clearly here, for once it was suspected that Hittite was related to IE, a number of puzzles in the decipherment could be solved, and this knowledge continues to help in the solving of the numerous problems which still beset this field of study. Because the general characteristics of IE were known, the interpretation of these difficult inscriptions, especially those written in Babylonian cuneiform, was made easier. This knowledge has also helped in the more recent elucidation of Linear B inscriptions in Mycenaean Greek alluded to above (p. 119). Hittite is now acknowledged to have close affinities with IE. Some scholars think it comprises another branch of IE, while others consider it a descendant of a sister of proto-IE, and speak of the larger family as Indo-Hittite.

Although proto-IE is a reconstructed language created as a way of explaining extant forms in the various documented IE languages, and although strictly speaking our reconstruction consists only of the formulas from which these extant forms can be most conveniently and expeditiously deduced, it is possible that something like proto-IE once existed as an actual language and that the reconstruction reflects some kind of historical reality. On this basis, various scholars, some of whom were convinced of the reality of the IE hypothesis, have attempted to reconstruct the culture of the alleged proto-IE speakers. The procedure has yielded interesting results, and has indicated the possibilities of fruitfully relating the results of comparative linguistics to those of archaeology and cultural anthropology.

The first thing to note about the IE hypothesis is that, in a very important sense, the linguistic scholars who discovered the IE relationship in languages may also have discovered something hitherto unknown about European and Asiatic prehistory. This relationship between languages has given us some impression, however vague, of a people or group of people who may have spoken a language somewhat like reconstructed proto-IE in the period before writing was known to Europe, and from whom various invading, neighboring, or migrating groups must have acquired the language, which somehow was diffused into countries like India, Asia Minor, Italy, Greece, and so forth. The fact of invaders speaking IE languages is not a hypothesis, but is substantiated in most cases by historical evidence. But no one really knows who these Indo-Europeans were. They may not have been one people at all, but rather an amalgam of peoples.

Attempts to localize the speakers of proto-IE have been made on the basis of shared vocabulary. This method is extremely difficult to use because we cannot be sure that words have retained their meanings. As Jelinek points out, "Whoever these people [proto-IE speakers] were, whatever their culture, they certainly knew milk, but the available linguistic evidence would not lead us to that conclusion." However, on the basis of certain plant and animal names, climatic and geographic terms, and so forth, it has been assumed that the proto-Indo-Europeans may have lived, just before the historical invasions or migrations, somewhere in Central Europe: possibly in the Danube basin or southern Russia.[5] The older assumption, influenced by the belief that IE speakers were the bearers of true civilization, was that the home of the original Indo-Europeans was somewhere in Asia.

The division of proto-IE into dialects is in accord with a natural phenomenon observed in all languages. In an age with poor com-

---

[5] See Vladimir Jelinek: "Linguistic Equations for the Study of Indo-European Culture," *Studies in Memory of Frank Martindale Webster*, Washington University Studies, N. S. Language and Literature 20 (St. Louis, 1951), 77–110. This article deals with the reconstruction of the culture of IE speakers from their supposed languages and elucidates the difficulties of the task.

munications, primitive political organization, and no writing, the development of dialects was even more rapid than today, when we have various forces tending to hold languages together. The movement of peoples must have led to the increase of dialectal differences, which eventually led to the development of separate languages (dialects mutually unintelligible). IE as spoken by various separated tribes became different languages after a time.

The various dialect divisions established by the comparative method may seem to imply a strict historical break between dialects. We might be tempted to say that IE first split into *centum* and *satem* languages and that then further splits took place—all clear-cut breaks. However, the facts argue otherwise. While various IE languages show distinct differences from each other, these differences do not all argue for the same divisions. In other words, dialect criteria crisscross. If the *centum-satem* division took place first, then it is hard to explain why certain *centum* languages show similarities to certain *satem* languages rather than to other *centum* languages. For instance, Balto-Slavic, a *satem* language, agrees only with *centum* Germanic, and with no other *satem* (or *centum*) language, in the use of a reflex of **m* as an inflectional suffix in certain cases of the noun and adjective. All the other IE languages, *centum* and *satem* alike, use a reflex of **bh* in these cases. If Germanic and Balto-Slavic had clearly separated from each other earlier, with the alleged *centum-satem* break, it is hard to see why they should agree on this feature.

This kind of evidence, and there is much more, has led to the rejection of the theory of strict dialect separation in proto-IE. In general, we now recognize that proto-IE already had dialectal distinctions which must have existed before any clear-cut breaks took place. Linguistic geography, which will be discussed in Chapter V, gives us a better picture of the spread of dialect features. Johannes Schmidt, another famous German linguist, argued in 1872 for a wave diagram, rather than a family-tree diagram, to represent these changes. Individual linguistic features propagate over contiguous areas; different features may spread into different areas. This realization explains the fact of crisscrossing similarities. Only in some cases need we postulate a clear-cut break.

In the case of the -m/-bh distinction, it may be that *bh* became *m* in a certain dialect of the parent IE language, and that this change was then preserved when the *centum-satem* division

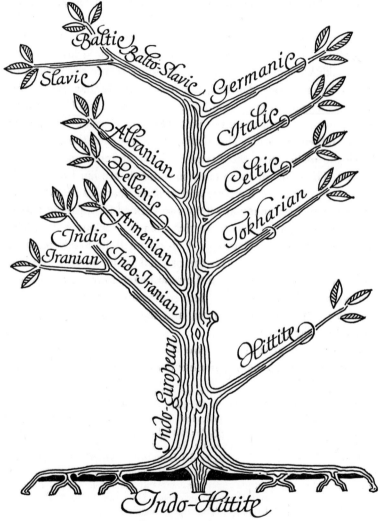

FIGURE 18. A highly simplified "family-tree" diagram of Indo-Hittite genetic relationships.

cut through this dialect. Or it may be that the feature $*bh>*m$ traveled from Balto-Slavic areas to the contiguous Germanic areas after the *centum-satem* break. In any case the reality of the dialectal divisions is much more complex than can be shown by any simple family tree diagram which pictures definite breaks. Figure 18, however, may help us visualize the divisions, if not the process itself.

When did proto-IE, or perhaps proto-Indo-Hittite, begin to lose its unity? We do know roughly the dates of certain invasions by IE-speaking peoples and must put IE unity before the earliest of these—before 2000–1500 B.C. But it is probable that the separation was a gradual affair. Paul Thieme writes: "Indo-European, I conjecture, was spoken on the Baltic coast of Germany late in the fourth millenium B.C." The Hittites were perhaps the earliest to leave the main body, the Aryan invaders of India and Iran the second. The dates of these early movements are hard to fix. The great civilizations of the Near and Middle East and the Mediterranean areas held many attractions to various IE-speaking tribes, and they descended into these rich areas in various waves. The last groups were the Germanic, Celtic, and Balto-Slavic peoples, who probably remained near the original IE home until the late pre-Christian centuries, when they too began to move northward and westward and to some extent southward. They carried their varieties of proto-IE with them, and these evolved into various separate languages.[6]

As we have already said, we do not definitely know what causes language change. It is clear that various causes operate at

---

[6] For an attempt to relate some of these assumed movements to the archeological evidence, see Hugh Hencken, *Indo-European Languages and Archaeology,* American Anthropological Association LVII No. 6, Part 3. Memoir No. 84, December, 1955. See also P. Bosch-Gimpera, *El problema indoeuropeo,* Con un Apendice de M. Swadesh. Universidad Nacional Autonoma de Mexico, Publicaciones del Instituto de Historia, Primera serie, Num. 45 (Mexico, 1960), which deals with some of the problems of the early prehistory of proto-IE speakers and the nature of their language, using archaeological and linguistic evidence. He tends to deny the unity of their culture and language. The above quotation comes from Thieme, *op. cit.,* 74.

various times. One is of special interest when migrations take place. When speakers learn a new language, they carry over some of the original language habits to the new language. The so-called substratum theory, which relies heavily on this fact, is looked on with some suspicion by many linguists because it has often been wildly applied to explain language changes. Irish speakers of English do carry over into English certain features from their original Irish language. This we do know. And we have ample evidence that such carry-overs are occasionally adopted by prestigeful speakers of the language, thus earning respectability and eventual general acceptance for these transplanted linguistic features. The whole Germanic consonant shift summed up in Grimm's Law has been explained by some linguists in this manner: The Germanic tribes, speaking some now unknown language, learned IE and consistently mispronounced it so as to produce the results we see today.[7]

The methods developed in the reconstruction of proto-IE were soon applied to other languages, which showed similarities greater than those that chance or borrowing could reasonably account for, and further families such as the Semitic, Finno-Ugric, and Altaic were discovered. The Far Eastern languages, the African languages, and the American Indian languages present numerous problems in the application of this kind of comparative method, but order is gradually being established and the general outline of the language families of the world is being filled in. Comparative linguistics of this sort has an excitement all its own, leading us as it may into the misty prehistoric period of mankind and giving us clues as to the development of man during his great formative period, which history cannot supply.

It must be pointed out that, in the past, most comparative linguistic work has consisted in family reconstructions such as we have shown in this chapter. But it must be remembered that

---

[7] See A. Meillet: *Caractères généraux des langues germaniques.* Seventh edition (Paris: 1949), 40–41. This would be an example of the use of one phonemic system in pronouncing words in another, as mentioned in Chapter I, p. 4.

languages may be compared with one another for any purpose. Strictly speaking, "comparative linguistics" need not be diachronic or heavily concentrated on phonological and semantic parallels. In the future we may expect more work in the comparison of languages in an effort to discover general, perhaps even universal, synchronic truths about language.

QUESTIONS

1. See what you can find out about the Hittite language and write a paragraph or two on it.
2. What is Tokharian?
3. Can the English word *back* be a descendant of the proto-IE root *bak*? Give reasons for your answer.
4. The OE word *pipor* 'pepper' and the Latin word *piper* 'pepper' are related in some way. Judging from the phonological correspondences involved, what type of relationship seems most likely? How does the history of the cultural contacts between the Romans and early Anglo-Saxons support the validity of your answer? See A. Baugh, *A History of the English Language*. Second Edition. (New York: Appleton-Century-Crofts, Inc.; 1957), 90–92.
5. What possible criteria could be used to differentiate dialect from language?
6. How do family classifications of languages differ from other possible classifications?
7. How would you go about showing the reasonableness of assuming that Old Church Slavonic *slabu* ('weak,' 'slack') corresponds to OE *slæpan* ('to sleep')?
8. What specific evidence has been used to deduce elements of the culture of speakers of proto-IE? Look in H. Bender: *The Home of the Indo-Europeans* (Princeton: Princeton University Press; 1922), and P. Thieme (see note 3, p. 117) for help in answering this question.
9. Discuss the validity of the use of the word "law" in speaking of sound changes.
10. What cultural and historical facts make it likely that *wigwam* and *papoose* were borrowed from American Indian languages?
11. In the year 2103 the previously uninhabited planet Venus is

settled by a small group of Albanians. As the population of the group increases, the Albanians split up into cliques and settle various widely separated parts of the planet. In the year 2846 you are among the first new group of people to arrive on the planet since the original settlement. You find that the population now speaks five different languages: Adap, Brit, Clak, Demin, and Eki. By a brilliant series of insights you compile the following sets of words, transcribed phonemically, which you assume to be cognate:

	A		B		C
bab	'father'	papa	'daddy'	bebe	'father'
stat	'week'	škak	'seven'	štet	'seven'
par	'money'	para	'coins'	pere	'money'
katir	'four'	kakir	'first'	ketir	'four'
drit	'lamp'	trika	'flare'	drite	'flame'
gur	'woman'	kru	'girl'	gru	'mother'

	D			E	
baba	'sire'		vovo	'father'
sat	'seven'		štot	'seven'
pala	'money'		poro	'valuable'
katil	'four'		kotir	'four'
dlita	'sunlight'		ðrito	'light'
glu	'lady'		ɣru	'woman'

PART I

From the evidence you have, perform the following feats of comparative linguistics:

1. List all the sets of phonemic correspondences deducible from the evidence. Then decide on a symbol to represent the most probable phoneme in the ancestral proto-Venutian for each set of correspondences. Make your list of this form:

A	B	C	D	E	PrV
b	p	b	b	v	*b
...	...	...	...	...	...

2. Now reconstruct the six probable proto-Venutian ancestors for the words in your collection:
   1) PrV *baba   'father'
   2) . . . .
3. Taking one daughter language at a time, how do you account

for the development of the modern forms from the ancestral language? Formulate general "laws" where possible. For example:

PrV *b>E v ⎫
PrV *d> E ð ⎬ Proto-Venutian voiced stops
PrV *g>E γ ⎭ become Eki voiced fricatives.

PrV *p>E p ⎫
PrV *t>E t ⎬ Proto-Venutian voiceless stops
PrV *k>E k ⎭ remain voiceless stops in Eki.

PrV *a>E o

. . .
. . .

PART II

Looking back now at all the steps you have taken since arriving on Venus:

1. How did your knowledge of Venutian settlement history help you in compiling your original list?
2. How has your work in reconstruction made you feel about your original insights into the relationships of the words in your list?
3. At what point was the meaning of the words in your list important for your work? How was it a hindrance?
4. Summarize the use of the meaning of words in doing this kind of comparative linguistics.

PART III

1. Another linguist in your expedition has compiled an etymological dictionary of Venutian in which he proposes that the following sets of words in modern Venutian languages are descendants of Albanian ancestors. By a close comparison of the corresponding phonemes, which sets seem reasonable to you and which seem invalid? Give your reasons.
   a. A gast 'six', B kašk 'six', E košt 'six'
   b. B pur 'man', D bur 'male', E vur 'boy'
   c. C reki 'brandy', D laki 'gin'
   d. A stip 'Venutian', D stip 'Venutian', E stip 'Venutian'
   e. A kur 'head', D klu 'top'
   f. A bret 'run', B prek 'run', C brit 'run', D blet 'run', E vrit 'run'
   g. A kuti 'box', B kuki 'box', C kuti 'crate'
2. If you discovered that in Earth Albanian the ancestor of A drit

'lamp' had been dríta while the ancestor of kuti 'box' had been kutí, what effect would this have on your answer to III. 1.g.? What would you now assume about the ancestors of A bab 'father' and A par 'money'?

3. In his preface to his dictionary, your fellow linguist writes: "From examples like baba 'sire' we can see that Demin is a very archaic language, since that form is identical with the original proto-Venutian form. By the same token, Eki is a strongly innovating language, as seen in the reflex vovo 'father' for the same item." Comment on this statement and its implications.

THE MORPHOLOGY
OF OLD ENGLISH

The history of the language which was to be called English passes out of the realm of systematic but speculative reconstruction when we come to that stage of it which is generally called Old English (or Anglo-Saxon); for this period (conventionally dated 700 to 1100) we find for the first time documents written in a language on the direct line of ancestry to modern English. The actual existence of these documents puts the study of our language in this period on a different course from that pursued earlier. We now have objective evidence for our reconstruction; we can appeal to material which exists—for the most part in great libraries and museums—and which can be studied by different scholars. Although it is true that interpretations of this material, especially the earlier remains, can and do differ, opinions of scholars can be checked against the evidence presented in physical, contemporary documents. The study of Old English is open to more than scientific conjecture, and can hence proceed with more confidence. We have evidence of the language recorded by native speakers, although it was not their intention, when they carved their inscriptions or wrote their literature or charters or laws or prayers or histories, to provide aid for modern scholars in their researches on the early stages of English. The availability of such material has a decisive influence on our methods of study.

If we can read the alphabet of the documents,[1] and in the case of Old English we can, we can recreate with some confidence the phonology, grammar, and lexicon of the language to be studied. Each involves certain special problems which we cannot discuss here; but, in general, by using our knowledge of related units in other languages, known later forms and their meanings, and contemporary translations made into and from the language, we can obtain our objective of interpreting the written records of a language no longer current. The recognized methods of historical study, the general techniques of descriptive linguistics, and knowledge of the later developments of the language (as in the case of English) will also be necessary for us to attain our goal of writing a description of a "dead" language.

The methods we have just mentioned—finding cognate units in genetically related languages, finding descendants in later standard and nonstandard varieties, finding translations from and into OE—all these are of great importance in helping us make reasonable guesses about a language no longer used today. However, the results of any or all of these methods require checking and confirmation. And this checking is done by inspecting the unit being investigated in its OE context. When the intensive scholarship which made OE come to life again for us was begun in the eighteenth and nineteenth centuries, there were many errors made, many guesses that later turned out to be wrong. But little by little at first, and then progressively more quickly, the pieces of the linguistic puzzle began to fit together in a way that proved the correctness of the individual guesses. The main confirmation of linguistic theories comes when all the individual hypotheses

---

[1] The first scribes of Anglo-Saxon (excluding those who used runes, if they indeed may be called scribes) used the current Roman alphabet, with the exception of a few signs (notably þ [*thorn*] or ð [*eth*], and a few others), to record OE. Their choice of letters gives us much help in reconstructing old pronunciation, although there are other methods of getting at it.

jibe—in this case, when the meanings tentatively assigned to individual units fit together to give us whole texts that make good sense. Constructing hypotheses that yield such meaningful results is an art, and at the same time it is the very essence of scientific method.

In this chapter we shall present one kind of description of the grammar of OE and one set of approaches to making such a description. Related but not exactly similar methods can be used to establish the phonology of the language. In Chapter VI we shall present quite a different kind of description of another "dead" language, Early Modern English, and shall employ quite a different set of approaches to that description. Each such description can be called *a grammar* of the language described.

When the language of the closely related tribes, the Angles, Saxons, and possibly Jutes, who apparently dwelt side by side on the eastern shore of the North Sea in what is today northern Germany and southern Denmark, began to manifest differences from the other West Germanic dialects spoken around them, to such an extent that the speakers became aware of this development, we may say that Old English was born. There is no one moment when we can say that a dialect of a language becomes a separate language; it probably takes some decisive nonlinguistic event to make a group of people conscious that their dialect has become a new language. Usually this event is political, for the linguistic consciousness of a people is closely related to its own sense of peoplehood or nationhood. In the case of the Angles, Saxons, and Jutes, this event was probably the invasion of England which began around the middle of the fifth century, an event which put a physical and political barrier between those who spoke West Germanic on one side of the English Channel and North Sea, and those who spoke West Germanic on the other.

This invasion, which began around 449 and must have lasted for a century—and even longer if we include full settlement of the English-speaking part of the British Isles—is not known to us in all its detail. Bede, the great English historian who died in 735, almost 300 years after the beginning of the movement across the North Sea, is our source for the names of these three Germanic tribes, the Angles, Saxons, and Jutes, but it is doubtful whether the matter is quite so simple. In particular, the Jutes, who are supposed to have settled Kent, the southeastern corner of England, and the Isle of Wight, pose a problem. The archaeological evidence seems to connect them with an area further south than the others, near the mouth of the Rhine and its lower reaches, rather than with Denmark and Schleswig-Holstein (the corner of Germany from which they are reported to have come). This area is within the territory which was occupied by the Germanic Frisians and Franks and which is today included in the Netherlands. The English language shows more affinities with Frisian than with the allegedly neighboring Old Saxon dialects;[2] in fact, some authorities argue for an Anglo-Frisian branch of West Germanic. Some scholars think there were no Jutes at all and that Bede made a mistake. Procopius, a sixth-century Byzantine historian, called the invaders of Britain Angles and Frisians; and Bede himself, after his preliminary classification, never speaks of the Jutes again, and calls his people either Angles or Saxons indifferently. There is some archaeological evidence to show that the Angles and Saxons invaded northern Holland (the home of some of the Frisians) before they moved on to Britain. In general, however, historians have accepted Bede's classification, and traditionally the invaders are called Angles, Saxons, and Jutes.

Whatever their names, their language was probably basically the same, and whatever dialects the study of Old English reveals probably developed after their settlement of the island. Some of these dialectal differences may have been stimulated by changes in the sister languages on the continent. There was much trade between England and the mainland, and innova-

---

[2] However, it is possible, indeed likely, that what we take to be Old Saxon, preserved mainly in two literary works, the *Heliand* and a translation of *Genesis,* has been much influenced by Old High German, and that spoken Old Saxon approximated closely Old English and Old Frisian and Old Dutch, although early examples of the latter two are not extant.

tions could easily have been carried over the English Channel. Recently it has been argued that some of the distinguishing features of the OE dialects were due to Frisian influence after the settlement in Kent, the nearest point to Friesland.[3]

The course of the invasion itself has to be reconstructed from incomplete accounts in Bede, the Anglo-Saxon chronicle, and Welsh traditions. This evidence can be supplemented from the evidence of archaeology and place names. This part of the story presents many difficulties, too, but it is of less significance to us in our study of the language than it would be to a historian. Suffice it to say that the Celtic peoples who inhabited Britain before the Germanic Angles and Saxons arrived were gradually defeated, enslaved, killed, assimilated, or pushed into the remoter parts of the island. In Wales they have maintained their own individuality and still speak the modern descendant (Welsh) of the Celtic language spoken in Britain before the invasions of the Germanic peoples.

Inasmuch as the documents we spoke of above do not exist in any number before the eighth century[4] and are not plentiful before the early tenth century, the evidence for the language these Germanic invaders spoke is much later than their first appearance in England. We therefore have a period of Old English when we are forced to rely on hypothetical forms. This blank period is divided into primitive Old English—running from about 400 to 500, including the period just before and just after the invasion—and prehistoric Old English—from about 500 to 700. Heuristically, this division is justified by the necessity of assuming that certain changes, especially in the sounds, took place around the time of the departure from the Continent,

---

[3] See David DeCamp: "The Genesis of the Old English Dialects, A New Hypothesis," *Language*, XXXIV (1958), 232–44. This article is an interesting example of the use of linguistic geography in attempting to solve the problem of the origin of OE dialects.

[4] There are some early, usually short, inscriptions from the seventh century written in runes, an alphabet the Germanic peoples used before they adopted a form of the Roman alphabet close to our own. Some collections of laws do date from the seventh century.

and that others took place on the island itself before the appearance of our first documents. We call the language spoken after written documents appear, from about 700 to 900, early Old English, and that spoken from 900 to 1100 late Old English. After that, because of the violent linguistic changes effected in English after the Norman conquest of the Anglo-Saxon kingdom (1066), the language gets a new appellation—Middle English. Our comments below on the morphology of OE are based on its late OE form.

The particular form of late OE which we shall analyze here is the standard literary variety which was used almost universally in this period. A kind of common accepted standard literary dialect had by this time been developed, based largely on the West Saxon dialect of OE. In fact most of our preserved records—literary and otherwise—of OE are written in this form of the language. Most earlier literary works written in other dialects had been transcribed into it, and the earlier texts are lost. A standard language meant that there was a prestigeful form of Old English which was widely understood, and that the scribes who wrote down literary, political, and legal documents were trained in the use of it. Although it is difficult to establish precisely their influence on the language, these scribes, as the preservers and transmitters of Anglo-Saxon culture, seem to have occupied an extremely important role in the process of standardizing OE.

This standardization was possible because England was politically unified earlier than the other countries of Europe and because, for many purposes, the local language was used instead of Latin. In the eighth and again in the tenth and eleventh centuries there was a kind of cultural renaissance in England, and in the later centuries a political unity based on the hegemony of the West Saxon kingdom. Its dynasty—that of King Alfred and his descendants—in the late ninth and tenth centuries became the rulers of all of Britain in Anglo-Saxon hands.

It is a remarkable fact in European history that England should have become unified so early and that a standard dialect should have been developed. The destruction of the Anglo-Saxon kingdom by the Normans in 1066 came as a terrible blow to the prestige of the English language, and it was not until the fourteenth century that it began to recover. In the tenth century, however, before this catastrophe overtook it, a form of English had succeeded in establishing itself as a respectable and widely used language, a standard for speakers of English.

Whenever or wherever they may have developed, various major dialects are characteristic of the earliest period of our language for which we have documentary evidence. These dialects never disappeared, but persisted with even greater differentiation into the Middle English period; however, in the later OE period, the West Saxon dialect, though sometimes with considerable intrusion from other dialects, was dominant in most written English. Since most of our preserved documents employ some special, literary style—aristocratic, legalistic, or religious—it is difficult to re-create the spoken language of the time. In living speech, however, nonstandard dialects other than West Saxon must also have been in continuous use, as the evidence of Middle English shows. We shall discuss this question at greater length in our next chapter.

Our knowledge of the Old English dialects is based upon two main sources: written and carved material, and place names. The evidence is not abundant except for West Saxon, but from it we can draw fairly sound conclusions. However, each document must be carefully checked against other material and, if the circumstances of its issuance are known, they too must be taken into consideration. Place-name study can be very valuable, but it is easy to see that the lack of variety of words represented can be limiting: there are many words of the type of -*ton* ('town'), -*tor* ('hill'), -*thwaite* ('village'), -*by* (as in *Granby*), but few verbs, few common nouns, etc. Fortunately, we do have some documents written in all the major dialects, and we can also reconstruct with caution forms from their descendants in Middle English, for which the material is richer.

Map 1. The Old English Dialects (approximate boundaries).

The major OE dialects distinguished by scholars are four. Their boundaries cannot be precisely delineated but one can make respectable guesses, partly from our general assumption that major geographic features like rivers and mountain ranges frequently constitute linguistic frontiers. (See Map 1.) These dialects are: Northumbrian, Mercian, West Saxon, and Kentish. Northumbrian, as the name implies, was spoken north of the Humber river. We have some short poems and runic inscriptions preserved in this dialect. Glosses—that is, interpretative comments and translations—written on several Latin works of the tenth century give us further information about Northumbrian. Mercian, which has some points in common with Northumbrian and which is sometimes grouped with it under the term Anglian, was in general spoken between the Thames and the Humber rivers. Our sources here are charters (various official and private documents) and various glosses. Some Anglian forms are preserved in predominantly West Saxon writings. Kentish was spoken in the southeastern corner of England south of the Thames. Charters, a small amount of literature, and a series of glosses on Bede's *Historia ecclesiastica* give us information about this dialect. West Saxon, spoken in the southwestern part of England, is preserved in the remaining bulk of OE literature and documents, although most of it is late—tenth and eleventh century. These manuscripts have mixed some non-West Saxon forms or spellings with their basic West Saxon forms. Besides these materials for all the dialects, we should mention place and proper names, sometimes found in Latin documents, as further sources of information in any quest to establish precise differentiating features of the various OE dialects.

To gain some rough idea of the kinds of phonological variation in the preserved forms of OE dialects, we may look at the words below. It is not always possible to distinguish between scribal habits in different parts of England and the actual pronunciations in different parts of England. However, there are various kinds of checks on the material, as for instance the differences in NE dialects.

West Saxon		Kentish	Anglian
weald	'forest'	*weald*	*wald*
nīehst	'nearest'	*nēst*	*nēst*
fyrht	'fear'	*ferht*	
ceald	'cold'	*ceald*	*cald*

Although there are phonological distinctions between North-umbrian and Mercian, the above table gives examples only of dialectal variants common to both, under their generic name —Anglian.

We will not attempt to present a phonemic analysis of OE in this book. However, in reading the OE forms as they occur in this chapter, a few hints may be in order about the general nature of the sounds we believe those forms to represent. There is considerable agreement among scholars as to the value of the OE letters, except in the case of the sequences of vowel letters. You may get some idea of how OE sounded by reading the OE spellings in this book as if they were NE phonemic transcriptions, with the following general exceptions:

1) *c* usually represents [č] before or after the letters *i, e,* and *æ;* [k] otherwise; *sc,* however, always represents [š]

2) *g* usually represents [y] before or after the letters *i, e,* and *æ;* [γ] or [g] otherwise; *cg,* however, always represents [j]

3) *þ* and *ð* represent [ð] between letters that represent voiced phones; [θ] otherwise

4) *f* and *s* represent [v] and [z], respectively, between letters that represent voiced phones; [f] and [s], respectively, otherwise

5) *y* represents [ü]

6) A macron written over a vowel letter or vowel sequence (e.g., ā, ēo) represents phonemic vowel length of that vowel or vowel sequence

There are many exceptions to these rules for *c* and *g* because the phonological values attached to these letters depend upon a variety of phonetic factors operating in the histories of the individual words in which they occur.

To go into the subject of phonological criteria distinguishing the OE dialects would involve much detail. As is suggested even by the few examples above, West Saxon generally has many more diphthongs than the other dialects, especially Anglian. Although for the most part the consonants in all OE dialects were the same, West Saxon and Kentish often have palatal consonants corresponding to velar consonants in Anglian, as in *ceald* above. This distinction between Southern and Northern dialects may still be seen in NE *church* as opposed to Scottish *kirk*. Scots, although much influenced by other varieties of English, especially London English, is a direct descendant of OE Northumbrian.[5]

These illustrate but by no means exhaust the kinds of criteria that can be used to distinguish the four main OE dialects. Other differentiating criteria could break down these four dialects further. For instance, the dialect situation in the Middle English period makes a division of Mercian into eastern and western areas probable, but because of the total absence of east Mercian materials scholars do not ordinarily make such a division.

A thoroughly reliable and consistent set of synchronic criteria is not yet available in treatments of OE; and we have not here presented the diachronic criteria that have been used, because they are meaningful only when the student already knows the relevant earlier and later forms. Nor have we qualified our statements about dialect divisions carefully enough to admit the actual presence of forms from one dialect in documents mainly written in another dialect. For example, there is evidence that particular spellings would originate in a major cultural center, such as Kentish Canterbury—focal center of the English church—and spread to other areas, to appear in this case as deviant forms in documents written in non-Kentish dialects; such deviant forms tend to obscure any neat, exhaustive set of identificatory criteria

---

[5] For a useful summary of the variations of vowels in the different OE dialects, see Joseph and Elizabeth Mary Wright: *Old English Grammar.* Third Edition. (London: Oxford University Press; 1925), 84–90, and Henry Cecil Wyld: *A Short History of English* (London: John Murray; 1914), 78–87.

we try to set up to distinguish the dialects from one another. With these necessary words of warning, we have said enough for our purpose here, which is merely to name and characterize the main OE dialects. We shall not delve further into the specific differences between those dialects. In the rest of this chapter, we shall not attempt to identify the specific dialect in which OE forms are cited; in general, however, we have mainly cited West Saxon forms of the period around 900 A.D.

The next thing to consider is the morphology—the grammatical characterization of words in OE. We will begin by discussing the technical terms that the linguist uses in his description of a language to designate the grammatical elements of that language. If one's philosophy of science allows, such elements may be considered to be pieces of reality which it is the linguist's task to discover and record, from the evidence presented by the actual discourses of the language. If one prefers a less committal attitude towards the nature of reality, these elements can be taken merely as the terms used to construct a simple coherent theory which will account for those actual discourses. In this chapter we will take the first view, on the whole, making it our task to show what kind of evidence we find in OE discourses that leads us to posit certain OE grammatical elements. In Chapter VI we will take the second view, and will try to show how a coherent theory can be constructed that will account for Early Modern English discourses.

Every linguistic unit has a characteristic form and a characteristic use. That is, given that a particular linguistic unit occurs, we can predict its particular form and use; conversely, given a particular form and use, we can identify the linguistic unit involved. As we have previously discussed, the elements in terms of which we specify the phonological form of a linguistic unit are called *phonemes*. Similarly, the elements in terms of which we specify the grammatical use are called **morphemes**.

To illustrate from NE, consider the two linguistic units *boy* /bɔy/ and *road* /ród/. Each of these, like all linguistic units, has a characteristic form and use; that is, being linguistic units, they make characteristic contributions to both the form and the use of the whole discourse in which they are embedded. Grammatically, *boy* and *road* differ in various ways: for example, *boy* is grammatically replaceable by *he*, *road* by *it*; we can say grammatically *She amazed the boy*, but not *She amazed the road*; we accept *A boy believed her*, but not *A road believed her*, etc. Next, consider the linguistic units *boy* /bɔ́y/ and *boys* /bɔ́yz/. Grammatically, these two also differ in various ways: for example, *boy* is replaceable by *he*, *boys* by *they*; we can say grammatically *The boy is tired*, but not *The boys is tired*; we accept *George is a mere boy*, but not *George is a mere boys*, etc. If we now consider the grammatical and phonological differences between *road* /ród/ and *roads* /ródz/, we shall find that these differences parallel the differences between *boy* and *boys* rather than those between *boy* and *road*. In order to account for the differences in these four linguistic units (*boy, road, boys, roads*) we shall find it expedient to identify three grammatical elements—three morphemes—which we may identify as {road}, {boy}, {-Z$_{pl}$}.[6]

We shall find that the morpheme {-Z$_{pl}$} has several different phonological forms:

{-Z$_{pl}$} = /əz/	= /s/	= /z/
roses /rózəz/	*docks* /dáks/	*boys*/bɔ́yz/
actresses /ǽktrəsəz/	*presidents*/prézɪdənts/	*roads*/ródz/
coaches /kóčəz/	*ships* /šíps/	*laws*/lɔ́z/
ledges /léjəz/	*giraffes* /jərǽfs/	*girls*/gɔ́rlz/

Each of these forms, each **morph,** is said to be an **allomorph** of the same **morpheme.** Many morphemes have only one allomorph: for example, {boy} and {road} have only the allomorphs /bɔ́y/ and /ród/, respectively. In general, different morphs which are allomorphs of a single morpheme are in **complementary distribu-**

---

[6] We will employ the convention here of enclosing the names of morphemes between braces. Remember in addition that phonemic transcriptions go between slants and that phonetic transcriptions go between square brackets.

tion; that is, they do not appear in identical environments. For example, the allomorphs of {-Z$_{pl}$} have the following distribution:

/əz/ appears only after one of the "sibilant" phonemes: /s,z,š,ž, č,ǰ/.
/s/ appears after any other voiceless phoneme; /p,t,k,f,θ/.
/z/ appears elsewhere.

It is useful in describing languages to distinguish between two large classes of morphemes: **lexical** and **grammatical.** Lexical morphemes are those whose grammatical characteristics can be accounted for by identifying them as members of morphological classes: for example, the grammar of {boy}, {man}, {uncle}, {gander}, {bull}, {stallion} can be more efficiently stated by identifying them all as masculine, animate nouns in a lexicon of English than by repeating the same rules for each of them separately in the grammar proper. That is, any unit identified as NOUN can, for example, be the object of the preposition *against* in NE; any unit identified as ANIMATE can be the object of the verb *amaze*; any animate noun identified as MASCULINE can be replaced by *he.* Grammatical morphemes are those whose special grammatical characteristics require independent treatment in the grammatical description: for example, {-Z$_{pl}$}, {be}, {by} all have special grammatical characteristics that require their special mention in grammatical rules. Because different descriptions of a language are possible, with different assignments of morphemes to the lexicon or grammar proper, linguists have shown great differences in their designation of morphemes as lexical or grammatical.[7] In addition, many morphemes are both lexical and grammatical; that is, some of their grammatical characteristics can be accounted for by their membership in lexical classes, but some of their characteristics require special mention: for example,

---

[7] The distinction between what we call *lexical* vs. *grammatical* here is parallel in large degree to what other linguists have called *full* vs. *empty, major* vs. *minor, lexical* vs. *formal* elements, *class* vs. *function* words.

{by} is just one more locative[8] preposition (a lexical class) in *He stood by the road*—notice that *at the road* or *in the road* or *along the road* would substitute very nicely here—but must be mentioned specially in a rule to provide for its appearance in *He was shot by his brother,* where the other prepositions fail as substitutes. Many prepositions, all conjunctions and pronouns, and a number of other morphemes (e.g., {the}, {one}, {too}) are, like {by}, both lexical and grammatical.

A useful general distinction in grammatical analysis is that between **free** and **bound** forms. A free form is a morpheme or morpheme-sequence that occurs without other morphemes to constitute a particular linguistic unit, while a bound form is a morpheme or morpheme-sequence that is accompanied by other morphemes to constitute a particular linguistic unit. If the linguistic unit involved is a word, we may speak of "word-bound" forms, if it is a phrase we may speak of "phrase-bound" forms, etc. Examples of word-bound morphemes in NE are {re-} as in *rename* /ri-ném/ or {-Z_{pl}} as in *boys* /bɔ́yz/. Similarly we may speak of phrase-bound forms like {at} in *at my house*; clause-bound forms like {although} in *although I like cabbage*; sentence-bound forms like {however}; and even discourse-bound forms like *Yes* and *Amen*. In each of these instances the bound form must be supplemented by additional morphemes to constitute whole linguistic units: for example, a whole discourse might be composed of "*Are you coming?*" "*Yes,*" but not of "*Yes*" alone. Free forms can simply be labeled with the name of the linguistic unit they constitute in a given discourse.

Grammatical word-bound morphemes are more commonly called **affixes**; lexical word-bound morphemes or morpheme-sequences are called **bases** (or **roots**). An affix that precedes a base is called a **prefix** and is denoted by placing a hyphen after the symbol for it: thus {re-} in *rename* is a prefix. An affix that

---

[8] {by} may also be a temporal preposition as in "Tom came in by ten o'clock"; an instrumental preposition as in "He won by cheating"; it has many other functions as well.

follows a base is called a **suffix** and is denoted by placing a hyphen before the symbol for it; thus, $\{-Z_{pl}\}$ is a suffix.[9]

As may be evident from the foregoing discussion, a linguistic unit displays two aspects of characteristic "use": 1) It is *used* with other linguistic units, it has characteristic privileges and limitations of occurrence in respect to other units—it has, in short, characteristic grammatical **valence**; and 2) it is *used* to say something, it has characteristic values as a tool of communication—it has, in short, characteristic **meaning**. Valence and meaning are two aspects of the same thing, namely, the use of a linguistic item. From either aspect alone it is possible to infer a large part, if not all, of the other aspect, and thus of the whole use. It is roughly true to say that the grammatical tradition by which most of the great "civilized" languages have been described is presented in terms of grammatical categories, in turn based largely on the aspect of meaning, while the "anthropological tradition," especially as it has been applied in the twentieth century to describe the "neglected" (also called "primitive" or "exotic") languages, has emphasized aspects of valence in grammatical presentations.

Morphemes—elements in terms of which the use of linguistic units is stated—can thus be said to be "carriers" of grammatical valences. Morphemes or morpheme-sequences that carry the same valences are said to belong to the same **grammatical category** by virtue of those shared valences. A given morpheme or morpheme-sequence belongs to as many different grammatical categories as the number of valences it shares with different groups of elements. We have already mentioned the grammatical cate-

---

[9] Phrase-bound morphemes are sometimes called **clitics—proclitics** if they must precede another morpheme, and **enclitics** if they must follow another morpheme. For example, *the* is a proclitic in NE (we have *the moon* but not *moon the*) and *one*, as in *a bad one* or *the green one*, is a postclitic. In the history of many languages we find many examples of words becoming clitics and the clitics then becoming affixes: in English, the ancestor of the word *like* became a clitic in phrases such as *sweet-like, man-like,* and eventually developed in turn into the affixes we find today in *sweetly* and *manly*. See also above Chapter II, pp. 80-81.

gories MASCULINE, ANIMATE, and NOUN in speaking of the shared grammatical properties of morphemes all of the same grammatical class: e.g., {boy}, {man}, {gander}, {uncle}, {bull}. The usefulness of such categories becomes even more apparent, however, when we want to describe the valences shared by items belonging to different classes: for example, the fact that *boy, rabbit,* and *rabbit-hunters* may grammatically fill in the blank in *The shot surprised the* ————., while *road, road-houses,* and *boyhood* may not, is describable by saying that *boy, rabbit,* and *rabbit-hunters,* although they clearly do not belong to the same morphological class, all belong to the ANIMATE grammatical category.

In morphological descriptions it is usual to distinguish two kinds of morpheme-sequences within a word: **derivational** and **inflectional** sequences. Derivational sequences are those which share the valences of a class of lexical morphemes; for example, sharing the valences of the class of morphemes that includes {boy} and {father}, we have the morpheme sequences in *bat-boy* and in *batter*. Derivational sequences like *bat-boy,* which are composed of lexical morphemes, are called **compounds**; derivational sequences like *batter* (a person who bats), which contain a grammatical affix as well as a lexical morpheme, are called **derivatives** of that lexical morpheme, and the grammatical affix involved is called a **derivational** affix. Morpheme-sequences within the boundaries of a word which do not share the valences of any class of lexical morphemes are called **inflections**; and an affix which forms inflections is called an **inflectional** affix. For example, in NE the inflectional suffix $\{-Z_{pl}\}$ forms sequences (like *boys* and *batters*) that have different valences from those of any class of lexical morphemes. To put it in another way, we might say that derivations do not add grammatical categories to the grammar of a language but that inflections do. This feature of inflections helps to account for the emphasis on inflection given by traditional descriptions, especially of Indo-European languages. Traditionally, "grammar" is often largely limited to, if not identified with, the display of the various types of inflections in a language. The display of all the inflectional or **inflected** forms with a given **stem**, that is, with a lexical morpheme or derivational sequence, is called the **paradigm** of that stem. In NE, both *name* and *rename* are stems—the first being a lexical morpheme, the second a derivational sequence—while *rename, renames, renamed, renaming* can be said to be the **paradigmatic forms** of the stem *rename*. In OE, the sets of paradigmatic forms are more extensive than in ME, and much more extensive than in NE; this fact accounts for the designation of OE as "an inflectional language," ME as "a language of reduced inflections," and NE as "an analytical language."

From the beginnings of our western grammatical tradition in early Greek grammars (in the second century B.C.) until the modern period (around the beginning of the twentieth century) descriptions of languages have been stated in terms of a standard set of grammatical categories that were taken to be universally applicable to all languages. Many of the traditional grammarians came to think that such standard grammatical categories—originally based on the analysis of only Greek and Latin—represented universal categories of thought, and thus that they were the only natural principles on which to base a description. It was not until the nineteenth century that the universality of the standard grammatical categories was seriously attacked by linguists; even now many linguists continue to present their grammatical descriptions as a display of how the standard grammatical categories are represented in the language being described. Until very recently, even when a linguist has realized that "future tense" in English does not operate as a category parallel to "past tense," he has felt called upon in his description of English to make an explicit statement (albeit a negative one) about future tense—an inheritance from our tradition of dividing grammatical categories in verbs into PRESENT, PAST, and FUTURE. Even our nontechnical everyday language employs terms derived from the classical tradition: for example, SENTENCE and WORD, not to speak of NOUN, VERB, ADJECTIVE, etc.

In this chapter we shall present a partial description of OE morphology in a traditional way. The paradigms are displayed as intersections of traditional grammatical categories; that is, the forms in a paradigm are presented in a kind of matrix whose columns and rows represent grammatical categories common to all the forms appearing respectively in those columns and rows. For example, in the following matrix of some of the paradigmatic forms of the OE stem *word* 'word' the forms in the columns represent the grammatical categories of number: SINGULAR and PLURAL; and those in the rows the grammatical categories of case: NOMINATIVE, ACCUSATIVE, GENITIVE, and DATIVE. Notice that a single form may belong in several different categories:

	SINGULAR	PLURAL
NOMINATIVE ACCUSATIVE	word	
GENITIVE	wordes	worda
DATIVE	worde	wordum

Such a presentation is justified on several grounds: 1) By and large, the traditional grammatical categories do reflect differences in both valence and form in OE. That is, to say that a given OE form is third person singular present indicative is to say something significant about its form and its valences. 2) As part of our cultural heritage, the traditional grammatical system must be learned by anyone who wishes to understand and use the enormous amount of profitable information which abounds in existing grammars and dictionaries. 3) The richness of OE in inflectional forms makes it a particularly appropriate vehicle for the demonstration of a system of grammatical description originally developed for Classical Greek and Latin, both of which were also highly inflected. 4) Modern descriptive linguistics has added little so far to our knowledge of OE. Few studies of OE have succeeded in matching, let alone surpassing, the insights into the language that we can gain from the better established traditions.[1]

The first set of grammatical categories we may distinguish are those called *parts of speech*: for OE we shall be particularly interested in the parts of speech called *nouns, pronouns, adjectives, and verbs*.

Parts of speech are large classes of whole words; in traditional grammars these classes are often defined by loose, heterogeneous, and often conflicting criteria. For example, if a noun is defined as "a word that names a person, place, or thing"; an adjective as "a word that modifies a noun"; a pronoun as "a word that takes the place of a noun"; and a verb as "a word that denotes an action or state," then how can we know how to classify the word *housing* in *We live in a housing project?* Doesn't *housing* here name a thing (compare *business*), modify a noun (as *residential* would do in the same sentence), take the place of a noun (in the sense that it serves the same kind of function as the noun *city* would serve in the same position), and denote an action (that of furnishing people with houses)? If the answer to any of these questions is "no," can the criteria by which we have determined our answer be stated clearly and consistently to apply to other problem cases? Do we really know what part of speech a word is on the basis of these definitions? Do "modifies" and "takes the place of" mean anything precise? What is the difference between "denote an action" and "name a thing" when the "thing" is itself an action (e.g., *cancellation*, the action of canceling)? How do our definitions account for the fact that we can identify the parts of speech even of words whose meaning we do not know? For example, in *The baffy scrill flasted my tander*, we unhesitatingly identify *baffy* as an adjective, *scrill* and *tander* as nouns, and *flasted* as a verb, although we would be hard put to defend our judgments on the

---

[1] The recent excellent grammars by Campbell and by Quirk and Wrenn offer good examples of the power of the traditional framework applied to the description of OE. Another recent work, the unpublished dissertation by George M. Motherwell: *Old English Morphemic Structure: A Grammatical Restatement* (Indiana University; 1959) tentatively proposes an approach to the grammar of the language which is outside the main tradition.

basis of the traditional definitions, since we could not say what modification *baffy* makes of *scrill*, what action is denoted by *flasted*, or what is named by *scrill* and *tander*.

For OE, these parts of speech are more satisfactorily defined in terms of the grammatical categories required to specify the grammatical characteristics of words belonging to paradigmatic sets; those grammatical categories are in turn established to account for the observed regularities in the use of words. Thus, an **OE noun** is a member of a paradigmatic set with a given *gender* and with variable *number* and *case*. An OE **adjective** is a member of a paradigmatic set with variable *gender, number, case,* and *definity*. An OE **pronoun** is a member of a paradigmatic set with a given *person*, and with variable *number, gender,* and *case*. An OE **verb** is a member of a paradigmatic set with variable *mood, tense, person,* and *number*.

OE Nouns

Below are three sample paradigms—**declensions**—of nouns in OE. It has been conventional since the early Greek grammars to use the nominative singular as a citation form—the form in which the word is referred to as a word; we have also inherited from the Greeks the notion that the other paradigmatic forms are somehow deviations or at least derivations from the citation form. Although for the sake of convenience we may follow the same convention here, we need not draw the inference that the

	stān 'stone'		*scip* 'ship'		*sacu* 'strife'	
Gender	MASCULINE		NEUTER		FEMININE	
Number	SINGULAR	PLURAL	SINGULAR	PLURAL	SINGULAR	PLURAL
Case						
NOMINATIVE	stān	stānas	scip	scipu	sacu	saca
ACCUSATIVE						
GENITIVE	stānes	stāna	scipes	scipa	sace	
DATIVE	stāne	stānum	scipe	scipum		sacum

word is "really," or even "originally," identical with its citation form.

These paradigms are typical of OE nouns in several ways: 1) With a very few exceptions, each noun has one and only one gender. 2) Not every potential difference in case is marked by an unambiguous case form; a given form—e.g., *sace*—may be used for more than one case. 3) The grammatical categories of gender, number, and case are relevant for the specification of the use of the noun form. But these particular paradigms are not representative of all nouns. For example, while the nominative-accusative plural form of many masculine nouns consisted of a stem morph (e.g., *stān*) plus the suffix morph -*as*, other masculine nouns had nominative-accusative plural forms consisting of stem plus the suffix -*e* (e.g., *Engle* 'Englishmen'), -*an* (e.g., *banan* 'killers'), or -*a* (e.g., *suna* 'sons'). For still other masculine nouns the nominative-accusative plural form consisted of the stem alone (e.g., *mōnað* 'months'), or of a special allomorph of the stem (e.g., *fēt* 'feet'; compare *fōt* 'foot'), on historical grounds traditionally said to have a "mutated" vowel. In NE we have some vestiges of several of these kinds of plural formation: -*as* survives (as -*s* or -*es*) to be our most productive plural morph; *feet* is still the plural of *foot*, etc. Similar remarks apply for the feminine and neuter plural forms. In general the variation in the composition of plural forms of nouns in OE was considerably greater than it is in NE, especially if we do not consider the foreign plurals in NE (e.g., *appendices*) which were lacking in OE.

In traditional grammars, nouns or adjectives which share a particular set of features (such as plural form ending in -*as*) in the composition of their paradigmatic forms are said to belong to the same **declension**. Similarly, verbs which share a particular set of features in the composition of their paradigmatic forms are said to belong to the same **conjugation**. The number of noun declensions in OE was large, from about eight to twenty, depending on whether one considers minor variations in the paradigms as establishing different declensions or merely different subclasses of the same declension. It has been traditional to define the OE paradigmatic classes by their historical origin: for example, to define a -*ja* noun declension because the prehistoric ancestors of a certain group of OE nouns all presumably had a non-final {-ja} suffix, even though by OE times this suffix no longer appeared on any of the members of the class. In this chapter we have not attempted a presentation of the numerous OE declensions and conjugations, because the traditional divisions make little sense without a fuller explication of OE prehistory than we could give here.

Although all of us are probably familiar with the terms "number" and "gender" as semantic categories ("number" tells "how many" and "gender" tells "what sex"), we are probably not equally aware of their use as grammatical categories. As grammatical categories, **gender** and **number** imply only a correlation of forms between words of different grammatical classes. In NE, for example, *this* is correlated with *stone* and with *is* in *This stone is heavy,* as opposed to the correlation between *these, stones,* and *are* in *These stones are heavy;* it is correlations like these that justify our speaking of grammatical categories of **singular** and **plural** for NE. Similarly, it is the correlation between *father* and *he, mother* and *she, book* and *it,* in sentences like *He is my father, She is my mother,* and *It is my book,* that justifies our speaking of **genders—masculine, feminine,** and **neuter,** respectively—in NE. Of course, grammatical categories often partially parallel semantic ones, and we may be led by the approximate parallels to conclude that the two kinds of categories can be completely equated. That this equation would be mistaken even for NE can be demonstrated by considering, for example, that a semantically unmistakable female, *vixen,* can be grammatically referred to either as *she* or *it* (contrast *wife,* which could grammatically be only *she*), or that a semantically plural bushel of grapes might be grammatically plural— *these grapes*—but an equal bushel of semantically plural *rice* could only be *this rice.*

For OE the correlations of gender apply not only to nouns

and pronouns, but also to adjectives and demonstratives. Note
that the correlation between semantic and grammatical gender
is much less consistent in OE than it is even in NE. For example,
in the illustrations below, while the semantically male *beorn*
'man' is a grammatically masculine noun and the semantically
female *fyxe* 'vixen' is a grammatically feminine noun, the semantically feminine *wīf* 'woman' is grammatically a neuter noun.
Many such instances are found among OE nouns:

sē	blinda	beorn	'that blind man'
seō	blinde	fyxe	'that blind vixen'
þæt	blinde	wīf	'that blind woman'

And correlations of number apply to nouns, pronouns, adjectives,
demonstratives, and verbs. For example:

Sē blinda beorn bærnde mīn scip. 'That blind man burned my
ship.'

Þā blindan beornas bærndon mīne scipu. 'Those blind men
burned my ships.'

The grammatical category of **case** rests on the notion of grammatical "government." We have already seen that grammatical
agreement or **concord** is the correlation between two or more
variable sets of word forms. **Government** is the term applied
when the selection of a word form out of a variable set of
forms is determined by its dependence on another word, while
the other word is unaffected in form by the first word. For example, in the NE sentence *He went with him and his brother
to those games,* the form *him* is selected—out of the set *he, his,
him*—because of its dependence on the word *with,* and we
therefore say that *with* "governs" *him.* Similarly the form *his*
is selected because of its dependence on—or we may now say
its "government by"—*brother. He* is the form that will generally
be selected when it is dependent on no other word: it is the
"citation form" of the word, used to refer to the whole set of
forms *he, his,* and *him.* In NE, these three forms are called **case**
forms of the word *he. He* itself, the independent or "ungoverned" form, is called the **nominative** case form. *His,* the form

governed by nouns, is in the **genitive** case (also called the "possessive" case for NE). *Him*, the form governed by prepositions (e.g., *with, from, in, by*), or by verbs (as in *I see him*), is in the **objective** case. The *cases* of a word are thus the forms about which it is relevant to state a relationship of government.

For OE nouns, as you see from the sample paradigms, we can distinguish four cases: **nominative, accusative, genitive,** and **dative.** The nominative case form is again the ungoverned one;[2] its principal use is as *subject* of verbs, that is, as the word (or words) which governs the form of verbs. To illustrate from NE, consider sentences of the form $\frac{\text{X likes Y}}{\text{X like Y}}$: the word that governs the choice between *likes* and *like* is the subject—if the subject is gender-distinguishing (*he, she, it,* or a subject that can be referred to by one of these), then the verb form *likes* is selected; if the subject is not gender-distinguishing in this sense (e.g., *I, you, we, they, the boys, the mother and her daughter*), the form *like* is selected. In OE, government of verb forms by the subject was much more extensive than it is in NE, as we shall see when we consider OE verbs.

The accusative case form (identical with the nominative form in many instances) was governed by certain prepositions—for the most part those with a semantic sense indicating directed movement through space or time: for example, the prepositions *in* meaning 'into,' *geond* 'throughout,' *wið* 'against, towards.' But the accusative case was mainly governed by verbs: the majority of verbs in OE governed the accusative case.

---

[2] Notice that we have said above that a case of a word is a form about which it is relevant to state a relationship of government, but here we say that the nominative case form is *ungoverned*. This apparent contradiction can be resolved if the *absence* of a relationship is construed to be a relevant statement about a form. Note, for example, that we would not say that any of the paradigmatic forms *fast, faster, fastest* in NE is ungoverned—such a statement would simply be irrelevant since none of the forms in the set *is* governed.

However, it should be admitted here that many linguists would consider such an argument to be sophistical. Indeed, some grammarians have considered the nominative "case" not to be a case at all.

The genitive case form was, as in NE, governed by nouns:
e.g., *eoforan Eadweardes* 'Edward's children,' *fyrdrinces gefara*
'warrior's companion'—here *Edward* is governed by *children*
and *warrior's* (*fyrdrinces*) by *companion*. In addition, it was
governed by adjectives—e.g., *wigges hrēmige* 'exultant of war'
(*wigges* is a genitive form of *wīg* 'war'); by some verbs—e.g.,
ne þorfte gemānan 'did not need a meeting' (*gemānan* 'meeting'
is a genitive form governed by the verb *þorfte* 'needed'); and by
a few prepositions with senses indicating the marginality of the
noun to the action—e.g., the prepositions *andlang* 'along' (as in
andlang þæs ealdan weges 'along the old road'), *wið* 'towards,'
tō 'until.'

The dative case was governed by many verbs, adjectives, and
prepositions. In general, the dative case was the neutral case to
use with prepositions, in contrast with the accusative, which
indicated directedness and the genitive, which indicated marginality (non-involvement). For example, the preposition *wið*
governing an accusative case form implied something like 'moving or directed against'; governing a genitive form, something
like 'towards, in the general direction of'; governing a dative
form, something like 'located opposite to, near.' With verbs,
the use of a dative case form generally indicated something involved in an action rather than the something upon which the
action was directed. For example, *him on bearme læg* 'it lay on
his lap' has *him* in the dative case, indicating that *he* is involved,
but not as the focal point of the action. A given verb may gov-
ern both a dative case form and an accusative case form in the
same sentence, the accusative case indicating the *direct object*
and the dative case indicating the *indirect object*: e.g., *Fæder,
syle mē minne dæl* 'Father, give me my share,' with *mē* 'me'
in the dative case and *dæl* 'part, share' in the accusative case.

OE Adjectives

On page 158 is a sample paradigm of the adjective *blind* 'blind'
in OE. Compare the categories and numbers of forms with those
for nouns on p. 152. There were some six to nine adjective de-

	SINGULAR			PLURAL		
Cases (Gender →)	MASCULINE	NEUTER	FEMININE	MASCULINE	NEUTER	FEMININE
INDEFINITE						
NOMINATIVE	blind	blind	blind	blinde	blind(e)	blinda
ACCUSATIVE	blindne	blind	blinde	blinde	blind(e)	blinda
GENITIVE	blindes	blindes	blindre	blindra	blindra	blindra
DATIVE	blindum	blindum	blindre	blindum	blindum	blindum
INSTRUMENTAL	blinde	blinde	blindre	blindum	blindum	blindum
DEFINITE						
NOMINATIVE	blinda	blinde	blinde	blindan	blindan	blindan
ACCUSATIVE	blindan	blinde	blindan	blindan	blindan	blindan
GENITIVE	blindan	blindan	blindan	blindra *or* blindena	blindra *or* blindena	blindra *or* blindena
DATIVE	blindan	blindan	blindan	blindum	blindum	blindum
INSTRUMENTAL	blindan	blindan	blindan	blindum	blindum	blindum

clension classes in OE, depending—as for nouns—on the importance one wishes to assign to minor variations in the paradigms.

For OE adjectives not only the grammatical categories of *case, gender,* and *number* are relevant, as they are for nouns, but also the category of **definity**. Forms labeled "definite" were used to imply that the reference of the forms was already identifiable by the listener or reader. In this way they had a grammatical function similar to that of the NE forms *the, my, his, that, this, he, she, her,* etc.; in NE we use *he* or *the man,* for instance, rather than *a man,* to indicate that our audience understands our linguistic reference, and *my friend,* rather than *a friend of mine,* if we assume our audience knows what *friend* we mean. In OE the definite forms of adjectives were used not only after words like *þæt* 'that,' *þis,* 'this,' and *his* 'his,' but also for comparative adjectives—e.g., *swiftran* 'faster'—and ordinal numbers—e.g., *ðridde* 'third'; in all these instances the linguistic reference would be assumed to be understood.

In addition, the category that for nouns is simply *dative case* is divided for adjectives into two cases: **instrumental** and dative. Of the kinds of "involvement" that the dative case of nouns might indicate, some were those in which the noun was a *means,* an *accompaniment,* or a *measure.* These "instrumental" functions were singled out for marking by special singular masculine and neuter adjective forms of adjectives and neuter forms of the demonstrative pronouns: *þȳ* or *þon* 'that,' or *þȳs* or *þis* 'this,' and *hwȳ, hwī,* or *hwon* 'what, who.'

An interesting vestige of the instrumental case is left in NE in sentences like: *The more, the merrier,* or *The faster you drive, the worse your chances of getting there.* The *the's* in such sentences can be traced back to the form *þȳ* cited above. A paraphrase to show the "instrumental" nature of *the* in those sentences might be: "With the more, by that much the merrier," and "By the degree of swiftness you drive, by that much less your chances of getting there."

If you examine the declension of OE *blind* above, you will

notice that most of the forms in the declension are composed simply of a stem *blind-* plus a suffix: *-e, -a, -es, -um, -re, -ra, -an,* or *-ena.* Let us attempt to describe such OE forms simply as sequences of morphemes, without resorting to identification of grammatical categories, with all the vagueness and circularity that such identification usually involves. The attempt is instructive: it will demonstrate the usefulness of organizing OE grammatical description according to paradigmatic categories.

For example, let us assume that the form *blindum* is treated simply as a sequence of the morpheme *blind-* plus the morph *-um.* Now how shall we describe the valence of the morph *-um?* We might say that it has "dative" functions, but that would fail to tell us why feminine singular datives do not have *-um.* If we were to say that it is masculine and neuter dative only, we would fail to account for its use for feminine plural datives. Then too we would have to account for its "instrumental" uses in plurals. For an accurate account of its valences, we would have to say something like: "dative and instrumental plural, and dative singular masculine and neuter." This description, though possible, is a mere list of functions, giving no sense of an organized system. In any case it does not avoid the use of terms for grammatical categories. If we had taken the morph *-e* instead of *-um,* the disorganization would have been even more apparent.

With all its faults, its redundancy and occasional looseness, the paradigmatic presentation of the morphology of languages like OE affords a picture of over-all structure that other kinds of presentation lack.

OE Pronouns

On pages 161 and 162 are paradigms for the principal OE pronouns. There was considerable variation in the forms of many of the pronouns—variation both according to the dialect of OE involved and according to the period of OE we are considering; that is, both geographical and chronological variation. We have included in our sample paradigm only a few of the variants that one actually finds in OE manuscripts.

| | | SINGULAR | DUAL | PLURAL |
		ic 'I'	wit 'we two'	wē 'we'
FIRST PERSON	NOMINATIVE	ic	wit	wē
	ACCUSATIVE	mē	unc	ūs
	DATIVE			
	GENITIVE	mīn	uncer	ūre

		þū 'thou'	git 'you two'	gē 'you'
SECOND PERSON	NOMINATIVE	þū	git	gē
	ACCUSATIVE	þē	inc	ēōw
	DATIVE			
	GENITIVE	þīn	incer	ēōwer

In order to place the grammatical category of **person** in proper perspective, we shall find it useful to characterize an act of language as involving four things: the language event itself (LE), the reported event (RE), the participant(s) in the language event (PLE), and the participant(s) in the reported event (PRE). We may now say that the category of person states the relationship between the PLE (the "speaker or listener") and the PRE (the "actor"). **First person** identifies one of the PLE, the speaker, as a PRE; **second person** identifies another of the PLE, the listener, as a PRE; **third person** implies that the PLE and PRE are different. In NE, *I* and *we* are first person, *you* is second person, and *he, she, it, they,* as well as all nouns, are third person.

The declensions presented above illustrate several characteristics of pronouns in OE. As a class they display more internal diversity than any other class; the third person pronouns have little in common with those of the first and second persons. Third person pronouns have distinct forms for the genders and for accusative and dative cases, and have considerable continuity of stem forms throughout their declension. First and second person pronouns distinguish gender by concord but not by form, do not distinguish (at the stage and dialect of the language we are con-

THIRD PERSON

PERSONAL

	MASCULINE 'he'	NEUTER 'it'	FEMININE 'she'	PLURAL 'they'
NOMINATIVE	hē	hit	hēō	hīē
ACCUSATIVE	hine	hit	hīē	hīē, hī, hēō
GENITIVE	his		hire	hira, heora
DATIVE	him		hire	him

DEMONSTRATIVE 'this, these'

	MASCULINE	NEUTER	FEMININE	PLURAL
NOMINATIVE	þes	þis	þēōs	þās
ACCUSATIVE	þisne	þis	þās	þās
GENITIVE	þisses		þisse	þissa
DATIVE	þissum		þisse	þissum
INSTRUMENTAL	þȳs			

DEMONSTRATIVE 'that, those'

	MASCULINE	NEUTER	FEMININE	PLURAL
NOMINATIVE	se	þæt	sēō	þā
ACCUSATIVE	þone	þæt	þā	þā
GENITIVE	þæs		þære	þære, þāra
DATIVE	þǣm, þām		þære	þǣm, þām
INSTRUMENTAL	þȳ, þon			

INTERROGATIVE 'who, what'

	MASCULINE	NEUTER
NOMINATIVE	hwā	hwæt
ACCUSATIVE	hwone	hwæt
GENITIVE	hwæs	
DATIVE	hwǣm, hwām	
INSTRUMENTAL	hwȳ	

sidering) accusative from dative forms, and do distinguish three different numbers—the distinction between **dual** and **plural** stems from Indo-European; it was generally lost by late OE times. Furthermore, there is a distinction in the third person between "personal," "demonstrative," and "interrogative" pronouns, a distinction lacking in the first and second persons.

Although NE has a considerably reduced set of pronoun forms as compared with OE, it is still true that pronouns as paradigmatic sets have undergone less change since OE times than any other part of speech. Corresponding to *ic, mē, mīn*, we still have *I, me, mine*; for *wē, ūs, ūre*, we have *we, us, our*; for *þū, þē, þīn*, we have *thou, thee, thine*; for *gē, ēōw, ēōwer* we have or had *ye, you, your*; for *hē, his, him*, we have *he, his, him*; for *hit* we have *it*; for *þis, þæt, hwa, hwæt*, we have *this, that, who, what*. Of course, many of the distinctions we make in NE for these are different from the distinctions of OE; and we have replaced a set of forms with new forms from Scandinavian: e.g., *they, them, their*. But by and large our system of pronouns in NE is the most "archaic" part of our grammar.

OE Verbs

On page 164 are illustrations of the two main conjugation classes of OE verbs.

Although there are various kinds of minor variation from the models exemplified by these verbs, most OE verbs belong to one of the two conjugation classes illustrated here: that is, to either the traditionally termed **weak** or **strong** class. "Weak" verbs are those whose preterite tense forms have an apical stop (*-d* or *-t*) suffix following the stem, while "strong" verbs are those whose preterite forms lack this suffix but do have a different vowel from that (or those) in the present tense forms. There are other differences between the two conjugation classes—such as the *-ed* past participle form for weak verbs as against the *-en* form for strong verbs—but the difference in preterite forms is sufficient to define the distinction. It is traditional to subdivide the strong verbs in Germanic languages into seven classes, characterized principally

dēman 'to judge' (WEAK)

FINITE — PERSON

PRESENT

NUMBER	INDICATIVE SINGULAR	INDICATIVE PLURAL	SUBJUNCTIVE SINGULAR	SUBJUNCTIVE PLURAL
FIRST	dēme	dēmað	dēme	dēmen
SECOND	dēm(e)st			
THIRD	dēm(e)ð			

PRETERITE

NUMBER	INDICATIVE SINGULAR	INDICATIVE PLURAL	SUBJUNCTIVE SINGULAR	SUBJUNCTIVE PLURAL
FIRST	dēmde	dēmdon	dēmde	dēmden
THIRD	dēmde			
SECOND	dēmdes(t)			

NON-FINITE

	SINGULAR	PLURAL
IMPERATIVE	dēm	dēmað
INFINITIVE	dēman	
PAST PARTICIPLE	(ge)dēmed	
PRESENT PARTICIPLE	dēmende	

teran 'to tear' (STRONG)

FINITE — PERSON

PRESENT

NUMBER	INDICATIVE SINGULAR	INDICATIVE PLURAL	SUBJUNCTIVE SINGULAR	SUBJUNCTIVE PLURAL
FIRST	tere	teraþ	tere	teren
SECOND	tirst			
THIRD	tirþ			

PRETERITE

NUMBER	INDICATIVE SINGULAR	INDICATIVE PLURAL	SUBJUNCTIVE SINGULAR	SUBJUNCTIVE PLURAL
FIRST	tær	tǣron	tǣre	tǣren
THIRD	tǣre			
SECOND	tǣre			

NON-FINITE

	SINGULAR	PLURAL
IMPERATIVE	ter	teraþ
INFINITIVE	teran	
PAST PARTICIPLE	(ge)toren	
PRESENT PARTICIPLE	terende	

by the vowels which the various forms of the stems had historically. These vowel alternations go back to IE ablaut series.[3] We
still preserve in NE some of the distinction between weak and
strong: compare *deem, deemed, deemed* with *tear, tore, torn.*
Over the years, however, the number of verbs in English that
preserve the historical characteristics of the individual strong
classes has decreased gradually, until today there are only some
seventy verbs (most of these, however, are among the most frequently used verbs in the language) that one might call "strong"
in NE.

The grammatical categories of person (first, second, and third)
and number (singular and plural) have already been discussed
for the other parts of speech. For verbs, distinctions in the category of person apply only to **finite** forms, those forms which are
governed (see p. 155) by the person and number of a subject:
that is, if the subject is the first person singular pronoun *ic*, a
first person singular finite verb form will be selected; if the subject is a third person plural pronoun or any plural noun, a plural
verb form will be selected, etc.

The **non-finite** forms do not have subjects, in the technical sense
we are using here. Roughly speaking, **imperative** forms are the
non-finite forms used to give second person commands; **infinitive**
forms are employed in "neutral" functions, such as that of citation
form for the whole verb (compare with the nominative case form
of nouns); **past participle** forms are employed in "resultative"
functions—to indicate, for example, completedness or passive-
ness of an action; **present participle** forms are employed in "con-
tinuative" functions—to mark duration of action in verb phrases,
and active characterization in noun phrases. It can also be argued
that present participles are derivational rather than inflectional
sequences—that is, that they are adjectives with verb stems
rather than verbs in their own right.

To understand the grammatical categories of **mood** it will help
to refer back to the scheme we used for discussing person. Re-

---

[3] See Appendix for details. For ablaut, see Chapter III, p. 108.

member that a language act involves two kinds of events—the language event itself (LE) and the reported event (RE); and two kinds of participant—participant in the language event (PLE) and participant in the reported event (PRE). Now, mood depends on the relation between the PLE and the RE: the **indicative** mood is neutral about that relation, in contrast to the **subjunctive** mood, which is used to display an attitude of the PLE toward the RE. For a clear-cut example, contrast the NE sentences *God helps us* and *God help us*. The first—in the indicative mood —does not involve the speaker in the reported event: he stands apart from that event as an observer. But the second—in the subjunctive mood—distinctly involves the speaker as a desirer of the reported event or at least as a commenter on that event.

Just as grammatical mood involves the relationship between the PLE and the RE, grammatical **tense** involves the relationship between the LE and the RE—roughly, the occurrence of the reported event in respect to the occurrence of the language event as a point of reference. **Preterite** tense forms in OE denoted the priorness of the RE in respect to the LE—that is, roughly for RE in the past time with respect to the LE. **Present** tense forms were used when the priorness of the RE to the LE was not involved— roughly, that is, for RE's in the present or future time with respect to the LE.

In many languages, inflected forms of verbs mark other grammatical categories. **Aspects** are grammatical categories that involve only the nature of the RE itself; for instance, the **perfective** aspect (in Russian verbs, for example) denotes RE's that are discrete, particular entities rather than continuous or general. In Germanic languages, including OE and NE, it is largely true that the aspects marked in various other languages by inflected verb forms are marked by combinations—called **periphrastic** constructions—with verbs. For example, in NE we have what has been called **progressive** or **durative** or **limitive** aspect in periphrastic constructions containing some paradigmatic form of *be* plus a verb form with the suffix *-ing*: e.g., *is talking, be living, has been holding, was nodding*. Similarly, we might talk about a **continua-**

tive aspect in *keep talking, kept nodding;* an **inchoative** aspect in *start talking, started nodding;* a **perfect** aspect in *have talked, had nodded,* etc.

Most Germanic languages also do not mark grammatical categories of **voice** by inflected verb forms. Voice categories involve the relationship between the PRE and the RE. **Passive** voice forms (as in Latin verbs) indicate that the referential emphasis of the RE is on the PRE, while **active** voice forms leave the matter of focus undetermined. In NE, and to a smaller extent in OE, a reordering of the sentence using periphrastic passive constructions mark what some other languages mark with single inflected verb forms: we have a passive construction in *The Danish army was never really defeated* as contrasted with the active *They never really defeated the Danish army.* OE uses this construction, but more frequently, like German or French, it reorders the sentence to begin with a word equivalent to "one" in NE.

Before leaving this general discussion of some of the features of OE morphology, a little space will be devoted to an aspect of word formation in OE which involves the combination of morphemes.

All languages which are alive have the power to create or form or borrow new words or give old words new meanings, to take care of new exigencies of communication. Every year hundreds of new words or new meanings come into modern English, dictated by inventions and discoveries, the desire for novelty, new ways of looking at things or ideas, new movements and developments. Correspondingly, certain words become obsolete or at least obsolescent. This process is a necessary one in all living languages, and OE was no exception.

In general, the ways new words or meanings are taken into the language are usually classified into three: the creation of new words by compounding and derivation or by neologistic fiat, the borrowing of foreign words, and the extension of the meanings of old words. Compounding (see p. 148) involves putting together two or more lexical morphemes; derivation involves putting together a derivational affix and one or more lexical morphemes. Enlarging a vocabulary by extending meanings may be illustrated by the word *channel*, which was adapted to television when that invention became practical and widely used. We have borrowed and still borrow many words from foreign languages. Sometimes a nation will not like to borrow too many foreign words, and will try to make up native equivalents. The Germans officially favor *Fernsprecher* ("far-speaker") for *telephone*, although many speakers of German do use the latter word. Icelandic is even more opposed to foreign borrowing than German. Modern English has no such qualms. OE speakers, on the other hand, preferred the German to the NE method and tried to make up words for foreign objects and notions with native morphemes. In other words, OE favored the first and third methods. Since the Norman Conquest, however, a great influx of French and Latin words have become English, and English speakers have been extraordinarily ready to borrow words from foreign languages.

However, we have never given up compounding and derivation of new words from native morphemes. We say, for instance, *houseboat* or *baby-sit* (compounding) or *unattractive* or *gangsterdom* (derivation). Sometimes we compose a new word on the pattern of a foreign word or phrase; this is called a **calque**. *Grandfather*, for instance, is formed on the pattern of the French *grandpère*.

OE used the methods of compounding and derivation a great deal, sometimes in the form of *calques* and more frequently not. Inasmuch as OE speakers did not borrow many foreign words as such, this alternative method was even more popular than in NE.

The process of compounding is especially characteristic of the Germanic languages.[4] All Indo-European languages possess this method of increasing their vocabularies, a fact which indicates that it was characteristic of the parent language. Both

---

[4] The best treatment of the subject in English is in Charles T. Carr: *Nominal Compounds in Germanic* (London: St. Andrews University Publications XLI; 1939), to which we are indebted for some of what follows.

derivation and compounding seem to have been present in proto-IE. The degree of employment of the two devices in the daughter languages, however, seems to depend on phonological factors which affected the extent to which morpheme forms were distinctly maintained. We notice, for example, that Latin and the Romance languages have tended to favor suffix formations, whereas Germanic ones have favored compounding. Perhaps, as Carr suggests in *Nominal Compounds in Germanic,* in Germanic languages the strong root accent tended to blur the phonological integrity of the derivational suffixes, and the development of a fixed word order then helped to establish compounding as a popular method of word derivation.

It is not always easy to identify compounds in OE, because words were not consistently separated in the manuscripts, and words that we suspect to have been compounded may appear separated by a space. Usually, however, a compound can be established by comparison of the same words in different manuscripts. In general, a compound has a meaning different from the sum of meanings of the individual morphemes, and as a check we find frequently that morphemes have special allomorphs in compounds.

In any case, we know that compounding was very common in OE. A few examples will suffice to illustrate the device: *Breostcofa* (literally "breast-chamber") means 'chest' or metaphorically 'heart'; *hellewite* means 'torment of hell'; *sæman* means 'seaman (sailor).' Note that in the first case we no longer have this compound in English. In the second case we might still use *hell-torment,* although it is no longer a standard compound with the same meaning. In the third, we still use the same compound with the same meaning.

Godspel (NE *gospel,* literally "good message") is a good example of an OE *calque* formed on the basis of the Greek εὐαγγέλιον (*evangelium*) which in its original form was a compound of the Greek words for 'good' and 'message.'

It is characteristic of derivational constructions for languages in general, and for English in particular, that predictive rules about their composition are of little value. We can have some confidence in rules we formulate to predict the occurrences of inflectional morphemes and can predict with some assurance the inflections of forms in a sentence or utterance, but derivational constructions can only be recorded after the fact. Each compound has a history of its own, although we do not usually know the circumstances of its original formation. Our knowledge of how even present-day compounds come to be formed is scanty. It is thus even less likely that we could understand the causative factors at work some 1000 years ago. In such matters, it is probably more scholarly to be silent.

QUESTIONS

1. What is a lexical morpheme, an inflectional morpheme, and a derivational morpheme?

2. Use a large Old English dictionary, such as J. Bosworth and T. N. Toller *An Anglo-Saxon Dictionary,* to break down the following OE words into their constituent morphemes and to determine which ones are affixes and which bases: *forgiefan* 'forgive'; *manigfeald* 'manifold'; *woruldþing* 'worldly affair'; *ymbsittende* 'sitting near (surrounding)'; *hearpestreng* 'harpstring'; *misthliþ* 'misty cliff'; *modigness* 'pride.'

3. See if you can show how the following OE and Latin words are *calque* pairs: *besilfran-*deargentare (cover with silver); *ymbgefretwian-*circumornare (adorn around or about); *efennis-*aequitas (truth or justice); *geleafsum-*credibilis (believable); *inlihtan-*illuminare (illuminate); *welgelicod-*beneplacitum (well-pleased); *mildheortnis-*misericordia (pity); *ðrines-*Trinitas (Trinity).

4. Classify the following OE words as derivations or compounds: *sārigmōd* 'mournful,' *soðfæst* 'truthful,' *breostweorðung* 'breast ornament,' *sunnandæg* 'Sunday,' *wērigmōd* 'depressed,' *deorcnes* 'darkness.'

5. How has the membership of verbs in the strong class and weak class changed during the history of English? You may use the books listed in the Bibliography (pp. 369-375) to help you formulate a general account, as well as to supply you with supporting details for your answer.

6. A high-school teacher tells you: "We must maintain the rules of grammar in order to maintain the time-tested distinctions of language; *I have spoke* is wrong because it obliterates the distinction between the past tense *spoke* and the perfect *have spoken*." Comment on this statement, both from what you can discover about the history of the forms involved and from what you know about how grammatical distinctions are made. Is the distinction between the past and perfect of *speak* dependent upon the distinction between *spoke* and *spoken?*

7. Compare traditional definitions of the following terms (you may use the Bibliography or conventional textbooks) with the use or definition they are given in this chapter:
   a) noun
   b) case
   c) verb
   d) gender
   e) adjective
   f) grammatical
   g) dative
   h) definite
   i) pronoun
   j) person

8. Using Wright's *Old English Grammar* (footnote 5, p. 142), make a simplified chart of the vowel variations between the major OE dialects (distinguishing Mercian and Northumbrian when necessary). Almost all these variations are limited to certain phonetic environments or by the origin of the sound in proto-West Germanic or Germanic. Indicate these limitations as Wright gives them. You may omit the vowels treated in Sections 194–210 inclusive.

9. The grammatical category of definity is operative in the OE adjectives, reflected in forms called definite and indefinite, or more commonly strong and weak. Explain this category in your own words and, referring back to Chapter III, point out its importance in IE (in particular, Germanic) classification of language groups.

V

THE DIALECTS OF
MIDDLE ENGLISH

Anglo-Saxon England was successfully invaded and conquered in 1066 by the Normans from northwestern France. Originally of Viking ancestry, the Normans had, by the eleventh century, become completely French both in language and habits. Their leader, William of Normandy, had himself crowned King of England in December 1066, and immediately began to reorganize the kingdom along Norman lines. In the process, he took away the lands and positions of the leading Anglo-Saxon noblemen and clergy and gave them to his own favorites; and since England was wealthier and more important than Normandy, he began to concentrate Norman power in conquered England. In 1204, France won back from Norman England the Duchy of Normandy for the French crown, although other parts of France, won or inherited earlier by the Anglo-Normans, were still not under French sovereignty. By this time, the Normans who had settled in England regarded themselves as English and England as their homeland. No longer under the political domination of the Continent, the English tried during the next two and a half centuries to extend their control over France, but ended by losing all their Continental dominions. It was not until the middle of the fifteenth century that England and France, although they continued to indulge in occasional wars, finally recognized each other as separate countries.

The effects of the Norman Conquest were felt throughout the fabric of Anglo-Saxon society. Innovations and changes of the first magnitude were made in every field of human endeavor; in law, architecture, government, warfare, literature, commerce, religious orders, social manners, and so on. Language was no exception. On the contrary, English was so profoundly influenced by this event and experienced such significant changes that we give a special name to the period of English after its effects begin to show themselves, from about 1100. We call it Middle English (ME). Further changes had become so extensive by around 1500 that a different term—Modern English (NE, for New English)—is used to describe the language after that date.

It should also be remembered that England had been subjected to another invasion—that of the Vikings—in the two centuries before the Norman Conquest.[1] Although this invasion—or series of invasions—had no direct political goal for the most part and was rather disorganized as compared to the Norman invasion, one important result of it was a substantial migration of Scandinavians into the northern and eastern parts of England; and these people, like the Normans, became assimilated to Englishmen, and like them left a mark on the English language.

These two waves of immigration had different impacts, however, on English. Unlike the Normans, who became noblemen and landowners, with retainers, and who constituted an imposed upper class, the Vikings settled down in close contact with their English neighbors. The fact that the Germanic language spoken by the Vikings (Danish and Norwegian—usually called

---

[1] For recent studies of the Vikings, see Johannes Brønsted: *The Vikings*. Trans. Estrid Bannister-Good (Pelican Books: 1960), and Holger Arbman: *The Vikings*. Trans. and ed. Alan Binns, Ancient Peoples and Places XXI (London: Thames and Hudson; 1961).

Old Norse [ON]) was closer to English than was Norman French facilitated contact and encouraged rapid assimilation. Language contact began almost at once between the Scandinavians and the English, and bilingualism must have been common from almost the very beginning. What students of bilingualism call interference—the influence of one language on another—began very early in the case of the Scandinavian settlement.

With the Normans it was different. Cut off for a long time from the people by social and language barriers, they were assimilated more slowly; language contact and interference were at first more restricted. Some Normans, and probably more Anglo-Saxons, must have been partially or wholly bilingual in order to make the transfer of orders and commands possible, but the total number was probably small until after 1204. Only after the loss of Normandy and the growth of English nationalism did Englishmen of Norman ancestry begin to learn English in large numbers, with subsequent strong French or Anglo-Norman interference. The few statistics we have bear this out. It is only in the thirteenth century that extensive borrowing from the French begins to show in our documents.[2] Such extensive borrowing, which would have been unlikely had the Anglo-Normans continued to maintain their original linguistic isolation from their Germanic compatriots, suggests that in this period a large number of Frenchmen must have been speaking or trying to speak English. The general high prestige of French must also have encouraged the speakers to carry over some of their words and phrases into their new language.

Scandinavian borrowing must have begun much earlier, probably long before the Norman Conquest, although OE documents

---

[2] See A. Baugh: *A History of the English Language*. Second Edition (New York: Appleton-Century-Crofts, Inc.; 1957), 213–15. These figures may be somewhat questioned because the literary and legal language on which they are based is very conservative in reflecting change. But even allowing for all this, the statement is probably true. See also the graph in A. A. Prins: *French Influence in English Phrasing* (Leiden: Universitaire Pers; 1952), 33.

show only a little Norse interference. Unfortunately, we do not
have enough documents which can be dated before 1300, coming from the areas where the Scandinavians settled, to give us
statistical support for this surmise.

When a man speaks two languages and successfully keeps
them apart, we have no bilingual problem. "Insofar as the bilingual succeeds in keeping the languages apart, he is two
separate speakers. . . . Whenever this condition is not met, there
is linguistic interference."[3] The characteristic features of ME and
NE may be said to be due in great part to linguistic interference, especially that of French, but also to some extent to that
of the Scandinavian languages, especially Danish. And this interference could only have been brought about by extensive bilingualism. Sometimes a whole word or phrase was taken
over from the source languages and anglicized and diffused into
existing English phonological and morphological patterns; sometimes a blend of both languages resulted; and sometimes the influence operated to affect the pattern of the English construction,
forming *calques,* semantic loans, and the like.[4]

Although our concern is primarily with English, it should be
noted that Anglo-Norman continued to be used in England at
least until the beginning of the fifteenth century and in legal
language until much later. The Norman French spoken in England was more and more influenced by English, particularly in
the matter of stress, and it claimed fewer and fewer speakers.
When French was spoken, the more prestigeful Ile-de-France dia-

---

[3] Einar Haugen: *Bilingualism in the Americas: A Bibliography and
Research Guide* (University, Alabama: Publications of the American Dialect
Society 26; 1956), 11. See this whole work and Uriel Weinreich: *Languages
in Contact, Findings and Problems* (New York: Publications of the Linguistic Circle of New York; 1953), for two excellent treatments of this
subject.

[4] For a good introduction to the French and Scandinavian element in the
English vocabulary, see Mary S. Sergeantson: *A History of Foreign Words
in English* (London: Kegan Paul, Trench, Trubner; 1935), 61ff. and 104ff.
On syntax, see H. T. Price: *Foreign Influences on Middle English* (Ann
Arbor: University of Michigan Press; 1947), and A. A. Prins: *French Influ-
ence in English Phrasing* (Leiden: Universitaire Pers; 1952).

lect was favored. The disappearance of Anglo-Norman may well explain the development of ME "high style," as the rhetoricians of the Middle Ages called the literary style proper for serious and elevated works, which we find occurring in English from about 1350 onwards. This style, in a very elaborate and Latinate form called *aureate*, flowered in the fifteenth and early sixteenth centuries, and may very well have been an attempt to fit English for some of the elevated duties that Anglo-Norman was felt to have performed in the past.[5] However, the story of Anglo-Norman, a much neglected subject, is not the theme of this book.

What were some of the immediate and long-range effects of the imposition of French upon English? Perhaps the most important was the elimination of a standard English (the West Saxon standard referred to in the previous chapter) as the cultural and administrative language of England. The learned upper-class speakers of English, and with them, the preserving and conservative linguistic center of English, were gone. English lost its high standing to French and Latin. No longer do we find documents or serious literature written in a widely accepted English dialect. For example, chronicles ceased to be written in OE, although one does extend to 1154; the new chronicles were written in Latin. Those works which were written in English were written in the local dialect of the writer; no established standard dialect remained from OE times. As a result, Middle English documents were written in a wide variety of dialects, no one dialect being universally accepted until well into the sixteenth century.

The growing nationalism of England, together with the loss of Normandy, and probably the lowering of status of Anglo-Norman

---

[5] This suggestion was first put forth by Fitzroy Pyle: "The Place of Anglo-Norman in the History of English Versification," *Hermathena*, XLIX (1935), 22–42. J. S. Purvis: *An Introduction to Ecclesiastical Records* (London: St. Anthony's Press; 1953), 12–13, gives 1520 as the earliest date when English begins to replace Anglo-Norman and Latin in legal documents; only in the eighteenth century is it finally triumphant. The earliest use of English in legal terminology is to form English *calques* on the original expressions.

as a dialect of French (with the rise of Paris and its Ile-de-France dialect), had by about 1250 settled the question of whether English was to survive at all as a national language. The next question was, which dialect of English would become the standard dialect—the cultural vehicle of court society, intellectual activity, and law court proceedings? Not until about 1350 did the rise of London begin to settle this question. We will tell this story in more detail later in the chapter.

By the time printing came in, most of the great European countries, certainly France, Spain, and Italy, each had an accepted standard dialect. But Caxton, the first English printer, still complains of his difficulties with English.[6] He writes, "Certainly it is hard to please every man, because of diversity and change of language." The dialect which was to conquer in England had been in a leading position for a long time by the 1470's, when he began his work, but many details were still unsettled. These were what bothered Caxton, who wanted his books to be understood all over England so that they could reach a large market. From its position in Anglo-Saxon times of being the first of all European languages to develop a standard form, English had badly receded by the fifteenth century. The necessity for establishing a new standard dialect had been forced on England by the Norman Conquest.

The second effect of the Norman Conquest on English flows from the first. Because English lost its status and became a language of peasants, certain changes in the language which we know were going on in late Anglo-Saxon times, but which could make little headway in writing against the conventions of standard West Saxon, were able to make themselves immediately apparent. There was no prestigeful cultural counterpressure to repress these changes and innovations. The elaborate inflections of the OE standard began to break down; that is, they no longer appeared

---

[6] For a recent brief treatment of Caxton and his influence on English, see Curt F. Buhler: *William Caxton and his Critics* . . . (Syracuse: Syracuse University Press; 1960). The quotation in the next sentence is Mr. Buhler's translation of the original from the preface to *Eneydos* given on p. 29.

in writing. The scribes were almost all Frenchmen and cared little and knew nothing about "correct" OE. They wrote, when they wrote English, pretty much as they heard it, using French graphemic conventions—still preserved in many NE spellings, e.g., in the French *ou* for ME *u* (as in *house*). As has been mentioned in the previous chapter, the role of scribes in the transmission of language and culture can be very great. The Norman Conquest destroyed the Anglo-Saxon scribal class, and with this destruction went the care for the preservation of outmoded forms. There was also no upper class speaking OE to remind the newer scribes of their linguistic duties. Suddenly, OE became colloquial, so to speak, and when we say that OE became ME, this is really what we mean, at least in the early years of ME. Early ME as seen in contemporary writing is simply colloquial, poorly (i.e., more accurately) spelled late OE, with perhaps a few French and Danish words added. Further changes took place, as we have suggested above, when the effects of bilingualism began to make themselves felt.

If we compare the written representations only, early ME is different from late ME, but not so different as both are from OE. The collapse of a standard written language allowed certain repressed or partially hidden developments in the current speech to come to light. These are manifest in the loss or reduction of inflection, the loss of grammatical gender, the burgeoning of various dialects, the adoption of French spellings, and a greater rigidity in word order which accompanied the loss of inflections. ME became a more analytic language than OE; that is, it relied more heavily on "function words" (free grammatical morphemes) and word order than OE. We will come back to these matters shortly.

A further effect of the Norman Conquest on English may have been to change the attitude of English speakers towards borrowing foreign words freely into their language. It was pointed out in the previous chapter that the speakers of OE preferred making up equivalents in native roots and words to borrowing foreign words directly. After the Norman Conquest all this was changed, and it is reasonable to assume that the influx of French speakers into England had something to do with it. Since the thirteenth century and possibly earlier, English has not hesitated to use foreign words as part of its own vocabulary. For the most part these words were reshaped according to English phonemic patterns and were thoroughly anglicized after a time, but they very often retained something of their foreign shape. Thus, to some extent, these foreign words did affect English phonemics, but for the most part English phonemics and phonology affected them. As one of the rare examples of the former in English, we may mention the fact that [v] and [f] were allophones of /f/ in OE, but in ME they became separate phonemes. In OE, [v] and [f] never contrasted. The [v] would appear only in the middle of an OE word. However, the French word *ver* 'spring' would on entering ME in its French form contrast minimally with OE *feor* > late OE *fer* 'far' and thus create a phonemic distinction between /f/ and /v/. To put it simply, ME speakers learned to hear the difference between the initial [v] in Early ME *ver* and the initial [f] in Early ME *fer*. Thus, the phonetic difference [f]-[v] assumed phonemic status and [v] was, so to speak, promoted from allophone to phoneme.

In most cases, however, the process went the other way and foreign words were anglicized into the English phonemic patterns. For example, the stress and accent pattern of English strongly altered the prominence of syllables in borrowed words; and many other phonetic changes accompanied these alterations, so that an original *nation* /nasión/ is preserved in NE as /nésǝn/ (in modern French it has become /nasyō/). As a result of fitting foreign borrowings into English syllable patterns, an example like the French *vrai* 'true' in *very* is hardly recognizable, so extensive has been the change.

Although there have been strong protests against this freedom to borrow, especially in the Renaissance and in the early nineteenth century, it has been characteristic of English since the later Middle Ages. This attitude of English speakers towards foreign words is probably an outcome, then, of the vast influx of

French words which the Norman invasion brought to England. English speakers became used to foreign words in their vocabulary. The large number of these words, mainly French and Latin, in our vocabulary is the final point in our list of the effects of the Conquest on English. Of all the Germanic languages, English is the most Frenchified and Latinate. Thousands of words were borrowed from French and Latin during the ME period—the French element through both popular and learned channels; the Latin mainly through a learned channel, the Church. In the latter case, the process probably went something like this. The Church, under the control of French speakers, did not hesitate to use Latin religious words in French. When the upper ranks became English-speaking in the thirteenth and fourteenth centuries, they continued to use these (as well as French) words in their English and many of them gained universal currency in English.

Now it is true that we should probably have a fair proportion of French and Latin words in English even if there had been no Norman Conquest. From the twelfth century on, French, as the language of the cultural center of Europe, and Latin, as the language of the Church and of intellectual endeavor, exercised a great influence on all European languages. But that the Norman Conquest intensified the effects of these two languages on English is evinced by the higher percentage of French and Latin words in English as compared with Dutch and German, and by the fact that in certain fields of human endeavor, such as law, government, and military affairs, the French element forms an overwhelming proportion of the English vocabulary. It was just in these fields, of course, that the Normans were predominant in England.

It must not be thought, however, that French and Latin gave English only a specialized or intellectual vocabulary. Some scholars have characterized the French and Latin words in English as fancy, effeminate, and sesquipedalian, the Germanic words as strong, masculine, and elemental. This generalization can be supported by some persuasive evidence (for example, compare the Romance words *ascend, reside, acquire* with the Germanic words *climb, live,* and *get*), but cannot stand without severe qualification. It is true that many of our homey and ordinary words are of Anglo-Saxon origin, but it is also true that many are of Romance origin. French words in English like *joy, face, cap, camp, force, gain, war, truck, catch, chase, state, stay, safe, save, porch, pose, file, tank, sue, plea, paint, pair, pay,* and so forth can hardly be considered fancy, weak, or even polysyllabic.

Now it is true that more Romance words in English are polysyllabic than Germanic ones, and they are often less immediate or homey than their Germanic counterparts. Part of the essential flexibility of our language comes from our having a variety of vocabulary which can express different shades of meaning, as in a large number of synonyms or near-synonyms of Germanic and Romance origin (e.g., *house* vs. *mansion, kingly* vs. *royal, fatherly* vs. *paternal*). Shakespeare can be as moving when he writes "the multitudinous seas incarnadine" as when he writes "to be or not to be."

The influence of French on English is seen not merely in the isolated borrowed words, however numerous, but also in phrases. A. A. Prins (see footnote 2 above) has collected a large number of phrases which were borrowed from or modeled on French ones, not all of them going back to ME times. It is amazing how pervasive this kind of influence has been. Any estimate of French influence on English must take into account this type of borrowing and calquing. For example:

English	*French Model*
plenty of	plenté de
to the contrary	au contraire
if need be	si besoin est
because of	par cause de
to make peace	faire paix
tender age	tendre âge

As we have seen, English is very receptive to new words and has even borrowed many Romance words which are nearly synonymous with already available Germanic words. This helps to explain why English has such a large vocabulary in comparison with German. It does not explain, however, why English tended to preserve so many of its older words in the face of competing new words. The historical and cultural reasons for this phenomenon are still not known.

If we look at the matter geographically, we see that there is a certain justice in English being a mixture of Germanic and Romance elements. The boundary between these two great language groups—the most important in Western Europe—hits the English Channel somewhere between Calais in France and Ostend in Belgium, very close to the point between the Continent and the British Isles where the English Channel, which joins the North Sea and the Atlantic Ocean, is at its narrowest. In a sense, beyond the barrier of the Channel the two language groups intermingle to form English, which embraces elements and characteristics of both families and which unites itself with both great European traditions.[7]

It must be kept in mind that English was an unimportant European language until the late eighteenth century. The regard in which a language is held is closely dependent upon the political and cultural importance of the people who speak it. It is not dependent upon its innate characteristics. Shakespeare and Milton were not universally admired until the eighteenth century, when the greatness of the British Empire was fully established. The English writers and thinkers who were admired abroad before that time wrote mostly in Latin. From the twelfth to the eighteenth centuries English occupied a place in the hierarchy of languages something like that occupied by Dutch today. There were a few people on the Continent who learned the language for various personal needs in communication, but it had little international scientific, cultural, or commercial importance. How different is the situation today, when English is the most widespread language in the world! For the sake of a critical perspec-

---

[7] We owe this way of looking at the matter to R. W. Southern: *The Making of the Middle Ages* (London: Hutchinson's University Library; 1953), 16 ff.

tive on the putative inherent superiority of some particular language, we must not forget the relative insignificance of English in the eyes of the world in the medieval and later periods; we should remember that history changes the status of nations and languages. It is clear today, for instance, that Russian and Chinese are on the rise and that French is on the decline. We can expect other shifts in the relative positions of languages as new centers of political power develop their strength.

Since the eighteenth century, however, English has been a very important language in the carrying on of the world's business and in cultural significance. It exhibits both advantages and disadvantages for widespread currency. On the one hand, its many points of similarity with Romance and Germanic languages as well as its many borrowings from other languages have helped to make and keep it cosmopolitan; a Frenchman, for instance, finds English easier to learn than German and a German finds English easier to learn than French. On the other hand, our inconsistent conventional spelling creates difficulties for all foreigners learning English. It is one of the greatest problems in the way of establishing English as the first "universal" language since the Latin of the Middle Ages.

Now let us look at some of the particular changes which differentiate ME from OE; later we will pass on to dialect study, which is the chief concern of this chapter. We will not discuss here the main phonetic changes or the influx in vocabulary but will concentrate on the changes which made English a more "analytic" language: the loss of inflections.

The factors making for the loss of inflections in late OE and early ME were threefold: the strong accent on the root or beginning of the word in OE, a characteristic shared with other Germanic languages; the speech mixture (or interference) which resulted from contact with a similar language, Scandinavian, and to some extent with a less similar language, French; and finally, the absence of a standard dialect, which would have tended to preserve certain distinctions. These factors, it must be urged, constitute reasonable explanations of what happened, rather than universal necessary or sufficient causes of language change. Note, for example, that both Czech and Irish have a root accent and both for a long time lacked a single standard dialect, but neither lost its inflections to the extent that English did. Nor could the second factor, the presence of foreigners speaking a similar language, have been decisive. For although it is true that in the north and east of England, in those areas where the Scandinavians settled in large numbers, the extensive loss of inflections developed earliest, in the south and southwest many inflections were also lost. Thus, none of the three forces can be demonstrated to have causal efficiency. At most one can say that they make the changes that did occur seem reasonable.

The first factor, a strong accent on the root or beginning of a word, especially of an inflected form of a verb, noun, or adjective, was operative in eliminating differences in the unaccented syllables of inflected words in late OE,[8] as the spelling confusions which crept into the manuscripts show. A large number of the inflected forms in OE ended in an unaccented vowel or an *m* or an *n*.[9] The final *m* in many of these forms became *n;* then, after an unaccented vowel, final *n* disappeared. In the meantime, the unaccented vowels themselves, perhaps first nasalized before a nasal consonant, generally became [ə], spelled *e*. The process may have gone like this: [um] > [un] > [ū̃n] > [ə̃n] > [ə̃] > [ə]; [ɛn] would suffer a quite similar fate. The unaccented vowel endings of OE had already become [ə]'s early, perhaps even in late OE. All these final unaccented [ə]'s (linguists call them *schwas*) of various origins, apparently disappeared in ordinary speech by about 1350.[1] As a result of all this, many previously

---

[8] Of course, in some forms, the ending did not disappear but was modified; for instance, the various forms of the past tense suffix of weak verbs, *-ed, -de, -od,* etc. > *-ed.*

[9] There are others; for example, the *-as* of a plural declension or the *-r* or *-st* of the comparative and superlative of adjectives. But note that we still preserve *-s* in the plural of nouns—indeed, we have vastly extended its use—and the *-r* and *-st* in many comparatives and superlatives.

[1] They probably were preserved for a longer period in poetry, as in Chaucer, who wrote most of his poetry in the last quarter of the fourteenth century.

distinct inflectional categories disappeared. This is also the way in which grammatical gender, so characteristic of OE, vanished. In those inflectional endings in OE composed of a vowel and *s*, the vowel became a schwa but was retained along with the *s* until at least the sixteenth century. This different phonetic development probably explains the preservation (and later extension) of the *s* in both genitive and plural of nouns.

The second factor, the close contact with Scandinavian speakers, made for a great deal of language interference with English. Language interference occurs in various ways, and one of the rarer ways is the interference with inflectional morphemes. When speakers of English and Scandinavian (and to some extent speakers of English and French) were in such close contact with each other over a long period of time, such interference was bound to take place. Given the close contact between two languages with a large number of words that differ only in their endings, it is reasonable to expect that simplification of some sort will occur. One can appeal to one's experience today, for instance, in trying to talk a foreign language which one knows imperfectly. An English speaker venturing to speak Italian, say, may use both the words *stazione* and *stazioni, limone* and *limoni,* and *nazione* and *nazioni* because of their similarity to English words, but he may well fail to make the distinction of final vowels and thus lose the difference between singular and plural in the Italian words. Some such process may have happened on both sides when Scandinavian and English speakers attempted to communicate with each other. Even though there were far fewer words similar in early ME and Old French, the same process may also have occurred between English and French speakers.

This type of interference between two languages, when prolonged over a long period of time, would have led to the elimination or modification of inflectional endings.[2] If we add to this fact the actual blurring of the distinctive endings of OE by the strong

---

[2] See the process as described by Henry Bradley: *The Making of English.* Reprint of 1948 (London: Macmillan and Co.; 1904), 25 ff.

root accent, it is easy to see why many of the endings would tend to disappear altogether or to be simplified.

The third factor, the absence of a standard written form of the language upheld by schoolmasters, scribes, editors, and rulers, allowed colloquial forms to appear in writing. No one could write angry letters to the press; no schoolmaster would be impelled to use his switch on this account. Nothing external operated to impose uniformity or "correctness" on the written language. As long as people could understand each other and communicate with each other, they could write as they pleased with impunity. And gradually the English inflections were simplified. The "decline" of English had set in some time before it was to become one of the greatest literary languages of the world.

We have already said something about dialects of a language, and now we must say more. Dialects—the term is used here for any distinctive varieties of a language—arise naturally from the inherent tendency of language, as of all mundane objects and institutions, to change. No two people, even when speaking the same language, speak exactly the same. At different periods or even different days or hours, the same person uses different kinds of speech. Yet the variability must remain within certain limits or the speaker will not be understood and accepted by his fellows. It is this necessity of being understood and accepted that acts as the most powerful brake upon language change.

Another factor which has been urged as a deterrent to language change is difficult to evaluate. We refer to the conviction held by speakers of a language that, except for vocabulary items, language does not change but conforms to permanently established norms. This conviction must have some force; it even blinds speakers to the fact that changes do occur. Most speakers of American English, for instance, are not aware that many speakers do not make any difference in the pronunciation of pairs like *latter-ladder* much of the time. The spelling makes people think that they are using [t] in one and [d] in the other.[3] The failure to distinguish between /t/ and /d/ in such positions is quite normal, but the idea of spelling correctness in our mind keeps many of us from being aware of our frequent practice. The more refined our acoustic instruments are, the more aware can we be of the actual variations in our pronunciation. The variability in idiom, syntax, and vocabulary is apparent to everyone, but the extent of these variations is not always appreciated.

In less civilized times there were fewer external hindrances to change, and the lack of facilities for communication tended to protect changes. The Indo-European hypothesis assumes that migrations and geographic barriers encouraged locally prevalent changes to become permanent. IE may at one time have been a single language whose dialects, separated over many centuries, developed into separate languages. Germanic was IE spoken by the Germanic peoples, and Latin was IE spoken by the Romans. The absence of a generally recognized standard form of the language encouraged these centrifugal tendencies.

Today, mass education and mass communication are spreading standard forms of IE languages more effectively than ever before. But they are apparently also spreading linguistic innovations more quickly to IE speakers than ever before. It is thus difficult to assess the present and to predict the future rate of evolution of IE languages.

Certain dialects of a language make good and become standard dialects or even separate languages, while others fail to make headway. Usually there are strong geographic, cultural, and social reasons for this difference in development. The late ME dialect of London, in various descendant forms, has succeeded in becoming the standard dialect of most of the speakers of English primarily because London was the commercial, political, and cultural center of England in late medieval times. Another factor which helped to make London English predominant was the large influx of population into late medieval London. This influx came from all

---

[3] For a recent study of these voiced *t*'s, see Donald J. Sharf: "Distinctiveness of 'Voiced *t*' Words," *American Speech*, XXXV (1960), 105–109.

over England, especially from the northern Midlands.[4] It assured the adoption of the London dialect by large numbers of people. And it was also to affect the very nature of that dialect as it became the standard for speakers all over England.

Nonstandard dialects are not debased versions of a standard dialect, as many people think, but dialects which have not happened to gain prestige in the society. They often preserve forms and features of the language which have been lost in the evolution of the standard dialects.

Contempt towards substandard dialects was widely, though not universally, felt in the eighteenth century. But the rise of the Romantic movement in the late eighteenth and nineteenth centuries, with its glorification of the peasantry, led to a burst of admiration for substandard, especially rural substandard, dialects. Both the underevaluation and overevaluation of these dialects resulted in many misconceptions. When they were highly admired, rural "sub-dialects" were said to be "pure" Elizabethan English or "pure" High German. This uncritical admiration was almost as false as the uncritical repugnance which had preceded it. Sub-dialects change too. They borrow words, pronunciations, and grammatical features from other dialects and languages, and although some of their pronunciations, words, and idioms are older than their counterparts in standard dialects, by no means all of them are. One result of the great enthusiasm for rural dialects, however, was the permanently valuable study and recording of them by their admirers.

For the most part, we have been talking so far only about geographic or regional dialects. But a language varies both with the geographic location and with the various complex social positions—including those of status and education, trade and profession, age and sex—of its speakers.

One of the most interesting types of social dialect is *slang*, a phenomenon widely recognized and used, but difficult to define.

---

[4] See the recent excellent study of Eilert Ekwall: *Studies on the Population of Medieval London* (Stockholm: Almquist and Wiksell; 1956), which shows how this population movement affected London English.

In its broad sense the word slang can designate almost any use of substandard linguistic features by speakers of standard dialects. At times speakers of a standard dialect will deliberately use such features to gain a certain effect—humor, intimacy, irony, and so forth. Every dialect, including standard dialect, binds its speakers together to some extent. But standard speakers may wish on occasion to identify themselves with groups in society who speak special nonstandard dialects and may then use phrases or words or pronunciations from those dialects.

Slang, in a narrower sense of the word, refers to the speech of social in-groups, notably adolescents, which aims at excluding outsiders. It is part of the defense which an in-group throws up to isolate itself and give itself a sense of superiority, perhaps the same motive which leads children sometimes to invent languages so as to exclude others, particularly adults. As slang expressions get widely known they lose their feature of exclusiveness, and new slang develops. All this helps to explain the ephemerality of much slang, although some slang words and phrases are long-lived (for example, *booze*), and others get taken into standard dialects (*mob* was eighteenth-century slang). Slang phrases or words are sometimes marked by vivid metaphors or implied metaphors. At other times, they are merely variations of socially acceptable words, as for instance *natch*, which was popular a few years ago for *naturally*.

In some countries, such as England, the socially accepted forms of speech play a large role in social and financial success. In the United States "good" English is not quite so highly regarded, although it would hardly be correct to say that it is ignored.

Many professions and trades have their own jargons or cants which are used naturally by their members and are often not known by outsiders. The cant of jazz has close relations with slang because adolescents, who in their rebellious conformity take to slang, are the chief audience for jazz. Certain exclusive or special activities like hunting and soldiering have their own vocabularies and pronunciations which the participants learn. There is no evidence that the large variety of social dialects is being lessened, although the current extension of education might be expected to lead to a leveling of the differences between them.

On the other hand, regional dialects seem to be losing their hold today, with the growth and extension of the means of communication and general social mobility. In a country like the United States, where a great part of the population is on the move, where radio, television, movies, and records penetrate everywhere, distinctions in speech based on location are gradually being eliminated. They will, however, certainly be with us for a long time yet.

All varieties of a language have their distinguishing features. Which particular varieties and which distinguishing features are useful to study depends on the goal of one's investigation. In delineating the main dialects of a language, the criteria are quantitative. When many distinguishing features characterize the speech of a large number of people, we may say that we have a major dialect or sub-dialect. This quantitative criterion rules out family dialects and the special idiolects of individual speakers. In studying the history of a language, we have normally been satisfied to study only the major dialects of that language. If we can satisfactorily analyze the major social and regional dialects of a language, we think we have done enough to understand the distinctions and differences that have been important in the history of that language. In particular cases, however, it may be necessary to study many minor dialects in order to understand some special historical linguistic problem.

In certain countries (not the United States), however, the problem arises of just what language a dialect belongs to. Related to this is the problem of determining when a dialect has become sufficiently different so that we should want to say that it constitutes a new language. Sometimes the fact is established, not by the linguistic criterion of mutual intelligibility or unintelligibility, but by political, historical, and cultural considerations.

Let us take an example of the first kind of question which can arise. We might say that if the speakers of Catalan, a language spoken in northeastern Spain and in adjacent islands like Majorca, can understand a given dialect, even with difficulty, then it is a dialect of Catalan. However, this rule cannot always be applied. A speaker of what is usually considered the Majorcan dialect of Catalan may have as much difficulty in understanding what is usually considered the Barcelonian dialect of Catalan as in understanding French, which is normally considered a separate language (although historically only another dialect of vulgar Latin). Consider that a local dialect speaker of Perpignan, which is on the other side of the Pyrenees in France (province of Roussillon), may understand much more easily a local dialect speaker of Figueras, which is on the Catalan (or Spanish) side of the border, than he may a speaker of Parisian or standard French, of which his language is considered a dialect. How can Majorcan and Barcelonian be considered different dialects of the same language, whereas Majorcan and French are considered different languages?

How have such questions been answered? Sometimes they have been answered historically and politically by saying that both Majorcan and Barcelonian are historically linked to Catalonia and hence, in spite of the linguistic difficulties involved in saying so, are both dialects of Catalan. At other times an answer has been found in what might be called "linguistic orientation." An inhabitant of Perpignan is linguistically oriented towards Paris; an inhabitant of Figueras is linguistically oriented towards Barcelona. Thus, although their local dialects may be relatively close to each other, they actually think of themselves as French and Catalan speakers, respectively. As education spreads, this problem becomes less acute; the inhabitant of Perpignan will study standard French in school, read French newspapers, and hear French on the radio and television, whereas the inhabitant of Figueras will do the same in Catalan (or Spanish, since the present Spanish government suppresses Catalan).

The standard cultural forms of the languages involved have already influenced and will continue to influence the local speech of these areas, and the inhabitants now hear more of the standard forms of the language of which they think their dialect is a variety.

With widespread education and communication facilities, the purely local dialect speaker is becoming more and more a rarity. On the basis of linguistic orientation, therefore, the inhabitant of Figueras is considered a Catalan speaker and the inhabitant of Perpignan a French speaker.

The popular notion of dialect division sometimes is in conflict with a linguist's definition, based, for instance, on some quantitative test of mutual intelligibility or some minimum percentage of common vocabulary. It is easy enough for the linguist to set up strict definitions of the dialect-language distinction, but strict application of these definitions would sometimes yield arbitrary and unsatisfying results.

The same answers have been applied to the second kind of question: namely, when have dialects become separate languages? Simply put, they have been considered separate when there have been political and cultural reasons for them to be regarded as separate units.[5] Again the question is partly one of linguistic orientation. When the speakers of a dialect consider that they are speaking a different language and when there are objective differences of some magnitude to back this belief, then the dialect may be regarded as a separate language. Danish and Norwegian could be considered separate dialects of the same Scandinavian language, but since the political separation of Denmark and Norway, Norwegian patriots have attempted to bolster the political independence of Norway by claiming that Norwegian is a separate language, and by encouraging the use of a dialect which emphasizes differences from Danish. There are many borderline cases. Is Ukrainian a dialect of Great Russian, or a separate language? Ukrainians in America consider their speech to be a different Slavic language from Russian. There are considerable

---

[5] The problems have been most lucidly discussed in *Linguistic Diversity in South Asia: Studies in Regional Social and Functional Variation*. Ed. by Charles A. Ferguson and John J. Gumperz (Bloomington: Indiana University Research Center in Anthropology, Folklore, and Linguistics, Publication 13; 1960). The Introduction to this volume presents an excellent summary of the problem.

differences between Ukrainian and Great Russian, and there is a literature in Ukrainian. Yet in Russia not all Ukrainians think of Ukrainian as a separate language. History may eventually decide the issue. But at present, Ukrainians out of Russia are linguistically oriented away from Great Russian; those in Russia are linguistically oriented towards Great Russian.

When the language boundary corresponds to sharper linguistic differences, as for instance the boundaries of Hungarian, a non-Indo-European language, with Czech, or the boundaries of German with Polish, there is less of a problem. When we are dealing with adjacent varieties of Romance or Germanic languages, however, the problem is likely to be more acute.

The varieties of linguistic differences which create dialects, sub-dialects, sub-sub-dialects, and so on are of various sorts—phonetic and phonemic, morphological and syntactic, and lexical. Dialects may thus vary in sounds, inflections, phrases, word order, or in choice of words. In the Scots dialect, which, though a dialect of English, has a tradition and standards of its own, we shall find phonological differences from NE as in *stane* [sten] for *stone;* lexical differences as in *lug* for *ear;* and morphological and syntactic ones as in Burns' "the best laid plans o' mice and men *gang aft agley*" (often go awry). In distinguishing dialects, however, the phonological distinctions are traditionally considered the most fundamental criteria.[6] This preference for phonetic criteria in classifying dialects should be examined a little.

From the fact that there are few phonological and inflectional elements, each with very frequent occurrence in a language, but thousands of lexical elements, it is clear that in general a phonological or inflectional difference between two dialects will be more pervasive and hence more characteristic than a lexical difference will be. Thus dialectal boundaries drawn on the basis of phonological features are more likely to be significant than those drawn on the basis of vocabulary differences (with the possible

---

[6] See Hermann Paul: *Principles of the History of Language.* Translated from the second edition of the original by H. A. Strong (London: Swan Sonnenschein, Lowrey, & Co.; 1888), 33–34.

exception of certain very common words, especially function words like *of* and *the*, which may in some cases also provide a pervasive characteristic dialectal criterion).

The matter is of special interest at the moment because of the current problem of classifying the major American English regional dialects. Up until some ten or fifteen years ago, American English was divided by most experts into three major dialects: General, Southern, and New England. Sub-dialects were, of course, also recognized. These divisions were all made primarily on a phonological basis, in particular the treatment of [r] in certain positions, the pronunciation of orthographic *a* in certain words (e.g., [ant] vs. [ænt] for *aunt*), the pronunciation of orthographic *o* in certain words (are *caught* and *cot* differentiated?), and the monophthongization and triphthongization of certain diphthongs (especially in the South).

However, as a result of the data supplied by the investigators for the *Linguistic Atlas of the United States and Canada*,[7] some linguists have urged a different classification, but one based largely on vocabulary differences. The conclusions to be drawn from the lexical evidence seem to disagree in part with those drawn from phonological evidence. The lexical evidence argues for a horizontal division of the United States into three major groupings: Northern, Midland (divided in turn into North and South Midland), and Southern. Each includes a large number of sub-dialects, depending on how many criteria one chooses to consider. The "Northern" speech area includes sub-dialects as diverse as those of New England; New York City; the Upper Hudson Valley; and the territory north of a line across northern Ohio, northern Indiana, and northern Illinois. Largely on the basis of a

---

[7] See Raven McDavid: "Regional Linguistic Atlases in the United States," *Orbis* V (1956), 349–86, and Hans Kurath: "Linguistic Regionalism," Chapter X of *Regionalism in America*. Ed. Merrill Jensen (Madison: University of Wisconsin Press; 1952), 297–310. A recent useful collection of phonological material from the *Atlas* files has been published by Kurath and McDavid in *The Pronunciation of English in the Atlantic States* . . . Studies in American English 3. (Ann Arbor: Michigan University Press; 1961).

shared vocabulary for certain test items, these linguists postulate a unity to this variegated Northern speech area. Now it is true that many of the informants for the *Linguistic Atlas* are from long-settled families and that for this layer of population the proposed classification may be sound. However, problems arise from this classification if it is extrapolated to the general population. For instance, the English of Cleveland, Ohio, is as much a part of Northern American English as that of Boston, Massachusetts, according to this classification. Columbus, Ohio, is in the Northern Midland dialect area. This might seem to argue that the speech of Cleveland today is closer to that of Boston, both being part of the same dialect area, than to that of Columbus. But this conclusion seems to contradict the general impression of the speakers in those cities that Clevelanders and Columbusites sound pretty much alike, while Bostonians sound radically different. That such a horizontal grouping exists is clear from the abundant evidence, but whether lexical evidence should take priority over phonological evidence in setting up regional dialect (as the term is commonly understood) boundaries is at least an open question.

In investigating the dialect of a particular locality for purposes of reconstructing dialect history, one should study the speech habits of someone born in that locality and, if possible, born of parents also born in that locality. There is so much mobility in American life today that it is not always easy to find the proper informants. For instance, upper-class Clevelanders who have been educated at eastern schools may very well speak more like Bostonians than the average Clevelander. These social facts must all be taken into consideration when studying a regional dialect.

For ME we shall be primarily concerned with regional dialects and not with the social dialects, because we do not have enough material to study social dialects in ME satisfactorily. Although there is a good deal of evidence for colloquial ME, much of it is inconclusive. In ME times, moreover, the differences between colloquial and literary varieties of the language were not so extensive as in NE times.

In order to study the regional dialects of ME, we must know

something about linguistic geography. **Linguistic geography** is concerned with the distribution of languages and language features through space. It is an indispensable subject in the study of dialect.

The most important tool of linguistic geography is the linguistic map, which enables the spatial distribution of speech elements to be graphically represented and easily handled. The construction of linguistic atlases, however, requires intensive investigations by well-trained investigators working according to a standard plan. The construction of linguistic maps is a major undertaking, requiring considerable time and—what has been more difficult to come by for such work—money.

Beginning in Germany in 1881, there appeared maps of linguistic features of various languages. France, Italy, and Germany have been much ahead of the English-speaking countries in this field; and there are linguistic maps in some profusion for all these countries, as well as for languages such as Catalan, Danish, Flemish, and Roumanian. For the United States and Canada, only the New England part of the *Linguistic Atlas of the United States and Canada* has been published, although a vast store of information on the language peculiarities of the remainder of the country has been collected. Linguistic atlases are in preparation for England, Scotland, and Ireland, but progress is slow.[8]

Of course, if completeness is the ideal, there can never be an end to the making of linguistic maps. Every linguistic atlas so far published or planned is a selective one; it must be so. If every feature of a language were put on a map the task would stretch to doomsday. What linguistic cartographers actually do is to pick out features of interest or importance for concentrated study. It is doubtful that every one of the millions of linguistic variations in a language would be of much scientific interest, since a point of

---

[8] For a monumental statement on the history and progress of dialect studies (up to its date of publication) and of the problems of dialect study of all languages, see Sever Pop: *La Dialectologie: Aperçu historique et méthodes d'enquêtes linguistiques.* Université de Louvain. Recueil de Travaux d'Histoire et de Philologie, 3 série, fasc. 8–39 (Louvain: 1950).

diminishing returns would soon be reached. At that point, more facts would probably not cause any changes in the linguistic generalizations which are the chief concern of linguistic science. However, one can never be absolutely sure. The incompleteness of all inductive processes is a universal principle of uncertainty. Just as we cannot be absolutely sure that the sun will rise tomorrow, so we cannot be absolutely sure that a new fact discovered tomorrow will not overthrow or at least show the limits of the present generalization.

How does the linguistic cartographer select the features which he chooses to study and record? He chooses those elements which he thinks will be helpful and important. He must be an experienced student and investigator of languages and must have a sense of what concerns most closely the establishment of linguistic generalizations. He must not be too narrow in his concepts, and he must be prepared to allow for the unexpected—to give even the unexpected a chance, so to speak, by the choice of his questions.

There is still dispute as to the proper method of collecting material for linguistic geography, and there are severe limitations imposed by time, money, and the availability of collectors. We have many mechanical aids today which were not available to investigators in the nineteenth century—the tape recorder and sound spectograph, to mention the two most important in current use. Linguistic atlases have been created on the basis of various methods of investigation, including written questionnaires, personal interviews, and combinations of both. Even the personal interview presents difficulties; for example, some informants tend to tell the investigator what they think he wants to hear or to distort their usual linguistic habits in their anxiety to be "correct." By patience and care, the investigator can, however, get at what he wants.

On the maps themselves there are two main indications of the distribution of features: individual signs for the location of each occurrence of a particular item, and **isogloss** lines. The latter are lines which mark the boundaries of linguistic elements. Isoglosses

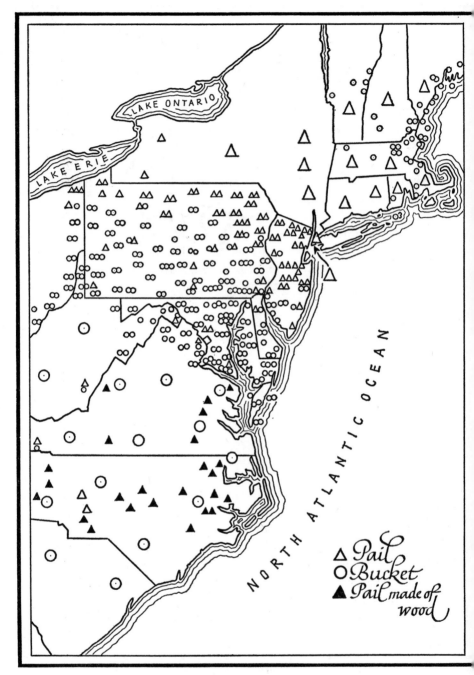

Map 2. A Linguistic Map.

(Adapted from Map 66 of Hans Kurath, *A Word Geography of the Eastern United States,* University of Michigan Press, by permission. Copyright 1949 by the University of Michigan.)

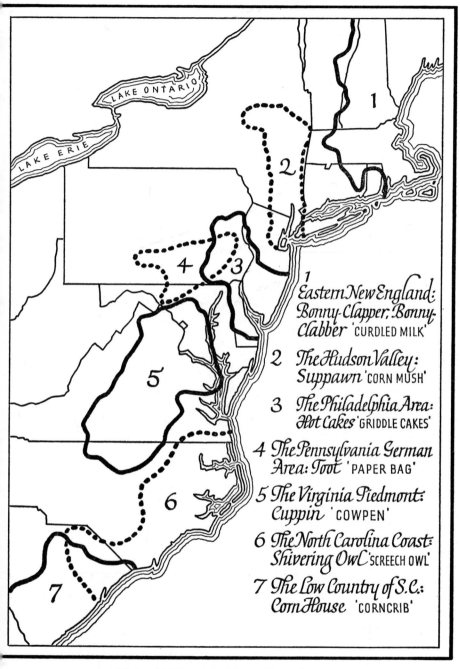

Map. 3. A Linguistic Map with Isoglosses.

may be more specifically named if desired: an **isophonic** line marks the boundaries of a sound feature; an **isomorphic** line marks the boundaries of a morphological feature, and so forth. See Maps 2 and 3.

When various features are marked by isoglosses on the same map, we sometimes get a bewildering variety of lines. However, somewhere isogloss lines may tend to coalesce; if we employ the quantitative principle mentioned above, such coalescences or bundles of isoglosses will be said to mark off the major dialect or sub-dialect boundaries (see Map 4). In other words, the collection of isoglosses along a certain line in space indicates that there are a number of differentiating features following the same path. These frequently, but not always, fall along major geographic features such as rivers or mountain ranges.

Of course, when a certain area has been marked out by a sign or an isogloss line, we do not mean to imply that every speaker in that area will use the particular linguistic feature so marked, but rather that the feature is relatively common on one side of the line and relatively uncommon on the other side of the line.

The full resources of even the linguistic atlases available to us have not yet been fully exploited, although we know in general what they can do. First of all, they provide a storehouse of graphically presented generalizations about dialectal variations in a language, in such a way as to enable us to be exact about linguistic and dialectal boundaries. Second, they can show the interaction between geography and history. They may corroborate historical facts or give us unexpected historical data. The earliest settlers of Marietta, Ohio, for example, came from New England, whereas most of the rest of southern Ohio was settled from the South. A linguistic atlas would mark off Marietta from the surrounding area and thus confirm certain historical facts. Suppose, however, that we did not have records of where the earliest settlers of Marietta came from. In that case, linguistic geography would give us an answer. In parts of Cumberland and Westmoreland, in the extreme northwest of England, we can tell from linguistic geography that certain valleys were settled by Norse-

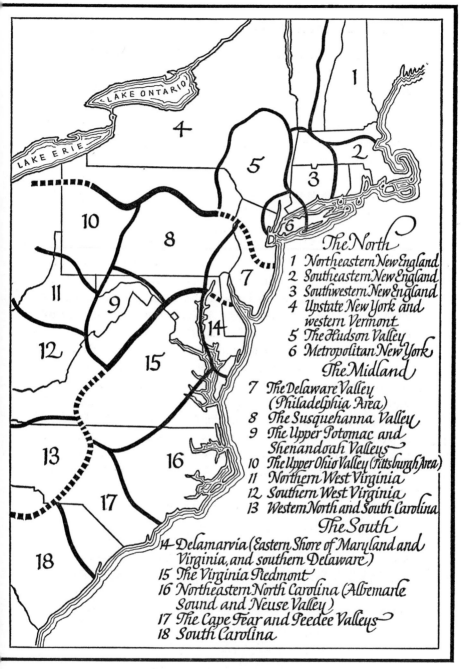

The North
1 Northeastern New England
2 Southeastern New England
3 Southwestern New England
4 Upstate New York and western Vermont
5 The Hudson Valley
6 Metropolitan New York

The Midland
7 The Delaware Valley (Philadelphia Area)
8 The Susquehanna Valley
9 The Upper Potomac and Shenandoah Valleys
10 The Upper Ohio Valley (Pittsburgh Area)
11 Northern West Virginia
12 Southern West Virginia
13 Western North and South Carolina

The South
14 Delamarvia (Eastern Shore of Maryland and Virginia, and southern Delaware)
15 The Virginia Piedmont
16 Northeastern North Carolina (Albemarle Sound and Neuse Valley)
17 The Cape Fear and Peedee Valleys
18 South Carolina

Map 4. Dialect Areas in the Eastern United States.

speaking invaders. The distribution of Celtic place names in England, and their phonetic forms, can tell us something about the chronology of the Anglo-Saxon invasion of Britain, for which we have practically no historical evidence.[9] The fact that the names London and Vienna are derived from Celtic words tells us that Celtic peoples must once have lived there, even though these cities are no longer in Celtic hands.

Another example of the way dialect distribution in space corresponds to historical movements of peoples may be seen in the contrast between the linguistic role of the river Thames as compared to that of the Rhine. The fact that dialect boundaries cross the Rhine in Germany at various places argues that the Germanic peoples moved from east to west (or from west to east) across the north-south line of the river, and that the movement was not up and down the banks of the river. In England, on the other hand, the Thames has historically been a linguistic boundary. In Middle English dialects, it is roughly the boundary of the Midland and Southern dialects. This would argue that the Germanic invasions of England went along both sides of the Thames River rather than perpendicular to it. We might guess from sparse historical documents that these early movements of Germanic tribes in Germany and in England actually did take place; but present-day linguistic stratification gives a firm foundation to this assumption.

When we have no documents at all, as in prehistory, linguistic boundaries, if they can be established, are most helpful in filling in our gaps in knowledge. Of course, the evidence must be used

---

[9] See Kenneth Jackson: *Language and History in Early Britain* (Cambridge, Mass.: Harvard University Press; 1953), 194–261, and "The British Language during the Period of the English Settlements," *Studies in Early British History*. Ed. N. K. Chadwick (Cambridge, England: Cambridge University Press; 1954), 61–82. The spatial distribution of place names may also tell us something about geographical features which have changed in the course of time. For instance, the place-name suffix *-ley* (<OE *lēah*) in Yorkshire tells us "of the existence of extensive woodland" (see London *Times Literary Supplement*, Jan. 5, 1962, p. 6, reviewing A. H. Smith: *The Place Names of the West Riding of Yorkshire* [Cambridge, England: Cambridge University Press; 1961]).

with caution, since movements and changes of which we are
not aware may have taken place later; and linguistic boundaries
are very difficult to establish in the distant past. But place names
tend to remain the same and linguistic habits are often very
conservative and both can, if cautiously interpreted, tell us a
great deal. Thus, the contribution of linguistic geography to the
study of history can be immense.

Third, linguistic atlases enable us to make sociological generalizations and to see the impact of social conditions on language. We can learn from linguistic geography how much
progress standard dialects are making, how prestigeful certain
forms are, how factors such as religion and social class affect
language.

Fourth, by examining the actual distribution of features we
may be able to find out unknown or uncorroborated facts about
the history of the language itself. We can frequently tell, just
by the way certain linguistic elements appear in space, which
of them are the oldest. These conclusions must be used with
caution, but they can be used. Leonard Bloomfield gives a good
example of how we can see that [u:] is the oldest vowel in
the Dutch words *muis* (mouse) and *huis* (house);[1] the intrusion
of other pronunciations in these words on the original area can
be directly established by inspection of present-day dialect
maps. Sometimes a linguistic map will show us the occurrence
of a feature in two separated areas. All things being equal, such
a distribution indicates to the historian of language that this
feature was once spoken over the entire area and that the
feature which separates the two is a later intrusion. As we may
see from Map 2, "the word *bucket* for a metal container used
to carry water, is known in eastern and northern New England,
throughout the Old South, and in parts of Pennsylvania, but
not in the Hudson valley and upstate New York, where *pail*
is the prevalent term. Since the use of *bucket* for this specific
article could hardly develop independently in two or more

---

[1] *Language* (New York: Henry Holt and Co.; 1933), 328–40.

places, we can infer that at some earlier time its geographical distribution must have been continuous."[2] Thus, linguistic geography is a valuable tool for the linguist, historian, anthropologist, and sociologist.

How do we construct linguistic maps of the past? We do not have living informants whom we can consult nor are time machines as yet constructed which enable us to make journeys into the past. There are two sound methods, however, if conditions make it possible to use them. One is to base our information upon correctly dated and localized documents of the past. The other is to use the form of traditional place names to mark dialectal habits. The difficulties of these two methods are obvious. There may be few or no localized and exactly dated documents available; and place names are rather limited in the range of words they use. Even if the physical document can be accurately placed in space or time, there is always the possibility that the scribe, author, or editor has had ideas of "correctness," or has certain peculiarities of language which he introduces in spite of the prevailing idiom or linguistic custom.

Most frequently, ancient documents, if they exist at all, can only be dated or localized approximately and are, therefore, of less value than other sources for accurate historical work. However, in spite of these problems, we can and do construct dialect maps of languages at earlier stages of their development and use them with some assurance.

Place names are tenacious and can help us somewhat in our quest for the linguistic past. Their location is more or less fixed and their dates of formation can usually be determined, if sometimes only roughly. Their phonetic shapes can be used for linguistic reconstruction. Isoglosses drawn to separate certain phonetic or lexical features of place names help us to establish boundaries. English place-name elements derived from the Latin *castrum* 'camp or military settlement' are particularly revealing, for instance. The word appears in various forms and

---

[2] Charles F. Hockett: *A Course in Modern Linguistics* (New York: The Macmillan Co.; 1958), 479.

spellings in English place names, but we are here interested only in whether the initial sound is [k] (spelled *c*) or [č] (spelled *ch*). There are a number of *-casters* in the north and northeast of England—*Muncaster, Hincaster, Lancaster, Tadcaster, Ancaster,* and so forth. In the rest of the country we usually find a form of *-chester,* where the initial [k] has become the palatal affricate [č] and the vowel raised to [ε]—as in *Manchester, Winchester, Rochester,* and so forth. If we draw an isogloss on a map of England to show this division we are at the same time showing, if only roughly, the northern limits of the OE West Saxon dialect, which we know palatalized the [k] before front vowels.[3] We can find other important information about the dialects of the past from the distribution of the place-name element *stretton: stratton* 'road or street settlement,' which reveals a former isogloss between West Saxon [æ] and Anglian [a]. Similarly, the presence of many Danish place names containing the elements *-thorp* ('village') or *-by* ('town'), as in *Linthorpe, Bishopsthorp, Grimsby, Rugby,* and *Derby,* enable us to plot the extent of the Scandinavian settlement.

A well-known study of Middle English dialects in relation to geography was undertaken by Samuel Moore, Sanford Brown Meech, and Harold Whitehall in 1935.[4] We shall base many of our comments on ME dialects on their notable and pioneering work. They did not take place names into consideration, but it is true that English place names help us more in the establishment of OE dialects than in that of ME dialects.

On the basis of only those documents and literary works from the Middle English period which could be localized exactly

---

[3] This would imply that the low back vowel [a] of the Latin was first fronted to [æ] (later [ε]) and then by phonetic assimilation palatalized the initial [k]. This example and the following are taken from Simeon Potter: *Modern Linguistics* (London: Andre Deutsch; 1957), 136 ff.

[4] Published as "Middle English Dialect Characteristics and Dialect Boundaries, Preliminary Report of an Investigation Based Exclusively on Localized Texts and Documents" in *Essays and Studies in English and Comparative Literature.* By Members of the English Department of the University of Michigan. University of Michigan Publications, Language and Literature XIII (Ann Arbor: University of Michigan Press; 1935), 1–60.

and whose dates could be fairly well determined,[5] the Michigan investigators were able to list ten distinctive dialect criteria whose approximate boundaries could be established, and which could therefore be plotted on maps. These ten criteria are: A) the treatment of the ME reflexes of the OE ā: whether it is [a:] (or [æ:]) or [ɔ:] in ME; B) the variation in the present indicative plural suffix: whether -(e)s, or -en, or -eth; C) the variation in the ME forms of NE *shall:* whether an initial [s] as in *sal, suld,* or *sold,* or a palatal [š] as in *shal* or *sholle;* D) the variation between *a* and *o* before *m* or *n* (but not *ng, nd,* or *mb*); E) the form of the third person plural of the pronoun in the accusative: whether there is an initial *h* as in *hem, him, hom* or an initial *th* as in *them* (the latter a borrowing from Scandinavian); F) the persistence of lip rounding in ME reflexes of OE *y* and *ȳ* and OE *eo, ēo;* G) the form of the present indicative third singular suffix of the verb: whether *-es* or *-eth;* H) the variation between *-eth* and *-es* in the present indicative plural (related to B); I) the ME reflex of OE initial *f:* whether *v* or *f;* J) the treatment of West Saxon OE *ea* and *ēa;* K) the form of the ending of the present participle: whether *-and, -end, -ind,* or *-ing.* It should be noted that the proper identification of some of these criteria depends upon a knowledge of the OE forms of certain ME forms and can only be applied by someone who knows OE.

These ten criteria (B and H are fundamentally the same) were considered to be the most satisfactorily documented criteria for determining boundaries, and were frequent enough to occur in a fair proportion of the material. They had all been noted before by ME dialect investigators, but few or none before the Michigan scholars had used them to obtain exact boundaries,

---

[5] For a recent study of the many problems in connection with ME dialects, with suggested further methods for attaining greater precision and for eliminating scribal habits from the material, see O. Arngart: "Middle English Dialects," *Studier i Modern Språkvetenskap* . . . (Stockholm Studies in Modern Philology) XVII (1949), 17–29. Arngart discusses at some length the value of place names in ME dialect investigations.

perhaps because they underestimated the value of the available material and of the resources of linguistic geography.

There are other dialect criteria, too, which mainly depend on documents that cannot be so clearly dated and localized as those used by Moore, Meech, and Whitehall—such as spelling conventions (the North, for instance, usually recorded the OE *wh* as *qu*, although this example probably reflects a sound change) or special predilections, such as *ho* for the feminine third person singular pronoun in the West Midlands, or the reflex of initial *s* in the South as *z*, or the Northern preference for *are* as the third person plural of *be*. But these criteria were ignored by the Michigan investigators, since the documents they relied on did not offer enough usable evidence.

As Moore, Meech, and Whitehall admit, more criteria would be valuable for greater precision, but the ME documents and literary works so far discovered do not provide the information needed. Since their purpose was to achieve as much precision as possible with respect to spatial distribution, the Michigan investigators did not use criteria which would not provide it. Their purpose was not merely to list dialect criteria, which for the most part were already known anyway, but to provide boundaries which would enable us to recognize the normal limits of ME geographic dialects.

As a result of their work, a new map of the English dialects became possible. (See Map 5.) Of this map, the investigators write: "We believe, therefore, in spite of the mixture of forms that appears in most (though by no means all) of our documents, in spite of the fact that the evidence in many cases consists of occasional spellings or minority forms, that these isophonic lines do reflect roughly at least approximate boundaries for eleven of the most important characteristics of the regional dialects of Middle English as they existed about the middle of the fourteenth century."[6] They go on to say that "if it were

---

[6] *Op. cit.*, p. 23. Note that the word *isophonic* is used; most of the criteria are purely phonological and in some sense all of them involve sound variations. See Appendix to this chapter for more recent work.

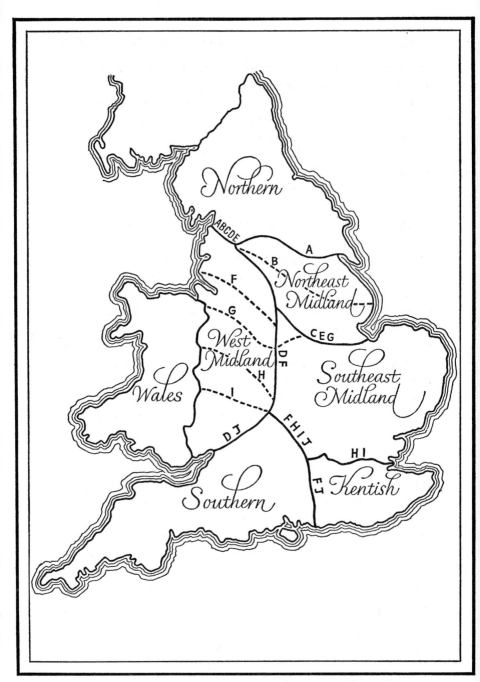

Map 5. Middle English Dialect Areas.

(Taken, slightly adapted, from Samuel Moore, *Historical Outlines of English Sounds and Inflections,* revised by Albert H. Marckwardt, Ann Arbor: George Wahr, 1960, p. 112, by permission.)

possible to determine accurately the boundaries of all the important dialect characteristics of Middle English, the resulting map would probably show fifty or more dialects rather than ten."[7] But many dialect criteria appear only rarely, and a map of the common characteristics is more important and usable than one with many more characteristics which are not often found.

The localized and dated documents on which the Michigan investigators based their conclusions are not completely reliable sources for dialect practice, although they represent the best that are available. We must remember that these documents are few in number compared to the total number of ME documents extant. They are not completely reliable, however, for a very important reason: even if we know where a document comes from and when it was written, we still cannot be sure that the scribe is following local, contemporary usage, or that he is following it in every particular. Scribes have personal predilections and prejudices which may differ from local habits. Also, by 1350 the influence of the London dialect was making itself felt all over England and especially in the Midlands and the South. A desire to follow the prestigeful forms of London English on the part of scribes who were all more or less educated may have interfered with local linguistic custom.

As one can see from all this, the application of criteria for dialect distinction in ME is not easy. There are very few purely unmixed samples—unmixed, that is, by our standards of what is characteristic of a certain dialect. The influence of London and the North was particularly strong throughout the late medieval period, and no doubt only a few people escaped it. If we had abundant evidence for the late eleventh and twelfth centuries we could perhaps present a more definite picture.

Of course, this confusion reflects what we are actually trying to establish—the state of the various forms of English in the fourteenth and fifteenth centuries. Standardization was even then on the march, and it shows its influence everywhere.

---

[7] *Op. cit.*, p. 24.

However, even allowing for these difficulties and uncertainties, we do have something to go on. Further discoveries of localized documents and perhaps place-name study will undoubtedly supplement this picture and enable a more accurate linguistic map to be drawn. Perfect accuracy will probably never be obtained, both for the reasons given above, which limited Moore, Meech, and Whitehall, and because there was dialect mixture at all times, which would lead to a great deal of crisscrossing of isoglosses.

As we have already said, linguistic features tend to follow geographic features: hills, rivers, marshes, and forests. Even small rivers, like the Ribble in Lancashire, can form important linguistic boundaries. The importance of the topographical and physiographical feature is not always related to the importance of the linguistic boundary. But in an age of poor communication, the geographical barriers tend to interfere strongly with the diffusion of linguistic features and hence form linguistic boundaries.

The general development of ME dialects from OE dialects, which has been known since the late nineteenth century, can be shown in the following chart.

OE		ME	NE
	West Saxon	Southern or SW	SW provincial dialects
	Kentish	Kentish or SE	SE ” ”
Anglian	Mercian	E. Midland	Standard NE[8] (in various forms)
		W. Midland	Western provincial dialects
	North- umbrian	Northern	Scottish and Northern English dialects

---

[8] Standard NE developed from one variety of East Midland—the London dialect. Other varieties of East Midland have to this day continued as local

On the basis of the work of Moore, Meech, and Whitehall, and that of others, one can list the significant features of the major ME dialects of the fourteenth century (see below). No single feature is sufficient to establish the geographic provenience of a document, and in some documents there will be contradictory evidence, but if a document contains a great number of Northern features we may say it is Northern. If it contains both Northern and E. Midland features, we may say it was written near the Northern-E. Midland boundaries. Occasionally we may get puzzling evidence when a document contains both Northern and Southern features. This case is very rare and is generally best explained by some unusual circumstance, such as a Northern scribe transcribing a Southern document. Note again that in order to identify some of the criteria a knowledge of OE is required.

The following chart is taken from Samuel Moore: *Historical Outlines of English Sounds and Inflections.* Revised by Albert H. Marckwardt (Ann Arbor: George Wahr Publishing Company; 1951), 116–7.

To these criteria others may be added; and from them all, we can draw the following picture (When referring to spelling, we underline the letter.):

   1) *Northern.* In general spoken north of the Humber River and a line to the west coast of England running somewhat

---

provincial East Midland dialects. Of course, most NE provincial dialects, if they exist at all, have been profoundly influenced by standard (London) NE, as has even Scottish. The latter, owing to geographic, national, and cultural factors, has been able to maintain its identity to a much greater extent than the other non-London English dialects. In fact it may be considered another standard variety of English, with a more independent history than the other NE standard dialects such as American, Australian, and Canadian English, which all developed from the London standard. A good general introduction to English nonstandard dialects past and present may be found in Walter W. Skeat: *English Dialects from the Eighth Century to the Present Day* (Cambridge, England: Cambridge University Press; 1912). More advanced students should see Joseph Wright: *English Dialect Dictionary* to which is appended an *English Dialect Grammar* (Oxford: Oxford University Press; 1898–1905). The latter was also printed separately in 1905.

Feature	Line	Northern	NE Midland	SE Midland	W. Midland	Southern	Kentish
OE ā	A	[aː]	[ɔː]	[ɔː]	[ɔː]	[ɔː]	[ɔː]
OE a before nasals	D	[a]	[a]	[a]	[ɔ]	[a]	[a]
OE ȳ, y, ēo, eo	F	[iː, ɪ, eː, ɛ]	[iː, ɪ, eː, ɛ]	[iː, ɪ, eː, ɛ]	[yː, ʏ œː, œ]	[yː, ʏ œː, œ]	[iː, ɪ eː, ɛ]
i-umlaut of ēa, ea; diphthongization of e by initial g, c, sc	J	[eː, ɛ]	[eː, ɛ]	[eː, ɛ]	[eː, ɛ]	[yː; iː, ʏ, ɪ]	[eː, ɛ]
Initial f	I	[f]	[f]	[f]	[f, v]	[v]	[v]
sal, shal, etc.	C	[s]	[s]	[ʃ]	[ʃ]	[ʃ]	[ʃ]
3d plural pers. pron.	E	them	them	hem	hem	hem	hem
3d sg. present indic.	G	-es	-es	-eth	-es, -eth	-eth	-eth
3d pl. present indic.	B, H	-es	-es, -e(n)	-e(n)	-e(n), -eth	-eth	-eth

ʃ = š
y = ü:
ʏ = ü
œ = ɛ
lip-rounded

Note that a somewhat different phonetic transcription system is used here from that in Chapter II.

northwest (Line A on Map 5). In the Middle Ages, Northern ME included what later became Scottish, as well as northern English provincial dialects such as that of Yorkshire.

1. OE ā appears as an unrounded vowel [a:] or [æ:], as in *stane* (NE *stone*) and *ham* (NE *home*) (North of line A on the map)
2. *-and* for the ending of the present participle (K above)
3. The spelling *qu* for OE *hw* and non-Northern ME dialects *wh*
4. The *-es* ending for the present indicative plural of the verb (B and H above)
5. *them* and *their* instead of *hem* and *here* for the accusative and possessive of the third person plural pronoun (E above)
6. *sal* and *solde* (or *sulde*) instead of *shal* and *shold* as in other dialects, reflecting a distinction between [s] and [š] (C above)
7. Preference for *are* rather than *be* in present plural of verb *to be*
8. [k] rather than [č] before front vowels (which may still be seen in the Scottish *kirk*, as opposed to NE *church*), probably due to ON influence
9. *at* commonly used for *to*

2) *West Midland.* In general spoken south of the Northern dialect line (line A on Map 5) and north of the Severn River and a line running west to the Thames (line D on map); the western portion of this Midland area to the Welsh-speaking area. In NE this dialect, insofar as it survives at all, has become the provincial dialects of southern Lancashire, Cheshire, Shropshire, Herefordshire, Staffordshire, parts of Worcestershire, and Gloucestershire.

1. OE *a* followed by *m* and *n* (except *ng, nd,* or *mb*) has become *o* so that we find *mon* for *man, nome* for *name, ronk* for *rank* (D above)

2. *-eth* for present indicative third person singular of verb in southern portion of area and *-es* in northern (B and H above)

3. initial *v* for *f* in southern portion (I above)

4. a preference for *-and* or *-end* in present participle (K above)

5. OE *y*, *ȳ*, *eo*, *ēo* retained as front round vowel (spelled *u*, or *ui* and *eo*, *o*, *oe*, *u*, or *ue*) (F above)

6. a preference for *ho* or *ha* as the third person singular feminine pronoun

3) *Southern or Southwestern.* In general spoken south of the Severn-Thames line and in the western portion of this area, the division being west of Kent, Surrey, and Sussex (line JF on Map 5). In NE, this dialect, insofar as it survives at all, has become the provincial dialects of Cornwall, Devon, Somersetshire, Dorset, Hampshire, and parts of other counties.

1. initial *v* for *f* (I above)[9]

2. OE *y*, *ȳ*, *eo*, *ēo* retained as in West Midland (F above)

3. *-ing* or *-ind* for present participle ending of verb (K above)

4. *-eth* for present plural indicative ending of verb (B above)

5. retention of late West Saxon *i*, *y*, *ī*, and *ȳ* which developed from early West Saxon *ea*, *ēa* by influence of following *i* or which developed from early West Saxon *e* preceded by *g*, *c*, or *sc* (J above). (In other dialects we usually find an *e* in this position. Compare Southern *huren* or *hiren* 'hear' with non-Southern *heren*.)

4) *Southeastern or Kentish.* In general spoken in the counties of Kent, Surrey, and Sussex (south of line HI and east

---

[9] Initial [s] is also usually voiced to [z] but is frequently still spelled *s* and is hence hard to detect in documents.

of line FJ on Map 5); in NE surviving as provincial dialects of these counties.

   1. initial *v* for *f* (I above)[1]
   2. *-ing* or *-ind* for present participle ending (K above)
   3. preference for *-eth* as present plural indicative ending of verb (B above)
   4. development of semi-vowel before *o* after *b* and *g* usually spelled with *u* (e.g. *guod* for *god* [NE *good*])
   5. preference for *e* over *i* in certain words like *pet* for *pit* (F above)

5) *East Midland.* In general spoken in the eastern part of the Midland area between the Thames and the Humber (south of line A, north of line HI, and east of D and FHIJ on Map 5); in NE surviving as Standard English (in most of its forms) and various provincial county dialects. In general,

   1. the absence of features listed above as characteristic of other dialects; in particular
   2. preference for *-en* in present plural indicative of verbs (B above) and
   3. *-end* for present participle ending (K above).

In general, the Southern dialects and the southern parts of the Midland areas are more conservative than the Northern in retaining relics of OE inflections. For instance, we find the past participle prefix *y-* (sometimes spelled *i-*) from OE (spelled *ge-*) in the Southern dialects as late as the fourteenth century. The more Scandinavian words there are in the vocabulary, the more Northern is the dialect using them. Some of the characteristics listed above for the various dialects can be used as negative evidence. The use of *hem* for *them*, for instance, although it would not tell you what dialect is being used, would usually eliminate Northern and northeast Midland as possibilities.

---

[1] See footnote 9 above, which also applies to Kentish.

As a conclusion to this chapter, a few words would seem appropriate on the development of London English, which was to form the basis of most other varieties of standard English, including American English.

London in the Middle Ages lay on the north side of the river Thames. Vast tracts of the southern side have since been added to it, not to speak of its expansion in all other directions, but in 1350, it was contained in what we today call the City. Some two miles to the west was the city of Westminster, where Parliament and the king's court were located. (In late Anglo-Saxon times the capital had been in Winchester, but was moved to London in the eleventh century.) London and Westminster have long since been joined by urban development, but in the period we are speaking of they were two separate settlements, and in the eleventh and twelfth centuries they had somewhat different dialects.

As we have already noted, the Thames was an important dialect boundary of ME and OE, going back to the days of the original settling of these lands by the Anglo-Saxon tribes. As a city or two cities on the north side of the river, London and Westminster should have been East Midland in dialect, yet the earliest London records show that London speech, if not wholly Kentish, was at least much impregnated by Kentish forms. Of course, any settlement on a linguistic boundary, even a river, is apt to show mixed characteristics. Linguistic features normally shade rather than break off sharply,[2] but the extent of Kentish in London speech might seem extraordinary, especially since the boundary is a sizable river and therefore crossed with more difficulty than most linguistic boundaries. However, at this point the Thames could be crossed easily by a bridge, and the activities of London tended to join it a good deal with the south towards the Continent or towards Canterbury, the primatial English See. These factors may explain the strong Southern element in early London English. Actually, however, localized London documents in English before

---

[2] For example, American English along the Canadian border, especially in New Hampshire, Vermont, and New York, shows a great many Canadianisms.

about 1250 are very rare, and it is possible that we have only a partial picture.

In the twelfth and thirteenth centuries, there were, as far as we can determine, differences in dialect between London, Westminster, and the small county of Middlesex which encompasses both, although not all investigators of early London English have kept them apart. By the fourteenth and fifteenth centuries, however, these dialects, which varied from each other only in a small number of details, had pretty much merged, and no distinction need be made for the late Middle Ages.

Besides these differences in early London documents reflecting City, Westminster, and Middlesex usages, the general influence of a convergence of dialects—Southern, Kentish, and Midland—make the task of an investigator of the early (twelfth- and thirteenth-century) London dialect difficult. We may also add the problem of a paucity of documents in the English of this period. As we have said, the early London dialect had many Southern characteristics. By the fourteenth century, however, possibly because of increased migration from the north,[3] the London dialect seems to have become pretty much East Midland and, as we have said, the three varieties—City, Westminster, and Middlesex—had coalesced; many of the Southern forms vanished.

The predominance of London as the cultural, legal, and governmental center finally made its dialect the educated standard which spread throughout the country; local dialects never died, however, and even when provincials spoke London English their speech would have a local flavor. But, as we mentioned above, there was still considerable variation in London and standard English, which persisted into the late sixteenth century and caused confusion to writers. The far north (Northern) also had a strong influence all over the East Midland area in the later Middle Ages, and standard English adopted many Northernisms such as *they*, *their*, *them*, *are*, *is*, and the *-s* ending on the present third person singular form of verbs (however, *-eth* persisted until the seventeenth century).

---

[3] See Ekwall's study mentioned above in footnote 4 on page 188.

The ascendancy of the East Midland is also to be explained by the presence of the two great universities in this language area, although Oxford was close to the West Midland border; by the use of London standards by great writers, such as Chaucer, Wyclif, and Gower; and by the fact that from the fifteenth century on, London was the center of the printing trade. All these factors helped the victory of London East Midland over the other ME dialects.

Even after a standard London English was established, the lower classes in London continued with their ordinary speech, which of course in the late fifteenth century was very like standard English. But as time went on, the language of the court and the upper classes spread over England, gaining prestige among educated people and undergoing a history quite apart from that of the uneducated lower classes in London. Language change is ceaseless. From this lower-class London speech a separate dialect developed, whose signs we can detect as early as the sixteenth century.[4] This dialect developed into **Cockney,** as we now call it. Brought into existence by social cleavages, it soon became a separate regional dialect. Meanwhile, standard London English was becoming that of a class rather than of a geographical district. Cockney has suffered the fate of most urban dialects; it is ridiculed and despised by the prestigeful speakers of standard dialects. Rural dialects leaped into favor among the romantic thinkers and writers of the nineteenth century, whose liberalism, however, never extended to urban dialects, which for some strange reason are considered to be made up of barbarisms and

---

[4] See, for the development of Cockney, William Matthews: *Cockney Past and Present, a Short History of the Dialect of London* (New York: E. P. Dutton & Co.; 1938). For a great mass of information on the development of standard and some nonstandard forms of spoken English in England, see Henry Cecil Wyld: *A History of Modern Colloquial English.* Third Edition (Oxford: Basil Blackwell; 1936). R. W. Chambers and Marjorie Daunt present a carefully chosen group of documents in London English, for the crucial period in the late fourteenth and early fifteenth centuries, in their *A Book of London English 1384–1425* (Oxford: Clarendon Press; 1931).

to be hopelessly corrupt. This attitude is unfortunately still wide-spread, in spite of all that linguistic investigation has shown.

Appendix:

Recent work on ME dialects[1]

In the past few years, Professors Angus McIntosh of Edinburgh and Michael Samuels of Glasgow have developed a new approach to Middle English dialectology which involves a rather strong criticism of the limitations of the method used by the Michigan investigators upon whose work part of this chapter has been based (pp. 205 ff., above). Inasmuch as their conclusions are still tentative and their methods not yet completely published, it does not seem fair or even possible to put them into the main body of this chapter. Yet their work is clearly of far-reaching impor-tance and bids fair to revolutionize both our knowledge of ME dialects and our methods of historical linguistic geography. Hence we shall, thanks to their kindness in letting us see some of their work and tentative conclusions, summarize their approach.

In brief, they emphasize the study of the written forms of words and morphemes in manuscripts and are much more willing than their predecessors in this field to use graphemic before phono-logical or phonemic analysis. They also want to use more ma-terial even if it cannot be exactly localized at first and limit the chronological range of admissible material (in their case mainly to 1350-1450, when documents are more numerous). They stress the importance of studying individual words in great detail and of making as many distinctions as possible. For example, they criticize Professors Moore, Whitehall, and Meech for only dis-

---

[1] Articles by Professor McIntosh ("A New Approach to Middle English Dialectology") and by Professor Samuels ("Some Applications of Middle English Dialectology") have recently appeared in the 1963 volume of *English Studies*.

tinguishing between the *th* and *h* forms of the third person pronoun when many more distinctions in this pronoun are to be found.

In the matter of dialect criteria, they call attention to various weaknesses in the approach of the Michigan investigators; the small number of items they record and plot on maps; the particular criteria they select (determined often by *a priori* considerations); their oversimplification; and their insufficient attention to all significant distinctions between the written forms of the texts. In the matter of the choice of textual sources by the Michigan investigators, they draw attention to the relatively small number of documents they use and their basis of selection; the slight use of literary texts; and, as already mentioned, the chronological spread.

As more and more specific material can be put on maps, it becomes possible to *fit* more and more documents into a narrow geographic area. The work will require many detailed maps of individual words. When this material is published, it should be possible to reconstruct a much more exact picture of ME dialects than is available at present, which will be of great value to historians and literary historians, to paleographers and linguists. In fact the whole problem of the genesis of standard English will be seen in a new light, and it will probably be much more complex than the general remarks in this chapter imply.

The Michigan investigators were pioneers and, like all pioneers, their work is to be superseded or at least enlarged into wider and at the same time more precise contexts. The work of McIntosh and Samuels is pointing the way to a reevaluation of the Michigan results and those of earlier investigators so as to give us a more detailed and exact picture of the state of ME dialects.

Some of the results, as of the spring of 1960, of the Scottish investigators' work on the written ME equivalents of the NE pronoun "she," are given on Map 6 on p. 221. It reproduces only the area around the Severn Basin running south from Shropshire and east from the Welsh border into Warwickshire. Tentative as it is, it does reveal the mass of detail they have uncovered and the kind of close work they are undertaking. It should prove to be im-

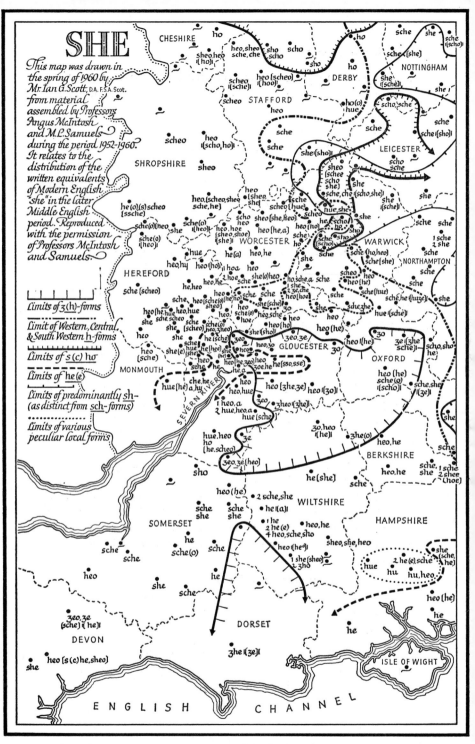

Map 6. "She."

mensely valuable. To identify the dialect, whether that of the scribe or of the author, of a ME text, it will, of course, be necessary to use more than one word or feature, but even one, if unusual, can be of help. In most cases, a group of criteria converging will be needed for this type of identification. To illustrate the method somewhat, however, try to answer the following question. If you came upon a piece of ME writing from the West Country which uses ȝeo, ȝe, or ȝo to spell the word for *she*, where would you tentatively and roughly place its origin on the basis of probability? And so on, using the additional information about other words on other maps, if you had them, you could determine with great accuracy dialect features of relatively small areas.

To lay down the principles used in distinguishing between the dialect of the scribe who may have "translated" his original into his own dialect and that of the author is too complex to go into here, but certain rimes and alliterating words can point towards the original from which the scribe copied. With care and proper safeguards such a distinction, which may be most important on occasion, can often be made by experts.

QUESTIONS

1. How do you explain *vixen* as the feminine form of *fox*? Consult the Oxford English Dictionary (OED) or (NED).
2. Looking at words such as *zet, zung, vine, vears,* and *vly* in the following nineteenth-century provincial dialect poem (the first stanza only being given), what would you say as to its provenience? Is it from the south, central, or northern part of England?

>A harnet zet in a hollur tree—
>A proper spiteful twoad (toad) was he;
>And a merrily zung while he did zet
>His stinge as shearp as a bagganet (bayonet);
>>Oh, who so vine and bowld as I?
>>I vears not bee, nor wapse, nor vly!

Put the stanza into standard American English.

3. How would you explain the fact that Scottish, which was originally Northern English, had a more prominent history than

the other varieties of Northern English, such as the Yorkshire dialect?

4. What are some of the linguistic features of the slang in vogue at your college?

5. Would you agree with Puttenham who wrote in his *Arte of English Poesie* in 1589, "After a speech is fully fashioned to the common understanding, and accepted by a consent of a whole country and nation, it is called a language." Discuss this statement in the light of the discussion in this chapter of a standard form of a language.

6. Observe the behavior of someone who speaks English with a foreign accent. What modifications of standard English does he make? If you know his original language, point out the ways in which this language has influenced or interfered with his English. How might this kind of language behavior explain certain features in the history of the English language?

7. What aspects of American history are reflected in American place names?

8. Make a list of things that you know have different names in different American dialects or sub-dialects. Look in H. Kurath, *A Word Geography of the Eastern United States*. Studies in American English I (Ann Arbor: University of Michigan Press; 1949), to see if these differences are recorded there. Try to list some lexical variants not in Kurath.

9. Look at the map of American dialects above on p. 201. Can you find any geographical features which seem to act as boundaries?

10. List five phonological, five lexical, and five grammatical differences between educated and uneducated American usage.

11. Why do you think London is so important in the history of the English language, and Washington so unimportant?

12. Can you think of any American urban dialect which, like Cockney, is looked down upon?

13. Write a short summary of reasons for the ascendancy of London English. In the light of what you have learned in this chapter, what would you say to the statement that standard NE achieved its superiority because of its innate characteristics?

14. Identify with reasons the ME dialects in which the following selections are written: þ = *th* and ȝ = *w* or *g* or *y* or *s*

a) þe kyng went furth, wrath and angry,
   Menand [urging on] his man full tendirly,
   And held his way all hym allāne,
   And richt toward þe houss is gāne
   Quhar he set trist [rendezvous] to mete his men.

b) and þo [when] hi [they: i.e., devils] weren ine ham [them], hise [them] adreynten [they drowned] ine þe ze [sea], ine tokninge þet þe glotouns ledeþ lif of zuyn [swine] and þe dyevel heþ [hath] y-leave to guo in ham and hise adrenche ine þe ze of helle. . . . Huanne [when] þe kempe [fighter] heþ his velaӡe [fellow] y-veld [felled] and him halt be þe þrote, wel onneaþe [with difficulty] he arist.

c) & wyth a luflych loke [look] ho [she] layde hym þyse
   wordeӡ: [words]
   Sir, ӡif [if] ӡe [ye] be Wawen [Gawain], wonder me
   þynkkeӡ,
   Wyӡe [man] þat is so wel wrast [disposed] alway to
   god,
   & conneӡ [can] not of compaynye þe costeӡ [manners]
   vndertake,
   & if mon [man: one] kennes [teaches] you hom to knowe,
   ӡe kest [cast] hom of your mynde.

GRAMMAR AND EARLY
MODERN ENGLISH

The term "grammar" has been and still is understood in several different senses in English. "Grammar" is used by many linguistic scientists as a name for the system—or better, the "systematic-ness"—of a language, for the particular set of consistent features that any language exhibits. For example, in NE it is a grammatical$_1$ fact that *very* may precede the words *old, clean,* and *talented* but not the words *predestine, say,* and *behave;* that the unaspirated phones [p], [t], and [k] immediately follow [s]; that we have one *sofa, alumna,* and *stoma,* but more than one *sofas, alumnæ,* and *stomata.* In this sense, the "grammar" of a language includes all the morphological, syntactic, and even phonological and lexical regularities that comprise a language system. We may use the term **structure** as an equivalent term for grammar$_1$.

"Grammar$_2$" is used to designate a *description* of grammar$_1$. Thus, if I say about the grammatical$_1$ facts above that *qualifiers* precede adjectives but not verbs; that within a word, *non-final phonemically voiceless stops* are unaspirated after /s/; and that the plural morpheme has different allomorphs depending on the class of noun stem that it follows, I am making grammatical$_2$ statements about English. As in any science, there are alternative ways of making statements which "account for" a body of facts, so that a particular grammar$_2$ should be taken as a theory about the grammar$_1$, rather than as the justification of grammar$_1$. Statements such as "It is ungrammatical to say *He is taller than her* because *than* is a conjunction rather than a preposition," are misleading because terms like "conjunction" and "preposition" are technical terms in descriptions of regularities and are not themselves determinants of what those regularities should be. The use of *because* in such statements suggests a confusion between grammar$_2$ and grammar$_1$. Such statements reverse the order of priority by implying that a label on a word determines its use, rather than the more reasonable alternative that the use of the word determines its label. If we want to avoid ambiguity, we may use the term **descriptive grammar** for grammar$_2$.

However, neither of these senses is commonly intended in our everyday talk about language. When someone says, "He has perfect grammar when he writes," or "Kids nowadays use terrible grammar," or "*Ain't* is ungrammatical," he means "grammar$_3$": namely, that variety of a language which enjoys prestige in a particular society. In Chapter VII we shall have more to say about grammar$_3$, which we may call **standard grammar**. Just as we talk about grammar$_1$, the structure of a language, in terms of grammar$_2$, a descriptive grammar, so we may talk about grammar$_3$, standard grammar, in terms of a grammar$_4$, which we may call a **prescriptive grammar**. The great bulk of what we usually refer to as "traditional grammar" is a mixture of prescriptive and descriptive statements.

Any of the grammars we have mentioned here may entail the special characteristics of discourses, sentences, phrases, word-groups, words, or phoneme sequences in a language. Sometimes the term **syntax** is used to apply only to grammars dealing with sequences larger than individual words, in contrast to the term **morphology**, for word-level grammars, and to the term **phonotactics**, for grammars of phoneme sequences. Sometimes the term "grammar" itself (grammar$_5$) is used only for morphology and sometimes (grammar$_6$) to cover both morphology and syntax.

In this chapter we will be interested in showing how a descriptive grammar of English might look, especially as applied to that historical period of English that we call Early Modern English (ENE). The particular approach that we will take here rests on the conviction that the best test of adequacy of a descriptive grammar is the ability of its rules to generate—that is, to specify, enumerate, or account for—all (and only) the discourses of a particular language. The descriptive grammar that results from such an approach may be called a **generative grammar**.

In contrast to grammars which require that descriptive statements be framed within a general grammatical tradition based ultimately on the study of Latin or Greek, and in contrast to **structural grammars** (like that we have presented in Chapter IV) which require that descriptive statements be framed as generalizations of observed particular occurrences, a generative grammar requires that its descriptive statements be explicit in specifying the construction of the sentences of a particular language—whether that specification satisfies the traditional grammar or not, and whether the sentences have already been observed or not.

SUMMARY OF DEVELOPMENT OF ENE

Before we take up the generation of a discourse in ENE, it will be useful to outline the ways in which English has been changing since OE times. To illustrate our points, we will look at three versions of the Lord's Prayer, one taken from an OE translation (approximately A.D. 1000), one from a ME translation (from the thirteenth century), and one from the ENE translation that we have come to know as the King James version (1611).

THE LORD'S PRAYER (Matthew 6: 9–13)

Old English

Fæder ure þu   þe   eart on heofonum, si   þin nama
Father our thou that art on heaven[s], may-be thy name
    gehalgod.
    hallowed.

Tobecume þin rice.   Gewurþe   ðin willa on eorðan swa
May-come thy realm. May-become thy will on earth   so
    swa on heofonum.
    so on heaven[s].

Urne gedæghwamlican hlaf syle us to dæg.
Our daily   loaf sell us today.

And forgyf us urne gyltas, swa swa we forgyfað urum
And forgive us our guilts, so so we forgive   our
    gyltendum.
    guilt-doers.

And ne gelæd þu   us on costnunge, ac alys us of
And not lead thou us on temptation, but free us from
    yfele.
    evil.

    Soþlice.
    Soothly.

Middle English

Fader oure þat art in hevene, i-halwed bee þi name.
Father our   that art in heaven, hallowed be thy name.

I-cume þi kingreiche, y-worthe þi wylle also is in hevene
Come thy king-realm, become thy will as is in heaven

so be on erthe.
so be on earth.

Oure iche-dayes-bred gif us to-day.
Our each-day's-bread give us today.

And forgif us oure gultes, also we forgifeth oure gultare.
And forgive us our guilts, as we forgive our guiltors.

And ne led ows nowth into fondingge, auh ales   ows
And not lead us not   into temptation, but deliver us

of   harme. So be hit.
from harm. So be it.

Early Modern English

Our father which art in heaven, hallowed be thy name.
Thy kingdom come. Thy will be done in earth, as it is in
heaven.
Give us this day our daily bread.
And forgive us our debts, as we forgive our debtors.
And lead us not into temptation, but deliver us from evil:
For thine is the kingdom, and the power, and the glory,
for ever. Amen.

The three versions of the Lord's Prayer above appear strikingly different, so much so that if we were not told, we might
very well not realize that we were dealing with versions of
the same discourse. Let us consider the differences under four
main headings: spelling, morphology, lexicon, and special textual
variation.

Spelling

Some of the spelling differences between the versions reflect
differences in orthographical practices over the years, rather

than actual phonological changes. For example, the replacement of the OE spellings þ and ð by ME *th* is of this kind. Another example is the ME spelling *ou* or *ow* (reflecting the French orthographical conventions which were influencing the ME scribes) for what had been written in OE texts as *u:* thus OE *ūre*>ME *oure* and OE *þū*>ME *thou*, OE *ūs*>ME *ows*. The OE digraph æ became more and more rare in ME texts, its place being taken usually by *a:* OE *fæder*>ME *fader*, OE *dæg*>ME *day*.

By the advent of printing, introduced into England by William Caxton in 1476, many ME spellings had become well established as visual representations of words, and printers today retain these spellings even though our actual pronunciations now are no longer accurately reflected by those spellings. In other cases, Caxton and later printers adopted new spellings according to some principle—often applied inconsistently—of phonemic representation of current pronunciations. For example, the retention of final *e* in the spellings *name, done, thine* (words pronounced by that time as single syllables) seems to be due to the visual conservatism of the printers, while the *ea* in *heaven, earth,* and *bread* seems to have been applied to a large number of words to represent a phoneme with a phonetic value something like [ɛ:], although the same *ea* spelling was also used to represent a different phoneme—something like [e:]—in words like *bead, weak, clean*, etc. The visual conservatism of spelling is perhaps most strikingly seen in the retention of so-called silent letters in NE: ME *gh*—which represented a phoneme with a phonetic value something like [x]—is preserved in the NE spellings *night, bought, through, tough*, etc.; *k* and *g* before *n* (in ME, [k] and [g] respectively) are retained in NE spelling of words like *knight, knife, gnat, gnaw*, even though those spellings do not accurately represent what was the current pronunciation of those words. And the result of the early NE printers' attempt to regularize spellings on phonemic principles is probably most evident in the way "long" and "short" vowel phonemes were distinguished in the orthography. A short vowel was written with a single vowel letter followed by at least two consonant letters if another vowel letter followed, while a long vowel was indicated by using either two vowel letters or one vowel letter followed by a single consonant letter plus another vowel letter. Thus, we owe our present spellings of "short" vowels in *batter, battle,* and *bat,* and "long" vowels in *baiter, bait,* and *bate,* to conventions employed by NE printers to represent ME differences in vowel length. The terms "long" and "short" vowels thus have some historical justification, in that they correspond by and large to differences in phonemic vowel length in ME. But in NE the ME differences of phonemic length in vowels have been replaced by other phonemic differences—mostly differences in vowel quality rather than vowel quantity. One should not make the mistake of thinking that in NE what are referred to traditionally as "long" vowels are prolonged "short" vowels.

Although some of the spelling differences between the versions of the Lord's Prayer—especially those between the OE and ME texts—thus represent only changes in orthographical conventions, a great many reflect the actual changes in pronunciation that had taken place. We shall consider these changes in two stages: those marking the transition of OE to ME, and those marking the transition of ME to NE. In summarizing these changes in the general way we do, we are in danger of making it seem as if the changes took place all at once, in all dialects, for all the words containing the specified original sounds. It must be emphasized that many of the generalizations given below are only roughly valid as stated, that they apply only for certain phonological environments not further specified here, only for certain dialects—we have been particularly concerned with the literary dialects here—and only gradually over a considerable period of time. Inspection of actual OE, ME, and NE texts would show how rough the formulations which follow really are.

Speaking generally, consonants have for the most part undergone fewer changes in the history of English than have vowels.

Among the consonant changes that did occur, the most important were the developments that created phonemic distinctions between [f] and [v] (as we have already seen), [s] and [z], [θ] and [ð], and [n] and [ŋ], which in the OE period were merely allophones of the same phonemes. The appearance of the spelling -*v*- instead of earlier -*f*- in words like *heofonum*> *hevene* records the fact that the phonetic difference between [f] and [v] had become phonemically significant and hence important to speakers of English. Other consonant changes were, for example, the disappearance of OE /h/ before other consonants (OE *hlaf*>ME *lof*); the disappearance of ME /k/ and /g/ before /n/ (as in *knight* and *gnaw*); the disappearance of ME /h/, phonetically probably [x] after vowels (as in *night*); the disappearance of ME /l/ before consonants in certain words (e.g., *talk, walk, salmon, should*); and the change of Early OE /g/ to /y/ next to front vowels and /w/ after back vowels and liquids (OE *dæg*>ME *day*, OE *gehālgod*>ME *i-halwed*).

In contrast with the consonants, the vowels of English have had an exciting history. Some of this history is obscured by the inaccuracy of ME and NE spelling systems in reflecting the changes in pronunciation, and the exact identification and dating of the changes are still matters for serious debate among scholars.

1) As we have already said in Chapter V, many of the distinctions between unaccented vowels in OE were lost by ME times; the most common spelling of unaccented vowels in ME was *e*, probably pronounced [ə]. In NE even this [ə] was lost in final position, although spellings with *e* were often preserved. In the following examples the vowels after the first vowel of each word are unaccented:

OE	ME	NE	
a	ə	—	OE *nama*, ME *name*, NE *name*
e	ə	—	OE *ūre*, ME *oure*, NE *our*
o, u	ə, ə	ə, —	OE *heofonum*, ME *hevene*, NE *heaven*

2) Words that had accented short vowels in ME, either inherited from short vowels in OE or newly shortened from long vowels in OE, retained short vowels in NE. In the transition from OE to ME, short /a/ and /æ/ merged into a single phoneme /a/, and this in turn became NE /æ/. In the transition from ME to NE accented short /ú/ became NE /ɜ/. In different dialect areas and at different periods, accented short /ü̇/ (usually spelled *y* in OE, *u* or *ui* in ME) merged with /í/ into a single phoneme /í/; in NE this has become /í/. In certain positions, accented short vowels in OE words (such as in *náma* mentioned above) became long in ME. Short "diphthongs"[1] in general merged with other short vowels. The following relationships are typical of short vowels:

OE	ME	NE	Examples
í	í	í	*willa*>*wylle*>*will*
ü̇	ü̇	í	*gylt*>*guilt*>*guilt*
ú	ú	ɜ	*ūs*>*ows*>*us*
e	e	έ	*heofonum*>*hevene*>*heaven*
ó	ó	ɔ	*on*>*on*>*on*
ǽ	á	ǽ	*æsce*>*ash*>*ash*
á	á	ǽ	*gehālgod*>*halwed*>*hallowed*

3) Words that had accented long vowels in ME, either inherited from long vowels in OE or lengthened from short vowels in OE, displayed radical changes in vowel quality in the transition to NE. These changes are so striking that they have been glorified by the name *The Great Vowel Shift*. In general, the

---

[1] The phonetic and phonemic status of the vowels written in OE with two letters (especially *ea* and *eo*) has been hotly disputed in recent years. Whatever these vowels were, whether phonetically single or double—i.e., monophthongs or diphthongs—whether phonemically distinct from simple vowels or not, whether generally consistent in graphemic representation or not, they were paired in OE as long vs. short, just like every other OE vowel. Vowel length and accent in English have never been represented reliably in the traditional orthography. It is conventional in historical linguistic scholarship to mark length and accent of vowels by adding a macron (e.g., *ēo, ā, ī*) and acute accent mark (e.g., *éo, á, í*), respectively, above the traditional spellings.

lower long vowels became higher and the highest long vowels became diphthongs, gliding from a low first part to a high second part. Modern spellings of the words involved usually reflect the ME pronunciations better than the NE ones. For example, the fact that *fight* is spelled with the same *i* letter that is used in *fit* reflects the ME relationship of long /i:/ in *fight* vs. short /i/ in *fit*, better than it shows the present relationship of /ay/ vs. /ɪ/. In the following illustrations, we have given a very rough "phonetic" representation of the vowels involved:[2]

OE	ME	ENE	LNE	Examples
ī				*mine, I*
ū̃	⟩ ī	> əi	> ai	*mice, fire*
ē	> ē	> ī		*we, teeth*
ǣ	> ɛ̄	> ē	⟩ i	*clean, cheese*
ū	> ū	> əu	> au	*mouse, our*
ō	> ō	> ū	> u	*to, tooth*
ā	> ɔ̄	> ō	> o	*loaf, stone*
	ā	> ɛ̄	> e	*name, lady*

Morphology

A second group of differences between the OE, ME, and NE versions of the Lord's Prayer is morphological. As we have said in Chapter V, most suffixes which consist in OE of a vowel or vowel plus nasal consonant become -*e* ([ə]) in ME and drop out altogether by the NE period:

OE heofon*um*	ME heven*e*	NE heaven
OE eorð*an*	ME erth*e*	NE earth
OE yfel*e*	ME ivil*e*	NE evil
OE ūr*e*	ME our*e*	NE our
OE nam*a*	ME nam*e*	NE name (with "silent" *e*)

Various other simplifications in word forms also took place in the historical development of English, with a net effect that can be roughly summarized as follows: The complexity of the inflectional system of adjectives, nouns, and verbs in OE is sharply

---

[2] See special note on page 285 at the end of this chapter.

reduced in ME, largely by reason of the simplification of the phonological structure of unstressed syllables; further reduction takes place by NE times, mainly by reason of the loss of the ME suffix -*e* (the vestige of many different OE suffixes, as we have seen), but also by reason of the loss of various other affixes as productive devices for forming new word forms—for example, the OE prefix *ge-*, which was sometimes retained in ME as *i-* (also spelled *y-*), disappeared almost without a trace in NE.[3] In the Lord's Prayer, notice that OE *gehalgod*> ME *i-halwed*> NE *hallowed* and OE (*ge*)*læd*> ME *led*> NE *lead*. The gradual elimination of inflectional suffixes from adjectives, illustrated in our text by the changes of OE *ure, urne, urum* all yielding ME *oure* and then NE *our*, was another factor accounting for the striking morphological simplification that has taken place in the history of English.

Vocabulary

Our different versions of the Lord's Prayer reflect a few of the enormous number of changes in the English vocabulary that have taken place over the last thousand years. The classification of these changes will be discussed in some detail in Chapter VIII. If we compare our three versions in chronological order the lexical changes that we observe in the texts appear to have been of two kinds: some of the words in earlier versions have been replaced in later versions by words borrowed from French or by words composed from native resources; and some words have slightly or drastically shifted their semantic ranges. For example:

EARLIER WORDS	REPLACED BY	SOURCE OF REPLACEMENT
OE *si*	*be*	from another verb in OE
OE *costnunge* ME *fondingge*	*temptation*	borrowed from French

[3] NE *yclept* is an archaic descendant of ME *icleped* or *ycleped*, in turn from OE *geclipod*, the past participle of *clipian* 'to call, to name.'

OE *ac* ME *auh*	*but*	from OE *butan* 'without'
OE *glytendum* ME *gultare*	*debtors*	formed from a French stem
OE *gewurþe* ME *y-worthe*	*become*	from another verb in ME
OE *alys* ME *ales*	*deliver*	borrowed from French
OE *rice*	ME *king-reiche*	*king* plus *reiche* 'realm'
	NE *kingdom*	*king* plus *-dom*
OE *swa*	ME *also*	*al* 'all' and *so* (from OE *swa*) 'as'
	NE *as*	contraction of *also*
ME *nowth*	NE *not*	an alternate negative form
OE *gedæ-ghwamlican*	ME *iche-dayes*	each day's
	NE *daily*	*day* plus *-ly* (from *-lic* 'like')
OE *gyltas*	NE *debts*	ME *dettes* (*b* introduced for etymological elegance)

SEMANTICALLY SHIFTED WORDS	FROM	TO
OE *swa*	'so, as'	ME and NE *so*
OE *on*	'on, in, at, into, against'	ME and NE *on*
OE *hlaf*	'loaf, bread'	ME and NE *loaf*
OE *syle*	'give, sell'	NE *sell*
ME *gult*	'guilt, sin'	NE *guilt*
ME *of*	'of, from, off'	NE *of*

Special Textual Variation

Finally, there are two kinds of special textual variation illustrated by our texts which do not bear directly on the historical development of NE. First, there are the differences that any two translations, even those made in the same historical period, may show because of variations in the skill, style, and taste of the translators and because of variations in the text from which the translations are being made. The difference in choice of words in translating the Latin word *malo* as OE *yfele*, ME *harme*, and NE *evil* indicates a difference in translation choices rather than a lack in ME of a word corresponding exactly to the OE and NE forms. Similarly, the NE translation *this day* obviously does not reflect a loss of the form *today*, whose ancestors appear in the OE and ME versions. And the absence of anything in OE and ME versions to correspond to the King James' "For thine is the kingdom, and the power, and the glory, forever," is not due to any linguistic deficiencies in those languages, but rather to the fact that the King James translators were working from original texts not available to the earlier translators.

The other kind of difference which might be misleading in trying to understand the historical development of English is that evidenced by the differences in the endings of OE *forgyfad*, ME *forgifeth*, and NE *forgive*. We have to do here with forms of three different dialectal proveniences: the OE *forgyfad* is a West Saxon form, the ME *forgifeth* is a Kentish form, and the NE *forgive* is a descendant—by the regular route of loss of vowel-plus-nasal suffixes—from the ME Midland form *forgifen* (originally a subjunctive plural shifted to the indicative plural in the North).

GENERATIVE GRAMMAR

Let us now turn our attention from the historical background of ENE to the description of ENE grammar. But before we can do this, we must raise some fundamental questions about the nature of our task.

What is the relation between a descriptive grammar and the language which it claims to describe? As we have indicated previously, a description is a theory that accounts for the phenomena being described. In spite of their otherwise invaluable contribution to the study of languages, neither traditional nor structural grammarians have provided an acceptable account of the nature of grammars as theories. In traditional grammars of English, the phenomena were usually accounted for by reference to categories of universal grammar—categories which often were mere extensions of the particular categories that had derived from the study of Latin and Greek rather than from a fresh investigation of the structure of English itself. In many of the descriptive grammars of the "structural" type, on the other hand, there has been an unfortunate overreliance on the ability of physical facts to speak for themselves.

To take an example of the weaknesses of both of these approaches, consider the ambiguous English sentence *She hates smoking cigars,* which can mean either that she doesn't like to smoke cigars, or that she dislikes cigars that have been left smoking in an ashtray. (We will ignore here the further ambiguity offered by the compound *smoking-cigars,* cigars used for smoking.) The traditional grammar would have no difficulty in accounting for the ambiguity: the word *smoking* can be either a present participle or a gerund, categories familiar to us from classical grammar and recognized in these sentences by inspection or introspection into the meanings of the two different sentences. But such an explanation rests on grounds that are inadequate for the appreciation of the particular grammatical structure of English. In the first place, the sentence is English, not Latin, and its grammatical description (as opposed, say, to its grammatical translation) should employ categories appropriate for English rather than Latin facts. In the second place, the appeal to differences in meaning is bound to be inconsistently applied. For example, consider the sentence *This has been a miserable day,* which has semantic, but not grammatical ambiguity. That is, the sentence might mean that the weather has been bad or that the speaker has had bad luck during the day; but no traditional grammar would infer from that semantic ambiguity that either *miserable* or *day* was grammatically different in the two cases. The use of differences in meaning to establish grammatical categories is thus unreliable.

Some structural grammars would also have no difficulty in

resolving the ambiguity of *She hates smoking cigars:* the ambiguity in the sentence is *merely* semantic, since the distinction one would have to make to account for the two meanings of *smoking* is not marked in English by a difference in phonological form. One problem here is that such an account would leave unexplained the consistency with which similar constructions are ambiguous. For example, substitute *She hates counting students, She hates playing fish,* or even *She hates helping hirelings,* for *She hates smoking cigars,* and the same ambiguity arises. And the explanation also fails to account for the observable effects of the difference between the two kinds of *smoking cigars* in the sentences: *Smoking cigars is disgusting* and *Smoking cigars are disgusting.*

A new approach, which is more likely to account satisfactorily for the ambiguity of *smoking cigars,* as well as for the construction of all English sentences, takes the job of accounting for grammatical facts as a problem of constructing a systematic set of rules (a *langue,* so to speak)—a generative grammar—from which all the sentences of a language and none of the nonsentences can be ultimately derived. To determine the grammatical analysis of the *smoking cigars* sentences will simply mean to state what specific rules in the grammar are applied to generate those sentences; in an ambiguous sentence, more than one set of rules can be applied. In the case we have been considering, one instance of *smoking cigars* can be generated by a "transformation" rule from an underlying *She smokes cigars,* and the other instance by a different transformation rule from an underlying *Cigars smoke.* And, if we can show that by applying a certain set of rules we can generate the discourse of a given language, we can say that in an important sense this set of rules "accounts for" that language, that it is indeed a descriptive grammar of that language.

Now, as a matter of fact, we do not yet have for any language —including NE, on which the most work has been done—anything like a complete set of such rules, that is, a complete grammar; nor is it likely that we shall have such a grammar within the near future. To attempt a complete generative grammar for a language like ENE, of which there are no native speakers living, would be presumptuous and foolhardy. What we will attempt here is a presentation of enough of the generative grammar of ENE to generate one discourse, namely, the King James version of the Lord's Prayer, as given on p. 229 above. We are particularly interested here in those rules of ENE grammar that have relevance to the generation of this discourse, but even this very limited number of rules will generate a very large number of possible sentences in addition to those in the Lord's Prayer. Most of the rules here are the same as for LNE (Late NE). A few of them are not. The amount of difference between the sets of rules gives us some measure of the difference between the two stages of the language, and the amount of similarity between the sets of rules is some measure of the similarity between the stages.

Now what form should the statement of such rules take? Consider the following attempt to state the construction of the first sentence in the Lord's Prayer *Our father which art in heaven, hallowed be thy name:* This sentence is composed of two parts, a vocative expression *Our father which art in heaven* and an imperative clause *hallowed be thy name*. The vocative expression is composed of a nominal *our father* plus a relative clause *which art in heaven*. The nominal *our father* is composed of a determiner *our*, itself composed of the pronoun *we* plus a genitive marker, plus the animate count noun *father*—one out of a very large number of such nouns. The relative clause *which art in heaven* is a transformation of the underlying sentence *thou art in heaven*, which in turn is composed of a nominal subject *thou* plus a predicate of the type *be* plus locative complement—one of several possible types of complement. *In heaven* is a locative complement composed of a locative preposition plus a nominal object; it illustrates one of the two types of locative constructions in English, the other being the locative adverbial. The form *art* is the automatic morphographemic (see below p. 272) resultant of present tense plus *be* after the subject nominal *thou* in the basic sentence, and is preserved in the relative clause transformation. The vocative expression as a whole is formed by a transformation which adds a nominal containing a proper name to a sentence. Such a description as this—and we haven't even begun the analysis of the second part of the sentence yet—is long-winded and confusing. It contains bits and pieces of several kinds of description; it loses the unity of the structure of the whole sentence under a mass of particular and sometimes irrelevant details. Its technical terms are undefined, and unclarified by their use in the statements themselves. It suffers from an annoying lack of direction in the ordering of its statements; very general statements are mixed indiscriminately together with very particular ones. Essential differences between the various kinds of statements made (compare the statement about *art* with that about the vocative transformation) are ignored without justification. Some of the individual statements are so cumbersome in form that it is difficult to make out just what they are saying, and harder still to see their relationship to other statements.

To overcome these deficiencies we may employ a special set of devices—devices well known to mathematicians and formal logicians, but not very widely used in the descriptions of historical languages. We shall present the rules of ENE grammar as a set of formulas ordered in such a way that technical terms are developed in successive formulas, so that a term becomes more and more "meaningful" as the rules progress; that is, it comes closer to the particularity of actual sentences.[4]

Specifically, we will start with the term *discourse* and break it down into component sentences. Then the components of the

---

[4] For fuller discussion of the principles involved here see Noam Chomsky: *Syntactic Structures* (The Hague: Mouton and Co.; 1957), and R. B. Lees: *The Grammar of English Nominalizations* (Bloomington: Research Center for Anthropology, Folklore, and Linguistics, Publ. #12; 1960) (*IJAL* XXVI Suppl. #3). Note that the term *formula* above is being used in a much more general sense than in Chapter III, when we discussed comparative linguistics. For two still useful older grammars of ENE in English, see those of Edwin A. Abbott and Herbert Sugden (see Bibliography at end of book).

sentence will be generated by a rule, and these components in turn will be broken down by further rules to yield sub-components, and so on and on until we arrive at lists of lexical units (dictionary items). All of the grammar to this point can be thought of as composed of **constituent-structure** rules—rules that specify the **immediate constituents** of a higher-level unit in terms of the lower-level units that compose it. Conversely, the rules can be considered to show how lower-level units "go together" to form higher-level units. Each rule takes an element on the left side of the written formula and indicates its constituent elements on the right side of the formula. For example, Rule 10: Pred $\rightarrow$ Aux + V_{phrase} says that a predicate has as constituents auxiliary plus verb phrase, each of which has its own constituents given in turn by later rules. Or if we read $\rightarrow$ as "generates," we may say that a predicate generates an auxiliary plus a verb phrase. Conversely, we will say that an element or sequence of elements on the right side of the formula is *generated from* or simply *is* an element on the left. For example, in Rule L7: $N_{an} \rightarrow$ father, debtor, dog . . . , we say that each of the items on the right *is* one of the class designated by the element on the left: in this case, *father* "is" an animate noun, *debtor* "is" an animate noun, etc. Thus the rule itself justifies and explains what we could mean when we say "X is a Y" in grammatical contexts. What does it mean to say that *father* is a noun in English? Our answer in terms of this grammar would be that *father* is generated from N_{an} which in turn is generated from Noun (see Rules 8 and 9 following).

From the constituent-structure rules come only a set of rather simple structures, called **kernel strings,**[5] which are limited in such a way as to exhibit only the most primary and irreducible rela-

---

[5] The terminology employed in this chapter differs in several respects from that introduced by Chomsky and followed by Lees (see footnote 4 above). For example, our application of *generates* and *is generated from* to individual rules differs from their application of such terms to the relationship between an axiomatic system and the theorems generated by it. Our use of the term *kernel* differs from their application of the term to the output of constituent-structure rules *after* obligatory transformations have been applied.

tions between parts. In order to generate the much more complex
structures that even the most ordinary of discourses actually display, rules must be stated that will modify, add to, subtract from,
and rearrange the simple structures resulting from application of
the constituent-structure rules. The rules in this second set are
called **transformations**. An example is the passive transformation
rule that we will meet on p. 263, Rule T3: $Nom^1 + (Aux) +$
$V_{trans} + Nom^2 + -M + X \Rightarrow Nom^2 + (Aux) + be + Comp$
$[-D_{part} + V_{trans}] + by + Nom^1 + -M + X$ which takes a sentence like *The play amused me last night* and transforms it into
I was amused by the play last night. With such a rule, the total
grammatical description can be enormously simplified, in that we
no longer need special statements to account for each separate
kind of passive construction in English, but can generate what is
common to all of them by means of this one rule. Thus, we do
not need to enter special descriptions into the grammar for *She
will be burned by the boiling water, George may have been held
captive by the kidnappers, The old man is made angry by youthful
rashness*; instead we generate them by Rule T3 from previously
generated sentences *The boiling water will burn her, The kidnappers may have held George captive, Youthful rashness makes
the old man angry.*

An even more important simplification permitted by transformation rules stems from the fact that there are several limitations on what can go with what in forming even simple sentences.
For example, English allows *The play amused me*, but not **I
amused the play*. (In this chapter an asterisk * is used to indicate
nongrammatical rather than hypothetically reconstructed forms.)
These limitations can be accounted for by proper grammatical
rules. But notice that the same limitations obtain in allowing for
I was amused by the play, but not for **The play was amused by
me*. In deriving passive sentences like *I was amused by the play*
only from previously generated sentences, these limitations are
preserved, and so they need to be accounted for only once, instead of having to be restated for every occurrence of *I, amuse*,
and *play*.

With only the kinds of rules we have mentioned up to this point, the discourses generated would be abstract entities, since the terms of the rules would have merely the status of formal elements generated by a set of formal statements. What we still need is a set of rules to translate the abstract elements into concrete representations. If we were dealing with speech, these would be **morphophonemic** rules, that is, rules for making formal (morphological) sequences into phonological sequences. Since we are primarily interested here in a written ENE discourse, we need instead **morphographemic** rules, that is, rules for converting formal sequences into graphemic sequences.[6] An example is Rule M3: [thou] + $-Z_{pres}$ + be $\rightarrow$ *art*, which yields the actually occurring graphemic sequence *thou art* from a sequence of formally defined elements. We shall need only a few such special morphographemic rules in this grammar, since the constituent-structure and transformation formulas, necessarily presented in visual form in a book, already yield graphemic sequences as their outputs.

The formulas presented in this chapter represent, of course, only a portion of the total grammar of ENE. However, we would claim that with even this restricted grammar, which includes constituent-structure rules, transformation rules, and morphographemic rules, we shall be able to generate the Lord's Prayer, as well as an infinite number of other discourses in ENE. The ability to generate all and only the discourses, potential as well as actual, of a language in the simplest way possible is the most reasonable requirement we can demand of a descriptive grammar. A grammatical analysis of a given linguistic unit will then be said to consist of the specific set of rules—or sets of rules, in the case of ambiguous units—from which that unit can be generated.

In the following formulations we will make use of a number of symbolic conventions and short cuts. The interpretation of the

---

[6] To get from graphemic to graphic sequences requires an additional set of rules of penmanship or printing. See Murray Eden: "On the Formalization of Handwriting," *Proceedings of the Twelfth Symposium in Applied Mathematics* (Providence: American Mathematical Society; 1961), 83–88.

formulas should become clear from the discussions following the rules; it will also be helpful for you to refer frequently to the list of abbreviations on pp. 254 ff. and to the lexicon on pp. 256-257, to remind you in more familiar terms what it is that the rules are saying.

CONSTITUENT-STRUCTURE RULES

1. $D \rightarrow D_{prayer}$
   $D_{conversation}$
   D_{sonnet}
   $D_{warning}$
   . . .

Our first rule says that there are several kinds of discourses, including prayers, conversations, sonnets, and of course many, many others. The structure of various discourse types is very insufficiently known, and we will not go deeply into the matter here. In our formulas we will use the convention of placing alternative readings under one another, instead of repeating the whole rule for each alternative. That is, Rule 1 is a shorthand way of writing:

$D \rightarrow D_{prayer}$
$D \rightarrow D_{conversation}$
$D \rightarrow D_{sonnet}$
$D \rightarrow D_{warning}$
. . .

2. $D_{prayer} \rightarrow S^1 + (S^n) +$ Amen.

Rule 2 specifies that a prayer will consist of at least one sentence (signified by the superscript ^{1}) and any number of other sentences (signified by the superscript ^{n}), and will end in *Amen.* In this formula and in subsequent ones, parentheses are used to enclose optional parts—that is, the rule may be read with or without the part enclosed between the parentheses. While it is difficult to characterize any given type of discourse exactly, we should note in passing that conversations typically contain question-answer sequences; that classical sonnets have a fairly fixed number of syllables with rimed syllables coming at certain regular intervals; that warnings can consist of single imperative sentences; etc. The plus sign is used in our formulas for the rules to separate parts of a sequence.

    3. S → Subj + Pred

Rule 3 says that a sentence consists of a subject and a predicate. This rule will hardly come as a surprise to people who have always been told that a sentence must contain a subject and a predicate in order for it to be a sentence at all. But the rule will not be so acceptable to those of us who are aware of the difficulty in finding subjects and predicates in phonological sentences (see Chapter II) like *Fire! Maybe tomorrow. How about him? Yes. Take it off!* The point here is that we can take the structure Subj + Pred as the basic one in a sentence grammar of English; sentences with other structures can then be derived from this basic structure by the application of various transformation rules, some of which appear later in this chapter. Thus, all the actual sentences of the Lord's Prayer are based on underlying subject + predicate structures.

    4. Subj → Nom

This rule says that the subject will be a nominal of some kind. In later rules we shall see other functions of nominal expressions. NE is characterized by a great wealth of **nominalization** transformations, that is, transformations that form new nominals from various sources within the language. We do not have space to treat such transformations in this chapter; let it suffice to mention such nominalizations as those illustrated by *smoking cigars, for X to smoke cigars, that X smokes cigars, to smoke cigars, smoking of cigars, cigar smoker, smoking-cigars, smoked cigars, cigar-smoking*—all transformations from the kernel structure *X smokes cigars.* Other kernel structures underlie nominals like *cigar-smoke, smoky cigars, cigar smokiness,* and to coin new, but possible, nominals—*cigardom* and *cigarhood.*

    5. Nom → Name
                (Det) + (Adjec) + Noun + ($-Z_{pl}$)

This rule describes the structure of the nominal—remember that the nominalizations such as *cigar smoker* or *smoking cigars* discussed under the preceding rule are derived from transformation rules rather than from this constituent-structure rule—as consisting either of a name or of a noun preceded by an optional determiner (See Rule 7) and an optional adjective, and followed by an optional plural marker. The fact that the determiner, adjective, and plural are optional is indicated by placing the appropriate symbol between parentheses. More complex nominals, such as those containing several adjectives or several nouns, are formed by transformation rules, most of which do not play a part in forming the discourse under investigation here and hence will not be discussed in this chapter.

6. Name → Name$_{prop}$
   Name$_{pron}$

This rule recognizes the grammatical similarity in NE of proper names and pronouns. Philosophers have frequently noted their logical similarity, but grammarians have typically not recognized their grammatical similarity in NE—for example, the severe restriction on the use of articles and adjectives before them both. Note that the categories Name$_{prop}$ and Name$_{pron}$ as used here do not correspond exactly to the traditional categories of proper nouns and pronouns: the traditional categories rest on considerations of meaning which reflect conflicting grammatical characteristics.

7. Det → Art
   Nom + -Z$_{gen}$

The fact that Det includes a possible Nom and that Nom in turn includes a possible Det implies the possibility of strings of Det, as in *my father's youngest brother's wife's former uncle's sweetheart*. In such strings, all articles except the first would be deleted by an obligatory transformation rule. Notice that the structure of rules prevents a Name from occupying any but the first position of such a string: *John's sister's husband* and *my sister's husband* are grammatical, but *sister's John's wife* and *sister's my wife* are not.

8. Noun $\rightarrow$ N$_{count}$

   N$_{mass}$

Unlike the student learning English as a foreign language—who is forced to become aware of the distinction between mass and count nouns almost as soon as he has learned his second English sentence—a native speaker of English, who may have studied his language for ten years in school, is likely to be unaware of the distinction, although it is of far-reaching importance in the language. It is, for example, the distinction that accounts for our saying *many coins* but *much money, a few songs* but *a little music, a chair* but not *a furniture, reports* but not *informations.*

9. N$_{count}$ $\rightarrow$ N$_{an}$

   N$_{inan}$

The distinction between animate and inanimate nouns is also grammatically important in English, even though it is not marked by any phonological characteristics. The fact that *we forgive our debts* is normally grammatical in a way that *posts forgive our debtors* is not rests on this distinction.

It should be pointed out, however, that here, as in other places in which grammatical distinctions are drawn, a given lexical item may belong to more than one grammatical class, and may have special class membership in the modified grammars specific to particular forms of discourse, such as those of certain literary styles. For example, in a fairy tale a post might indeed forgive debts, the lexical item *post* having moved from the N$_{inan}$ class to the N$_{an}$ class.

Rules 4–9, plus the lexical rules on pp. 256-257 and the morphographemic rules on pp. 271 ff., generate all the subjects of the constituent structures underlying the Lord's Prayer: *thou, thy name, thy kingdom, thy will, we, thine.* For example, *thy kingdom* may arise by generating Nom from Subj (Rule 4); Det + Noun from Nom (Rule 5); Nom + -Z$_{gen}$ from Det (Rule 7) and N$_{inan}$ from

Noun (Rules 8 and 9); Name$_{pron}$ from Nom (Rules 5 and 6); then, by the proper lexical rules, the sequence thus generated— Name$_{pron}$ + -Z$_{gen}$ + N$_{inan}$—becomes thou + -Z$_{gen}$ + kingdom, which in turn is converted by morphographemic rules into *thy kingdom.*

10. Pred → Aux + V$_{phrase}$

Rule 10 implies that auxiliaries can be considered apart from the rest of the predicate, that the rules which account for their use need not be confused with the problems of the verb phrase proper. This separation of problems makes possible a great step towards the clarification of such questions as verbal tense, mood, voice, and aspect (the difference between *I go, I am going,* and *I have gone*) in English. We need not think of English verbal forms in terms of the conjugation of whole verbs. For example, the so-called future perfect forms *I shall have been washed, you will have been washed, he, she, it will have been washed, we shall have been washed,* etc., can be viewed as really quite simple and regular combinations of pronoun plus auxiliary plus verb phrase; Rule 10 enables us to handle in a simple way even such traditionally neglected monsters as *they could have been being washed.*

11. Aux → Tense + (Mod) + (have + -D$_{part}$)

This rule affords very great simplicity in the statement of the structure of ENE predicates. In effect, it says that an auxiliary is composed of tense, optionally a modal form (i.e., can, may, will, shall, must, need), and optionally *have* plus a "past participle."

12. Tense → -Z$_{pres}$
-D$_{past}$

One of the implications of this rule is that English has exactly two grammatical tenses, not the whole bevy of chronological "tenses" that complicate many grammars. The value of this statement can be appreciated if you try to make consistent correlations between time and tense in a set of sentences such as:

Grammar and Early Modern English 250

Plato writes very well, I write my last paper tomorrow, I shall write him right now, I am writing him now, I am writing him tomorrow, I have written him now, I wrote it yesterday, if I wrote now, if I wrote it tomorrow, I hope the elevator is running, I hope the elevator was running, I wish the elevator were running.
The statement that English has only two tenses accords very well with its membership in the Germanic language family: the two-tense verbal system is one of the characteristics of Germanic that distinguishes it from the other Indo-European families. The labeling of numerous other constructions in English as "tenses" tends to obscure this fact. The other so-called tenses are accounted for by certain particular selections of alternatives from various grammatical and lexical rules.

13. $V_{phrase} \rightarrow be + Comp$
$$V_{group} + (Loc) \quad + (Tm)$$

This rule distinguishes two kinds of verb phrases: those composed of *be* plus a complement plus an optional expression of time, and those composed of a verb group plus an optional expression of location plus an optional expression of time. The order here of (Loc) and (Tm) reflects an attempt to account for the greater naturalness of *I looked at my watch in the library before five o'clock,* in comparison with *I looked at my watch before five o'clock in the library,* as well as the possible ungrammaticality of **He ate yesterday there.* Of course, the existence of transformational rules which can, with special effect, change the order of items that is generated by constituent-structure rules prevents us from saying for a given sentence with both Loc and Tm that it is constructed in the *only* possible order.

14. $Comp \rightarrow Nom + (Loc)$
Adjec
Loc
$-ing + V_{group} + (Loc)$

Rule 14 implies that *be* is followed either by a nominal plus an optional locative expression, or by an adjective or by a locative alone, or by an -ing verb group plus optional locatives. Not included are, for example, expressions of time or manner; we don't have *The table is today* nor *They are carefully.* Some traditional names for Nom in this rule are *predicate nominative, subjective complement, predicate noun;* for Adjec the term *predicate adjective* has most frequently been used; for -ing+ V$_{group}$ the term *present participle* is used—together with the preceding *be,* it forms what are called *progressive* constructions.

    15. Loc $\rightarrow$ P$_{loc}$ + Obj
            Adv$_{loc}$

A locative—roughly, an expression of location—is composed of either a locative preposition plus an object, or a locative adverb.

One advantage of describing a language by this technique of generating particular from general categories is illustrated by this rule. By this description the similarity of function between certain adverbs and prepositional phrases, such as *in heaven* and *there,* is seen to be a grammatical fact, not merely a semantic one. Yet the identity of grammatical function does not obscure the difference in structure between the two; thus, an important limitation of certain kinds of modern descriptive grammars—their recognition of grammatical categories when and only when those categories are marked by features of physical form—is removed without a consequent loss in the validity of the description.

    16. Obj $\rightarrow$ Nom+-M

This rule says that an object is composed of a nominal plus a specific suffix. By a later morphographemic rule, -M will turn out to leave a directly observable effect in ENE only in the graphemic forms *whom, them, him, me, thee, you, her,* and *us.*

    17. Tm $\rightarrow$ Adv$_{tm}$
            (P$_{tm}$)+Obj [Noun=N$_{inan\,tm}$]

This rule gives a formulation of the structure of expressions of time. Such an expression is composed of either an adverb of time or an optional preposition of time plus an object.

The formula here includes a new convention for the use of square brackets: the brackets enclose symbols that designate a special restriction on the preceding symbol. In this case, the formula says that if Obj contains Noun, Noun may only be of a special subtype $N_{inan tm}$; that is, it must be a noun such as *day, year, month,* etc.

18. $V_{group} \rightarrow V_{trans} + Obj$
$V_{mid} + Obj$
$V_{intrans}$

We have already divided verb phrases into two kinds of structures in Rule 13. In this rule we subdivide the second of those kinds, the verb group, into three further types: 1) transitive verb plus object, 2) "middle" verb plus object, and 3) intransitive verb. A transitive verb can be characterized as having both an object and a passive transform (*we do thy will* and *thy will be done*), a middle verb as having an object but no passive transform (*we have debtors,* but not **debtors are had*), and an intransitive verb as having no object and hence no passive transform (not **we come thy kingdom* and hence not **thy kingdom be come*).

19. $V_{trans} \rightarrow V_{trans_1}$
$V_{trans_2} + Obj$

Transitive verbs divide into two main types. As a consequence of this rule and Rule 18, the first type will have only a single object (in traditional grammars called the "direct" object), while the second may have a second object (called "indirect" object). As a consequence of this rule *God delivers us* and *God forgives us our debts* will be generated from kernel strings.

20. $V_{trans_1} \rightarrow V_{trans_{dir}} + Dir$
$V_{trans_{und}}$

This rule further breaks transitive verbs with single objects into two subtypes: the first is followed by a "directive" expression, while the second is not. The difference accounts for the fact that *Lead us not into temptation* is grammatical English, but **Hallow us not into temptation* is not.

21. $Dir \rightarrow P_{dir} + Obj$
Adv_{dir}

This rule permits alternative ways of expressing "direction"; for example, instead of *lead us not into temptation* we might have *lead us not away*, and instead of *deliver us from evil* we might have *deliver us thence*.

The rules we have presented to this point will account for all the basic constituent structures in the Lord's Prayer, as well as those in an indefinitely large number of other discourses in ENE. It is significant that these rules also suffice to generate a large number of the kernel structures of LNE—an indication of the extent of basic similarity between these two stages of English. Differences between the two stages will begin to appear in various rules after this point, but will not be of sufficient importance to override the fact that English has maintained in large part the same underlying structure over more than three and a half centuries.

Résumé of Constituent-Structure Rules

1. $D \rightarrow D_{prayer}$
   $D_{conversation}$
   . . .
2. $D_{prayer} \rightarrow S^1 + (S^n) + Amen.$
3. $S \rightarrow Subj + Pred$
4. $Subj \rightarrow Nom$
5. $Nom \rightarrow Name$
   $(Det) + (Adjec) + Noun + (-Z_{pl})$
6. $Name \rightarrow Name_{prop}$
   $Name_{pron}$
7. $Det \rightarrow Art$
   $Nom + -Z_{gen}$
8. $Noun \rightarrow N_{count}$
   N_{mass}
9. $N_{count} \rightarrow N_{an}$
   N_{inan}
10. $Pred \rightarrow Aux + V_{phrase}$
11. $Aux \rightarrow Tense + (Mod) + (have + -D_{part})$

12. Tense → $-Z_{pres}$
     $-D_{past}$

13. V_{phrase} → be+Comp
                                            $+(Tm)$
     $V_{group}+(Loc)$

14. Comp → Nom+(Loc)
     Adjec
     Loc
     $-ing+V_{group}+(Loc)$

15. Loc → $P_{loc}+Obj$
     Adv_{loc}

16. Obj → Nom+-M

17. Tm→Adv_{tm}
     $(P_{tm}) + Obj$ [Noun = N_{inantm}]

18. V_{group} → $V_{trans}+Obj$
     $V_{mid} +Obj$
     $V_{intrans}$

19. V_{trans} → V_{trans_1}
     $V_{trans_2}+Obj$

20. V_{trans_1} → $V_{trans_{dir}}+Dir$
     $V_{trans_{und}}$

21. Dir → $P_{dir}+Obj$
     Adv_{dir}

Symbols used in formulas	Suggested interpretation
Adjec	adjective
Adv_{dir}	adverb of direction (directional adverb)
Adv_{loc}	adverb of location (locative adverb)
Adv_s	sentence adverbial
Adv_{tm}	adverb of time
Art	article
Aux	auxiliary
Comp	complement
Conj	conjunction
D	discourse

Symbols used in formulas	Suggested interpretation
$D_{conversation}$	conversation
D_{prayer}	prayer
D_{sonnet}	sonnet
$D_{warning}$	warning
Det	determiner
Dir	expression of direction
$-D_{part}$	participle
$-D_{past}$	past tense
Loc	expression of location
Man	expression of manner
Mod	modal (auxiliary)
-M	objective case
Name	name
$Name_{pron}$	pronoun
$Name_{prop}$	proper name
Nom	nominal
Noun	noun
N_{an}	animate noun
N_{count}	count noun
N_{inan}	inanimate noun
$N_{inan_{tm}}$	time noun
N_{mass}	mass noun
Obj	object (of verb or preposition)
P_{dir}	preposition of direction
P_{loc}	preposition of location (locative preposition)
P_{tm}	preposition of time
Pred	predicate
Q	qualifier
S	sentence
Subj	subject
T_m	expression of time
Tense	tense (of verbs)
V_{group}	verb group

*Symbols used in
 formulas* — *Suggested interpretation*

Symbol	Interpretation
$V_{intrans}$	intransitive verb
V_{mid}	middle verb
V_{phrase}	verb phrase
V_{trans}	transitive verb
V_{trans_1}	transitive verb with 1 object
V_{trans_2}	transitive verb with 2 objects
$V_{trans_{dir}}$	directional transitive verb
$V_{trans_{und}}$	undirected transitive verb
$-Z_{gen}$	genitive
$-Z_{pl}$	plural
$-Z_{pres}$	present tense
W, X, Y	any grammatical sequence

LEXICAL RULES

To generate the Lord's Prayer we shall also need a set of **lexical rules** which generate the **lexicon** used in the Lord's Prayer. We shall discuss the difference between lexical units and grammatical units immediately following this alphabetically arranged list of lexical rules. Lexical units used for the generation of the Lord's Prayer appear in italics; a few other items are included to give some indication of the membership of the particular lexical classes. We adopt the convention here of listing the alternative members of each class as a series separated by commas. The list for most of the rules represents of course only a tiny portion of the total membership of each class.

L1: Adjec → *daily*, old, good, loathsome
L2: Adv_{dir} → away, thence, hence
L3: Adv_{loc} → here, there
L4: Adv_{tm} → *forever*, today
L5: Art → *the, this*
L6: Mod → can, may, must, shall, will, need

L7: $N_{an} \rightarrow$ *father, debtor,* dog, lady, god, cow
L8: $N_{inan} \rightarrow$ *debt, kingdom, name, day,* sword
L9: $N_{inan_{tm}} \rightarrow$ *day,* year, hour, month
L10: $N_{mass} \rightarrow$ *bread, evil, glory, power, temptation, will*
L11: $Name_{pron} \rightarrow$ I, *thou,* he, she, it, *we,* ye, they
L12: $Name_{prop} \rightarrow$ *earth,* England, *Our Father, heaven,* John Donne, William
L13: $P_{dir} \rightarrow$ *into, from,* in, to, under
L14: $P_{loc} \rightarrow$ at, *in,* on, under, by
L15: $P_{tm} \rightarrow$ at, during, for, in
L16: $V_{trans_{dir}} \rightarrow$ *lead, deliver,* put, take
L17: $V_{trans_{und}} \rightarrow$ *do, hallow, forgive,* help
L18: $V_{mid} \rightarrow$ *have,* resemble, weigh
L19: $V_{intrans} \rightarrow$ *come,* live, listen
L20: $V_{trans_2} \rightarrow$ *forgive, give,* tell

To understand the difference between what we call "lexical" units and those we call "grammatical," consider Rule 13:

$$V_{phrase} \rightarrow be + Comp$$
$$+ (Tm)$$
$$V_{group} + (Loc)$$

Each of the terms on the right side of this formula serves as part of the definition of the constituent structure of the V_{phrase}. We call such terms—that is, terms generated by general grammatical rules—**grammatical units.** The "meaning" of a grammatical unit is always difficult to state in anything but vague, subjective, and circular terms: e.g., *Comp* designates what completes the verb, *Tm* designates an expression of time, *be* joins a subject with a complement, V_{group} designates an action or state, *Loc* designates an expression of location.

In contrast, most of the **lexical units** generated by lexical rules have "meaning" in a more usual and less vague sense. For example, the lexical units generated from the grammatical unit N_{mass} by Rule L10 include *bread, evil,* etc. All lexical units generated from the same grammatical unit by the same lexical rule are said to belong to a single lexical class, namely, that designated by the grammatical unit; thus, N_{inan} not only designates a grammatical unit but also a **lexical class.**

By virtue of being generated from a particular grammatical unit, a lexical unit is said to have the **valence** of that unit, which is to say that it has the grammatical properties of that unit. Thus, *bread* has the valence of an inanimate mass noun. A lexical item may have multiple valences if it belongs to more than one lexical class: for example, *forgive* has the multiple valences V_{trans_2} and $V_{trans_{und}}$ which account for its appearance in *forgive us our debts* (V_{trans_2}) and *forgive our debtors* ($V_{trans_{und}}$), respectively. Differences of meaning generally attend such differences in valence. But lexical items belonging to different lexical classes may still share a valence if they go back to the same grammatical unit in their generative "histories." For example, *father* and *I* both have the valence of nominals, although they belong to different immediate lexical classes, since both are generated indirectly from Nom. Since the individual lexical units within a lexical class have by definition the same valence, the choice of one rather than another has no effect on the grammatical structure of a sentence; in contrast, the choice of one grammatical unit rather than another changes, by definition, the grammatical structure. Thus, *He is our father* and *He is our debtor* have the same grammatical structure, since *father* and *debtor* belong to the same lexical class; but *He is our father* and *He hallows our father* have different grammatical structures, since *is* and *hallows* are generated from different grammatical units (*be* and V_{trans_1}, respectively).

Before proceeding to the transformation rules of ENE, let us see how application of the rules we have presented so far will generate one of the kernel structures that underlie the Lord's Prayer.

Starting with Rule 1 we generate a prayer (D_{prayer}) as the particular discourse (D) we want. From Rule 2 we generate a sequence of sentences ($S^1 + S^2 + \ldots$) followed by Amen. Now we will apply Rule 3 as many times as is necessary to generate the various subject+predicate (Subj+Pred) structures that underlie the resultant sentences of the discourse. We can diagram what we have done so far as follows:

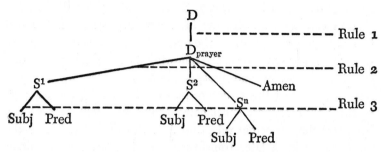

Now, continuing the generation of one of the constituent sentences, we apply Rule 4 to generate a nominal (Nom) from the subject (Subj); apply Rule 5 to generate a determiner (Det) plus a noun (Noun) from the nominal; apply Rule 7 to generate a nominal plus genitive for determiner; apply Rule 5 again to give us a name (Name) for this new nominal; and apply Rule 6 to generate a pronoun ($Name_{pron}$) for the name. This series of steps can be diagrammed:

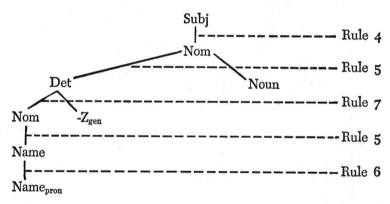

From Noun we can generate a count noun (N_{count}) by Rule 8 and then an inanimate noun (N_{inan}) by Rule 9. At this point we may shift to the lexical rules to select *thou* for our $Name_{pron}$ and *kingdom* for our N_{inan}. This long series of steps yields for S the sequence $thou + -Z_{gen} + kingdom + Pred$.

You can see that describing the generation of even a simple sequence as this requires a large amount of space, if each step is spelled out in words. However, the use of diagrams allows us to present the same information in rather succinct form. We will therefore present the rest of the derivation of the kernel structure underlying this sentence in the following diagram. Remember that the transformation and morphographemic rules which come later will convert this structure into the form actually occurring in the Lord's Prayer: specifically, *thou*+-Z_{gen} will become *thy* by a morphographemic rule, and Aux will be deleted from the verb phrase by a later transformation rule. The final resultant sentence will then be: *Thy kingdom come.*

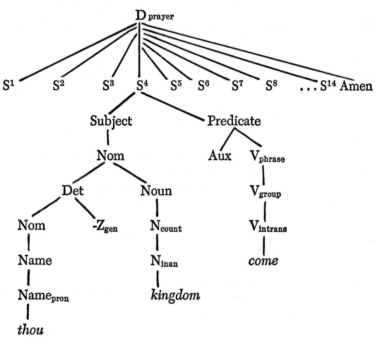

The following fourteen kernel structures need to be generated as the basis of the resultant sentences in the Lord's Prayer. The numbers of the immediate-constituent rules needed for the generation of those structures are indicated in parentheses.

As an exercise, construct diagrams like the one above for a few of these structures.

Lord's Prayer

Sentence 1: a. Our father+Pred (1–6, L12)

          b. thou art in heaven (1–6, 10–16, L11, L14, L12)

          c. Subj+Aux+hallow thy name (1–3, 10, 13, 18, 19, 5–9, L17, L11, L8)

Sentence 2: thy kingdom+Aux+come (1–10, 13, 18, L11, L8, L19)

Sentence 3: a. Subj+Aux+do thy will+in earth (1–3, 5–9, 10, 13, 18–20, L17, L11, L10, L14, L12)

          b. Subj+Aux+do thy will+in heaven (same as for a.)

Sentence 4: thou+Aux+give us our daily bread+this day (1–6, 10, 13, 18, 19, 5–9, L11, L20, L1, L10, L5, L9)

Sentence 5: a. thou+Aux+forgive us our debts (1–6, 10, 13, 18, 19, 16, 5–9, L11, L20, L8)

          b. we+forgive+our debtors (1–6, 10–13, 18–20, 7, 8, L11, L17, L7)

Sentence 6: a. thou+Aux+lead us+into temptation (1–6, 10, 13, 18–21, 8, 9, L11, L16, L13, L10)

          b. thou+Aux+deliver us+from evil (same as for a.)

Sentence 7: a. thine is the kingdom forever (1–14, 17, L11, L5, L8, L4)

          b. thine is the power forever (1–14, 17, L5, L11, L10, L4)

          c. thine is the glory forever (same as for b.)

TRANSFORMATION RULES

From the rules we have presented so far, actually none of the sentences in the Lord's Prayer can be generated in all their complexity. What is needed is a set of rules that will combine, rearrange, subtract from, and otherwise modify the basic sentences generated from the constituent-structure rules, that is, a set of **transformation rules**.

Transformation rules are of two kinds: those which take one already generated, single sentence and transform it into a new sentence, and those which combine two sentences to form one new one. We will call them respectively **single-base** and **double-base** rules. All but one of the transformation rules we consider here are optional; in a more exhaustive grammar we would also have to consider more transformations that are obligatory.

Single-Base Transformations

In the following formulas the structure of the **source** sentence is indicated on the left side of ⟹ (which can be read "is transformed into") and the **transform** is indicated on the right side. Those parts of the structure that remain unaffected by the transformation are indicated by the general symbols W, X, or Y.

Rule T1 (Subjunctive): $X + Aux + V_{phrase} + Y \Rightarrow X + V_{phrase} + Y$

This transformation forms what may be called "subjunctive" sentences from the "indicative" sentences—to use traditional terms—which the constituent-structure rules generate. The process is simple: merely drop out the Aux constituent of the source sentence. In LNE the corresponding transformation is restricted to source sentences whose subject is *you*, but in ENE the rule applies for any subject. Thus, in ENE, the transform sentence *Thy kingdom come* is possible with *thy kingdom* as subject of the source sentence; in LNE such sentences exist only as frozen vestiges of the ENE system. The fact that in many cases—the Lord's Prayer is an outstanding example—whole sentences or even sections of the King James version of the Bible have been memorized intact by so many LNE speakers may obscure this difference. To demonstrate to yourself that the difference does exist, try transforming a LNE sentence such as *Your train has arrived* into **Your train arrive*. You will notice either that the transform seems wholly ungrammatical to you, or that it is incongruously (and probably humorously) archaic; that is, it has been formed by what is recognizably an ENE rule.

In the Lord's Prayer T1 has been applied in the following cases:

1) Nom + Aux + hallow + thy name $\Rightarrow$ Nom + hallow + thy name
2) thy kingdom + Aux + come $\Rightarrow$ thy kingdom + come
3) Nom + Aux + do + thy will + X $\Rightarrow$ Nom + do + thy will + X
4) thou + Aux + give + our daily bread $\Rightarrow$ thou + give + our daily bread
5) thou + Aux + forgive us our debts $\Rightarrow$ thou + forgive us our debts
6) thou + Aux + lead us + X $\Rightarrow$ thou + lead us + X
7) thou + Aux + deliver us + X $\Rightarrow$ thou + deliver us + X

T2 (*Thou* ellipsis): thou + V_{phrase} + X $\Rightarrow$ V_{phrase} + X

This transformation eliminates *thou* if a V_{phrase} immediately (that is, with no intervening Aux) follows—a condition that exists after the application of T1. Thus, T2 takes the transforms above that result from T1, and further transforms them.

1) thou+give us our daily bread$\Rightarrow$give us our daily bread
2) thou+forgive us our debts$\Rightarrow$forgive us our debts
3) thou+lead us+X$\Rightarrow$lead us+X
4) thou+deliver us+X$\Rightarrow$deliver us+X

T3 (Passive): $Nom^1 + (Aux) + V_{trans} + Nom^2 + \text{-M} + X \Rightarrow$
$Nom^2 + (Aux) + be + Comp\ [\text{-}D_{part} + V_{trans}] + by + Nom^1 + \text{-M} + X$

This important rule forms a passive sentence out of an active sentence with a transitive verb, by interchanging the subject and the object of the verb, introducing *be* plus a new kind of complement composed of the "past participle" of the verb, and placing *by*[7] before the former subject. It is interesting to note that in ENE the passive transformation did not apply to progressive constructions (e.g., there was no transform *Our daily bread is being given us* from *X is giving us our daily bread*); this fact is accounted for in this grammar by including *be+-ing* in the V_{phrase} (see Rules 13 and 14) rather than in the Aux (see Rule 11). For LNE *be+-ing* has become part of the Aux.

---

[7] In ENE, *of* could also be used as an alternative agential preposition.

In the Lord's Prayer T3 is applied twice, in both cases to sentences already transformed by T1:

1) X + hallow + thy name + M $\Rightarrow$ thy name + be + -D_{part} +

Nom^1 + V_{trans_1} + Nom^2 + M $\Rightarrow$ Nom^2 + be + -D_{part} +

hallow + by + X + -M

V_{trans} + by + Nom^1 + -M

2) X + do + thy will + -M $\Rightarrow$ thy will + be + -D_{part} +

Nom^1 + V_{trans} + Nom^2 + -M $\Rightarrow$ Nom^2 + be + -D_{part} +

do + by + X + -M

V_{trans} + by + Nom^1 + -M

T4 (*By* ellipsis): $X + by + Nom + -M + Y \Rightarrow X + Y$

This transformation makes possible the elimination of the "agentive" construction $(by + Nom + -M)$ from the transform sentences resulting from T3. T4 is a useful stylistic device in English to apply in those instances in which the writer or speaker does not want to specify the doer of an action, but does want to specify the action and its object. In both of the instances above to which T3 has been applied, T4 has also been applied.

1) thy name be + -D_{part} + hallow + by + X $\Rightarrow$ thy name be + -D_{part} + hallow

2) thy will be + -D_{part} + do + by + X $\Rightarrow$ thy will be + -D_{part} + do

T5 (negative): a) $X + Mod + Y \Rightarrow X + Mod + not + Y$
b) $X + have + Y \Rightarrow X + have + not + Y$
c) $X + be + Y \Rightarrow X + be + not + Y$
d) $X + V_{group} + Y \Rightarrow X + V_{group} + not + Y$

This rule consists of four parts, each to apply only if none of the previous ones applies. It says, in effect, that a negative sentence may be formed by placing *not* after Mod, *have*, or *be* if they appear in the source sentence, but after the whole verb group (which, remember, may include Obj; see Rule 18) if one of these does not appear. Thus we would have in ENE:

T5a) you can lead us ⇒ you can not lead us
T5b) you have led us ⇒ you have not led us
T5b) you have courage ⇒ you have not courage
T5c) you are courageous ⇒ you are not courageous
T5d) you lead into temptation us ⇒ you lead into temptation
       us not

In the Lord's Prayer, we get by T5d: lead + into temptation
+ us ⇒ lead + into temptation + us + not. In LNE, T5d is eliminated and instead a rule is applied which automatically
attaches *not* (as well as Tense) to a form *do* that appears in questions and emphatic sentences (*Do you lead us?* and *You DO
lead us*) as well as negative ones (*You do not lead us*). In ENE
texts these negative constructions with *do* also appear, but the
negative transform without *do* is more typical.

T6 (Genitive nominalizer):

$$X + Nom^1 + \text{-}Z_{gen} + Nom^2 + Y \Rightarrow X + Nom^1 + \text{-}Z_{gen} + Y$$

This transformation allows a genitive form of a nominal to
"take the place of" the whole larger nominal of which it is a
part in the source sentence. That is, we can have *Shakespeare's
are the best* instead of *Shakespeare's plays are the best, I like hers*
instead of *I like her face*, and, for the Lord's Prayer, *Thine is the
kingdom forever* instead of *Thy kingdom is the kingdom forever*.
A morphographemic rule (see M1, p. 271) takes care of the
difference in form between *her* and *hers, thy* and *thine* in such
examples.

T7 (Object transposition):

a) $X + Obj\ [Nom \neq Name_{pron}] + Tm \Rightarrow X + Tm + Obj + Y$
                           Loc   Loc
b) $X + Dir + Obj + (not) + Y \Rightarrow X + Obj + (not) + Dir + Y$

Rule T7a reverses the order between an object and a following
expression of time or of location. It operates in the Lord's
Prayer to transform *X + our daily bread + this day + Y* into *X +
this day + our daily bread + Y*. Notice that the rule cannot be

applied if the object is a pronoun; that is, we could not have
Give this day us our daily bread or *Give this day it*. The
transformation seems to have the stylistic effect of giving the
expression of time or location a closer tie to the verb itself.

Rule 7b is the only obligatory transformation rule in this grammatical sketch. It is provided to move the directional expressions
generated by Rule 20 into position after objects and the negative
not, providing the proper order of words in *lead us not into
temptation*.

T8 (Emphatic transposition):

$$\text{Subj} + X + \text{be} + \text{Comp} \Rightarrow \text{Comp} + X + \text{be} + \text{Subj}$$

By this rule the subject and complement may be reversed for
purposes of emphasis. For example, *The kingdom is thine* becomes by this transformation *Thine is the kingdom; He was a
coward* may be transformed into *A coward was he; I am cold*
into *Cold am I; Thou art in heaven* into *In heaven art thou*. In
LNE such transforms are unusual and have a distinctly archaic
and literary flavor, and the rule which generates them belongs
to a special set of rules—a special grammar, so to speak, for the
generation of literary devices. Another such rule has already
been referred to: that which converts inanimate nouns into
animate ones, thus allowing *posts* or *automobiles* in fairy tales
and in metaphorical speech to *cower* in the wind or to *stare* at
the people passing by.

Double-Base Transformations

The single-base transformations we have considered take
single source sentences and form them into new sentences. Now
we shall see how another set of transformations takes two or
more source sentences and combines them to form new structures. In stating the formulas for these double-base transformations, we will join the two source sentences together by a pair
of braces { }, placing on top that source sentence (called the
matrix sentence) which provides a constituent structure for the

resultant transform. That is, the new sentence will have the same constitutent structure as the matrix sentence, with any new parts assigned to the constituent which they replace in the matrix. For example, in TT1 below, the sequence Name$_{prop}$, S replaces S, and is thus itself an S; in other words, if a vocative is appended to a sentence, the whole resultant sequence is itself a sentence.

The formulas for these, as well as for many of the other rules in this chapter, are far from being as refined and as general as they will eventually have to be. A certain crudity and *ad hoc* quality is bound to characterize grammatical statements focused, as these are, on the explanation of a particular text rather than a whole language. Linguists will have to improve on these formulas in the future: linguistics continues to be interesting largely because there is so much room for improvement in the description of all existing grammars.

To account for the first part—*Our father, which art in heaven* —of the first sentence of the Lord's Prayer, three double-base transformations are needed. We number them here in the order in which they must be applied to yield the resultant sentence that we want.

$$\text{TT1 (Vocative):} \quad \left\{ \begin{array}{c} S \\ X + \text{Name}_{prop} + Y \end{array} \right\} \Rightarrow \text{Name}_{prop}, S$$

This rule states that a new sentence may be formed by adding a proper noun to any sentence (no matter from what derivational source, as indicated by the use of X and Y here), separating the two constituents by a comma (in speech, by an intonation terminal). The proper name serves as a "vocative," designating the person or thing being directly addressed. Examples like, *Ed, this is my birthday* or *Chicago, why can't you grow up?* or *Mr. Wilson, please move over!* show that the rule still applies in LNE. For the Lord's Prayer, the transformation yields *Our Father, hallowed be thy name.*

$$\text{TT2 (Apposition):} \left\{ \begin{array}{c} X + \text{Nom}^1 + Y \\ \text{Nom}^2 + \text{Aux} + \text{be} + \text{Nom}^1 \end{array} \right\} \Rightarrow X + \text{Nom}^1, \text{Nom}^2, + Y$$

This formula presents a rule by which nominals "in apposition" can be generated; nominals which "refer to the same thing" (as traditional grammars put it) can appear in sequence, with the second nominal separated from the rest of the sentence by commas (intonation terminals in speech). The semantic property of "referring to the same thing" is replaced here by the grammatical property of appearing on two sides of an "equational" sentence; that is, the two nominals involved must appear as subject and complement of *be* in a source sentence. For the Lord's Prayer, the Nom[1] involved here is *Our Father* and the equational sentence that acts as source is *Thou art our Father.* The resultant transform, then, would be *Our Father, thou, hallowed be thy name.*

$$\text{TT3 (Relative clause)}: \begin{Bmatrix} X+\text{Nom}^1+Y \\ \text{Nom}^1+\text{Pred} \end{Bmatrix} \Rightarrow X+\text{Nom}^1+\text{which Pred}+Y$$

This formula accounts for many of the "relative clauses" (a term from traditional grammar) of ENE in a somewhat oversimplified way. Actually, as in LNE, there are various other types of relative clauses in ENE, but to account for them here would lead us too far afield. An important thing to note here is that it was still possible in ENE to use *which* in relative clauses referring to persons; *who* came to replace the earlier *which* in such cases, and eighteenth-century grammarians who argued for preserving the "traditional" distinction between *who* and *which* were guilty of a misunderstanding of the historical facts.

What the formula says in effect is that a nominal in the matrix sentence may be expanded by inserting after it *which,* followed by the predicate from a second sentence of which the nominal concerned is the subject. For example, from the matrix sentence *I live in the city,* and the sentence—with *the city* as subject—*The city is beautiful at night,* the transform *I live in the city which is beautiful at night* is generated, with the predicate *is beautiful at night* attached to *the city* by *which.* For the Lord's Prayer, the matrix sentence is *Our Father, thou, hallowed be thy name* (a resultant transform generated by TT2); the second source sentence is *Thou art in heaven,* with *thou* as subject; and the resultant transform is *Our Father, thou which art in heaven, hallowed be thy name.*

Now another single-base transformation is required to delete the pronoun *thou*, to yield the sentence which actually occurs in the Lord's Prayer:

T9 (Pronoun deletion): $X + Nom + Name_{pron} + which + Y \Rightarrow$
$X + Nom + which + Y$

Rule TT4 (Sentence conjunction): $\left. \begin{array}{c} S^1 \\ S^2 \end{array} \right\} \Rightarrow S^1, Conj + S^2$

Rule TT4 combines sentences by means of conjunctions to form a new sentence. By repeating the rule again, using these new sentences, still larger sentences can be generated.

The formula introduces a new symbol, Conj (conjunction), and thus implies a new grammatical and lexical class. In the Lord's Prayer, the representatives of that class are *as, and, but,* and *for.* This class is a peculiar one, not only in that it is generated in a transformation rule rather than in a constituent-structure rule, but also in that each of its members must be individually mentioned in later special rules; that is, each conjunction is itself a small grammatical unit.

At this point, we must introduce a new set of single-base transformation rules which will make certain modifications and deletions of parts of the "conjoined" sentences generated by Rule TT4. For example, we need a rule that will transform the sequence *Thy will be done in earth, as thy will is done in heaven* (from TT4) into *Thy will be done in earth, as it is in heaven.* To state these rules we might use more formulas, but we would find that we can put the rules more clearly without the use of formulas. The rules all involve modifications made for conjoined sentences whose corresponding parts are identical.

T10 (Subject and object pronominalization): If conjoined sentences have identical expressions either as subject (Subj) or object (Obj), the second expression may be replaced by a pronoun.

Example: *thy will* be done in earth *as thy will* is done in
　　　　　 Subj　　　　　　　　　　 Conj　Subj
heaven ⇒ thy will be done in earth as it is done in heaven.

T11 (Subject deletion): If sentences conjoined by *and, but,*
　　or *or* have identical expressions as subject, the second sub-
　　ject may be deleted.
Example: *thine* is the kingdom forever *and thine* is the power
　　　　　 Subj　　　　　　　　　　　 Conj　Subj
forever *and thine* is the glory forever ⇒ thine is the kingdom
　　 Conj　Subj
forever and is the power forever and is the glory forever.

The particular pronoun chosen in these "pronominalizations"
depends on what the subject is: *he* replaces a singular masculine
noun, *she* a singular feminine noun, *we* a nominal plus *I*, etc.
The rule covering such pronominals is rather complicated, and
will not be discussed further here.

T12 (Complement deletion): If conjoined sentences have
　　identical complements (Comp), the second complement
　　may be deleted.
Example: thy will be *done* in earth *as* it is *done* in heaven
　　　　　　　　 Comp　　　　 Conj　 Comp
⇒ thy will be done in earth as it is in heaven.

T13 (Deletion of auxiliary plus *be*): If conjoined sentences
　　have identical auxiliaries plus *be*, the second occurrence
　　of that sequence may be deleted.
Example: thine *is* the kingdom forever *and is* the power
　　　　　 Aux+be　　　　　　　　　 Conj　Aux+be
forever and the glory forever ⇒ thine is the kingdom forever
and the power forever and the glory forever.

T14 (Deletion of "adverbial" expressions): If conjoined sen-
　　tences have identical repeated expressions of time (Tm),
　　place (Loc), or direction (Dir), either of the repetitions
　　may be deleted.

Example: thine is the kingdom *forever and* the power *forever*
                         Tm Conj   Tm
and the glory *forever* $\Rightarrow$ thine is the kingdom and the power
Conj   Tm
and the glory forever. (The rule would also permit the deletion
of the third *forever* here instead of one or both of the first two.)

MORPHOGRAPHEMIC RULES

In illustrating the previous rules we have often written many
of our examples in conventional English orthography. As we
have previously indicated, however, the terms of a grammatical
rule are abstract entities; we need a special set of rules to convert these sequences of abstract entities into the forms that
appear in writing or speech. We call these rules **morphographemic** for writing, **morphophonemic** for speech.

Because our purpose here is to indicate what a grammar
could be like rather than to present that grammar in its most
rigorous form, we will be content in this chapter with presenting
only a few morphographemic rules—those necessary to generate
the Lord's Prayer in its final form. Furthermore, we will omit
here a discussion of the rules that account for our writing the
lexical units in rules L1–L20 as we have written them; and we
will also not mention those rules by which the terminal punctuation, spacing between items, and typography (including
capitalization of letters) of the actual text are generated.

All of the following morphographemic rules are obligatory;
that is, if the conditions on the left side of the formula are
present in a sentence, the rule must be applied.

M1: a. thou + -Z_{gen} → *thine*
       b. *thine* + consonant → *thy*

The **genitive** (also sometimes called "possessive") form of
thou appears in the Lord's Prayer both as *thine* and *thy*. In OE
the form from which the *thine* is descended had been *þīn*. In
ME *thine* developed a special form *thy* (also spelled *þi* and *thi*)

that was used when a consonant followed, *thine* being maintained otherwise; e.g., *thy name*, but *thine eyes* and *it is thine*. In ENE, some writers (including the King James translators) followed the same practice, while others used *thy* whenever a noun followed in the same nominal, with *thine* employed otherwise, in what we call "absolute" constructions: thus, *thy name* and *thy eyes*, but *it is thine*. A similar development explains the forms *mine* and *my* from OE *mīn*. Note that in LNE we have *my* if a noun follows in the same nominal but *mine* otherwise. We have a vestigial trace of the earlier rule to preserve *mine* before a noun beginning in a vowel in the archaic *Mine eyes have seen the glory of the coming of the Lord*.

Other pronouns developed special "absolute" forms (which are generated by T6; see p. 265) on the analogy of the genitive forms of nouns which ended in -*s*. Thus *hers, ours, yours, theirs* came to be used as the absolute forms of *her, our, your*, and *their*. *His* was already provided with an -*s*, and *its*—when it appeared at the end of the sixteenth century to replace *his* as the genitive form of *it*—developed an -*s* ending for the non-absolute as well as absolute form.

M2: *we* + -Z_{gen} → *our*

M3: Subj [thou] + -Z_{pres} + be → Subj + *art*
If the subject is *thou*, the present tense form of be is *art*.

M4: Subj [Noun] + -Z_{pres} + be → Subj + *is*
      [he]
      [she]
      [it]
If the subject is a singular noun, or one of the pronouns *he, she*, or *it*, the present tense form of *be* is *is*. It should be pointed out that certain nominalizations (see p. 246)—e.g., *to do justice, asking questions, parting*—are always grammatically singular; they may be thought of as substitutes for *it* in this rule.

Rules M3 and M4 provide special forms, *art* and *is*, for the combination -Z_{pres} + be—that is, present tense forms of *be*—after particular subjects. Similar rules would be required to yield the forms *am, are, was, were,* and *wert.* This special morphographemic complexity for *be* is the historical result of the fact that the ENE forms stem from three different earlier verbs. Forms of OE *bēon* were the ancestors of *be* (as well as *been* and *being*); OE *wesan* provided the forms that were to become ENE *was, were,* and *wert;* and a third set of anomalous forms, themselves inherited from proto-Indo-European—as evidenced by corresponding anomalies in the other Indo-European languages —provided the ancestors of *am, art, are,* and *is.*

M5: Subj [Noun + $-Z_{pl}$] + $-Z_{pres}$ + V_{group} → Subj + V_{group}
       [we]
       [ye]
       [they]
       [I]

This rule says in effect that if the subject is a plural nominal, the present tense will have no graphemically marked effect on an immediately following verb group; in more traditional terms, the plural, present-tense forms of verbs (not including *be*) are "uninflected." In the Lord's Prayer, *we* $+-Z_{pres}$ + *forgive our debtors* →*we forgive our debtors,* by this rule.

In a complete generative grammar of ENE we would need, of course, a morphographemic rule to provide also for the present-tense form of a verb whose subject is a singular noun or *thou, he, she,* or *it* (or a nominalization substituting for *it*). For the variety of ENE used in the King James Bible (a variety that was slightly archaic even in its own time), that rule would simply convert $-Z_{pres}$ in such cases into a morphographemic *-eth,* added to the verb. In other varieties of ENE (including that from which standard LNE developed) either *-eth* or *-es* might be used; e.g., in Shakespeare's dramas one finds both *loveth* and *loves, standeth* and *stands,* etc. Modals are uninflected in NE in the present tense, and a special rule is thus also required to make $-Z_{pres}$ + Mod → Mod.

In a complete grammar, we would need additional morphographemic rules to provide for converting $-D_{past}$ into graphemic forms. In NE, unlike OE, the morphographemic form of -D$_{past}$ does not depend on the number—singular or plural—of the subject. In addition to a rule providing for the so-called regular past-tense forms ending in *-ed* (e.g., *hallowed, delivered, loved*), special morphographemic rules would be required for the "irregular" past-tense forms of verbs (e.g., *came, did, gave, forgave, led*) and of modals (*should, would, could, might*).

M6: -D$_{part}$+do→*done*

Many special morphographemic rules like M6 would be necessary in a complete generative grammar of NE to account for the many "irregular" forms that occur. We should observe that an "irregular" form is not irregular in the sense that there is *no* rule that determines its formation—if that were true we might just as well have *°didded, °doned,* or even *°fifi* as the "past participle" form of *do*—but only in the sense that the rule is restricted to a small number (even one) of the members of a grammatical class.

In the design of a generative grammar, it is economical to have any special rules that apply to only a few members of a grammatical class listed *before* the general rule that applies to most other members of that class. It is then possible to state the general rule without giving exceptions, since the "exceptions" have already been taken care of by their own special rules. It is on the basis of this principle that M6, which forms only the past participle of *do*, precedes M7, which forms the past participle of the great majority of verbs in both ENE and LNE.

M7: -D$_{part}$+V → V+*-ed*

This rule, which provided for the form *hallowed* in the Lord's Prayer, is the rule for the "regular" formation of past participles of verbs in NE. Notice that past participles formed by this rule are graphemically identical with regular past-tense forms: *hallowed* (past participle) and *hallowed* (past tense), *delivered* (past participle) and *delivered* (past tense), etc. But the *grammatical* difference between the two that is felt intuitively by native speakers of English is accounted for in a generative grammar as a difference in their generative "histories," that is, a difference between the two sets of rules by which they are generated.

M8: $N_{count} + -Z_{pl} \rightarrow N_{count} + -s$

As it stands, this formula accounts for the form *debtors* in the Lord's Prayer as well as for the majority of plural forms for count nouns in ENE. However, it is inadequate to provide for plural forms like *men, mice, sheep, children,* or even like *kisses* or *fishes* (with *-es* rather than *-s*). A complete grammar of ENE would, of course, require rules that would provide for forms like these, but for our limited purpose here Rule M8 will suffice.

M9:

who		whom
they		them
he		him
I		me
thou	$+ -M \rightarrow$	thee
ye		you
she		her
we		us
Noun		Noun

We have now about finished our sample generative grammar of ENE. In several places we have suggested how some of the rules might be supplemented and modified in a fuller grammar, but it is in order here for us to indicate some of the major pieces still missing from the grammar.

In the first place, at a number of points in a complete grammar it would be important to specify the order in which the rules were to apply. Our sample grammar does suggest some such order by its numbering of rules—for example, Rule T2 does not apply unless T1 has previously been applied—but it does not adequately stipulate the necessary ordering of rules: for example, in an adequate grammar it would have to be stipulated that M3 must apply before TT3 in order for the sequence $thou + -Z_{pres} + be$ to be converted to Subj $+$ art, before *which* is inserted between *thou* and $-Z_{pres}$. If we failed to make that stipulation, we should have in the Lord's Prayer *Our Father, which is in heaven,* instead of *Our Father, which art in heaven.*

Our constituent-structure rules here generate many of the grammatical units that play a role in ENE grammar, but they do not generate many others that would be required for a complete grammar. For example, in a complete grammar Rule 3 would be expanded to include the possibility of a "sentence adverbial" (Adv$_s$), like *surely* or *in other words;* thus Rule 3: (Adv$_s$) + Subj + Pred. Similarly, Rules 18 and 19 would be expanded to include the possibility of expressions of "manner" (Man), such as *gradually* or *in a hurry* after transitive and certain intransitive verb groups. A new rule for generating "qualifiers," (Q) like *very* or *quite*, before adjectives should also be introduced. Even more numerous than the rules for introducing such addition of new elements into the grammar are the new rules for subdividing lexical units already generated in our sample grammar into more and more special classes. For example, it is apparent that within the N$_{an}$ class, subdivisions are necessary to account for the differences in pronominalization that are found in conjoined sentences; e.g., *father* is replaced by *he, mother* by *she, insect* by *it*. That is, our complete grammar must provide grammatical **gender**. Similarly, the V$_{trans}$ class must be divided into various subclasses —for example, to provide for the difference between those transitive verbs like *eat* and *finish*, which are subject to a transformation that would optionally delete the object of the verb (e.g., *He ate his bread quickly* and *He ate quickly, He has finished the book* and *He has finished* are all possible), and those transitive verbs like *devour* and *bring* which are not subject to such deletion of the object (e.g., *He devoured his bread quickly* but not *He devoured quickly, He has brought the book* but not *He has brought*).

In addition to the new lexical classes thus to be created by new grammatical units in the constituent-structure rules, there would have to be in a complete grammar an enormous additional number of lexical units generated by the grammatical units we have already listed in our sample grammar. The number of additional units required is different for each of the lexical classes (Mod is almost completely given in our sample, while N$_{inan}$ could be expanded by thousands of new units). A total listing of lexical units —that is, a complete lexicon of a language—would be a prodigious task, perhaps a task so large that we might never hope to complete it for any actual historical language. A traditional dictionary is, in large part, a lexicon of a language; but even our largest and best dictionaries, which may list half a million entries or so, do not present complete lexicons of any historical language. It must not be assumed from this that any speaker therefore necessarily employs a lexicon of more than half a million lexical units; many of the items in a large dictionary will be unknown to any given speaker, and many more of the items may be derived by additional grammatical rules from items already generated from other parts of the lexicon. But in any case, the lexicon that any normal adult speaker of a language uses will be large enough to enable him to say anything he wants to say.

We have just suggested that many of the items that a traditional dictionary lists as entries may be derived by grammatical rules from existing grammatical sequences. It is probably obvious that *Our Father,* which is generated in our sample grammar as a single lexical unit from $Name_{prop'}$, could alternatively have been generated as a transformation of the sequence $we + \text{-}Z_{gen} + father$ into a proper name. It is perhaps not so obvious that, for example, *gravedigger* may be generated from *X digs graves* by a transformation rule like:

$$TT_5 \text{ (Agentive nominal)}: \begin{cases} X + N_{count} + Y \\ W + V_{trans} + (Det) + Noun + \text{-}M \end{cases} \Rightarrow X + Noun + V_{trans} + \text{-}er + Y$$

That is, a new count noun can be formed of an object of a transitive verb plus *-er.*

Rules like TT_5 may productively form new units in English that play the same grammatical role—that is, have all the same valences—as lexical units generated by lexical rules. The new units, together with the lexical units, can be called the **words** of the language. Words, in this special sense (for another sense of "word," see pp. 326-327), are thus of two kinds: **simple** = generated by lexical rules, and **derived** = generated by transformation rules. A further useful distinction divides derived words into two classes: **compound**, in which a single lexical unit (in TT5 represented by N_{count}) is replaced by a word containing two or more lexical units (*grave* and *dig* in the transform *gravedigger*), and **derivative**, in which a lexical unit is replaced by a word containing a single lexical unit. An example of the latter is *womanish*, formed by a rule that might be formulated:

$$\text{TT6 (Adjective in -ish):} \begin{Bmatrix} X+\text{Adjec}+Y \\ W+\text{be}+\text{like}+(\text{Det})+\text{Noun} \end{Bmatrix} \Rightarrow$$
$$X+\text{Noun}+\text{-ish}+Y$$

(For the values of W, X, and Y, see p. 256.) Here a single lexical unit, *woman*, appears in the transform to replace a lexical unit represented by Adjec in the matrix sentence.

Transformation rules like TT5 and TT6, sometimes called **derivational** rules, are very numerous in ENE. Just how numerous they are is a matter of disagreement among linguists. The question hinges on our decisions about the economy of distributing the generation of words between lexical rules and transformation rules. For example, in our sample grammar L1 generates the word *daily*. But if we had thought it more economical to do so, we might have omitted *daily* from that rule and introduced a transformation rule which would derive *daily* from *day*, and, in general, an adjective ending in *-ly* from N_{inantm}. Such a rule could also be used to derive *weekly*, *monthly*, and *yearly*. However, with all the special limitations we should have to introduce into the grammar somewhere in order to prevent a consequent derivation of *°centurily*, *°minutely*, *°decadely*, which are all ungrammatical, we might well have a more economical grammar by simply generating the words that *are* grammatical by lexical rules. Thus, the question of how many derivational rules a grammar has, and consequently which of the words in the language are simple and which are derived, rests on technical considerations involving the economy of the grammar,

Some linguistic theorists have proposed that only those derivational rules should be included in the grammar proper which apply quite generally to the lexical classes they involve—not lexical classes to be set up *ad hoc* for the purpose of a particular derivational rule, but ones that exist in the grammar to account for other common features of their members. For example, in the case of *daily, weekly, monthly,* etc., but not in that of **centurily, *decadely,* etc., we could arbitrarily posit *day, week, month,* etc., as a special subclass of $N_{inan_{tm}}$, and that would allow us to make a derivational rule that was applicable to every member of that class; but since the members of such a subclass would have no other grammatical properties in common that would justify setting them apart from words like *century* and *decade,* that solution would have to be rejected.

It has been suggested that these derivational rules rejected from the grammar proper should be included in a special grammar— so to speak, a grammar of the lexicon—which *would* generate words like *centurily* and *decadely.* These words are available to users of a language, even though at any particular time they might be considered ungrammatical. In the past, many such words as *scientist* and *knowledgeable* have gone from this "available" status to an "acceptable" one, while others have gone the way of Shakespeare's *unpregnant* and *forgetive,* from an "acceptable" to an "available" status.

A striking characteristic of Elizabethan, and especially Shakespearean, literature is the great number of derivatives employed, derivatives that for our own time are available but not used: for example, *feverous* (Macbeth, Act II, Scene 3), *in the grapple* (Hamlet, Act 4, Scene 6), *so crimeful in nature* (Hamlet, Act 4, Scene 7). One should be cautious about assuming from this, as many scholars have done, that ENE employed derivation much more freely than LNE; an ENE speaker, struck by the number of derivatives used in LNE that were available but not used in ENE, might similarly make the mistake of concluding that LNE was a language that employed derivation without restraint.

In addition to derivational rules, many more transformation rules would be needed for a complete grammar of ENE. To mention only a few, our sample lacks transformation rules for forming questions of various kinds; rules providing for "post-nominal modifiers," as in *that man there, a heart unfortified, a breeder of sinners;* rules to adjust the order of grammatical elements in relation to one another and to introduce changes in order for various stylistic purposes; rules to provide for the conjunction of grammatical units other than whole sentences—e.g., *a dull and muddy-mettled rascal,* with conjunction of two adjectives; rules to provide "gerund" nominalizations, as in *for fear of opening my lips* (with the nominalization *opening my lips* transformed from $X+Aux+open\ my\ lips$) or "infinitive" nominalizations, as in *To be or not to be—that is the question;* and rules to provide for many kinds of elliptical expressions, including those that are so characteristic of conversational discourse—e.g., all the "incomplete sentences" in the following sequence from *Hamlet,* Act 1, Scene 2:

HAMLET: Hold you the watch tonight?

ALL: We do, my lord.

HAMLET: Arm'd, say you?

ALL: Arm'd, my lord.

HAMLET: From top to toe?

ALL: My lord, from head to foot.

HAMLET: Then saw you not his face?

HORATIO: O yes, my lord; he wore his beaver up.

HAMLET: What, look'd he frowningly?

HORATIO: A countenance more in sorrow than in anger.

HAMLET: Pale or red?

HORATIO: Nay, very pale.

HAMLET: And fix'd his eyes upon you?

HORATIO: Most constantly.

HAMLET: I would I had been there.

HORATIO: It would have much amaz'd you.

HAMLET: Very like, very like. Stay'd it long?

HORATIO: While one with moderate haste might tell a hundred.

BOTH: Longer, longer.

HORATIO: Not when I saw't.

HAMLET: His beard was grissl'd—no?
HORATIO: It was, as I have seen it in his life, a sable silver'd.
HAMLET: I will watch to-night; perchance 'twill walk again.
HORATIO: I warr'nt it will.

Finally, we have barely hinted at what some of the morpho-graphemic rules would be in a complete grammar. In order to develop those rules, we would want to introduce the concept of the **morpheme**: an element of the grammar which is directly converted by morphophonemic rules into a sequence of graphemes or phonemes; or to put it in another way, a linguistic unit which is concretely manifested in actual discourses. The manifestations of morphemes are called **morphs**, the morphs of any one morpheme being termed its **allomorphs**. *Heaven*, -Z$_{pl}$, and *be* are all morphemes. The morpheme *heaven* is manifested by the allomorphs *heaven* or *heav'n* (only in poetry) graphemically, corresponding to /hɛvən/ or /hɛvn/ phonemically. The morpheme -Z$_{pl}$ has a number of allomorphs: phonemically it has /əz/ after most morps ending in /s,z,ž,š,č,ǰ/, /s/ after most morphs ending in other voiceless phonemes (e.g., /dɛts/ *debts*), /z/ after most morphs ending in other voiced phonemes (e.g., détərz/*debtors*), /ən/ after the morph /aks/ *ox*, etc. The morpheme *be* has a variety of allomorphs, both graphemic and phonemic, in the forms *be*/bi/, *am* /æm/, *is* /ɪz/ *are* /ar/, etc.

The term **grammatical category** may be used broadly to refer to grammatical elements that do not have an immediate concrete manifestation in discourses; thus, the abstract elements SENTENCE, NOUN, TENSE, etc., are grammatical categories in this sense, since they must be converted into specific morphemes before they can be represented graphemically or phonemically. Contrast these with grammatical units like *by*, *be*, *-ing*, *-M*, or lexical units like *bread*, *give*, *daily*, all of which are immediately convertible into sequences of graphemes or phonemes.

As we have already indicated, the morphographemic rules in our sample grammar fail to indicate the spacing and terminal punctuation between items in the written discourse—for speech, this would correspond to a failure of morphophonemic rules to account for phonemic disjunctures. Such a failure is important in view of the fact that we would like to extend our use of the term **word** to include not only lexical units and their derivational equivalents, but also any sequence which appears in writing bounded by spaces or terminal punctuation (punctuation marks other than the apostrophe and hyphen)—for speech, any sequence which appears bounded by silence, disjunctures, or terminals. Assuming that such morphographemic and morphophonemic rules would be included in a complete grammar of ENE, and hence that we can speak meaningfully of *words* in that language, we can now define a number of terms that are useful in talking about the grammar of a language.

First, we may distinguish two kinds of words: those which contain—i.e., are generated from—lexical units we will call **lexical words;** all others we will call **grammatical words.**[8] For example, *debt, debts, debtor, debtors, tempt, tempted, temptation, this, have* (as a V_{mid} meaning "possess"), and *by* (as a P_{loc}) are all lexical words; *be, is, amen, have* (as part of Aux in Rule 11), and *by* (as part of the transform of Rule T3) are all grammatical words.

Next we may distinguish two kinds of components of lexical words: **roots** are the lexical units underlying lexical words, **affixes** are all the non-root morphs in lexical words. For example, the lexical word *debtors* has the root *debt* and the affixes *-or* and *-s; gravediggers* has the roots *grave* and *dig* and the affix *-s; unknown* has the root *know* and the affixes *un-* and *-n.*

We may distinguish affix morphs according to the relation of their positions to the root: a **prefix** is an affix that precedes the root—e.g., *un-* in *unknown, per-* in *perforce* and *peradventure,* or *over-* in *overgrown;* a **suffix** is an affix that follows the root— e.g., *-or* and *-s* in *debtors, -n* in *unknown, -ful* in *sinful.* It is conventional to cite affixes with a hyphen indicating the position of the root in respect to an affix. Since most morphemes have al-

---

[8] Compare Chapter IV, p. 145.

lomorphs of one kind—i.e., roots, prefixes, or suffixes—it is conventional to transfer this nomenclature to the morphemes themselves. Thus the morpheme $-Z_{pl}$ is itself called a suffix, because its main allomorphs are suffixes.

Compare the following singular and plural nouns:

Noun	Noun $+ -Z_{pl}$
1. cat	cats
2. ox	oxen
3. brother	brethren
4. mouse	mice
5. deer	deer

The word *cat* in the first example is a root morph. Now, in the word *cats* we clearly want to say that we are dealing with the same morph of the root *cat* plus an allomorph *-s* of the morpheme $-Z_{pl}$. In the word *oxen* we again have a root identical with *ox*, but now a different allomorph *-en* of the morpheme $-Z_{pl}$. In *brethren* we seem to have the same allomorph of $-Z_{pl}$ as in *oxen*, but a different root allomorph from that in *brother*. We can account for this difference by a morphographemic rule that gives *brother* the special allomorph *brethr* before $-Z_{pl}$. Notice that we can now conveniently account for the plural form *mice* by saying that it consists of a special allomorph *mice* of the root *mouse*, plus $-Z_{pl}$; but since $-Z_{pl}$ is not directly represented by a morph here, we may say that in *mice*, $-Z_{pl}$ has a **zero** allomorph. Finally, in the plural form *deer*, we may say again that $-Z_{pl}$ is present, but as a zero allomorph; the root *deer* happens not to have a special allomorph before $-Z_{pl}$.

Some affixes are generated by the constituent-structure rules: e.g., $-Z_{pl}$ by Rule 5, $-Z_{gen}$ by Rule 7, $-D_{part}$ by Rule 11, $-Z_{pres}$ and $-D_{past}$ by Rule 12, -ing by Rule 14, and -M by Rule 16. Such affixes are called **inflections** or **inflectional affixes**. In NE all inflectional affixes are suffixes; in OE the prefix *ge-* (see p. 235) was inflectional. It is interesting to note that in all Indo-European languages, as well as in many other languages, inflectional suffixes far outnumbered inflectional prefixes. As was remarked on pp. 234-

235, the number of different inflections has decreased greatly from OE to NE—so much so that some linguists have wanted to classify the two stages of English as belonging to two entirely different kinds of languages, OE being classified as an "inflectional language" and NE as an "analytical language." Such distinctions are not viewed today as so important or as so characteristic of languages as they were formerly, but you will still encounter the terms in numerous accounts of languages.

Other affixes are generated by transformation rules, particularly in derivational rules: e.g., *-er* in *gravedigger*, *-ish* in *womanish*, as well as *un-* and *-n* in *unknown* (the latter perhaps introduced by Rule T3). Such affixes may be called **derivations** or **derivational affixes.** The number of derivational affixes in ENE is probably very great—how great depends on whether we choose to consider words like *confess, profess, prevent, circumvent, duteous, reconcile, tyranny, euphony,* and many other words borrowed from Latin, French, and Greek, as simple lexical units or as derived words in English.

CONCLUSION

This recital of deficiencies in our sample grammar is far from complete, and yet it is sufficient to make one ask, "If such a grammar is so bad, why bother with it?" To justify, though not relieve, the frustration implied in this question, one must examine the kinds of historical grammars of our language that we already have. He will find in these grammars a great amount of interesting material —exact histories of particular words and groups of words, of particular sounds and groups of sounds, of particular grammatical features and groups of grammatical features. He will profit from such an examination, and may acquire enough fascinating information to satisfy his curiosity about the origins and development of his language. But if he wants a grammar that will provide a theoretically sound framework, a structural base for that grammatical description and explanation; if he wants to see wholes behind the parts, the forest as well as the trees, he must eventually confront a grammar of grammars, a systematic account of what it might mean to describe a language. This chapter falls short, far short, of providing such an account. But if it suggests the outline of how a grammatical description might be made explicit, it will have achieved its purpose.

SPECIAL NOTE

The same chart (p. 234) may be reinterpreted phonemically to suggest the steps by which the changes might have taken place:

OE		ME		ENE		LNE	Examples
/ih/	>	/iy/	>	/əy/	>	/ay/	*mine, I*
/uy/							*mice, fire*
/eh/	>	/ih/	>	/iy/	>		*we, teeth*
/æh/	>	/eh/	>	/ey/		/iy/	*clean, cheese*
/uh/	>	/uw/	>	/əw/	>	/aw/	*mouse, out*
/oh/	>	/uh/	>	/uw/	>	/uw/	*to, tooth*
/ah/	>	/oh/	>	/ow/	>	/ow/	*loaf, stone*
		/ah/	>	/eh/	>	/ey/	*name, lady*

This analysis depends on a formulation of English phonemes different from that presented in Chapter II. It derives from the basic work of George L. Trager and Henry L. Smith, Jr., *An Outline of English Structure* (Norman, Okla.: Battenburg Press; 1951), as extended by others to periods other than NE, e.g., Robert P. Stockwell, "The Middle English 'Long Close' and 'Long Open' Mid Vowels," *Texas Studies in Literature and Language,* II (1961), 529–38. The relevant differences between the Trager-Smith reformulation of vowels for NE and that presented in Chapter II can be tabulated as follows:

Chapter II		Reformulation
I	- - - - - - - - - - - -	i
i	- - - - - - - - - - - -	iy
ɛ	- - - - - - - - - - -	e
e	- - - - - - - - - - -	ey
ʊ	- - - - - - - - - - -	u
u	- - - - - - - - - - -	uw
ɔ	- - - - - - - - - - -	ɔh
o	- - - - - - - - - - -	ow

The Trager-Smith argument for analysis of the long narrow vowel as vowel plus /y/ or /w/, and of the long wide vowel as vowel plus /h/, lacks persuasiveness for specific single dialects of English, but for certain comparisons of dialects, and for a coherent account of historical changes in the language, the Trager-Smith analysis offers several attractive features. Suffice it to point out that the separation of vowel from semi-vowel components permits a neat statement of the general shift of long vowels in the history of English:

/h/>/y/   after front vowels
/ h/>/w/   after back vowels
/ y/>/ y/
/w/>/w/

Before semi-vowels: low vowels>mid
mid vowels>high
high vowels>/ə/>/a/

Or diagrammatically:

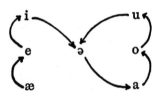

Such a formulation would claim that at each shift of a long-vowel nucleus—the part of a syllable that consists of a vowel with or without a following semi-vowel—only one of the constituents is changed. If the semi-vowel is /h/, it finally becomes /y/ (after front vowels) or /w/ (after back vowels.) If the semi-vowel is /y/ or /w/ it remains, and only the preceding vowel changes.

QUESTIONS

1. In what sense(s) of the term *grammar* are the following ungrammatical in NE:

    a)   George don't talk too good.
    b)   George doesn't talk many good.
    c)   George doesn't talk like he should.
    d)   George doesn't talk very shdenj.

2. What is the ancestry of the NE vowel /e/ (Trager-Smith /ey/; see Special Note above)? Choose ten or more words in which the vowel occurs in NE and look in a dictionary (the NED is useful for this purpose) for the etymologies of those words. Try to classify the kinds of sources from which the vowel has stemmed.

3. Which effects of the "Great Vowel Shift" probably account for the word "Great" in its name?

4. How does the notion of a grammar as a *theory* bear upon the notion of grammar as the pronouncement of authoritative grammarians?

5. Find or compose ten ambiguous English sentences, five of which are semantically, but not grammatically, ambiguous, and five of which are grammatically ambiguous. Can you find an example of a grammatically ambiguous but semantically unambiguous sentence?

6. a) Make a grammatical analysis of the fifth sentence of the King James version of the Lord's Prayer, using grammatical categories like those of Chapter IV rather than the generative framework of this chapter.

    b) Now make a grammatical analysis of the same sentence by stating the constituent-structure rules, the lexical rules, and the transformation rules by which it can be generated, as presented in this chapter.

    c) Evaluate the kinds of analysis, in respect to their relative comprehensibility, precision, usefulness, flexibility, etc.

7. Construct constituent-structure diagrams like the one on p. 260 for the kernel structures underlying Sentence 6 of the Lord's Prayer.

8. Restate Rule T7 in conventional grammatical terms. Discuss whether there is any economy in the symbolic formulation as compared to your restatement. Test two or three of the other rules in this chapter to see whether the symbolic formulation is more economical than the discursive formulation.

9. Search a short scene from a Shakespearean play or a short chapter from the King James version of the Bible for differences from the ordinary English of today. State what these differences are, using the terms and classificatory system of this chapter wherever helpful.

THE PROBLEM OF CORRECTNESS AND GOOD USAGE 1600–1850

The changes that took place in the writing and speaking of English between 1600 and 1850 were few compared to those of the preceding centuries. The general effect of old-fashionedness which the reading of a piece of eighteenth- or early nineteenth-century prose gives us today is primarily due to matters of style and rhetoric—that is, to the way the language was used—rather than to differences in phonology, grammar, or vocabulary—that is, to differences in the linguistic system itself. This is not of course to deny that changes in the latter, especially in the vocabulary, have occurred, but rather to affirm the underlying conservatism in the structure of the standard language during that period. Historical or diachronic linguistics, as such, is traditionally less concerned with such stylistic and rhetorical changes of fashion than with phonological, grammatical, and lexical changes, although the former cannot be completely separated from the latter.

The greatest change bearing on English which took place in these two centuries, however, is in the attitude of English speakers toward their own language. In 1582, Richard Mulcaster had written: "The English tongue was of small reach stretching no farther than this island of ours and not there overall." At the beginning of this period English was still a minor language in Europe; by the end it had become one of the major languages of the world. At the beginning of this period, it was not felt that English was a suitable language for all purposes, especially for scholarship and science;[1] by the end it was one of the few basic languages for international communication in trade, politics, science, and scholarship. In the seventeenth and eighteenth centuries, speakers of English were often apologetic about their language, and felt that it lacked importance, dignity, and standards; by 1850, this feeling had disappeared and speakers of English believed English was a proper language for all types of communication, had a great tradition, and existed in a "correct" form.

This change in attitude, which we now take so much for granted, will be the main subject of this chapter, although we will briefly discuss some of the other and more concrete changes first. The linguistic self-confidence of speakers of English vis-à-vis other languages is not shared by speakers of Dutch, Hungarian, and Finnish. Of course, native speakers of any language can be confident of their language within the sphere of its particular use, but the speakers of relatively few languages, such as English, French, Chinese, Spanish, German, or Russian,[2] can enjoy the confidence that theirs is a language of great international importance.

This extraordinary development in the destinies of English had nothing to do with the innate qualities of English itself, but rather with the political, cultural, and scientific success of English-speaking peoples. Of course, looking at English as an international

---

[1] For instance, Isaac Newton, who died in 1727, wrote all his scientific works in Latin.

[2] A relatively recent phenomenon, corresponding to the rise of Russia politically, culturally, and scientifically in the past fifty years.

language, we can stress its advantages for the adult learner, such as its paucity of inflections and its international vocabulary, but we must not overlook its disadvantages, the most notable of which is its difficult traditional spelling. However, it is doubtful whether on the whole English is easier to master as a foreign language, even ignoring its difficult spelling, than any other language. It is as complex and irregular in its ways as other languages are in theirs. A French or German speaker finds English easier to learn than Finnish, even with the latter's easy traditional spelling, but this is merely because English shares so many linguistic features with these languages. International linguistic respectability is not a measure of a language's innate qualities.

Before discussing the rise of English in the minds of its own speakers and of the world in general, we will devote a little space to the major formal and semantic changes in English since 1600. We will pay a little attention to changes in style preferences, but we will mainly consider these changes under various headings: orthography, punctuation, vocabulary, phonology, inflections, and syntax. The major changes have been in the first three groups. Some of these changes have already been discussed in the preceding chapter.

In orthography, the greatest change has been the establishment of standardized spellings of words. Until the eighteenth century there was considerable variation in spelling; English spelling in Shakespeare's time was not normalized as it is at present. This lack of standardization appears both in the number of particular spellings in ENE which have been replaced by others in LNE times, and in the variation of graphemic representation of words that we find in ENE itself. The great dictionaries of the eighteenth and early nineteenth centuries, together with an increasing desire on the part of printers and businessmen to have standard spelling, were important factors in accounting for our present sense that there is a "correct" spelling for every word. As we have noted previously, there had already been an increase of standardization in orthographical practice by 1600 tending to simplify the confusion of different ME spellings.

Older NE spelling used the allograph ſ frequently for the grapheme *s* except at the end of a word. The graphemes *u*, *v*, and *i* could each represent either a vowel or a consonant, depending on what the adjacent graphemes were. *-ick* or *-ique* rather than *-ic*, at the end of words like *logic* and *music* were usual spellings. Older (and still standard in British spelling) *-our* is now spelled *-or* at the end of words like *honor* and *color* in American English. *-ie* appeared at the end of words like *obscurity* or *antiquity*. More frequent doubling of consonants and gratuitous final *e*'s were common, as in *generall* and *olde*. Occasionally, older spellings show a single consonant where we now use two, as in *originaly* and *strictnes*. Some miscellaneous examples of other differences in spelling are *sence* for *sense, conceipt* for *concept, toung* for *tongue, spatious* for *spacious*. It must be remembered that these words may also be found in ENE texts in modern spelling form or in yet other variations. It was not felt necessary, as it is today, to spell a word always in the same way.

Punctuation conventions also varied from present practice. The apostrophe in the genitive case was not universally used, and we find many phrases like *in her Maiesties Courte*. On the other hand, the apostrophe was frequently used in the past participle of weak verbs, in forms like *call'd, lov'd,* and so forth. The roles of the colon and semicolon were rather fluid. Both spelling and punctuation differences give a slightly strange aspect to a printed page of an older book.

In vocabulary and idiom we find the greatest changes of all. These are of different sorts—some in the range of meanings of words, some in the degree of formality the words present, some in the frequency of use. Let us look at two passages of older literary prose, which will give us some examples of vocabulary change as well as of spelling and punctuation. The standard we use to discuss them is modern American literary English.

Nowe, as for my ſaucie preſſing vppon your expected fauor in crauing your iudgment, I beſeech you let me make thys excuſe: that whereas true Gentilitie did neuer withdrawe her louing affection from Lady Learning, so I am perſwaded, that your worshyppe cannot chuſe, but continue your wonted fauourable benignitie towardes all the indeuourers to learning, of which corporation I doo indeede profeſſe my ſelfe one ſillie member.

For ſith the wryters of all ages, haue ſought as an vndoubted Bulwarke and stedfaſt ſauegarde the patronage of Nobilitye (a ſhielde as ſure as can be to learning) wherein to ſhrowde and ſafelye place their ſeuerall inuentions : why should not I ſeeke ſome harbour for my poore trauell to reste and ſtaye vppon, beeing of it ſelfe vnable to ſhyft the carping cauilles and byting ſcornes of lewde controllers? (William Webbe, *A Discourse of English Poetry*, taken from the dedication to Edward Sulyard, written 1586).

First, note the spelling and punctuation, in the light of our discussion above. Now let us look at some of the words and expressions which have changed. In standard forms of English today, *saucie* is descriptive of a small child's impertinent behavior, not that of a serious, grown man; we would today say *presumptuous*. *Pressing uppon your expected fauor* would now be reworded into something like *hopeful appeal to your kindness*. The word *iudgment* here implies a *favorable* judgment, unlike its present broader meaning. The use of *beseech* here would be far too strong today. *Lady Learning* makes use of the rhetorical trope of personification of abstract nouns, which rarely appears in modern prose. The expression *your worshyppe* is far too obsequious for modern tastes. The word *usual* would replace *wonted* and the word *kindness, benignitie*. In this text, *sillie* means "poor" or "mere." The *corporation* of learning referred to would no longer make much sense to us. The word *sith* means "since." We would no longer use *inuentions* to speak of literary compositions. *Trauell* as "work" and *lewde* as "ignorant" are both archaic.

Let us look at a piece of prose from the middle of the eighteenth century, almost two hundred years later. This passage was written by Lord Chesterfield about Samuel Johnson's forthcoming Dictionary.

We have at present two very different orthographies, the PEDANTIC, and the POLITE: the one founded upon certain dry and crabbed rules of etymology and grammar, the other singly upon the justness and delicacy of the ear. I am thoroughly persuaded that Mr. Johnson will endeavour to establish the former; and I perfectly agree with him, provided it can be quietly brought about. Spelling, as well as music, is better performed by book than merely by the ear, which may be variously affected by the same sounds. I therefore most earnestly recommend to my fair countrywomen, and to their faithful or faithless servants, the fine gentlemen of this realm, to surrender, as well for their own private as for the public utility, all their natural rights and privileges of misspelling, which they have so long enjoyed, and so vigorously exerted.

Here the parallel form *the one . . . the other* is distinctly old-fashioned. *Based* would almost certainly replace *founded upon*. *Crabbed* would be peculiar today in describing *rules*. *Justness* would be replaced by *sensitivity* or some such word. *I am thoroughly persuaded* is today so very formal as to be almost unusable. *Practiced* would replace *exerted*. Some of the punctuation and the use of capitals strike us as old-fashioned. Yet all in all we may see from a comparison of these two passages that the second is much closer to present-day usage than the first.

Turning to the changes in sounds, let us take up some of the major developments. After the period of the Great Vowel Shift was over, the changes that were to take place in English phonology were few indeed. The exact dates of those that did occur are often not certain. Even the exact time of the Great Vowel Shift has not been definitely established, although we do know that it was still in progress well after the Modern Period had begun. Some of these phonological changes are early (1350–1550) and some late (1550–1700).

To mention changes in the consonants, initial /θ/ was replaced by /ð/ in a number of common words (all "pointing" words) like *the, they, that, this, there,* and so forth. Final /f/, /s/, and

/θ/ became voiced if preceded by an unaccented vowel. ME /hɪs/, for instance, became NE /hɪz/; /of/ became /əv/; the -/əs/ allomorph of the plural morpheme became -/əz/. ME *faces* /faːsəs/ became NE /fesəz/. The ME phone [x] generally disappeared in NE, but if it came after /ɪ/, the vowel was first lengthened to [iː], later to become /ay/. ME *right* [rixt]> NE /rayt/. In a few cases, [x] was replaced by [f] as in *enough*. The phoneme /l/ vanished before /k/, /m/, and /f/ if the preceding vowel was ME [a] or [ɔ]. ME *talk* [talk]>NE /tɔk/. The loss of the /l/ took place before Shakespeare's time. The phoneme /r/, phonetically a trilled resonant in ME and ENE, acquired its present NE allophones, and even disappeared in certain post-vocalic positions in some dialects. The ME and ENE accented pronunciation of -*tion* /sión/ gave way to the unaccented /šən/ in the seventeenth century: Shakespeare's *nation* /nesión/>LNE (Late Modern English) /néšən/.

Let us briefly mention the major vowel changes after the Great Vowel Shift. Accented final /é/ in ME French borrowings like *pity* /pité/ became /i/ as in /píti/. Accented ME /ɛː/ or /æː/ had become /eː/ by Shakespeare's time, and in most dialects (not Anglo-Irish, however) unlike the /eː/ from ME /aː/, which remained, usually later developed into /i/. Shakespeare's *clean* /klen/ became LNE /klin/. In some cases when followed by /d/, /t/, or /θ/, the vowel was shortened to /ɛ/ as ME *deed* /dæːd/>NE *dead* /dɛd/. The ENE /ú/<ME /ó/ in many words has the reflexes in LNE /ʊ/ or /ə/, except in the north of England and Scotland. This process still seems to be going on, as may be seen in the variant pronunciations of *roof* and *hoof* in LNE. ME /o/ apparently had two allophones: [ɒ] and [ɔ]. This variation is reflected in American NE, where we find for *horrible* either [hɒrəbl] or [hɔrəbl], or even [harəbl]. Words containing the ME diphthong /iu/ developed variants with /u/ instead. The diphthong /iu/ was retained after labial or labiodental consonants, as in *beauty* and *view*, but became /u/ after /r/. The variation may still be seen in the alternate pronunciations of *tune* as /tyun/ or /tun/. This diphthong /iu/,

accented on the first vowel in ME, shifted its accent to the second vowel /yú/, in initial position or after /h/ and /k/ in NE: compare ME *use* /íus/ with NE /yús/. Finally, it should be noted that since 1600 there have been numerous other changes in word accent, mainly those in which the accent in borrowed foreign words has moved from later syllables to the first syllable of those words.[3]

In morphology, it may be said that by the eighteenth century present-day habits as a whole prevailed in the standard dialect of English. However, we do find some developments since 1660 worth mentioning. For example, the form *ye* became increasingly archaic and *you*, originally *ye* + -M (the objective case), took its place. *Thou* and *thee* became limited to special uses, and *you* was used for both singular and plural. *Its*, perhaps created by analogy with *his*, replaced *his* or *it* as the genitive form of *it*. (In Shakespeare's plays *its* is not very often found.) A number of previously "strong verb" forms were replaced by weak ones: for example, *clomb* disappeared from standard English in favor of *climbed*. The eighteenth century saw the full development of the "progressive tenses," that is, constructions with *be* + -ing + verb groups (e.g., *was building*), but it was not until the end of that century or even later among some grammarians that the passive transformation of such constructions (e.g., *was being built*) found ready acceptance as standard English. The -s suffix in plural nouns was used pretty much as today, although in Shakespeare we still find an -n in occasional words like *shoon* for *shoes* or *eyne* for *eyes*.

We have already pointed to some of the syntactic differences

---

[3] The above changes can be studied in greater detail in Samuel Moore: *Historical Outlines of English Sounds and Inflections*. Revised by Albert H. Marckwardt (Ann Arbor: George Wahr Publishing Co.; 1951), 130 ff., to which the above account is indebted. For the pronunciation of English in the sixteenth and seventeenth centuries, see R. W. Zachrisson: *Pronunciation of English Vowels* (Göteborg: W. Zachrisson; 1913), Henry C. Wyld: *A History of Modern Colloquial English*. Third edition (Oxford: Basil Blackwell; 1936), Eric John Dobson: *English Pronunciation, 1500–1700*, 2 vols. (Oxford: Clarendon Press; 1957), Helge Kökeritz: *Shakespeare's Pronunciation* (New Haven: Yale University Press; 1953).

between older NE and present-day English in the two passages quoted above. A few further changes may be noted. Shakespeare or Ben Jonson could begin a question with a verb rather than only with an auxiliary as today. "Say you so?" "Looks my love well?" are constructions not used today. Phrases like "This my friend" for "This friend of mine," "If any chance to behold himself" for "If anyone chances to see himself," "the whilst" or "the while" for "while," "I am sure I am none such" for "I am sure I am not like that," "I did long to tell it you" for "I longed to tell it to you," "Why bring you him not up?" for "Why don't you bring him up?" (See Chapter VI, p. 265), "the King's son of England" for "the King of England's son'—all illustrate differences between English syntactic constructions of 1600 and American English ones of 1960. These examples illustrate, but obviously do not begin to exhaust, the kinds of syntactic differences in the English of the two periods.

As we said at the beginning of this chapter, important as all these changes in the structure and constitution of English are, an even more important development has been the change in attitude towards English which has developed during the modern period on the part of speakers of English.

Western civilization grew up under the shadow of the great prestige of Latin, and for many centuries Latin remained the sole respectable language of learned communication in the West. This inherited respect for Latin led at the outset to the depreciation of the popular spoken languages known as vernaculars. A different language from that spoken by the people generally served as the language of culture and learning in Western Europe. This situation led to a double standard. Latin was a noble and fixed language, so it was thought. The vernacular was merely useful. One did not have to worry much about the vernacular; it served ordinary purposes of communication. The fact that the vernaculars changed or displayed variations in forms, and existed in various dialects, was not, as far as we know, a matter that created concern among most people.

Taking a broad view of the history of the languages of Western Europe, we may say that what we see in the past thousand years is the gradual replacement of Latin by various vernaculars, and the corresponding rise in the prestige value of particular dialects of these vernaculars. Looking at the Western languages objectively, what we find is that those varieties or dialects of each language have developed prestige exactly to the extent that the *users* of those varieties or dialects have been looked up to by other users of these languages. Certain varieties are prestigeful, others are not, and which is prestigeful can vary according to historical circumstance. As one socially dominant class—the ruling class or cultural elite—is replaced by another, the dialect of the new dominant classes gradually becomes considered the desirable, the *standard* dialect. Other speakers who wish to rise socially ("upwardly mobile" as the sociologist calls them), or merely to do "what is right," imitate this dialect and favor its being taught to their children.

Latin came to the West in a relatively fixed form. With some changes, the Latin used by the great writers of the past, stabilized in grammars and rhetorics and taught in schools, was considered the language par excellence. It had written grammars and dictionaries which could be appealed to. The schoolmasters in the grammar schools—and by "grammar" was meant *Latin* grammar—had inculcated a notion of correctness in the use of language. Of course, medieval Latin had undergone changes and was not the same as classical Latin, but it was fairly close to it. And besides, medieval teachers of Latin were convinced that there was one precariously right way of using Latin and many slovenly wrong ways.[4]

This notion of correctness was at first not believed to apply

---

[4] Medieval Latin developed forms and usages of its own and became a language in its own right with a great and extensive literature. But it was considered by most of its users to be fundamentally the same as classical Latin, and notions of what was thought to be classical correctness were applied to it. Inasmuch as it was largely, though not exclusively, a written language, it tended to be more conservative than the vernaculars. The *Vulgate,* the translation of the Bible by St. Jerome into fourth-century Latin, exercised a great influence on its forms. For a good short introduction to medieval Latin, see Karl Strecker: *Introduction to Medieval Latin.* English translation and Revision by Robert B. Palmer (Berlin: Wiedmannsche Verlagsbuchhandlung; 1957).

strictly to the "degenerate" vernaculars; until authoritative grammars and dictionaries were written to lay down the laws, there were no laws, it was thought, that could be violated. By the late eighteenth century, this lack of "authority" was to be remedied for English. In general we may say that the period 1350 to 1650 saw the gradual acceptance of the London dialect of English as the "proper" one for vernacular speakers in England and even to some extent in Scotland, and the development of an elaborate vocabulary to deal with a multitude of subjects, some new and some old. The period 1650–1825 saw the development of English dictionaries and grammars which could be appealed to as the arbiters of correct usage. At the same time, as we have said, the prestige of English rose internationally, an accidental development in the sense that it was a by-product of the rise of English arts, commerce, and military power. By 1825, English had a prestigeful, "correct" form, which was stabilized more or less in dictionaries and grammars.

To account for the displacement of Latin and the rise of standard vernacular dialects would take us deep into social and cultural history. Here we can do no more than suggest a few possible reasons for this phenomenon.

The rise of nationalism in Europe is closely connected with the rise of the vernaculars. Large, autonomous, self-seeking units of political power became the accepted political organizations of Europe. The rise of national political independence favored the rise in prestige of national languages at the expense of a dominating international one.

Protestantism, with its emphasis on the accessibility of liturgy and Scripture to all, favored the vernaculars at the expense of Latin. This in turn influenced Catholic practices, not indeed to admit the vernacular into general use in the liturgy, but to produce vernacular versions of the Bible and a large number of religious classics in the vernacular.

The material rise of the townspeople and the peasant also favored the vernaculars. With more money and more leisure, but with little or no Latin, these people provided a market for serious or semi-serious written works in the vernacular. Orders of friars (such as the Franciscans) who used the vernacular in sermons and religious works to provide for these people were founded in the thirteenth century. The church as a whole increasingly took over this task.

Certain technological advances in printing and in means of communication, both for commerce and pleasure, made the use of the vernacular in written form more sensible and profitable. Both printing and the rise of commerce favored the vernacular over Latin, and they were also powerful forces for standardization of the vernacular.

The collapse of the landed aristocracy and the accompanying rise of a commercial and financial society stimulated the vernaculars. The bourgeois in the seventeenth and eighteenth centuries who felt unsure of himself socially wanted to be able to speak and write correctly as much as he wanted the other social graces. This desire was increasingly catered to in the eighteenth and nineteenth centuries by the large number of grammars which prescribed correct usage, often based on the particular prejudices of the writers rather than on the observation of standard practice. Almost to a man, the writers of these grammars favored the notion of one "correct" form, in the face of their numerous disagreements about what that one form was.

The emphasis on reason and order, in the seventeenth and eighteenth centuries, encouraged the desire for standards in vernacular usage. The idea that man was rational and that his speech reflected his reason became widespread. The applicability of universal grammar, in large part erroneously based on Latin grammar, was stressed throughout the eighteenth century. The notion of universal grammar goes back, however, to the Middle Ages. A normative concept of a fixed human nature was widely held, and language, as the true reflection of that nature, had also to be essentially fixed.

In England, the high reputation of the French Academy, founded in the mid-seventeenth century as a regulating body for good usage in the respected French language, stimulated many Englishmen to the hope that a similar academy could be established for English. Jonathan Swift provides a good example of how some early eighteenth-century writers felt about the subject. He thought English was badly corrupt and needed refining and fixing.[5] He writes in *The Tatler* for September 26–28, 1710: "I would engage to furnish you with a catalogue of English books, published within the compass of seven years past . . . wherein you shall not be able to find ten lines together of common grammar or common sense . . . These two evils, ignorance and want of taste, have produced a third; I mean the continual corruption of the English tongue, which without some timely remedy, will suffer more by the false refinements of twenty years past, than it hath been improved in the foregoing hundred." Swift tried hard to establish an English Academy to provide standards for English, a task briefly undertaken previously by the Royal Society (the English scientific society founded in 1660) before it concentrated exclusively on experimental science. Although many educated Englishmen would continue to favor the setting up of authoritative standards, the project for an academy was to fall through, and by the mid-eighteenth century the cause of a formal regulating body was regarded as hopeless, many even boasting that the English feeling for liberty would never allow the restrictions of an official academy. Dr. Johnson, in the Preface to his Dictionary in 1755, wrote "If an academy should be established . . . which I, who can never wish to see dependance multiply, hope the spirit of English liberty will hinder or destroy . . ."[6]

---

[5] For a recent study of Swift's attitude to English, see Annette P. Thorpe, "Jonathan Swift's Prescriptions Concerning the English Language," *CLA Journal* III (1959–60), 173–80. The quotation following is taken from George H. McKnight and Bert Emsley: *Modern English in the Making* (New York and London: D. Appleton-Century-Crofts, Inc.; 1928), 313–14.

[6] Quoted in Albert C. Baugh: *A History of the English Language*. Second edition (New York: Appleton-Century-Crofts Inc.; 1957), 325. This book in Chapter IX (pp. 306–55) gives a good introduction to the whole subject of the problem of linguistic authority in the eighteenth century. There were also attempts in America to set up an academy to regulate

Furthermore, changes in approved Latin style favored in an indirect way the rise of the vernaculars. The Renaissance humanists wanted to get back to the Latin of Cicero and Virgil and away from medieval and scholastic Latin, which was closer in syntax and vocabulary to the Romance vernaculars. They hated the medieval period so much that they extended their hatred to its form of Latin. They were obsessed with the idea of corruption and felt that the barbarous Middle Ages had corrupted the pure classical Latin—an idea that dies hard and is still current. The classical writers became the models in school. The result of this changed attitude towards Latin led to the introduction of a more difficult (for Western European speakers) Latin, and ultimately destroyed in large measure Latin as an international language.

However much classical Latin waned as the international language of science and learning, it strongly influenced English (and other Western languages) in vocabulary and syntax and above all, as we have said, as a model of a correct language which could be transferred in general to the vernaculars. It is probably true that if Latin had not served the function of the prestige language of Western Europe, varieties of the vernaculars might well have done so; prestigeful forms of language seem to be present in all societies. But because Latin was a foreign and completely incomprehensible language to those not versed in it, the prestigeful varieties of the vernacular languages which replaced it in Western Europe succeeded to the reverence which had formerly been paid to Latin learning.

The influence of Latin on the English vocabulary we will discuss briefly in Chapter VIII. Here, we may sum up its influence on English syntax in B. Trnka's words:

> This influence of Latin [on English in the early modern period] is to be seen on the one hand in the inclination to use the passive voice more frequently, the accusative and

---

the language; see Allen Walker Read, "American Projects for an Academy to Regulate Speech," *PMLA*, LI (1936), 1141–79.

infinitive construction [e.g., "I helped him *to complete the job*"], and the absolute participle constructions [e.g., "*The dawn having come,* he got up"], in a more precise use of the tenses, and in the imitation of Latin word order; and on the other hand it is to be traced in the growing tendency to limit the use of the nominative and infinitive construction, of the infinitive constructions, and of the use of the personal pronoun with the imperative, and so on.[7]

The whole subject of classical Latin influence on English syntax needs extensive investigation, but we may take Trnka's summarizing statement as a good brief presentation of at least its major influence on the syntax of the English verb.

The various forces listed above may be seen as the general causes of the displacement of Latin and of the corresponding rise of the vernaculars, until they attained complete victory as the proper medium of every kind of expression for their native speakers. This rise may also be seen in the increasing self-consciousness of those speakers about their native language. Apparently, it was not until 1125 that anyone raised questions in writing about the native language of Englishmen. In that year the English historian William of Malmesbury, in his *History of the Popes,* made the first comment we have preserved on the English language. In this comment we find a complaint about the corruption of English, which is attributed to both Danish and Norman influence, and a reference to the superior prestige of French. William also comments on the variety of pronunciations of English, in contrast to Anglo-Norman. He divides English into Southern, Midland, and Northern dialects; as a Southerner he was very prejudiced against the Northern dialect.[8] Besides

---

[7] *On the Syntax of the English Verb from Caxton to Dryden* (Travaux du Cercle Linguistique de Prague 3). (Prague; 1930), 11. For a more general treatment of the subject from a European point of view see Franz Blatt, "Latin Influence on European Syntax," *Classica et Mediaevalia* XVIII (1957), 133–78.

[8] Quoted in *The Critique of Pure English from Caxton to Smollett.* Collected by William A. Craigie (S.P.E. Tract No. LXV). (Oxford: Clarendon

complaints about English, about its corruption and even about
its fondness for monosyllables,[9] we also find national pride in the
language in the Middle Ages, especially in the fourteenth century
and later. Sometimes this defense of English took an apologetic
tone. A writer would justify his use of English by the fact that
he could be more widely understood. For instance, the author of
the Northern English Homily Cycle writes in justification of his
using English:

> And both clerk and layman
> Can understand English
> Who were born in England
> And long have been dwelling therein,
> But all men certainly cannot
> Understand Latin and French.
> Therefore methinks it is alms
> To work some good thing in English
> That both learned and lay may know.[1]

Other writers are unabashed about their use of English and
boast a little too loudly of it. The writer of the *Cursor Mundi*,
a long historical work written about 1300, stresses in his pro-

---

Press; 1946), 115. This pamphlet contains a number of valuable comments
on English by Englishmen down to the eighteenth century.

[9] Thomas Palmer, a Dominican friar, in arguing against the attempt to
translate the Bible into English as had been done in the late fourteenth
century by Wyclif and his followers, uses as one of his arguments that
English was too barbarous to convey the beauty, dignity, and subtleties of
Biblical Latin (as in the *Vulgate*). He says English is too monosyllabic and
lacks adequate figures of speech. His whole discussion is most interesting.
The Bible must be translated word for word or sentence by sentence, he
says, but deficiencies of English vocabulary make this impossible. English
is deficient in both letters and words. English sounds like the grunting of
pigs or the roaring of lions. Presumably his comment on the deficiency in
letters means that English sounds are different from those of Latin. He
also makes the point that English hardly observes grammatical rules, which
means that it did not observe Latin rules. The whole passage in the original
Latin is quoted in Margaret Deanesly's *The Lollard Bible* (Cambridge,
England: The Cambridge University Press; 1920), 418 ff.

[1] Quoted by Albert C. Baugh, *op. cit.,* 172 note.

logue that French is for Frenchmen but English is for English-men. Robert Holcot, a Dominican friar, some thirty or forty years later accused William the Conqueror of deliberately trying to destroy English spirit by destroying the English (Saxon, as he put it) language.

Throughout the fifteenth century, although by then the battle to use English for ordinary purposes was won, we find an increasing concern for the honor and glory of English. Around 1422 the London brewers begin a resolution advocating the use of English in their proceedings as follows: "Whereas our mother tongue, to wit, the English tongue, hath in modern days begun to be honorably enlarged and adorned; for that our most excellent lord King Henry the Fifth hath, in his letters missive, and divers affairs touching his own person, more willingly chosen to declare the secrets of his will [in it]. . . ."[2]

The first English printer, William Caxton, in his prefaces continually discusses the status of English, and the difficulties of translating foreign works into it (for many of the books he printed were translations). Typical is this comment, taken from part of the introduction to his *Eneydos,* a translation from the Old French. Speaking of his preliminary translation of a few leaves of the work, he writes:

And whan I sawe the fayr and straunge termes therein I doubted [suspected] that it sholde not please some gentylmen which late blamed me, saying that in my trans-lacyons I had over curyous termes which coulde not be vnderstande of comyn peple and desired me to vse olde and homely termes in my translacyons. And fayn wolde I satisfye every man and so to doo toke an olde booke and redde therin and certaynly the englysshe was so rude and brood [broad] that I coude not wele vnderstande it and also my lorde abbot of westmynster did do shewe to me late certayn euydences wryton in olde englysshe for to reduce it in to our englysshe now vsid. And certaynly it was wreton

---

2 *Ibid.,* 183.

in suche wyse that it was more lyke to dutche than englysshe;
I coude not reduce ne brynge it to be vnderstonden. And
certaynly our langage now vsed varyeth ferre from that
which was vsed and spoken whan I was borne. For we
englysshe men ben borne vnder the domynacyon of the mone,
whiche is never stedfaste but ever wauerynge wexynge
one season and waneth & dycresseth another season.

The sixteenth and seventeenth centuries produce a torrent of
comments on English, which reveal both its rapidly growing
status and the problems, especially those of vocabulary, which
then beset it. Nor does a certain defensiveness about writing in
English disappear. English nationalism under Elizabeth I and
James I reached a peak of enthusiasm which is reflected in these
comments on the language. Chaucer, Gower, and Lydgate, late
medieval writers who wrote in English, were esteemed as "orna-
ments of our tongue," as evidence that great writers could use the
vernacular, though not necessarily as models of the correct use
of that vernacular.

During the seventeenth and eighteenth centuries, the practical
problems of writing authoritative English grammars and dictionaries occupied the minds of many thoughtful writers. Sometimes their concerns with correctness reflect the provincial fears
of the Scottish and American writers, for some of them were
Scotsmen and even Americans. But in general the concern with
making English perfectly respectable was widespread among
users of the language.

Although Elizabethan critics and rhetoricians were agreed on
the dialect of English they could recommend, they did not provide any detailed guides for the writing and speaking of English.
Custom and usage were considered sufficient. George Puttenham,
in his *Art of Poesy* (1589), writes:

> Our maker [poet] therefore at these days shall not follow
> Piers Plowman, nor Gower, nor Lydgate, nor yet Chaucer,
> for their language is now out of use with us: neither shall
> he take the terms of Northern-men, such as they use in daily

talk, whether they be noblemen, or gentlemen, or their best clerks, all is a matter; nor in effect any speech used beyond the river of Trent. Though no man can deny but that theirs is the purer English-Saxon at this day, yet it is not so courtly nor so current as our *Southern English* is; no more is the far Western man's speech. Ye shall therefore take the usual speech of the Court, and that of London and the shires lying about London within sixty miles, and not much above.

Puttenham devotes only two slight chapters to errors in English as contrasted with, say, the emphasis modern books give to the subject.[3] In spite of his awareness of the "best" dialect of English, he did not think it worthwhile to dilate on errors in grammar. He would recommend a general model for writers, but he did not think it necessary to go beyond that.

The Elizabethan or Stuart speaker or writer, unlike the modern one, found few statements of rules or prescriptions about his own language, nor did he apparently desire them. Although there are English grammars written before 1660, it was not until the period after the Restoration that correctness became a widespread concern and linguistic authorities were sought. It is not to be supposed that the Elizabethan was not aware of his language and its status, or that prestige was not attached to certain forms of the language. But the matter did not in his view deserve the passionate concern it was to get in later centuries, nor did he consider it necessary to raise the kind of questions which needed to be answered by language authorities. It is probable that in any period certain forms of a language are considered more worthy of imitation, more prestigeful, more correct than others. But a systematized doctrine of correctness, which grammars and dictionaries provided, did not come into existence until the eighteenth century.[4] From this doctrine of correctness stems traditional prescriptive grammar.

---

[3] Pointed out by Gladys D. Willcock, in "Shakespeare and Elizabethan English," *Shakespeare Survey* 7 (1954), 22.

[4] Studied by Sterling A. Leonard: *"The Doctrine of Correctness" in English Usage 1700-1800,* University of Wisconsin Studies in Language

In this chapter we shall be interested in coming to an understanding of what is meant by "correctness" in usage, and to an appreciation of its significance for the present day. To achieve this purpose we have made and will continue to make reference to the history of the concept for whatever insights that history affords us into its present meaning. It is not, however, our aim to present here anything like an exhaustive account of the history of the doctrine of correctness, together with the necessary documentation from grammatical and lexical treatises and compilations; that work has already been largely done for us.[5]

In the preceding chapter we discussed some of the various meanings of the word *grammar*. In this chapter we are concerned specifically with the prescriptive grammar of English, the grammar that states what *standard* English is. The linguistic scientist who undertakes to write a prescriptive grammar—and we must disagree with those who would claim that such an undertaking is beyond the proper scope of linguistic science—faces the difficult task of discovering and recording what the specific characteristics of the prestigeful dialects are. This task necessarily involves not only his ability to describe what he observes but also his judgment in deciding whether what he observes is in fact prestigeful in the society for which he is writing his grammar. On the basis of both his observation and his judgment, the prescriptive grammarian is in the best possible position to make recommendations to members of the society as to what

---

and Literature No. 25 (Madison: 1929). Reissued (New York: Russell & Russell, Inc.; 1962).

[5] Besides the Leonard work cited in the preceding note, the student may profitably study the following: George H. McKnight: *Modern English in the Making* (see note 5, p. 300, above); Albert C. Baugh, *op. cit.*, 306–55; W. F. Bryan, "Notes on the Founders of Prescriptive English Grammar," *Manly Anniversary Studies*, (Chicago: University of Chicago Press; 1923); Ivan Poldauf: *On the History of Some Problems of English Grammar before 1800*, Prague Studies in English LV (Prague: Filosofické Faculty University Karlovy; 1948); Karl W. Dykema, "Where our Grammar Came From," *College English*, XXII (1960–61), 455–65 (on the Latin grammatical tradition); Otto Funke: *Die Frühzeit der englischen Grammatik . . .* (Schriften der literarischen Gesellschaft Bern, neue Folge der Neujahrsblätter IV). (Bern: H. Lang & Cie.; 1941).

forms they *should* use in order to achieve the results they desire.

The two-part nature of the prescriptive grammarian's task has been grossly misunderstood in the past. "Liberal" grammarians have sometimes assumed that the linguist can perform the first part of the task without reference to the second, that he can simply describe the "facts" of standard grammar without introducing any judgment of those facts. "Traditional" or "conservative" grammarians have sometimes assumed that the second part of the task is independent of the first part, that decisions can and must be made about what features the standard dialect *ought* to have, whether or not the standard dialect in fact does have those features.

Even more serious is the misunderstanding that the ordinary layman has about the nature of prescriptive grammar, because his notions about what he calls "grammar" belong to the very center of his views about himself and his relationship with society. To attack his cherished misconceptions in this matter is to threaten his whole attitude, his whole adjustment, to the society in which he finds himself. Let us look more closely at these misconceptions of the linguistically naïve man.

Most people regard grammar as a series of prescriptions which have the sanctity of most mysterious authority and which are beyond discussion as the basis of how things are to be said. Such people find no objection to the label "purist" that others give to them or that they give themselves. Strictly speaking, to be a "purist" in linguistic matters is to suffer from an insufficiency of knowledge about language. To be concerned with good usage and good English is not the mark of the purist, for all people should be concerned with these matters; his mark is rather the sacred authority with which he invests his own notion of good usage. This purist attitude, extended to lexical matters, gives rise to the feeling that a word has a "real" meaning.[6] What we have here is an hypostatization of certain usages. These are regarded as not merely conventional but innately right and built into the mysterious nature of the English language. However, in their

---

[6] See below Chapter VIII, p. 353.

teaching of "correct" English, English teachers are not teaching an English which has some absolute virtue over all other English dialects; rather, they are quite properly teaching a prestige dialect which has social advantages. The expressive advantages of the prestige dialect are due to the intelligence and educational superiority of its speakers, and not to the innate characteristics of that dialect.

The purist's wrath is often curiously selective. People often strain at a gnat and swallow a camel. Certain particular examples are frowned on; others are accepted without question. When one considers the thousands of instances of functional shift in English,[7] that is, the change of a word to a new grammatical valence, it is curious that so much fuss should have been made some years ago over the functional shift of the particular nouns *contact* and *loan* to verbs. Besides such generally shared selectivity, any individual may have his own grammatical shibboleths. Certain usages irritate some people more than others. Often the cause can be traced to a zealous schoolmistress or parent, who emphasized the heinousness of a particular grammatical or lexical usage.

In their attitudes toward these matters, such people reveal a refusal to accept two cardinal characteristics of historical languages: their essential arbitrariness and their essential susceptibility to change. The first recorded reference ever made to the English language by a speaker of English, as we have seen, was a lament over its corrupt state. This has been a recurrent complaint ever since, and seems to reflect a general feeling that the world is going to the dogs.

Many of the locutions objected to in traditional prescriptive rules have a long history in English and have been used by great writers. The distinction between *like* (preposition) and *as* (conjunction), which has been insisted upon so firmly, has little historical justification. Shakespeare, Robert Southey, Cardinal Newman, and William Morris, among other great English writers, used *like* "incorrectly." Yet this same use arouses great protesta-

---

[7] Discussed below in Chapter VIII, pp. 338–341.

tions today. If one wants to be considered an educated person today, it is wise not to use it in writing because it has become a shibboleth to so many people, but one must not think that the distinction as drawn in our traditional grammars is justified by historical or logical considerations. Eventually, the status of the distinction may change, or it may not.

Probably all linguistic communities have some feeling for status and social distinctions as revealed in language, when that language is accepted as the normal means of communication by all groups in a community. The kind of language used, like the kind of material possessions, is a status symbol in society. Sometimes there are societies in which different languages function as social markers. As we have seen, Latin and French in earlier England had such roles. A notable example of this, frequently cited though possibly inaccurately reported, was to be found in the Antilles, where men spoke one Indian language—Carib— and females another—Arawakan—although an Antillan had to understand both.[8]

When different languages within a community do not function as distinct social markers, different dialects of the same language may play the role of marking social or even biological distinctions. However, it must not be thought that a speaker knows or even uses only the dialect which is considered characteristic of his group. Especially in modern societies, with the facilities they provide for public education and mass communication, most speakers of a particular dialect have ample opportunity to acquire the linguistic characteristics of other dialects, including the standard one, and thus may find themselves linguistically at home even outside their own dialect groups. The variety gives them a chance to take different roles depending on their audience and particular desires. A cultivated male speaker who "knows better," for instance, may deliberately use

---

[8] See Willem L. Graff: *Language and Languages, An Introduction to Linguistics* (New York and London: D. Appleton and Company; 1932), 431. There are, probably in all societies, words or phrases which are considered especially masculine, feminine, or even childish.

slang or vulgar language or feminine language or any other variety, in order to gain special effects.

The traditions of various language groups about dialects of their own language affect the speaking and writing habits of their members. Different societies place different values on "correct" usage. Englishmen are much more alive to dialectal variations as social markers than are Americans, and Frenchmen are more concerned with "good" French than most Englishmen or Americans are with "good" English. These attitudes must be taken into consideration when the matter of "correctness" in language is being considered.

What is demanded for linguistic sophistication in the matter of good usage is an awareness of the complexity of the problem and some historical perspective. Prescriptive grammar must be based on a sensible descriptive grammar. If educated people prefer "he isn't" to "he ain't," the former is preferable for anyone who wishes to be accounted educated in speech and writing. In the long run, of course, what educated people *prefer* tends to follow what other educated people are actually *doing* in their use of language. But what educated people *do* in their language is also sometimes determined by what is prescribed or believed to be prescribed. A classic example of the latter is the pronunciation of the suffix *-ing* as /ɪŋ/. Apparently in the eighteenth century it was universally pronounced /ən/, as preserved in the speech of most speakers of nonstandard English and many speakers of standard English (e.g., speakers of standard Southern American English) but prescriptive schoolteachers, largely because of the spelling, reintroduced /ɪŋ/ as the mark of educated usage. And today it is such a mark in General (or Northern and North Midland) American English.

In the last analysis the criterion for correctness should be a practical, not a logical one. To put it in terms of a medieval dichotomy, *consuetudo* (custom) rather than *veritas* (truth) is the relevant consideration. A time-honored way of expressing it was to say that usage was the criterion of correctness. However, usage alone is not enough, as "usage" is not a simple matter to determine. What also interferes with attempts to identify "what is correct" simply as "what is used," is the fact that the users themselves *believe* that usage is based on logic, as Samuel Taylor Coleridge believed, when he wrote in his *Biographia Literaria,* XVII, that the "rules of grammar . . . are in essence no other than the laws of universal logic, applied to psychological materials." This notion has been reinforced historically by the prestigeful association of universal logic with Latin grammar, although even assuming a "universal grammar" to be possible, we certainly have no right to assume that it would correspond to the grammar of Latin.[9]

From what we have said up to here it will be obvious that an understanding of the role played by prescriptive grammar is crucial to an understanding of the usage doctrine. If a prescriptive grammar is conceived to be the codification of educated English present-day usage as far as that may be determined, then to be "grammatically correct" is simply to speak or write as educated people do. If, on the other hand, prescriptive grammar is identified with reason or with the language of reason, Latin, then grammar is completely normative and not at all descriptive. In other words, grammar becomes metaphysically sanctioned, and can be used to make speakers and writers conform to "reason." A more sensible alternative position to both of these is that prescriptive grammar has both descriptive and normative aspects, that the norms should be derived from accurate observation and description of the actual *use and effect* of language. People are often loath to accept this view because they refuse to believe that language is essentially conventional. Because they do not do so, they may actually say and write artificially "correct" forms, and in the end may even force the artificial forms into the standard grammar.

From what we have written, it should be clear that the subject of "correctness" in language is by no means a simple matter. It is curious that, in practice, holders of either view of correct-

---

[9] See Karl W. Dykema, "Where our Grammar Came From," *College English,* XXII (1960–61), 455–65.

ness discussed above usually themselves use the same kind of educated language. The only effective differences between them lie perhaps in their attitudes toward innovations in usage and in their degrees of optimism about the future of English. The linguistic "authoritarian" tends to disapprove of all innovations, except perhaps those of vocabulary for new inventions, and to lament the ever increasing corruption of English, as William of Malmesbury did in the twelfth century. The linguistic "libertarian" is less unhappy about innovations and feels that English can take care of itself, as it did for hundreds of years before people in the seventeenth century began to worry about the state of English.

Most people do not make a strict distinction between style and grammar; much of the lamenting about "poor grammar" is actually over poor style. Much more serious than "like" as a conjunction is a poor feeling for rhetorical fitness and logical organization. A piece of writing can be perfect grammatically and yet poorly written because the sentences are jerky, because the thoughts are not well organized, because of a misunderstanding of the tone of particular words, and for a myriad of other stylistic reasons. Such matters are not properly the concern of linguistic science but rather of rhetoric.

In the last half of the eighteenth century we find a vast number of grammars and rhetorics of English. Earlier there had been simple grammars of English, often for foreigners, but until the second half of the eighteenth century, they were few and very elementary. In studying the origin of many of our traditional grammatical rules these grammars are most instructive, for in them we find most of the forerunners of the traditional rules which we now take for granted, for better or for worse. Most of these grammars claim to accept some principle according to which usage determines the rule, but then go on to apply this principle in a most arbitrary and peculiar way. The influence of Latin grammar is obvious in most of them, as when Latin-type vocative and dative cases are ascribed to the English noun. Most of them confuse letters and sounds, and many are picayunish about small matters. But, what is of most significance for us today, they do not carefully distinguish description from prescription. Of the various eighteenth-century grammarians studied by Professor Baugh,[1] only Joseph Priestley seems to have practiced what he preached, in his grammar *Rudiments of English Grammar* (1761), and carried out the task, which all of them set themselves, of describing educated usage.

It has generally been assumed in recent studies of status distinctions in language that socially vertical variations fall into dialect divisions in pretty much the same way that geographically horizontal ones do. A corollary of this assumption is that, since a regional dialect is determined by investigating the language behavior of the residents of that region, so a status dialect is determined by investigating the language behavior of the people with a given status.[2] Good usage is taken to be the usage of educated or highly placed persons, and poor usage the usage of the other groups in society. This view, as we have already implied, is much too simple a view of the problem. For one thing, in many socially mobile societies, such as the American one, class distinctions cannot always be consistently drawn. We all know of people in high places to whom we would assign low status if our judgment were to be based only on their linguistic production, and the lowly butler with the dandy dialect is a well-established stereotype: no elaborate demonstration is necessary of the imperfect correlation between linguistic and social status. We cannot definitively assign a prestige value to a linguistic item, merely by observing which people use it most often.[3] The

---

[1] *Op. cit.*, 330 ff.

[2] For a fairly recent study of the status significance of a dialect (spoken by Negroes of a Washington alley), see George N. Putnam and Edna M. O'Hern: *The Status Significance of an Isolated Urban Dialect*, Catholic University of America Dissertation, Supplement to *Language*, XXXI (1955), Language Dissertation No. 53. See also John L. Fischer, "Social Influences on the Choice of a Linguistic Variant," *Word*, XIV (1958), 47–56.

[3] This oversimplified attitude weakens the effectiveness of Charles Carpenter Fries, *American English Grammar*, National Council of Teachers of English, English Monograph No. 10. (New York and London: D. Appleton-Century Company; 1940), in spite of its very valuable material.

prestige classification of a given item is in fact a statement of judgment by a particular listener or group of listeners: the judgment may or may not reflect the "real" status of the speaker, but it will very probably reflect differences of judgmental bases characterizing different classes of listeners. In other words, the judgment may be a comment on the judge rather than on the judged.

That the audience judgment of the "quality" of the speech can play an active part in actually creating that quality may be seen in two linguistic phenomena—baby talk and pidgin languages. It has long been noticed by careful observers that it is not babies and illiterate natives who create baby talk and pidgin languages respectively, but adults and members of the socially dominant class. The child who is trying to speak English as his parents speak it makes mistakes. The parents think he *wants* to speak in such a way and address him in what they think is his form of the language, in effect making it harder for him to learn what is correct. The same kind of situation in various parts of the world, as in Melanesia, for example, has given rise to creolized forms of English known as pidgin English. The native tries to speak English properly and cannot succeed at first. The "civilized" speakers, with a sense of linguistic superiority, attribute mistakes to the innate inferiority of the speaker and patronize him by speaking in the same way. They think they will make the native understand them more easily if they adopt "his" language. The listener in both cases has shaped the language for the speaker.

The status of the speech of a given speaker is determined by the judgment of the members of the community in which that speech is used; therefore, an adequate assignment of prestige values to linguistic phenomena must take into account the status-assigning behavior of the judges themselves. If we are serious in wanting reliable information about the probable social consequences of any given linguistic behavior, our study of the "high status" dialect will be incomplete without the controlled investigation of differential judgments on that behavior. *Between you and I* may seem "classy" to listeners of one status rank, neutral to listeners of a second, careless to listeners of a third, illiterate to listeners of a fourth, socially aggressive to listeners of a fifth, and so on. We should not take for granted that all speakers of a given language will make the same judgments about one another.

In practice, the issue is solved by those who control schools, write grammars, and edit dictionaries. Many of us place our trust in linguistic matters in those who control the normal channels of education and communication. The spellings, the pronunciations, the vocabulary, and the grammatical usages of those favored groups who command our intellectual respect are those which carry prestige. That certain locutions do carry prestige with editors, writers, educators, and publishers is a fact, and it is essentially these men who are in positions to assert what is considered good usage in general, and to exercise the most effective sanctions over other people's use of language. We accept the correction of editors on our books and of our schoolteachers in our schools, and take the word of the makers of our dictionaries to settle linguistic disputes. And indeed, this is in general probably the most sensible thing for us to do. However, we do need to recognize that if we have any education at all, we speak and write different varieties of English in different circumstances, and that our "authorities" for standard English are not authorities for all other varieties as well. If you want to know the proper use of a piece of teen-age slang, the best authority is a teen-ager, not a middle-aged schoolteacher or dictionary-maker.

Let us look at some of the linguistic points on which the eighteenth-century grammarians concentrated. Most of these are still issues in prescriptive grammar today. One important concern was the problem of agreement—agreement between subject and verb, noun and pronoun. "You was" was strongly condemned for its lack of analogy with *you are*, although one could easily have made a logical case for it for the singular *you*. The grammarians were also concerned with the number of the verb after *a number of* or *none* (<*no one*) and gave varying recommendations. And they wrestled with the matter of a singular verb after two or more subjects, frequently used by eighteenth-century writers. We also find in these writers the use of *their* in reference to *everybody*, and *these kind of*; the decision of the grammarians in each case was to object to these usages on grounds of logic. Another point which concerned the eighteenth-century grammarians was the vague reference of pronouns, usually *which* or *this*. Most of the grammarians felt that an explicit antecedent for these words was logically necessary.

A subject that we now see as being more often the concern of rhetoric than of grammar is the matter of parallelism. Eighteenth-century grammarians insisted on having scrupulously parallel constructions after *not only . . . but* and *either (neither) . . . or (nor)*. Some of them went further and insisted on the same kind of detailed parallel constructions with *and* and *but*.

Functional shift aroused opposition from the authorities, particularly the use of adjectives for adverbs. "He is real good" is a modern parallel to "It is *prodigious* cold" of the eighteenth century, and both expressions have been strongly condemned. Yet *very* itself, if we go back far enough, is an example of the very same shift. "It is *very* cold" originally meant "It is true cold." But time has a way of sanctifying old grammatical "errors."

Problems of case also aroused the older grammarians, especially choice of pronoun forms after *than* and *as* and the verb *to be*. Here the recommendations differed, especially in the case of *as* and *than*. A related problem was the use of the genitive forms before the gerund, as in "I rejoice at *his* leaving so quickly," rather than "I rejoice at *him* leaving so quickly."

Among matters in a miscellaneous category, we may mention their favoring the article *the* before a gerund and *of* after it when no possessive pronoun is needed; and their disapproval of contractions such as *'em* for *them* or *don't* for *doesn't*, of "misplacement" of modifiers like *only*, and of redundancies such as *as yet, from hence*, and *approved of*.

As a typical example of actual educated eighteenth-century practice, Boswell's usage conforms in some ways to the grammarian's recommendations (when his usage is consistent), but in other ways it does not.[4] Boswell's usage was more inconsistent

---

[4] We have been following the points used by Esther K. Sheldon in her article "Boswell's English in the *London Journal*," *PMLA*, LXXI (1956),

than that of most modern writers and as such typifies the lack of conformity of actual eighteenth-century educated English to the recommendations of the grammarians. Facts like these support the view that the recommendations of most eighteenth-century grammarians were in large part based not on educated contemporary usage but on a Procrustean use of Latinish grammar, misapplied logic, or plain prejudice.

It is instructive that many of the points "settled" by grammarians in the eighteenth century are today still a major concern of our school grammars. Only a few seem no longer to need special attention by language reformers. The circumstances of the origin of these grammatical recommendations, continued in a persistent educational tradition into our times, should make us cautious about taking too seriously laments about the present state of the language and about its special susceptibility to corruption. Corruption is an old accusation, as baseless when it was first made as it is today. "Errors" in grammar often have long, respectable histories, and do not afford evidence of a *new* spirit of linguistic destructiveness.

English dictionaries, like English grammars, arose out of Latin models. The oldest dictionaries in English were medieval glosses on Latin works, and lists of hard Latin or occasionally French words. With the great influx of new words in English in the Elizabethan period, a demand arose for dictionaries of hard English words. The first one, by Robert Cawdrey, appeared in 1604.

We have no intention of giving a history of English dictionaries in this chapter, any more than we have done for English grammars. The information is available elsewhere.[5] But a few key

---

1067–93. She uses them to evaluate Boswell's English in terms of the recommendations of the contemporary grammarians.

[5] For the early history of English dictionaries up to Samuel Johnson's *English Dictionary*, see De Witt T. Starnes and Gertrude E. Noyes: *The English Dictionary from Cawdrey to Johnson, 1604–1755* (Chapel Hill: The University of North Carolina Press; 1946). For Dr. Johnson's dictionary, see James H. Sledd and Gwin J. Kolb: *Dr. Johnson's Dictionary: Essays in the Biography of a Book* (Chicago: University of Chicago Press; 1955).

dictionaries deserve mention because of the crucial role they played in the development of our linguistic self-confidence. English dictionaries show a great dependence on each other historically. Lexicographers of English have tended to model their work on the dictionaries of their predecessors and to some extent on the great French and Italian dictionaries. The development of the English dictionary to the point where it included all the information which we now normally expect of a dictionary was slow. Samuel Johnson's great dictionary of 1755 improved on existing tradition by including a large number of illustrative citations, and by indicating the place of the accent on words, although it did not further specify the pronunciation and did not always base its definitions on uses that could have been illustrated from the writing of Johnson's own time. On the other hand, the tradition did establish for Johnson the need to include a grammar and a history of the language. Modern dictionaries often give a short history of the language in the preface but usually omit the grammar. Johnson brought such thoroughness and authority to his work that his dictionary exerted an almost Mosaic influence over the later eighteenth century and the nineteenth century, and was not fully replaced until, in 1928, The Philological Society completed *The New English Dictionary* (NED), also called the *Oxford English Dictionary* (OED). Johnson's dictionary is still valuable to us today because it is a perceptive record of eighteenth-century English by one of the people who had the most to say about what English should be.

For a list of American dictionaries up to 1861, see Eva Mae Burkett: *A Study of American Dictionaries of the English Language Before 1861*, submitted . . . for the Degree of Doctor of Philosophy . . . George Peabody College for Teachers, Abstract of Contribution to Education No. 187 (Nashville: 1936). For the later history of English dictionaries, see M. M. Mathews: *A Survey of English Dictionaries* (London: Oxford University Press; 1933), and the excellent short summary by Harold Whitehall in the front part of *Webster's New World Dictionary of the American Language*. College Edition. (Cleveland and New York: The World Publishing Company; 1953), xxxii–xxxiv. On Noah Webster, see Harry F. Warfel: *Noah Webster, Schoolmaster to America* (New York: The Macmillan Company; 1936).

Between Johnson and the *NED*, the American Noah Webster completed two versions of a great dictionary, the second of which appeared in 1828 and established a tradition of fine dictionary-making in the United States. Between 1755 and 1858, when plans for the *NED* were laid, the world had seen a notable development of linguistic knowledge and science. This development made possible great improvements in the lexical treatment of English. Just as Noah Webster's dictionaries showed an advance in accuracy and completeness over Johnson's, so the *NED* surpassed both. The aim of the *NED* was frankly historical: to illustrate by quotations the changing meanings of all the words in the English language since about 1100, to provide accurate etymologies, and to give all variant spellings. As might be expected, this ideal could not be completely attained, but the final product yielded a wealth of accurate information about the development of the English vocabulary and gave English-speaking peoples one of the great dictionaries of the world. A supplement to the *NED* was produced in 1933, and another is being planned.[6]

Because of the large degree of arbitrariness of English spelling, the many specialized meanings of words, the very large vocabulary in English, the great number of "hard" words[7]—words made up from foreign roots—the dictionary has come to occupy a very important place in the writing, and to some extent in the speaking, of the users of English. Educated speakers of other important languages rarely consult a dictionary of their own language; English speakers, even well-educated ones, do so frequently. As a result, English-speakers give the dictionary an aura of authority and a degree of respect unknown or rare among speakers of other languages. This respect creates dangers which should be recognized. The dictionary and the traditional prescriptive grammar have been made final arbiters of correctness in English; and although this is quite useful as a unifying force for a language

---

[6] See R.W. Burchfield, "O.E.D.: A New Supplement," *Essays and Studies 1961* (London: John Murray; 1961), 35–51.

[7] On hard words in English, see Chapter VIII, p. 332.

whose millions of speakers lack any geographical, political, or social unity, it is necessary that their claims to authority be qualified. We have briefly examined the claims of prescriptive grammar; now we must turn to the dictionary.

It is noteworthy that most people refer, as we have done above, to "the dictionary" rather than to a particular dictionary. All dictionaries are assumed to be saying the same things about words; yet there are actually a good many differences even among equally authoritative and reputable dictionaries. If we include "supermarket" dictionaries, which are often poorly edited and unreliable and some of which are mere reprints of poor nineteenth-century dictionaries, the differences will appear even more clearly.

No dictionary can give a complete listing of all words in the language, and for ordinary purposes such completeness is not necessary. But some dictionaries—*The Webster Third New International* and the *NED*, for instance—are very comprehensive, the latter especially for the older and learned words and for most common words in active use. The various college or desk dictionaries—*The American College Dictionary (ACD)*, *Webster's New World Dictionary (NWD)*, *The Merriam-Webster New Collegiate Dictionary*, *The Concise Oxford*, and Funk and Wagnall's *Standard College Dictionary*—are suitable and complete enough for most normal purposes. For special American English usages and developments, the *Dictionary of American English (DAE)*, and *A Dictionary of Americanisms*, ed. M. M. Mathews, may be recommended. *The Century Dictionary*, compiled before the First World War, is still a mine of useful lexical information and along with the NWD is especially good for etymologies. The University of Michigan Press is at present putting out, fascicle by fascicle, an excellent dictionary of Middle English (*MED*).

Most reliable editors of dictionaries arrive at their judgments after examining large collections of citations illustrating the uses of words. The meaning of a word is determined by considering the context in which it appears. By looking at helpful citations of words in the context of current writings and speeches, a skillful editor can come to some conclusions about the present meaning and usage of a word. But not all citations are equally helpful. A bare statement like "This gorilla is large" would not tell us much about the meaning of the word *gorilla*, but a sentence like "The fierce untamable gorilla approaches nearest, in physical conformation and in certain habits, to man," does provide important clues to the meaning of the one word if we already know the meanings of the other words in the rest of the sentence. Of course, many more citations and the expert help of zoologists would be needed to make our definition suitably precise. The most useful citations for lexicography will contain defining actions or characteristics of the word to be defined, and will embed that word in a context of already known words, since we obviously do not define the unknown by other unknowns. The earliest known citation is not always the most helpful, and in some cases adequate citations cannot be found. Most dictionaries rarely print citations to support the judgment of the editor, but some, such as the *NED* and *DAE*, are quite generous in their illustrative citations.

Dictionaries may give us a considerable amount of information about words besides their spelling and meaning. They tell us their etymologies, their general range of usage (some words are colloquial, i.e., normally used only in speech; some are provincial; some are Scottish; some are technical; etc.), and something of their syntactic use in sentences. Many present-day dictionaries are also miniature encyclopedias and have valuable appendices containing a variety of useful information.

Conscientious makers of dictionaries do not conceive their task to be the determining of correct rules for the use of words. The editors of reputable dictionaries do not claim to legislate what is correct in language, but merely to record what is used and by whom. A recent dictionary-editor writes, "This dictionary records the usage of the speakers or writers of our language; no dictionary founded on the methods of modern scholarship can prescribe as to usage; it can only inform on the basis of the facts of usage.

... It is not the function of the dictionary-maker to tell you how to speak, any more than it is the function of the mapmaker to move rivers or rearrange mountains or fill in lakes. A dictionary should tell you what is commonly accepted usage and wherein different classes of speakers or regions differ in their use of the language."[8]

In other words, modern dictionary-makers look upon themselves as neutral recorders of what other people do. It is the layman who looks upon them and the dictionaries they make as authorities who establish laws that create and regulate the use of words.

However there is a sense in which the average person is not entirely wrong, for the making of a dictionary is not wholly the impersonal act that its own makers may claim it is. Human judgment must inevitably come in when the huge masses of data with which the dictionary-maker begins must be organized, reduced, and reported in the final form of the dictionary. A dictionary is really the interpretation of the state of English usage by its particular editors and their friends—more accurately, by its chief editor and whoever that editor considers an authority to judge that usage.

A conscientious editor does make an attempt, by gathering material, to determine the "objective" facts. To establish the "facts" of English usage is frequently considered a simple task. Actually it is extremely difficult to do so for various reasons. The sample upon which the lexicographer draws, no matter how many millions of citations he takes, will always represent much less than all usage; his sample will be especially unfair to spoken English because of the difficulty of obtaining sufficient data uncontaminated by the intermediation of writing. For any usage, the editor must decide whether "enough" citations have been gathered to "establish" it. Moreover, any speaker or writer at different times uses different varieties of English, depending upon the impression he wishes to make in different social environments

---

[8] Clarence L. Barnhart in the General Introduction to the *American College Dictionary* (New York: Random House; 1958 edition).

and on his own judgment of what is proper or appropriate; determining the intention of the user of a word is by no means easy. Even the mere keeping of statistical records, when thousands of words are involved, is a most complicated and formidable task. In all this, the dictionary-maker conscientiously tries to be sensible and objective. Nevertheless, it is exactly his own sensitivity to language that finally determines whether the dictionary is "accurate," whether it provides a reliable guide to what the user's society will consider prestigeful.

If one wishes to use English acceptable to educated judges, one does well, by and large, to follow the information recorded in dictionaries, because dictionary-makers do occupy that important place to which we have referred above: they are the conventional authorities to whom one is willing to leave judgment in matters of word usage. One can, then, take the dictionary as a guide and use its information as recommendation. But one must understand what he is thereby doing. Otherwise such an assumption may lead to a blind submission to what one man has judged as educated usage, and to a repugnance toward accepting legitimate changes in language. One must not overlook or undervalue the reality of language change; and it is no demonstration of enlightenment to recognize those changes that have taken place long enough ago to find their way into a dictionary, while at the same time automatically withholding acceptance of more recent changes *merely* because they have not yet gained favor with one of the few dictionary-editors. Dictionaries are for the most part commercial ventures and often do not discourage the idea that they have a special authority. Dictionaries also occasionally enshrine out-of-date usages. However English speakers are well provided with good dictionaries, which provide indispensable help in their use of language.

QUESTIONS

1. Take the following passage from Joseph Addison's *Spectator* No. 165 (1711) and put it into American English. Then discuss the chief differences between the two versions, in spelling, punctuation, words (in their meaning or tone), grammar, and style.

   I have often wished, that as in our Constitution there are several Persons whose Business it is to watch over our Laws, our Liberties and Commerce, certain Men might be set apart as Superintendants of our Language, to hinder any Words of a Foreign Coin from passing among us, and in particular to prohibit any French Phrases from becoming Current in this Kingdom, when those of our own Stamp are altogether as valuable. The present War has so Adulterated our Tongue with strange words that it would be impossible for one of our Great Grandfathers to know what his Posterity have been doing, were he to read their Exploits in a Modern News Paper.

2. In Chapter V we discussed language contact which involved the impact one language has upon another. Apply this notion to English social dialects and show from your own experience how one dialect of English can affect another.

3. How would you write a declension of the English noun if you were to model it on the Latin cases: nominative, genitive, dative, accusative, ablative, vocative? If you do not know any Latin, look up the definitions of the cases you don't know in an English dictionary.

4. Write a short essay on "correct" English, making use of some of the ideas discussed in this chapter.

5. How would you account for the dictionary habit of speakers and writers of English?

6. In evaluating what English is used by educated speakers, why is the role of the judge especially important?

7. List some of the difficulties which would be encountered in endeavoring to determine what is cultivated English.

8. Discuss the role of the hearer or audience in determining the status of words or phrases in a language.

THE ENGLISH VOCABULARY
AND ENGLISH
WORD FORMATION

Of all the elements of language, it is the word which is most widely recognized. To many people, a language is a collection of words which must be learned, and even the most illiterate of speakers usually has an awareness of this unit. Apparently, if Edward Sapir is correct, this consciousness of words is active among speakers of all languages, including those which lack a traditional writing system.[1] This strong psychological feeling is supported by the way in which sentences are divided in writing, and by the strong emphasis on vocabulary learning in schools.

This widely identified language element is, however, very hard to define, in spite of its apparent psychological reality. There have been numerous attempts to define *the word* in a more objective fashion, but they are all more or less unsatisfactory. Leonard Bloomfield writes, "for purposes of ordinary life, the word is the smallest unit of speech."[2] Charles Hockett proposes as a definition,

---

[1] *Language* (New York: Harcourt Brace and Company; 1921), 32 ff.
[2] *Language* (New York: Henry Holt and Company; 1933), 178.

"a word is any segment of a sentence bounded by successive points at which pausing is possible."[3] Neither of these definitions, if literally interpreted, would produce units which always correspond to what we think of as words.

In this chapter what we shall discuss is best understood in terms of what was presented in Chapter VI above. We will not deal with all "words," but only with certain ones which may best be considered as lexical units. It may be recalled that certain elements in sentences appear in the grammatical rules for generating correct sentences in English, and other elements appear in the lexicon of English. A lexical unit is an element introduced into sentences by a listing rule. Nonlexical, i.e., *grammatical,* elements form an integral part of a grammatical rule. We shall be here concerned with the elements in the English lexicon. It is characteristic of lexical units that they are closely associated in the mind of the speaker with the notion of reference. They are signs referring to events, objects, ideas, and the like. They may thus be called "referential units," corresponding for the most part to what a dictionary takes as words. In this chapter we shall be concerned with the classification of such words and with their social and cultural history in English.

All words are not equally common in use, in terms of their actual frequency or in terms of the varieties of speakers who use them. Some are widely known; others are known only to a specialized group. The words which are rarely used, or if frequently used are used only by a small group of people, may be considered to be on the periphery of the vocabulary. Those which are frequently used and widely known belong to the core.[4]

Certain regions favor certain words and certain classes, trades, or professions use specialized words. These words have a geo-

---

[3] *A Course in Modern Linguistics* (New York: The Macmillan Company; 1958), 167.

[4] We cannot use frequency alone as the test for certain terms; *gene,* for example, must be very frequently used by geneticists, whereas a term like *colt* is rarely used. Yet *gene* is not in the core English vocabulary, whereas *colt* is. A greater number and variety of people would know the meaning of the latter word than that of the former.

graphic or social localization, and so may not be understood out of their normal context. Then there are learned, archaic, or obsolescent words, which are known only by scholars or historians or by people who have looked them up in dictionaries. Some of these words belong to what is often called a "recognition vocabulary." All speakers of a language recognize the meaning of more words in the language than they will ordinarily use. A recognition vocabulary belongs to the living language only in a special way. It is part of the heritage of a speaker of a language; it may be dipped into on occasion, and must be turned to when great masterpieces of the past are read. Many words in English exist for most people only in Shakespeare's plays, in Milton's *Paradise Lost,* or in other literary works.

Words, then, are "in" a language in different degrees and in different ways. The words left in the vocabulary after we have eliminated localisms, trade and professional words, and literary words may be called the **core vocabulary** of a language. These may be pronounced differently in different parts of the area over which they are spoken, or by different social groups, but if the language has any unity there is a basic general vocabulary common to most speakers of it. It is with this core vocabulary that speakers feel most secure, intimate, and familiar.

The sense of security manifested in the use of these core words may be seen in the unwillingness of speakers to be corrected when they use them. A speaker of English will probably accept correction if he is told that he is misusing the word *hemoglobin* but would find it absurd to hear that he is misusing the word *table.* The sense of familiarity may be seen in the widespread, almost universal knowledge of these words. For ordinary purposes a speaker of English never has to look such words up in the dictionary. The sense of intimacy may be seen in the fact that in moments of stress such words immediately come to his mind. No speaker of English would shout *Conflagration!* in the presence of an uncontrolled fire.

In Chapter V we mentioned that many speakers of English feel that words of Romance, Latin, or Greek origin are fancy or literary or academic. We pointed out that this feeling is selective. Many speakers do not feel that *enemy* is fancy or specialized, in spite of its Romance origin. *Foe,* on the other hand, which is part of our Anglo-Saxon word heritage, is a fancy word in NE. *Deem,* of OE origin, is fancier than *judge,* of Romance origin. The origin of a word, therefore, cannot determine whether or not it is part of the core vocabulary. But there are more words of non-Anglo-Saxon origin than words of Anglo-Saxon origin in the peripheral vocabulary, and more words of Anglo-Saxon origin are in the core vocabulary than are out of it. This fact accounts for the widespread notion that non-Anglo-Saxon words are fancier than Anglo-Saxon words.

Even within the core vocabulary, some words are more central (or, common) than others. *They* is more central than *minnow,* yet both may be said to be core words. One cannot be scientifically exact in characterizing words in this way, but their general position in the language can usually be determined.

Words are continually entering languages in these different categories, or moving into another category, or falling out of active use. Some are made up for a special occasion (**nonce-words**) or in special circumstances, and are never used again— indeed never get into dictionaries at all. Others "catch on" and become part of the general or core vocabulary. Other words are accepted by special groups, e.g., astronomers. What causes a word to be accepted or not is unpredictable, but after the event we can sometimes give a plausible explanation of why the word did or did not catch on. We can explain it as we explain any historical event after the fact, as historians can give us the causes of the American Civil War; in 1859, no one could have predicted it with certainty, although no doubt many who thought about it could have guessed correctly. Why words like *againstand* 'resist', *againrising* 'resurrection', *forthinking* 'repentance', and *unworship* 'dishonor', which John Wyclif used in the fourteenth century, did not survive, it is not easy to say. Many words like these apparently had only a brief history in English before they disappeared.

West Germanic became English when it was carried into the British Isles in the fifth century. English, then, began with a vocabulary taken from West Germanic, consisting of many words inherited from IE and affected by the sound "laws" by which IE sounds became Germanic and West Germanic ones; of some words which seem to be peculiar to Germanic or to West Germanic (their cognates are unknown elsewhere); of a small number of words borrowed from Latin, mainly indicating culture objects originally unknown to the Germanic peoples; and of a very small number of words borrowed from neighboring Celtic tribes on the Continent. This group of words may be considered the original word hoard of English. This hoard is not, of course, identical with our present core vocabulary, but it did contribute a great deal to it, perhaps more than what was contributed by later innovations and borrowings. We may reconstruct it by eliminating from the vocabulary of our extant documents those words which were borrowed or made up after the invasion of Britain, as far as we can determine them, and by adding to it the native Germanic words which turn up only in ME documents or in NE. The preserved literature and epigraphic material of OE displays only part of the total vocabulary of OE. If a word has not found its way into a document at some time, we may mistakenly assume therefore that it did not exist. Some words, however, which because of their form must go back to the original OE vocabulary, get recorded only in Middle or Modern English times—sometimes only in provincial dialects. We may add these late-attested words to our original vocabulary. In addition, there were in OE many words which died out without ever being recorded—lost to us forever.

As we have said above, not all words in a language are equally common. Some words are rarely if ever used, others are used only by various segments of the population, whereas still other words recur again and again. When estimating the relative importance of various parts of the English vocabulary, we should keep in mind not only the number of words in each of these categories but also their frequency of use. Old Norse, for instance, has probably not contributed as many words to the NE vocabulary as, say, Italian, but the words which come from Old Norse are much more frequently used in English than those from Italian. More of them are in the core vocabulary. No Italian word has penetrated into the general common vocabulary of English as deeply as, say, the Old Norse words for the third person plural pronoun—*they, their, them.* We may say that Old Norse has had a greater influence on English than Italian has, even though the actual vocabulary percentages in a dictionary will not show it.

The OE word hoard which persists in NE has been estimated at somewhat less than 35 per cent of the whole NE vocabulary, on the basis of the words listed in the *NED*, a large but by no means exhaustive collection of English words.[5] The figure given for the total Germanic element in the NE vocabulary is 35 per cent, including compounds and Scandinavian borrowings added to the core vocabulary since OE times. Yet because of the frequency with which these words are used, it would be misleading to say that NE is only 35 per cent Germanic. If the frequency of occurrence were the criterion, rather than the number of words in dictionaries, the percentage would be much higher—well over 50 per cent, it may reasonably be assumed. Koziol gives figures for individual writers and estimates that about 88 per cent of Chaucer's words are of Germanic origin, 86 per cent of Shakespeare's, and 90 per cent of Tennyson's.

For a fundamental reason, it is impossible to fix the total number of words in any natural language: a language has inexhaustible resources available for making up new words. Whenever speakers of a language are faced with a situation calling for a new word, they can find a way of constructing one which they can make more or less understandable to other speakers of the same language.

Speakers of a language have three general possibilities open to them in increasing the vocabulary of the language: 1) the crea-

---

[5] The figure is taken from Herbert Koziol: *Handbuch der englischen Wortbildungslehre* (Heidelberg: Carl Winter's Universitäts Buchhandlung; 1937), 8.

tion of new words out of the morphemic and phonemic resources of the language, 2) the extension of the uses of words already in the vocabulary, and 3) the borrowing of words from other languages. Societies differ in their employment of these methods. Some societies avoid borrowing in language as much as possible; others, like present-day American society, have no hesitancy about borrowing at all. We showed that, as a result of the Norman Conquest, English society became very receptive to borrowing, but before that event—in the OE period—it favored the first two methods. What Ernst Leisi has called *dissociation* set in after the Conquest.[6] Leisi means that the normal Germanic method, still widely used in Modern German, of making up new words from morphemes and words already in the language, was abandoned in favor of widespread borrowing. This borrowing has created most of the English "hard words." An extensive English dictionary is full of such hard words, mostly of Romance (especially French and Latin) origin. In German the word *mündlich* 'oral' is derived from *Mund,* the word for "mouth." But in English we have *oral,* a borrowing from Latin, instead of a possible but nonexistent *mouthly,* which we might have formed with clearly associated native elements. Such is of course not the case for all our related words: we have *father* and *fatherly, good* and *goodness.* Nevertheless, many of our words which are related in meaning are not related in form, and this **dissociation** is an important feature of the modern English vocabulary.

A viable language must have means of creating new vocabulary elements. The particular ways in which this extension of vocabulary takes place are affected by various historical and social factors which operate or have operated among the speakers of that language, but we can say in general that all languages that stay alive do so by employing, to a greater or lesser extent, all three of the methods mentioned in the preceding paragraph.

The words of a language preserve a great deal of social history, and the story of their entrance into and employment by a

---

[6] *Das heutige Englisch, Wesenzüge und Probleme* (Heidelberg: Carl Winter Universitätsverlag; 1955), 58 ff.

language is full of interesting material which has only indirectly to do with the structure of a language, but which is a compendium of the impact of culture on language. The etymologies of words reflect folk habits and wit, superstitions and beliefs, irony and taboos. The details of these etymologies are interesting in their own right, but our concern in this chapter is rather with the classification of the mechanism by which the English vocabulary was built and is being built. A good deal of this discussion is not scientifically exact, for the mechanisms introducing new words into a vocabulary are still not completely understood.[7] However, certain categories, some of them overlapping, have been useful in the past, and we will make use of these.

Let us turn to the first class—the creation of new words out of morphemic and phonemic resources already available in the language. Words which function as only one part of speech may be extended to other parts of speech or from one grammatical role to another grammatical role; words already in the language may have to be modified for the sake of precision or clarity; and words may be needed to name new objects, events, or concepts. Let us look at these various methods as they are applied to the creation of new words out of the resources of the language.

When a new word enters English, it comes in with a given grammatical function or set of valences. *Domination,* for instance, came into English from French in the fourteenth century as a noun. The verb *dominate* does not appear in English until 1611— formed by what is known as "back formation," which we shall shortly discuss, to provide English with a verb parallel to the noun. Although back formations are not the most common type of grammatical extension, the process of coining verbs parallel to nouns, or nouns to verbs, or verbs to adverbs, and so forth, is quite common and is one of the main types of word formation in English.

Perhaps the oldest method of extending a word from one gram-

---

[7] A step toward a formalization of some of these mechanisms has been made in a monograph by R. B. Lees, *The Grammar of English Nominalizations.* (See Bibliography at end of this book, p. 372.)

matical function to another is known as **ablaut** or **vowel gradation,** to which we have referred in Chapter III. *Ablaut* is best
known to students of the history of English as the method once
used in proto-Germanic to form inflectional forms of strong verbs,
as may still be seen in NE *sing, sang, sung.* It is a type of formation
once active, but is now fossilized in NE and other Germanic languages. But *ablaut* was also used for word derivation, in particular
for extending words from one part of speech to another. Vowel
gradation is a characteristic feature of proto-IE, and appears in
various roles in the various branches of IE. Vowel gradation in
word derivation is preserved in NE in such distinctions as *sing*
(verb), *song* (noun); *shoot* (verb), *shot* (noun); *bind* (verb),
band (noun); *strike* (verb), *stroke* (noun).[8] However, it is no
longer used in NE for making new words.

Closely related to ablaut, and also old, is what is known as
umlaut or **vowel mutation.** In *umlaut* the vowel phoneme in one
syllable has been influenced by phonemes in the following syllable. In proto-Germanic, higher or more fronted allophones of
vowels appear when an /i/ or /e/ or /y/ followed in the next syllable of the same word. When the /i/ or /e/ or /y/ disappeared,
as they did in these positions in prehistoric OE, the allophonic
differences in the preserved syllable became phonemic differences. *Umlaut* is a form of phonetic assimilation. This process
may explain certain more recent changes, such as the raising of
/ɛ/ to /ɪ/ in *pretty* /prɪti/, which was once pronounced /prɛti/.

In older English, and especially in proto-Germanic and proto-
West Germanic, the "i-umlaut" (an umlaut change due to an
/i/ or /y/) is very common, largely because of the use of /y/
as a common derivational suffix, having causative and other functions. As we have said, this suffix usually disappeared, but it left
a mark in the changed vowel. We see the effects of this preserved
in NE *drink* and *drench,* where the second verb was originally

---

[8] Sometimes the part of speech shift has been obscured by later developments. *Shoot* was originally only a verb and *shot* a noun, but *shoot* is now
also used as a noun. For some IE ablaut series in Germanic and OE, see
Appendix.

a causative verb. *Drench*<proto-Germanic **draŋkyan* ("to cause to drink"), the causative of **driŋkan* ("to drink").[9] I-umlaut has also operated in the past to produce distinctions between parts of speech, as in *whole* : *heal* and *drop* : *drip*. In NE, it no longer operates to produce new words.

As we have seen, i-umlaut phonemic distinctions in English resulted from the disappearance of older suffixes. Suffixation is still widely used in many languages to shift parts of speech by derivation.[1] Suffix derivation in NE is still quite productive of new words, although certain particular suffixes have lost their productivity. Derivation was also used in OE. We have for instance from OE times a series of adjective-verb parallels in such a set as *black* : *blacken*, *white* : *whiten*, *straight* : *straighten*, and so forth. Adverbs in OE were made by various endings, one of which was *-lice*, the ancestor of our *like*. This ending later developed into *-ly*, which we still use generally to make adverbs out of adjectives.[2] Abstract nouns are formed from other adjective and noun endings, such as *-hood*, *-ness*, *-ship*, *-dom*, etc., some of which are no longer very productive. Today our most productive bound lexical morpheme for forming abstract nouns is *-ness*. We have words like *cleverness*, *goodness*, *closeness*, *uneasiness*, *consciousness* and neologisms like *up-to-dateness*. We make "agent" nouns with suffixes such as *-er*; e.g., *greaser*, *eater*, *climber*, *fixer*, and so forth. We have feminizing suffixes, the most popular today perhaps being *-ette* as in *drum-majorette*, *usherette*, *Rockette*. Older ones, which are fossil suffixes (no longer productively used), include *-ster*, as in *spinster*,[3] *-ess*, as in *abbess*, *Jewess*, and *-trix*, as in *executrix*.

---

[9] The variation between [a] and [i] is due, incidentally, to ablaut.

[1] See above Chapter IV, p. 148. The adding of prefixes is also called *derivation*; on this see below. Derivation can be thought of as the creation of new words by adding a bound morpheme—usually a prefix or suffix—to a word already in the language.

[2] We also have some adjectives ending in *-ly*, e.g., *gentlemanly* from *gentleman* and *goodly* from *good*, also created by suffix derivation.

[3] The suffix *-ster* is still active as an agent ending as in *punster*, *oldster*, *trickster*, etc. It lost its feminizing force quite early—as early as the ME period—especially in the North.

A popular method today of making verbs out of adjectives and nouns is the use of *-ize,* as in *personalize, memorize, characterize.* English does not have many **diminutives,** i.e., suffixes which indicate smallness or irreverence, either of affection or of scorn. The suffix *-ling,* as in *gosling,* and *-let,* as in *piglet,* indicates the sense of smallness in diminutives, probably their oldest function. Adjectives are frequently made out of nouns by adding a *-y,* as in *mossy, rosy,* but *-y* or *-ie* (two spellings representing the same phoneme and morpheme) is also used as a diminutive as in proper names like *Johnny, Tommy,* or in common nouns like *commie.* English is, however, not rich in diminutives, as is Russian or Italian. A suffix of originally Greek origin, *-ism,* has in recent years, because of its frequent use in designating political movements of our times, become a word in its own right. The suffix *-ist* is related to it and is used to create adjectives out of certain nouns. Adding *-ic* to *-ist* in some words gives a particular twist to an adjective, something like "tending toward." To say "He is communistic" is not the same as saying "He is a communist." The suffix *-ish* had a recent vogue in making up adjectives. We even find humorous adjectives or nouns like *eightish,* in a sentence like "I'll be over at eightish."

Although the number of suffixes in English seems rather fixed, as compared with the apparently unlimited number of words, new suffixes continue to come into the language, even though slowly. It is instructive to look at two recent developments: the newly productive *-type* and *-wise.*

-type is now widely used in popular speech in phrases like "executive-type man," "interesting-type movie," or "wall-type telephone." Here a noun is becoming a suffix under our very eyes. It is true that prestigeful speakers of English have not yet adopted this suffix widely in writing, and it is still not considered "good" usage by everyone. Even if it is never fully accepted by prestigeful speakers, it will have left its impact on the language. With adjectives, *-type* seems to add either a classifying or a modificatory element to the noun it goes with. In "an interesting movie," the semantic stress is on the quality of the particular

movie. In "an interesting-type movie," the semantic stress is on placing this particular movie among the whole class of interesting movies. Or it may mean that the movie is not completely interesting but only partially so. The whole phrase probably arose from the elision of *of* in phrases like "an interesting type of movie," the *of* being spoken in a reduced form as [ə].

With a noun, the development is even more interesting. If we say "a wall telephone" we cannot modify *wall* with *very* or *more*, as we normally can with adjectives, whereas we may say "a more wall-type telephone." *-type* here has become a suffix which may make an adjective out of a noun.

-wise is another example of a new suffix, or rather a revival of a noun which was used as a suffix in older English. This word, which appears in its older form in words like *likewise, edgewise,* was often confused with *-ways*. In its modern revival, however, it usually has the meaning of "from the point of view of" or "in respect to" as in "Propaganda-wise, it is a good move." The construction functions as a kind of adverb. The older use could also make an adverb out of a noun or adjective, but in a somewhat different sense—"in the manner of" as in "crab-wise" or "ship-wise."

Another kind of word creation has already been referred to: **back formation.** In this process a new stem is created by cutting off what is taken to be an affix from an existing word, on the analogy of other pairs of words; the new stem may appear with other affixes. Consider the word *domination* mentioned above. On the analogy of existing pairs like *relate* : *relation* or *donate* : *donation,* a verb *dominate* was formed to fit into the pattern. Even when exact analogies do not exist, we may create a shortened form of a word for a different grammatical function. *Enthuse* from *enthusiasm* provides such an example. One is usually unaware that these parallel forms are back formations, unless he happens to know or to discover from a historical dictionary like the *NED* which form was historically prior.

Words ending in the singular with *-s* are sometimes turned into plurals, and an *s*-less form is created for the singular. We got our *cherry* this way from the Old French singular *cérise* and *pea* from OE singular *pise*. We also hear substandard forms like *Chinee* and *Portugee* for individual Chinese or Portuguese.

Back formation, then, involves the extraction of a stem from what is taken to be a sequence of morphemes. The reverse of the process is **affixal derivation**. If, for instance, *dominate* had come into English before *domination,* then *domination* might have been formed by adding the suffix *-(t)ion*. Here are some more examples of back formation: *reminisce* from *reminiscence; grovel* from *groveling* (an old adverb), *peddle* from *pedlar.* Often back formation is used for humorous purposes, as for instance *reluct* from *reluctance* or *to hamburg* from *hamburger.*[4]

By far the most common method of extending a word into another part of speech in English is known as **conversion** or **functional shift**. This method provides English speakers and writers with a rich source of new words: almost the whole vocabulary of English itself. In most Western languages, different grammatical functions are indicated by different affixes. French verbs in the infinitive form have the suffixes, *-er, -ir,* or *-re.* German infinitives end in *-en.* English infinitives have no characteristic ending at all. *Play,* for instance, can be either a verb or a noun; only its particular role in a sentence determines which it is. The same is true of most parts of speech. There is no affix form which universally differentiates one part of speech from another. Conversion may be due to the loss of endings in the ME period, which we discussed above in Chapter V.[5] Because of this lack of distinctive endings, it was easy to shift words from one grammatical function to another.

---

[4] For further examples and some discussion of back formation, see O. Jespersen, "A Few Back-Formations," *Englische Studien* LXX (1935), 117–22.

[5] Hans Marchand, in his excellent book, *The Categories and Types of Present-Day English Word-Formation, A Synchronic-Diachronic Approach* (Wiesbaden: Otto Harrassowitz; 1960), 295 ff., denies that the loss of inflection gave rise to conversion (which Marchand calls "derivation by a zero morpheme"). His opinion seems too categorical, although the loss of inflections is perhaps not the only factor involved.

Whatever the explanation, it is certainly true that speakers of English shift words with great freedom from one part of speech to another, without making any formal changes except those attached to them by virtue of their new roles. (We may legitimately add an inflectional *-ed* to a noun functionally shifted to a verb.) When a formal change is made, as, for instance, the adding of *-en* to make a verb out of an adjective, we do not call this conversion but affixal derivation. We have in English two verbs *black* and *blacken*. The first is an example of conversion; the second is not. Broad use of conversion began in English in the early ME period, at roughly the same time the endings began to disappear,[6] and we have used it extensively ever since.

In English much functional shifting continues to take place, even though it occasionally arouses protests[7] and occasionally makes for ambiguity. English poets make good use of this freedom. Here are some characteristic examples from Shakespeare: "The hearts that *spaniel'd* me at heels" (*Anthony* 4. 12. 21); "To hear my nothings *monster'd*" (*Coriolanus* 2. 2. 81); "*stranger'd* with our oath" (*Lear* 1. 1. 207); "I'll . . . *blanket* my loins: *elf* all hair in knots" (*Lear* 2. 3. 10); "I shall see Some squeaking Cleopatra *boy* my greatness" (*Anthony* 5. 2. 220); "With news the time's with labour, and *throes* forth Each minute some," (*Anthony* 3. 7. 81); "I'll *devil-porter* it no further" (*Macbeth* 2. 3. 18).[8] Given our willingness to accept various kinds of

---

[6] For a study of early conversion in English, see Donald W. Lee: *Functional Change in Early English,* A Dissertation . . . in the Faculty of Philosophy, Columbia University (Menasha: George Banta Publishing Co.; 1948), and Evelyn Konkol: *Die Konversion im Frühneuenglischen in der Zeit von etwa 1580 bis 1600, Ein Beitrag zur Erforschung der sprachlichen Neuprägungen Der Kyd, Marlowe, Peele, Greene, Spenser und Nashe,* Inaugural-Dissertation . . . der Universität Köln. (Privately printed: Cologne; 1960).

[7] There has been so much conversion in English, and it still continues to such an extent, that it is curious that certain functional shifts, like that of *contact* from noun to verb, should have been so much objected to. However, by now, *contact* as a verb seems to be established. *Loan* as a verb has also met such selective resistance.

[8] We have taken these examples from the excellent article by Bogislav von Lindheim, "Syntaktische Functionsverschiebung als Mittel des barocken

conversion in English, especially in poetry, we are tempted when reading the lines from Archibald MacLeish's poem "You, Andrew Marvell," "To feel the always coming on The always rising of the night,"[9] to take "always" (normally an adverb) as a converted noun until the word "of" reveals that it suggests a converted adjective.

Some shifts are more common than others, of course, but conversion in general is widespread in both speech and poetry. Many of these shifts become accepted in standard usage. As in back formation, one has to know something of the history of the language to recognize what has been shifted in many accepted older conversions. Such knowledge is necessary to know that *plow* (verb) is an ME conversion of *plow* (noun) and that *pay* (noun) is an ME conversion of *pay* (verb). We also have a number of abbreviated adjective-noun phrases in NE in which the noun is lost, such as *private* from *private soldier,* which deceptively look like simple conversions.

There are limitations on functional shift in NE in spite of its wide range of applicability. Adjectives in NE, for instance, are generally shifted directly only into abstract or plural nouns. As nouns, *the good,* does not mean, for example, *the good man* but ordinarily only good people in general or *good* as a philosophical attribute, and *the grotesque* usually means the *quality of grotesqueness.* The enclitic *one* must be used if we wish to indicate a particular person, as in *the handsome one is over there.* Another kind of limitation operates on words which already have similar forms in another part of speech. For instance, we have the pair: *temptation* (noun) and *tempt* (verb). We would not shift *temptation* to a verb. We do not say: "I will *temptation* him," except as a jocular threat (with emphasis on *him*). The substandard shift of *suspicion* (noun) to a verb, when we

---

Stils bei Shakespeare," *Jahrbuch der deutschen Shakespeare-Gesellschaft* XC (1954), 229–51.

[9] By permission of the publisher, Houghton Mifflin Company (Boston: Massachusetts; 1952) from *The Collected Poems of Archibald MacLeish* by Archibald MacLeish.

already have the verb *suspect*, is curious. Here the difference in form may explain the conversion: many speakers of English do not associate *suspect* with *suspicion*.

Another method of deriving new nouns and verbs may be seen in the accent shift which remains in a number of verb-noun parallel words in NE, all with a prefix. The accent on the second syllable is characteristic of the verb in these parallel words and no doubt goes back to an OE accent pattern. In OE there are different accent rules for prefixed verbs and for prefixed nouns. The verbs always have an accent on a root syllable. Many of these parallels are of French origin, but most of them came into the language when accent rules like those of OE still prevailed. In most such words the verb is the older form, and when it was shifted to a noun the accent also shifted forward. This may be seen in the following pairs: *prótest* (noun) — *protést* (verb); *réfuse* (noun) — *refúse* (verb); *pérfume* (noun) — *perfúme* (verb); *óbject* (noun) — *objéct* (verb). Sometimes a change in meaning followed, as may be seen in *réfuse* and *óbject*. The method is still occasionally productive, as in the recent *prétest* (noun) — *pretést* (verb).

New words are also created in English by prefixing. Here the modification does not shift grammatical function. We have a large list of prefixes which, added to various roots, indicate various modifications of existing root meanings—repetition, negativity, originality, interrelationship, opposition, heightening, falsity, and so forth. Jespersen lists a number of prefixes in English which operate in various ways.[1] Most are of Latin or Greek origin, and while some are no longer productive, many of them are still used to form immediately acceptable new words. Here is his list: *Up, in, an, a, n, no, non, un, dis, de, mis, mal, anti, contra, counter, gain, with,* and *ex* (these indicate negativity or related notions); *for, pro, super, sur, hyper, a, epi, in (il, im, ir), en (em), intra, intro, by, circum, peri, inter, cis, trans, preter, extra, ultra, through*

---

[1] See *A Modern English Grammar on Historical Principles*, Part VI (London and Copenhagen: George Allen & Unwin Ltd. and Ejnar Munksgaard; 1954 Reprint), 464 ff.

(or *thorough*), *sub, hypo, infra, fore, pre, ante, post, mid, co-, syn, meta, para, be, ana, re, retro, demi, semi, hemi, uni (un), mono (mon), bi, poly, pan, panto, proto, neo, palaeo (paleo), pseudo, auto, vice,* and *arch* (*archi*). The mere list suggests vast possibilities of word creation, and Jespersen has not by any means included all English prefixes: think of *micro* and *tri* for instance.

We have already discussed the derivational process of compounding in Chapter IV in connection with the morphology of OE. However, a little more needs to be said with emphasis on NE. Every word in English has a certain **valence**, a capacity for combining with other words to form sentence units. Every grammatical class has its own valence rules. We can ordinarily combine an adjective with a noun as in *a blue towel* but not a noun with an adjective (we cannot say *a towel blue*). In compounds, however, the constituent units lose the valences they have outside the compound. We cannot ordinarily say *the apple tall tree* but must say *the tall apple-tree,* nor can we say *an eating apple-tree* although *tall tree* and *eating apple* are both perfectly respectable combinations in English. The constituents of a compound lose the grammatical power they have when uncombined. *-tree* in *apple-tree* does not have the grammatical characteristics of *tree,* but *apple-tree* as a whole has.

Compounds also have distinctive accent and juncture patterns. Sequences of words are separated by disjuncture, symbolized in our phonemic transcription by a space, while constituents of a compound are connected by a juncture, symbolized by a hyphen. In compounds one of the elements loses its accent. *Long Ísland* /lɔŋ-áyland/ is an example of a compound in which the first element has lost its accent. *Wátchmaker* /wáč-mekər/ is an example of a compound in which the second element has lost its accent. Except in fast speech all compounds, then, have a phonological juncture, but not all junctures indicate compounds: *dilate* and *motto* may have junctures between their syllables, but they are not compounds. This phonological characteristic is of much help in identifying ambiguous phrases as compounds or word sequences. A *dóctor's óffice* /dáktərz-ɔfəs/ is a compound, whereas a *dóctor's óffice* /dáktərz ɔ́fəs/ is not.

It should be noted that orthographic habits are not dependable in determining compounds, for some are written as one word, some are hyphenated, and some are spelled as separate words.

These two principles of valence and phonological structure enable us to identify compounds in English with some degree of security, but a classification of types of compounds on other bases is also of value in understanding this phenomenon of the English vocabulary. In the past there have been attempts to classify compounds by semantic criteria and by the parts of speech involved. Sometimes, but less frequently, syntactic criteria have been used, but until very recently not with great consistency.

Certain types of compounds reflect an old type of IE word formation, for we find similar compounds in many IE languages. The Sanskrit grammarians, many centuries ago, skillfully devised a plan of classification of the compounds in their language. They used both semantic and syntactic criteria. *Apple-tree* is a compound in which, they said, the first word modifies or limits the second word. Another (and in English, less common) type of compound consists of elements of equal rank like the NE *producer-director.*[2]

In more modern times other semantic (sometimes partially syntactic as well) criteria, such as "action-actor," "action-goal," and so forth have been used. But there are many differences of opinion as to the semantic categories, and none of them seem to avoid ambiguities and alternate possibilities.

The second method—identifying the parts of speech involved —has also been used in modern times. Compounds in English are made up of various parts of speech and the resultant word

---

[2] This type of compound, although probably used in proto-IE, is very rare in the older stages of English but has become very common in NE. For a study of this type, called copulative in English, see Anna Granville Hatcher: *Modern English Word-Formation and Neo-Latin, A Study of the Origins of English (French, Italian, German) Copulative Compounds* (Baltimore: The Johns Hopkins Press; 1951).

may be yet another part of speech. A *get-together,* for instance, is made up of a verb and adverb, and the resultant compound is a noun. We may join together nouns, as in *apple-tree,* or adjectives with nouns, as in *bluebell,* adverbs with nouns, as in *upbeat,* verbs and nouns, as in *scofflaw* and *spoilsport,* and verbs and adverbs, as in *knowhow* or *breakup,* to take a few possible combinations.

However, this kind of classification is also unsatisfactory. It does not allow for the different relational meanings which arise from the combining of the same parts of speech. It does not account for the ambiguity of a compound like *fire-screen,* which may be either something that screens a fire or a screen made of fire. It would put together compounds such as *apple-tree* "a tree which bears apples" and *producer-director* "a man who is both a producer and a director."

A more promising approach, though not free of problems, has recently been attempted by Robert B. Lees, who takes a thoroughgoing syntactic approach. He regards compounds as reduced sentences or as transforms of complete sentences. He classifies nominal compounds into nine types: a transform subject-predicate, as *girl friend* (reduced from a sentence like "This girl is a friend"); a transform subject-middle object,[3] as *arrowhead* (reduced from a sentence like "The arrow has a head"); a transform subject-verb, as *talking machine* (reduced from a sentence like "The machine talks"); a transform subject-object, as *steamboat* (reduced from a sentence like "The boat makes steam"); a transform verb-object, as *pickpocket* (reduced from a sentence like "He picks pockets"); a transform subject-preposition object, as *garden party* (reduced from a sentence like "The party is in the garden"); a transform verb-prepositional object, as *grindstone* (reduced from a sentence like "John grinds knives on a stone"); a transform object-prepositional object, as *wood alcohol* (reduced from a sentence like "They make alcohol from

[3] A middle object is the object of a verb which cannot be transformed into an ordinary passive sentence. "The arrow has a head" cannot in English be made into a passive sentence of the type, "The head is had by the arrow." See above, Chapter VI, p. 252.

wood"); and finally proper nouns like "Marshall Plan," of which
there is no all-embracing sentence source.[4]

Compounds need not be limited to the joining of two words.
Sometimes we find what Jespersen calls string compounds,
which consist of more than two words, as for instance a *house-to-house call* or a *cat-and-dog fight.*

In English we also have what may be called **separable compounds** made up of a verb and another part of speech, frequently
an adverb or preposition. There are many of these in the colloquial language. A speaker of colloquial English may say *ascend*
or *mount* but prefers *climb up* or *get up;* may say *endure* but
prefers *stand up to;* may say *surrender* but prefers *give in.*
Those which are separable compounds must be sharply distinguished from verb + prepositional phrase. The *get on* in *He
got on it* is not the same as *He got it on.* In the latter case we
have a genuine separable compound, as the position of *it* shows.
In most separable compounds the valence limitation on the
verb (if it is transitive, as here) is shown by the fact that the
it (or any suitable pronoun) may not follow *on* or whatever
completing word follows. In separable compounds, juncture
cannot of course be used as a test. Valence is a more helpful
test. It is sometimes suggested that the possibility of the substitution of a single verb for the verb + completing word is
the test of whether the group is a genuine compound. But as
we may see from the examples above, this test will not work
well; *mount* may be substituted for *He got on it,* but there is
no single verb substitute for the separable compound in *He
got it on.*

The range of these separable compounds can be illustrated
from the many combinations possible with a common verb like
get. Think of *get in, get out, get under, get up, get down, get
over, get through, get across, get along, get even with, get off,
get round, get ahead, get about, get at, get away, get back, get
by, get down to, get nowhere, get on, get to,* and *get together.*
Some of these separable compounds have been made into regular

---

[4] *The Grammar of English Nominalizations,* International Journal of
American Linguistics, Part II of XXVI (1960).

compounds and functionally shifted to nouns, as *get-up, get-away* show.

There are also **pseudo-compounds** in English, often of a playful type, like *chit-chat, zig-zag, knick-knack, hanky-panky, hurdy-gurdy,* which make use of rime or alliteration or even vowel gradation of a sort. Their accentual pattern and juncture make them sound like compounds, but they are pseudo-compounds because their elements are ordinarily not free morphemes. In this book we will treat them as reduplicated words (see p. 347).

As was pointed out in Chapter II, many compounds lose their juncture after a while. They are then recognized as former compounds only by scholars. *Daisy* (day's eye) and *holiday* (holy day), and many proper names like *Johnson* (John's son) or *Cambridge* (bridge over the Cam river), are good examples. These words can be regarded as compounds only from an historical point of view. Synchronically regarded, they are no longer compounds.

English poets have always been great compounders, as well as converters, of words, especially to form epithets which give a freshness, immediacy, and force to their language. Here are some from a very great compounder—Gerard Manley Hopkins: *wanwood, mind-wandering, weed-winding, after-comers, couple-colour, fresh-fire coal, chestnut-falls, wind-beat whitebeam, flake-doves, piece-bright, wimpled-water-dimpled, not-by-morning-matched, girlgrace, dare-gale, fresh-bound, gold-vermilion, beam-blind.*[5]

The term **root creation** covers a great variety of methods which have in common the creation of a new root to form a new word. Such a root may be called a "coined word." A few are created out of nothing, although they generally fit into ordinary English phonemic and morphemic patterns. *Blurb, nylon,* and *kodak* are examples of this method.

---

[5] On the whole subject, see Bernard Groom: *The Formation and Use of Compound Epithets in English Poetry from 1579.* S. P. E. Tract No. XLIX (Oxford: Clarendon Press; 1937).

Onomatopoeia is the term given to root creation when the attempt seems to be made to imitate in a word some natural sound. On close inspection, very few turn out to be genuinely onomatopoeic. *Meow* and *hiss* seem to be reasonably close to the natural sounds they reproduce, but many so-called onomatopoeic words only vaguely suggest the noises to which they seem to refer. Often the association is made only after the word has been created. Some words may have been originally more onomatopoeic than they now are, but like other words in English have since undergone sound changes. Because of our erroneous conviction that our words are truly related to what they refer to, we may find ourselves discovering onomatopoeia everywhere. The sound of *charm* actually may seem to indicate 'charm,' and so on.[6]

There is a conventional element in so-called onomatopoeic words which must be understood. A rooster really does not say *cock-a-doodle-doo*, but we may regard this word as an attempt, however poorly executed, to reproduce its sounds, and we may therefore call the word onomatopoeic in a loose sense. There does seem to be an attempt in many so-called onomatopoeic words to reproduce, if not the sounds, at least the repetitive quality or the sheer noisiness of certain natural sounds. Continuousness of sounds may be indicated in some languages by repetition or length or even by continuant sounds. Interruptions may be indicated by stops which interrupt the flow of air in the oral cavities (e.g., *rat-a-tat*) or loud resonant sounds by resonants.

Reduplicated words which make use of rime or other repetitions of sound are another group of root creations. These words sometimes suggest intimacy and affection and partially make up for our lack of diminutives. *Fuddy-duddy, ding-dong, goody-goody, boogie-woogie, teeny-weeny, hocus-pocus, willy-nilly,*

---

[6] The difficulty of separating a sound from that which is signified by it is well illustrated in negative fashion by the story of the Frenchman who thought the most beautiful word in English was *cellar door*. It is impossible to think of an English speaker choosing this word if asked what the most beautiful word in English was.

super-duper are examples. The type *cancer-schmancer* has recently been borrowed from Yiddish and has had some vogue. Most of these words are not appropriate to formal varieties of English.[7]

Somewhat similar to this method of reduplication is the formation of words around semantically suggestive sound sequences. For instance, at the beginning of words, /kl/ may suggest some attention-drawing noise, as is attested in English by a number of words suggesting such noises: *clack, clatter, clap, clash, click, clang, clank, clamor.* New words employing this initial sound combination may easily be made up and perhaps even accepted by other English speakers.[8] For example, imagine meanings for *clurg, clish, cleaky, clarf. Fl,* which denotes rapid movement, seems to be a constant element in words in English like *flee, flicker, flow, flutter, fling, flit,* and so forth. Final symbolic sounds can also be found in a large number of words in English. *-ash* is one persuasive example, as we may see in *dash, flash, pash, crash, bash, gash,* and so forth. In all this, however, it must be pointed out that these sound sequences are not consistent in their suggestivity: *-ook* might suggest a curve in *crook* and *hook,* but hardly in *book.* In the initial sound clusters above, the formal unifying principle is alliteration; in the final sound clusters the formal unifying principle is rime. The use of suggestive sound sequences to form new words is still productive in English, as may be seen in the recent words *squirch, snook,* and *clutterfly,* although these also illustrate other word formation processes.[9]

---

[7] For a list of these in English, see Henry B. Wheatley: *A Dictionary of Reduplicated Words in the English Language,* Appendix to the *Transactions of the Philological Society* for 1865 (London, 1866).

[8] Whether /kl/ and similar suggestive sounds should properly be regarded as morphemes has been seriously debated by linguists. Since for describing the grammar of English there seems to be no particular advantage gained to treat them as such, we do not recognize morphemic status for them here.

[9] See, for example, Morton W. Bloomfield, "Final Root-Forming Morphemes in English," *American Speech* XXVIII (1953), 158–64, Dwight L. Bolinger, "Rime, Assonance, and Morpheme Analysis," *Word* VI (1950),

Blends or **portmanteau words** are another type of root creation which has some extension in English word creation. *Blending* is the making of a new word by uniting of other words. *Smog* from *smoke* + *fog* and *brunch* from *breakfast* + *lunch* are two examples of the process. The most frequent uses of such blends are in comic and fanciful writing, and in commercial advertising writing. *Motel* from *motor* + *hotel,* initiated for its value in advertising, has by now become a perfectly serious word in American English. Lewis Carroll is especially associated with similar devices and has even left us a poem composed of many blends. Some of these strange words are, however, composed of semantically suggestive sounds rather than composed by uniting parts of separate words. The first verse of *Jabberwocky* runs:

> 'Twas brillig, and the slithy toves
> Did gyre and gimble in the wabe;
> All mimsy were the borogoves,
> And the mome raths outgrabe.

False splitting has also contributed to the formation of new words in English. What happens in such splitting is a false word division, following a loss of disjuncture. *Tawdry* for instance comes from *Saint Audrey* with the *t* getting attached to the Audrey. The word actually is a shortened form of *Saint Audrey's lace,* which referred to cheap cloth kerchiefs worn around the neck in the sixteenth century. *Nickname* preserves an initial *n* from *an;* its original form was *ickname* (ME, *ekename:* literally *also-name*). The *n* of *numpire* and that of *napron* was attached to the *a* of the indefinite article to make our *umpire* and *apron,* both examples of word splitting in the reverse direction. The Spanish word for orange *naranja* (taken from the Arabic) was falsely split in French after *une* 'a or one' to make the French *orange.* We borrowed the word after it was falsely divided by the French.

With the great increase in governmental, quasi-governmental, military, and international agencies in recent times, many new convenient names have been needed for them. The most popular methods are to designate them by a word made up of the initial letters (or sometimes several beginning letters) of a descriptive name or by a word made up of the *names* of these initial letters. These created words are called **acronyms**—words made up from the peaks or points of words (from Greek *acro-* 'peak' and *onyma-* 'name'). This process may be seen in words like *NATO* (*N*orth *A*tlantic *T*reaty *O*rganization), *UN* (*U*nited *N*ations), *WPA* (*W*orks *P*rojects *A*dministration—during the Roosevelt era). Sometimes the name is chosen first and a descriptive expression afterwards. *CARE*, an organization for feeding destitute people abroad, preceded its fuller name *C*o-operative for *A*merican *R*elief *E*verywhere. Commercial firms sometimes use acronyms for advertising purposes, as in *Nabisco* from National Biscuit Company.

New words are sometimes created by what is known as **folk etymology**. Learned foreign words are assimilated to English on the basis of some general resemblance to English words. *Place Pigalle* in Paris became to many *GI*'s in the last war *Pig-alley*. This method of rendering the unfamiliar familiar has operated on a number of words in the past. The elements which appear need not always make sense in NE, but they usually do have some associational resemblance to existing words. There is sometimes a problem in making the foreign word fit into the English phonemic pattern. The plethora of chickenburgers, chiliburgers, shrimpburgers, etc. in American eateries results directly from a folk-etymologizing of *ham-* out of *hamburger,* a beef concoction originally associated with the city of Hamburg, Germany, rather than with the hind meat of a pig. *Crayfish* is a folk-etymologizing of Old French *crévice* in the Middle English period. The *goose* of *mongoose* was suggested by the Indian *gus* of *mangus,* the Marathi word for this animal. Because of the association with church bell towers, Old French *berfrey* was reformed into English *belfry.*

A large number of words are created from proper nouns or

names. Often an invention or product is associated with the name of its creator. We have words like *pompadour, mackintosh, zeppelin, sandwich, silhouette* which are derived from the names of their inventors. Sometimes personal characteristics or activities are associated with particular people, and words formed from their names live on long after these people are dead, as for instance in *bowdlerize, mesmerize, lynch, boycott, McCarthyism, quisling.* Besides personal names, place names are sometimes used for a particular characteristic feature, such as *Canadian* in *canadian* bacon. *Champagne* was first used in France to indicate the wine of the district of Champagne, but soon the word stood by itself and was borrowed into English. The same is true of most other wines and liquors, such as *burgundy, moselle, bourbon, bordeaux, scotch, cologne* (the last alcoholic, though potable only at your own risk). *Damask* is ultimately from Damascus and *tweed* from the river Tweed. Literary characters sometimes give their names to types of people or activities—*shylock, pander.* The names of scientists have been and continue to be drawn on to designate scientific units or elements like *watt, ampere, ohm, einsteinium.* Proper names are in this way still a frequent source of new words.

Whether new or old, words in English are subject to a process known as **shortening** or **abbreviation,** by which polysyllabic words or phrases are reduced in length. Sometimes both words continue in the language with different meanings, as in the case of *cute* and *acute* or *sport* and *disport.* Sometimes both long and short forms are differentiated by degree of formality: a *professor* rarely refers to himself as *prof.* Swift and many others in the early eighteenth century objected to the word *mob* (from Latin *mōbile vulgus*), but it has since become a part of standard English. Hardly anyone speaks of *a zoological garden,* but *zoo* is very common. Sometimes we preserve one or two words from a phrase or formula and use it for the whole idea or document which it embodies or begins. We have words like *affidavit* (Latin: "he has made oath," used in legal documents when they were written in Latin); *quorum* (Latin: "of whom [plural]," from the wording of a document appointing someone to an official body); *habeas corpus* (Latin: "[that] you have the body," a phrase in a legal document requiring that a prisoner be brought before a court at a certain time and place to determine the legality of his detention); *dirge* (from *Dīrige*, the first word of a verse in the Psalms used in the Office for the Burial of the Dead)—all of which show this process. Cities are often known by clipped forms—*Frisco* for *San Francisco* or *Philly* for *Philadelphia*. These particular shortened forms often serve the same function as diminutives in other languages.

Shortening is a widespread phenomenon in English and is widely operative at present, especially in slang formations. The different types of shortenings have been analyzed in some detail by scholars.[1] The relation of stress to the part of the word retained has also been studied. For example, when they shorten words, children tend to preserve the stressed syllable, as in *fessor* for *professor,* while the shortened forms of adults, who are subject to the influence of the visual form of the word, do not generally maintain the stressed syllable.

We now turn to the second of the general ways by which languages enlarge their vocabularies—extending or changing the meanings of words already in the language. The analysis and classification of these changes is an important branch of **semantics,** which may be defined as the study of word meanings or, to put it in another way, of the uses of words in communication and related functions. Although some solid results have been attained, semantics is a subject which has not yet been definitively organized and developed. We know that ideas, superstitions, events, beliefs, the influence of certain individuals, historical accidents may all affect the meanings of words, but there are at present conflicting and mostly confusing theories of how to analyze these effects. The study of semantic changes takes us into the study of culture in its broadest sense and often tells us a great deal about the culture of past and present societies.

---

[1] See for instance the chapter in Marchand (footnote 5 on p. 338 above), 357 ff.

In studying the changing meanings of words, one must beware of the attitude to which we have frequently alluded in this book—the attitude towards words which regards them as naturally bound to their meanings. The widespread belief that by knowing the word or name of a thing or person or concept, we somehow magically control that thing, person, or concept, is closely related to this attitude and is part of a primitive legacy from the past which we may carry within us.

Words mean what human societies make them mean. This is a basic principle in the scientific study of word meanings. If all English speakers tomorrow interpreted *black* as 'white,' then *black* could only be properly used where *white* is now called for in utterances. It is a common error to think that each word has a "real" meaning and that change in word meanings is evidence of linguistic degeneration. The earliest meanings of words do not determine what the present meanings should be. The meaning of words today is determined by their present use, not by their former use. All words have ranges of meanings which change over periods of time, some to a greater and some to a lesser extent. Although *man* still means, as it did in OE, 'man,' its total range of meanings has changed; for example, one of the notions included in its earlier range has been taken over by the word *husband*. A word never exists in isolation in a language; it is always part of a field of related words. Words change in relation to their word-field as their meanings change or are modified. In the case of *man*, the range of meanings has shifted only slightly. On the other hand, the range of meanings of the OE *deor* 'animal' has narrowed considerably to NE *deer*. A deer could be called a *deor* in OE, but so could a lion or a tiger. In NE we may not ordinarily use *deer* to indicate a lion or a tiger; *animal* has taken over its function.

To take any other view is to fall into what has been called the **etymological fallacy**. What a word once meant in a foreign language, or in OE or in ME or in early NE, does not guarantee the "real" meaning of the word. The "real" meaning of a word is what the users of the language think it means. If we try to argue for some other principle by which words "have" meaning, we are forced into an impossible situation of inconsistency. If we insist, for instance, that *dilapidated* must only be used for stone structures because it contains the Latin word for *stone (lapis)* in it (as was done in the nineteenth century and even later), then there is no reason why most of our words should not be objected to. *Meat*, for instance, meant 'food' in ME— even as late as the sixteenth century. The same logic which insists on *dilapidated* being limited to stone constructions should also insist on *meat* as the class to which tomatoes and asparagus belong. People who object to shifts in meaning on "purist" grounds are curiously selective. Words borrowed from foreign languages seem to be peculiarly subject to purist attention. Here too the sensible attitude to take is that once a word enters another language it becomes part of the new language and undergoes whatever changes fate or fortune creates for it.

One way of looking at changes in word meaning is to think of every use of language as a kind of creative act, in which we are making an unconscious decision to apply words having general, potential ranges of meanings to a particular situation. There are thousands of men with whom one comes in contact, and the word *man* becomes in each particular case applied to a different one (or sometimes to a whole class) each time the speaker decides to use it. In an appropriate context one may praise a boy by calling him a "man," or may insult a woman by calling her "mannish."

Many more complicated situations arise with less universally accepted usages. Shall one say "between you and I" or "between you and me?" The decision depends on the effect one wishes to make. If a person wishes to be accepted in certain circles, he may use one rather than the other. A particular usage does not get or have a status assigned to it by some remote "authority" or by some hypostatized "rule of grammar"; rather it *has* the status that the users of the language themselves assign to it. The particular usages one adopts are determined by a wide variety of factors. Since we wish to imitate certain speakers and make certain effects at certain times, we use certain words rather than others. The continual requirement that we select words in particular situations from the store of potentialities offered by the language makes it inevitable that words will change their ranges of meanings. If we hear speakers use certain words in new contexts and wish to emulate them, we will also use such words as they do. Or we may ourselves employ new meanings for old words and may or may not be imitated by others. As new meanings lose their deliberate quality and become automatic or "natural," they may be said to become part of the language system itself.

The purist fear that shifts in meaning bring about irreparable losses in useful semantic distinctions is groundless. The speakers of a living language develop all the words they need, for if they need them the words will be brought into the language in one way or another. If a distinction such as that held until recently between *disinterested* and *uninterested* breaks down, no irreparable harm has been done. If speakers need the distinction here, they will maintain it by using other words in the language, such as *impartial* and *indifferent*. If a distinction disappears and is ever needed again, the requirement may be met by reviving old words, by using synonyms, or by developing new words. *Gaggle*, for instance, is an old word that designated a flock of geese at a time when speakers had use for a special word for a group of geese. It is now occasionally used in a transferred sense for gabbing women, and it could be revived (or another word used) if we ever went back to tending geese. Distinctions in words are continually being lost. Language, like nature, can afford to be a prodigal wastrel.

The way in which particular applications of a word become generalized and incorporated into the language system should be looked at a little more closely. Sometimes the range of meaning of a word comes to be restricted by the accident of prevalent circumstances to one set of its potential applications. For example, we can imagine a situation in which there were many small men; the word *man*, because of the smallness of the men, could easily come to be thought of as applying only to small men, and this application might become generalized.

We may see the process at work in the history of a word already referred to, *meat*, which in ME had the central meaning of 'food.'[2] The range of meanings of *meat* included the flesh of animals, just as *man* can mean a small or a large man. Perhaps a sudden increase in meat eating led to a heavy use of this word in this sense. In any case, *meat* lost its general meaning of 'food,' and became confined to the flesh of animals, driving out the older word *flesh*. A new general word was needed, and *food* was supplied. Changes in the range of meanings of a word often move in this fashion, although the older central meaning is not always lost. *Meat* may eventually refer only, say, to 'steak' if the same process goes on.

Another kind of semantic development may result from the repeated deliberate application of a word for its figurative associations. We may see this development in *buxom*, which originally meant "yielding." It was metaphorically used of the flesh of females, and eventually this semantic component was extended to its present range in NE. This second process—deliberate metaphoric association—may also be illustrated by the word *meat*. By metaphorical extension, *meat* can also mean the heart or center or important part of anything, given meat as the central part of a meal. We may say, for instance, that his report has no *meat* in it, a statement which means that his report lacks a central force or importance. But this meaning has not driven out the earlier meaning. When the nonfigurative meaning of *meat* was 'food,' it could also be used metaphorically, as when Richard Rolle in the fourteenth century spoke of sin as being the "devil's meat."

Another good example of a shift in meaning by metaphoric association may be seen in the word *fret*, which in ME referred primarily to (voracious) eating by animals, as its cognate in German *fressen* still does. In NE, however, in the core vocabulary, it exists only in the sense of "worry," and probably arose from the idea that worry eats into one. Around 1200, Orm wrote, "Hat lufe towarrd Godess hus me frettethth att min herrte" (Hot love towards the house of God torments me [eats] at my heart). We still say,

---

[2] The description of the process here is somewhat indebted to L. Bloomfield: *Language* (New York: Henry Holt and Company; 1933), 425 ff. Bloomfield's description is based in part on Hermann Paul's work.

"What's eating you?" *Hleor* meant 'cheek' in OE; from the historical point of view its modern descendant *leer* has only a figurative meaning.

Extension of meaning is the acquiring of a new meaning of a word without the loss of the old one. Shift of meaning is the acquiring of a new meaning of a word which replaces the old one, as with *buxom* or *fret*.

Metaphor and association are of the essence of the use of words, and lead in many cases, but not always, to extensions and shifts of meaning in the language. To analyze these metaphoric and associative forces has been one of the purposes of much semantic analysis in the past. The factors involved are so many and so often associated with particular historic and social contexts that such analysis is a task of the greatest complexity. The remainder of this section will be devoted to a brief discussion of some of these factors, without any attempt to present a definitive analysis.

Analogy of some sort is at the basis of many changes in word meaning. The thinking part of man is contained in his head; therefore we may use *head* to represent the thinking part of an organization, as in the *head* of the business. The similarity between the function of the human hand and the pointers on a clock led to the word *hand* being extended to the pointers.

Emphasis is another force which makes for change of meaning. Words to express strong approval or disapproval are often chosen because they are striking, but after constant repetition they stop striking, and stronger words are sought. In Shakespeare's time words like *amazing* and *terrific* were very strong. Today they often indicate no more than mild surprise or approval.

Words may leap into favor or fall into desuetude because of extra-linguistic changes in a society. *Broadcast* was a rather specialized word as a verb in 1910, but by 1960 it had become very active, all owing to its application to radio and television uses.

Chance phonetic similarities may play an important role in word histories. Older English had two words which in their NE forms are *queen* and *quean*, the latter meaning "harlot." They were phonemically distinct until the seventeenth or eighteenth century, the former being pronounced /kwin/, the latter /kwen/, in the sixteenth century. Some speakers may even have pronounced both alike. The similarity or identity in sound of two words which embarrassingly clashed in meaning probably led to the virtual disappearance of one. *Quean* had synonyms whereas *queen* did not,[3] and hence the former disappeared.

Other factors also make for change in meanings and use of words. One of them is the persistence of prescientific linguistic attitudes, many based on word magic. **Euphemism** and **word-taboo** are terms used to describe the desire to avoid certain words because of a feeling that they may either cause something unpleasant to come about or may indicate a disrespect towards the objects or persons named.[4] The effect of these feelings may be seen in all natural languages. In English we tend to avoid the direct words for certain physiological functions and activities, and to substitute milder words or periphrastic locutions for them. These substitute words are in turn frequently felt to be too strong, and new substitutes come into the language. The name for the "lavatory," for instance—itself a euphemism—, continually changes. In English we have had in the past few centuries words like *jakes, privy, water-closet, W.C., toilet, bathroom, men's* (or *women's*) *room*, and so forth. Because of the euphemism *sexual intercourse*, a respectable general word *intercourse* is now used with caution in polite conversation. Words like *death* and *cancer* are frequently avoided. The Greeks called the *Furies*, whose task it was to carry out vengeance for unpunished crimes, the kindly ones (*Eumenides*), in order to placate them. The rate of rejection of certain words is so great that it is actually difficult to find the original meanings of certain words in a language. Practically all

---

[3] On these words, see Edna Rees Williams: *The Conflict of Homonyms in English*, Yale Studies in English 100 (New Haven: Yale University Press; 1944), 83–9. This book gives other examples of the conflict of homonyms in English.

[4] For a good discussion of this attitude towards words and of various psychological attitudes which affect word meanings and use, see Robert M. Estrich and Hans Sperber: *Three Keys to Language* (New York: Rinehart & Company, Inc.; 1952).

the "four-letter words" in English which we think of as the "real" words for certain taboo activities are only euphemisms themselves, as the comparative method shows. The proto-IE roots in most cases reveal the older meanings of these words from which we can infer their original euphemistic employment.

Words undergo changes in popularity, and euphemism and word-taboo help us explain the decline of certain words as well as the increase in popularity of others. Humor, word-play, puns, and simple faddishness are other forces which tend to increase or decrease the popularity of words.

Words frequently get strong emotional associations or charges, and are consequently changed in their use and meaning. These changes are due to various psychological and cultural factors. The study of the changes in word meaning and popularity leads us into the subconscious and into old, perhaps forgotten, cultural conflicts.

It is usual to distinguish several kinds of changes in meaning, not necessarily mutually exclusive. Narrowing or specialization is the limiting of the range of meanings of a word. *Meat* provides one good example. *Hound* was once the word for any kind of dog. *Town* originally referred to any 'enclosed place,' but now refers to a kind of 'city.' An *undertaker* once meant a man who for pay might undertake anything for someone else. Now it is limited to undertaking funerals. It is possible that the pun in this word for undertaking funerals led to its great popularity and hence to its taboo association with other uses. ME *dress* had a broader meaning than its present descendant. Widening or generalization is the opposite process. *To land,* for instance, was originally applied only to travel in ships; now it is used for airplane travel as well. *Dog* once referred to a particular type of dog.

Degeneration or **pejoration** is the process whereby words come to be limited to designate unpleasant or disapproved things or notions.[5] For instance, *silly* in its OE form meant 'blessed' or 'happy.' *Cunning* originally meant 'knowledge' as a noun or 'knowl-

---

[5] On pejoration in English, see Hindrik Schreuder, *Pejorative Sense Development in English I,* Academisch Proefschrift . . . aan de Universiteit van Amsterdam . . . 1929. . . . (Groningen: P. Noordhoff; 1929).

edgeable' as an adjective. *Peculiar* originally meant 'of one's own' or 'special'; now it usually has a pejorative sense. **Elevation** or **amelioration** is the opposite process.[6] In OE *cniht* meant 'boy' or 'servant,' but by the ME period it had been elevated to its present meaning 'knight.' *Lord* and *heaven* have been elevated because of their religious uses. *Luxury* originally meant 'lewdness,' but was elevated into designating feelings of pleasure in general and finally to what created such feelings. It has now completely lost its exclusive association with sex. It is easier to find examples of pejoration than amelioration in English, but both processes have been and still are at work.

Various other types of classification of word changes are used. Various kinds of mental association affect the passage of words from one meaning to another. OE *ceace* meant 'jaw'; now the meaning is 'cheek.' Here we have an example of **metonymy**, in which meaning is transferred from something to something else near it in space. **Synecdoche**, another type of association, occurs when the part stands for the whole, as when we say, "He is fifty *winters* old."

Words have diverse fates and undergo very dynamic and curious transformations. They may extend or shift not only their meanings but also their level of usage. Some old slang words become respectable, like *mob;* some never do and yet remain in the language for years, like *bones* for 'dice' and *booze* for 'liquor.' Some literary words become colloquial; other colloquial words become literary or archaic. *Divan* affords an example of a word which, if we take it throughout its history in various languages, has undergone extensive and curious changes. Originally a Persian word meaning a 'brochure,' it took on the meanings of a 'collection of poems,' a 'register,' a 'military pay-book,' an 'account-book,' 'a room where an account-book was kept,' an 'account office' or 'customs-house,' a 'court' or 'council of state' (with which meaning it appeared in written English in 1586); then it acquired

---

[6] Studied in English by Gerrit Albertus van Dongen in *Amelioratives in English* I, Academisch Proefschrift . . . aan de Universiteit van Amsterdam . . . 1933. . . . (Rotterdam: T. De Vries Dz.; 1933).

the sense of a 'hall' (in English in 1597), and finally the chief piece of furniture in such a hall.

Nouns, adjectives, and verbs—members of large lexical classes —seem to be subject to more change than pronouns or conjunctions—members of small lexical classes. And the various English dialects do not always show the same changes. *Fall* for 'autumn' was a popular English word in the seventeenth century. It is still popular in American English, whereas it has fallen into disuse in England, although it is generally known there because of its frequency in written American English. Words may develop and hold special meanings in only one dialect of a language, whether regional or social. *Case* (verb) has a special meaning in gangster jargon, which it does not have, at least as yet, in other dialects of English.

Perhaps the most striking way of adding to vocabulary is by borrowing words from foreign languages. English is particularly rich in borrowed words, and its speakers since the Norman Conquest have been ready to accept them. Usually, outside of the speech of bilingual speakers, these foreign words become adapted to the English phonemic pattern and become indistinguishable from other words. As we have previously discussed, an English word or phrase modeled on a foreign word or phrase is called a *calque*. In estimating the influence of foreign languages on English, we must count not only the borrowed words, but also the **calques** and **semi-calques** which we owe to the foreign language. Semi-*calques* or phrasal *calques* (such as 'cut short' based on the French *couper court* or 'in vain' based on the French *en vain*) are actually more common than *calques*, of which the OE *godspel* 'good teachings' (NE *gospel*) from Greek εὐαγγέλιον 'good teachings' and OE *lȳtelmōd* 'small mind' (in NE literally 'little mood'), from late Latin *pusillanimis* 'tiny mind' are good examples (the latter has not survived as a compound in NE).

As we have said earlier, the degree of penetration into the English vocabulary must be considered in evaluating the influence of foreign languages on the English vocabulary. Some foreign words remain part of a specialized vocabulary. A botanist must use a large number of Latin words to designate species and genera of plants. These words are "in English," but only in particular dialects. Italian musical terms which have a wider circulation than botanical Latin terms, because music is more popular than botany, are also in English in a special way. Most of them are not in the core of the English vocabulary. Other foreign words on the periphery of English designate foreign objects which are rarely seen or used in English-speaking lands, such as *mosque, hookah, junk* (Chinese boat), and so forth. Then there are learned or literary words known only to educated speakers of English, such as *raison d'être, Weltanschauung, quid pro quo.* Such words, many of which are of Latin or French origin, may be used rather frequently in certain contexts—mainly writing and formal speeches—but less often in everyday speech. And finally, there is the central core of ordinary English words which all normal speakers of English use and understand.

Remember that in the core vocabulary the number of words inherited from OE is higher than it is in most of the specialized vocabularies. An exception is the specialized vocabulary of farming, which because of antiquity may contain an especially high proportion of OE words. But words, as we have already said, may change their position within the over-all vocabulary. Sometimes former core words, like *foe* or *cast* (in the sense of "throw"), become learned or literary. Sometimes words move from the periphery into the core. *Vodka* has become a core word with the sudden rise of popularity of this drink in the past few years. *Broadcast*, as mentioned above, is another good recent example, but there are many more, older ones, including almost all the originally French and Latin and Old Norse words of the present core vocabulary.

Sometimes words which are literary in one part of the English-speaking world are part of the core in others. A number of borrowed Spanish words are in everyday use in the southwest of the United States, whereas in other parts of the United States they are learned or literary. All speakers of English use different varieties of language in different situations, and many words belong to more than one dialect.

In languages with various standard varieties, what may be called **interdialectal borrowing** frequently takes place. In recent years, British English has borrowed extensively from American English. This process goes back to the seventeenth century, when new objects or institutions discovered in America, mainly those of the American Indians, were named in America and the terms exported to England. As years went on the flow of words continued, and by no means all of them designated objects foreign to the British. The impact of American technology and culture on Great Britain, Australia, New Zealand, Canada, and South Africa, not to speak of non-English countries, has been great in recent years, and this impact has led to extensive word borrowing.

The movement has of course not all been one-way, for throughout the eighteenth and nineteenth centuries British words and pronunciations were being borrowed by American speakers. The flow to America has not ceased, but it is now less strong than the movement the other way. The influence of American English on British English has alarmed Britishers, especially those who are linguistically naïve.[7]

Words are sometimes borrowed from the archaic vocabulary of the same language. *Weskit* is a good example in recent English. In some languages there is much borrowing from older archaic forms of the same language or of a closely related one. Modern Hebrew and Hindi provide many examples.

Words are often borrowed from a secondary rather than from the source language. *Potato* of American Indian origin came into English from Spanish. *Chocolate* of similar origin came from French which borrowed it from Spanish. Oriental words have come through French (*orange* and *sugar*), Italian (*algebra*), and even Latin (*lapis lazuli*). Many of our Latin and Greek words have come into English through French. In fact, most of the American Indian, Persian, and Arabic words, and a fair number

---

[7] For a good study of very recent American influence on British English, see Brian Foster, "Recent American Influence on Standard English," *Anglia* LXXIII (1955–56), 328–60. See also Gustav Kirchner, "Recent American Influence on Standard English: The Syntactical Sphere," *Zeitschrift für Anglistik und Amerikanistik* V (1957), 29–42.

of classical words in English are not direct borrowings but are **secondary borrowings**. Many of these words are **international words,** that is, words found (in various forms) in many languages.

Sometimes the same word is borrowed twice in two different forms, called **doublets** (if borrowed thrice **triplets**). *Zero* and *cipher* are doublets from the Arabic *sifr. Chase* and *catch* are doublets, one borrowed from the Ile-de-France type of French, the other from Norman French.

Areas of knowledge like science, which are actively moving and changing, require many new words. These are frequently made up from Greek and Latin morphemes and ordinarily do not enter the core vocabulary unless there is some particular development which makes the scientific use popular. The vocabulary of atomic physics was not known to the general public until the explosion of the atom bomb. Not all new words in science are made up from borrowed roots; all the other devices of word formation are also available and are also used. New inventions which reach the people bring new words in their trail. Television brought into English many new words and added new meanings to old words like *channel.* Rocketry has a vogue at present, moving to the English core vocabulary items like *blast off, nose cone, missile, orbit,* and *satellite.*

It must not be thought that language speakers necessarily borrow foreign words either because their own language lacks a suitable word or because their own language could not create or extend a suitable word out of its own resources. The causes of word-borrowing are complex and are not fully understood as yet. We may conjecture that prestige, tradition, and historical accident all enter into the process. By studying borrowing carefully and in the context of the recipient language, we may understand the reasons for certain individual borrowings.[8] It is important in the

---

[8] For a recent study of ME word-borrowings in the field of religion, which takes cognizance of their lexical and cultural context especially in the recipient language, see Hans Käsmann: *Studien zum kirchlichen Wortschatz des Mittelenglischen 1100–1350, Ein Beitrag zum Problem der Sprachmischung.* Buchreihe der Anglia, Zeitschrift für englische Philologie 9 (Tübingen: Max Niemeyer Verlag; 1961).

"borrowing" situation not merely to concentrate on the donor language as has so far largely been the procedure, but also to study the relevant circumstances, if they can be re-created, in the recipient language. Empiric studies in word-borrowing which take the whole situation into consideration are badly needed. Although we do have some information to go on, it may be some time before adequate generalizations about word-borrowing can be made.

There is no point in listing a large sample of the enormous number of borrowed words in English. There are good general books on the subject[9] and any number of special monographs. Any good dictionary will provide etymologies of English words. It is enough for our purposes here to know that French, Latin, and Old Norse have been the major donor languages to the English vocabulary, and that Italian, Spanish, Greek, German, Dutch, Celtic (Irish, Gælic, and Welsh), Hebrew, and Arabic have also made important contributions to the English vocabulary. To these, and to a number of other languages with which speakers of English have had close contact, English owes a vocabulary which is cosmopolitan and varied, affording us units in which we can express ourselves exactly and vigorously.

QUESTIONS

1. Show how *diamond* and *adamant, grammar* and *glamour* are doublets. Show how *inch, ounce,* and *uncial* are a triplet.
2. To what parts of the English vocabulary do the following words belong? That is, are they specialized, learned, core, foreign, or names for foreign objects? Some may be in several categories. Are any in different categories in different localities or social groups? *Bamboo, tulip, pogrom, care, leotard, cybernetics, sulphuric acid, salami, beat, sheik, paradise, alkali, fortissimo, cigar, matador, mesa, encyclopedia, naïveté, banal.*

---

[9] See, for instance, Mary S. Serjeantson: *A History of Foreign Words in English* (New York: E. P. Dutton & Company; 1936), and J. A. Sheard: *The Words We Use* (London: André Deutsch; 1954).

3. Show how the ME word *dress* has been narrowed in meaning.

4. How would you classify the type of word creation seen in the underlined word in the sentence, "They're *fabricious*," used in an advertisement for fabrics in *The Manchester Guardian Weekly* of May 24, 1956, p. 16. What are its elements? What type is seen in the underlined word in the sentence, "If you do *magazine* it, I would rather be paid per month, like other contributors"—Richard D. Blackmore in a letter to his publisher on February 8, 1865, quoted in *Nineteenth-Century Fiction*, X (1955), p. 181. What chances do you think these words have to get into the English core vocabulary?

5. Show how folk etymology operated in the form of the word *mushroom*. Can you think of a possible semantic reason for the first element?

6. Show how euphemism has operated in the history of the following words: *idiot, enceinte, unmentionables, gosh darn, insane.*

7. Try to discover the facts about the following back formations from the *NED: burgle, greed, difficult, suckle.*

8. Comment on the following statement: "Every word is born with a meaning; its determination is precise; it is the symbol of a definite idea . . ." Ralcy Husted Bell: *The Changing Values of English Speech* (New York: 1909) 123.

9. What kind of transformation in meaning has taken place in the word *edify?*

10. Etymologically considered, *mortician* (connected with the French word *mort* meaning 'death') is less euphemistic than *undertaker.* Yet *mortician* widely replaced the latter. How do you account for this? Why is *funeral director* widely used today for *mortician?*

11. Take a longish scene from one of Shakespeare's plays and list the compound epithets he uses.

12. Using whatever etymological information you can find, show the connection in each of the following pairs of words: *blood* and *bless; tidy* and *tide; wealth* and *well.* Show how phonetic assimilation and i-umlaut have operated in the case of *bless.*

13. Look up the meaning of the following processes in a dictionary: *aphesis* and *apocope.* Show how one or the other of these two processes has operated in the history of the following words: *cheat, lunge, miss* (unmarried female), *photo, spite, cab, venture, chap* (fellow), *spend.*

14. What is the difference between extensions and shifts of meaning? Give some examples other than those used in this chapter to illustrate both processes.

Appendix

THE EVOLUTION OF THE ROOT VOWELS
IN THE FIRST SIX CLASSES
OF OE STRONG VERBS*
(The seventh, and last, class is a composite.)

(IE ablaut series)

(OE STRONG VERB CLASSES)

Root Vowels	Infinitive	Preterite Singular	Preterite Plural	Past Participle†	
IE e/o/—/—+ i:	bīdan[1] (to stay)	bād[2]	bidon	biden	I
IE e/o/—/—+ u:	bēodan[3] (to command)	bēad[4]	budon[5]	boden[5]	II
IE e/o/—/—+—:	bindan[6] (to bind)	band[8, 6] (bond)	bundon[7, 5]	bunden[7, 5]	III
IE e/o/ē/—+—:	beran (to bear)	bær[8, 9]	bǣron[10]	boren[7]	IV
IE e/o/ē/e + —:	metan (to measure)	mæt[8, 9]	mǣton[10]	meten	V
IE o/ō/ō/o + —:	faran[8] (to go)	fōr	fōron	faren[8, 11] (færen)	VI

and various other ablaut series of IE involving ǎ, which fell together with this series in Germanic (see 8, 12 below)

(The first class may be distinguished by a root vowel i, which [with the ablauting vowel] forms the second element of a diphthong; the

* This scheme has been worked out by Professor H. M. Smyser of Connecticut College to whom we are much indebted.

† These four forms of the strong verb are known as the **principal parts** of the strong verb; if we know these we may deduce all the other forms of the verb by paradigms.

second class by a similar root vowel u; the third, by liquid or nasal + consonant; the fourth by a single liquid or nasal; the fifth by a single consonant other than liquid or nasal. But this description is useful only to a degree.)

NOTES

[1] IE ei > OE ī.

[2] IE oi > Pr. Gmc. ai > OE ā. (Pr. Gmc = Proto-Germanic)

[3] IE eu > OE ēo.

[4] IE ou > Pr. Gmc. au (cf. 8, below) > OE ēa.

[5] IE u > OE o except when followed by i, j, or u in the next syllable or immediately by a nasal; the vowel of the pret. pl. ending was originally -u- (not -o-); hence the root -u- of *budon* is retained.

[6] IE e before a nasal + consonant > i in Pr. Gmc.; a + nasal often becomes o in OE.

[7] IE vocalic ṇ (*bṇd-) > un in Pr. Gmc.; IE vocalic ṛ > or in OE.

[8] IE o > Pr. Gmc. a.

[9] Pr. OE a > æ except when followed in a next syllable by a, o, or u (this rule is proximate).

[10] IE ē > OE (West Saxon) ǣ.

[11] Though the original pa. ppl. ending was -an, this -an had become -en before the raising described in 9, above. *Færen* is thus the original form of the OE pa. ppl.; the a of the form *faren* is due to analogy with the infinitive.

[12] IE ā > Gmc. ō.

See for more details on the evolution of these vowels, E. Prokosch, *A Comparative Germanic Grammar* (Philadelphia: Linguistic Society of America; 1939), 164 ff.

Selective Bibliography

This list of books is confined to those written or available in English which can serve as supplementary readings to the text. It is not a complete listing of books and articles used in the preparation of this book nor does it aim at a complete listing of useful supplementary reading for the student. It merely serves to help students to explore the various aspects of the subject of language and of the history of English in more detail than is provided in this book. Some of the items listed, especially in the more general groupings, contain useful material for more than one classification.

LANGUAGE IN GENERAL

Bloch, Bernard and George L. Trager: *Outline of Linguistic Analysis*. Baltimore: The Linguistic Society of America; 1942.

Bloomfield, Leonard: *Language*. New York: Holt, Rinehart and Winston; 1933.

Brown, Roger William: *Words and Things*. Glencoe, Ill.: The Free Press; 1958.

Carroll, John Bissell: *The Study of Language: A Survey of Linguistics and Related Disciplines in America*. Cambridge, Mass.: Harvard University Press; 1953.

Gleason, Henry A: *Introduction to Descriptive Linguistics* revised ed. New York: Holt, Rinehart and Winston; 1961.

Graff, Willem L.: *Language and Languages: An Introduction to Linguistics*. New York and London: D. Appleton and Company; 1932.

Gray, Louis Herbert: *Foundations of Language*. New York: The Macmillan Co.; 1939.

Hamp, Eric P.: *A Glossary of American Technical Linguistic Usage*. Utrecht: Spectrum; 1958.

Hockett, Charles Francis: *A Course in Modern Linguistics*. New York: The Macmillan Co.; 1958.

Jespersen, Otto Harry: *Language: Its Nature, Development and Origin*. London: Allen and Unwin; 1922.

Potter, Simeon: *Modern Linguistics*. London: André Deutsch; 1957.

Sapir, Edward: *Language: An Introduction to the Study of Speech*. New York: Harcourt, Brace and World; 1921 (also in paperback: Harvest Books).

Saussure, Ferdinand de: *Course in General Linguistics,* trans. Wade
Baskin. New York: Philosophical Library; 1959.
Schlauch, Margaret: *The Gift of Language,* (earlier edition: *The
Gift of Tongues*). New York: Dover Publications; 1956.
Sturtevant, Edgar Howard: *An Introduction to Linguistic Science.*
New Haven, Conn.: Yale University Press; 1947 (also paper-
back: Yale University Press).
Whorf, Benjamin Lee: *Language, Thought, and Reality: Selected
Writings.* Cambridge, Mass.: Technology Press; 1956.

PHONETICS AND PHONEMICS: GENERAL AND ENGLISH

Heffner, Roe-Merrill Secrist: *General Phonetics.* Madison, Wis.: Uni-
versity of Wisconsin Press; 1949 (and later editions).
Hockett, Charles Francis: *A Manual of Phonology,* Indiana Uni-
versity Publications in Anthropology and Linguistics, Memoir
11. Bloomington, Indiana, 1955.
Jakobson, Roman and Morris Halle: *Fundamentals of Language.* The
Hague: Mouton; 1956.
Jones, Daniel: *An Outline of English Phonetics.* Sixth edition. New
York: E. P. Dutton; 1940.
────── *The Phoneme: Its Nature and Use.* Cambridge, England:
W. Heffer & Sons; 1950.
Joos, Martin: *Acoustic Phonetics.* Language Monographs no. 23.
Baltimore: The Linguistic Society of America; 1948.
Kenyon, John Samuel: *American Pronunciation: A Textbook of
Phonetics for Students of English.* Eighth edition. Ann Arbor,
Mich.: George Wahr Publishing Co.; 1940.
Kurath, Hans and Raven I. McDavid, Jr.: *The Pronunciation of
English in the Atlantic States.* Ann Arbor, Mich.: University
of Michigan Press; 1961.
Pike, Kenneth Lee: *Phonetics: A Critical Analysis of Phonetic Theory
and a Technic for the Practical Description of Sounds.* Ann
Arbor, Mich.: University of Michigan Press; 1943.
────── *Phonemics: A Technique for Reducing Languages to Writing.*
Ann Arbor, Mich.: University of Michigan Press; 1947.
Thomas, Charles Kenneth: *An Introduction to the Phonetics of Ameri-
can English.* Second edition. New York: Ronald Press; 1958.
Ward, Ida Caroline: *The Phonetics of English.* Fourth edition. Cam-
bridge, England: W. Heffer & Sons; 1945.

HISTORY OF ENGLISH

Baugh, Albert Croll: *A History of the English Language.* Second edition. New York: Appleton-Century-Crofts; 1957.

371 *Selective Bibliography*

Bradley, Henry: *The Making of English.* New York: The Macmillan
Co.; 1904, (reissued 1951).
Brook, G. L.: *A History of the English Language.* London: André
Deutsch; 1958.
Bryant, Margaret M.: *Modern English and Its Heritage.* Second Edi-
tion. New York: The Macmillan Co.; 1962.
Jespersen, Otto Harry: *Growth and Structure of the English Language.*
Ninth edition. Oxford: Basil Blackwell; 1948 (also in paper-
back: Anchor Books).
Marckwardt, Albert H.: *American English.* New York: Oxford Uni-
versity Press; 1958.
——— *Introduction to the English Language.* New York: Oxford
University Press; 1942.
Potter, Simeon: *Our Language.* Pelican Books A 227. Harmonds-
worth, England; 1950.
Robertson, Stuart: *The Development of Modern English.* Second
edition, revised by Frederic G. Cassidy. New York: Prentice-
Hall, Inc.; 1954.
Wrenn, C. L.: *The English Language.* London: Methuen & Co., Ltd.;
1949.

STRUCTURE OF ENGLISH

Curme, G. O.: *A Grammar of the English Language,* Vols. II and
III (Parts of Speech, Accidence [II] and Syntax [III]). Bos-
ton: D. C. Heath and Company; 1931–35.
Francis, Winthrop Nelson: *The Structure of American English.* New
York: Ronald Press; 1958.
Fries, Charles Carpenter: *American English Grammar.* New York:
Appleton-Century-Crofts; 1940.
——— *The Structure of English: An Introduction to the Construc-
tion of English Sentences.* New York: Harcourt, Brace &
World; 1952.
Hill, Archibald A.: *Introduction to Linguistic Structures: From Sound
to Sentence in English.* New York: Harcourt, Brace & World;
1958.
Jespersen, Otto Harry: *A Modern English Grammar,* 7 vols. Heidel-
berg: Carl Winter; 1909–49.
——— *Essentials of English Grammar.* New York: Holt, Rinehart
and Winston; 1933.
Kellner, Leon: *Historical Outlines of English Syntax.* London: Macmillan and Co.; 1892 (reprinted 1924).
Kruisinga, E.: *A Handbook of Present-Day English.* Fifth edition, 3
vols. Groningen: P. Noordhoff; 1931.

Moore, Samuel: *Historical Outlines of English Sounds and Inflections.* Revised by A. H. Marckwardt. Ann Arbor, Mich.: George Wahr Publishing Co.; 1951.

Nida, Eugene A.: *A Synopsis of English Syntax.* Norman, Okla.: Summer Institute of Linguistics; 1960.

Onions, C. T.: *An Advanced English Syntax.* Third edition. London: Kegan Paul, Trench, Trubner & Co., Ltd.; 1911.

Poutsma, H.: *A Grammar of Late Modern English,* 5 vols. Groningen: P. Noordhoff; 1904–29.

Roberts, Paul: *English Sentences.* New York: Harcourt, Brace & World; 1962.

Sledd, James: *A Short Introduction to English Grammar.* Chicago: Scott, Foresman; 1959.

Sweet, Henry: *A New English Grammar: Logical and Historical,* 2 vols. Oxford: Clarendon Press; 1891–98.

Trager, George L. and Henry Lee Smith, Jr.: *An Outline of English Structure.* Studies in Linguistics, Occasional Papers 3. 1951. Reprinted, Washington, D.C.: American Council of Learned Societies; 1957.

Zandvoort, Reinard W.: *A Handbook of English Grammar.* London: Longmans, Green; 1957.

COMPARATIVE LINGUISTICS

Collitz, Hermann: "A Century of Grimm's Law," *Language* II (1926), 174–83.

Hudson-Williams, T.: *A Short Introduction to the Study of Comparative Grammar (Indo-European).* Cardiff: The University of Wales Press Board; 1935.

Pedersen, Holger: *Linguistic Science in the Nineteenth Century,* trans. John Webster Spargo. Cambridge, Mass.: Harvard University Press; 1931.

Prokosch, Eduard: *A Comparative Germanic Grammar.* Philadelphia: Linguistic Society of America; 1939.

MORPHOLOGY AND SYNTAX

Chomsky, Noam: *Syntactic Structures.* The Hague: Mouton; 1957.

Elson, Benjamin and Velma B. Pickett: *Beginning Morphology-Syntax.* Santa Ana, Calif.: Summer Institute of Linguistics; 1960.

Harris, Zellig Sabbetai: *Methods in Structural Linguistics.* Chicago: University of Chicago Press; 1951.

Lees, Robert B.: *The Grammar of English Nominalizations.* Bloomington, Ind.: Research Center in Anthropology, Folklore and Linguistics. *International Journal of American Linguistics*, Part II of XXVI (1960).

Nida, Eugene A.: *Morphology: The Descriptive Analysis of Words.* Second edition. Ann Arbor, Mich.: University of Michigan Press; 1949.

DIALECTS, ENGLISH DIALECTS AND LANGUAGE CONTACT

Craigie, William A. and others: *The Scottish Tongue: A Series of Lectures on the Vernacular Language of Lowland Scotland . . .* London: Casswell & Company, Ltd.; 1924.

Dieth, Eugene: "A Survey of English Dialects," *Essays and Studies* XXXII (1947), 74–104.

Haugen, Einar: *Bilingualism in the Americas: A Bibliography and Research Guide,* Publications of the American Dialect Society 26. University, Alabama, 1956.

Kurath, Hans: "Linguistic Regionalism," Chapter X of *Regionalism in America,* ed. Merrill Jenson. Madison: University of Wisconsin Press; 1952.

—— *A Handbook of the Linguistic Geography of New England* (Linguistic Atlas of New England Vol. I). Providence, R. I.: Brown University Press; 1939.

McDavid, Raven I. and Virginia G. McDavid: "Regional Linguistic Atlases in the United States," *Orbis* V (1956), 349–86.

McIntosh, Angus: *An Introduction to a Survey of Scottish Dialects.* Edinburgh: Thomas Nelson; 1952.

Matthews, William: *Cockney Past and Present: A Short History of the Dialect of London.* New York: E. P. Dutton & Co.; 1938.

Moore, Samuel, Sanford B. Meech, and Harold Whitehall: "Middle English Dialect Characteristics and Dialect Boundaries." *Essays and Studies in English and Comparative Literature,* University of Michigan Publication, Language and Literature XIII. Ann Arbor, Michigan: University of Michigan Press; 1935, 1–60.

Skeat, Walter W.: *English Dialects from the Eighth Century to the Present Day.* Cambridge, England: Cambridge University Press; 1912.

Weinrich, Uriel: *Languages in Contact: Findings and Problems.* New York: Linguistic Circle of New York; 1953.

OLD ENGLISH

Brook, G. L.: *An Introduction to Old English.* Manchester: University Press; 1955.

Campbell, A.: *Old English Grammar*. Oxford: Clarendon Press; 1959.
Elliott, Ralph W. V.: *Runes: An Introduction*. Manchester: University Press; 1959.
Quirk, Randolph and C. L. Wrenn: *An Old English Grammar*. London: Methuen & Co., Ltd.; 1955.
Wright, Joseph and Elizabeth Mary Wright: *Old English Grammar*, Third edition. London: Oxford University Press; 1925.

MIDDLE ENGLISH

Clark, John Williams: *Early English: A Study of Old and Middle English*. London: André Deutsch; 1957.
Dickins, Bruce and R. M. Wilson: "Characteristics of Early Middle English" in *Early Middle English Texts*, ed. Bruce Dickins and R. M. Wilson. New York: W. W. Norton & Co., Inc.; 1951.
Mossé, Fernand: *A Handbook of Middle English*, trans. James A. Walker. Baltimore: The Johns Hopkins Press; 1952.
Roseborough, Margaret M.: *An Outline of Middle English Grammar*. New York: The Macmillan Co.; 1938.
Sisam, Kenneth: "The English Language in the Fourteenth Century," Appendix to *Fourteenth Century Verse and Prose*, ed. Kenneth Sisam. Oxford: Clarendon Press; 1925.
Wardale, E. E.: *An Introduction to Middle English*. London: Kegan Paul, Trench, Trubner & Co., Ltd.; 1937.
Wright, Joseph and Elizabeth Mary Wright: *An Elementary Middle English Grammar*. London: Oxford University Press; 1932.

MODERN ENGLISH

Abbott, Edwin A.: *A Shakespearian Grammar* . . . New ed. London: Macmillan and Co.; 1881 (and later editions).
Dobson, Eric John: *English Pronunciation, 1500–1700*, 2 vols. Oxford: Clarendon Press; 1957.
Kökeritz, Helge: *Shakespeare's Pronunciation*. New Haven: Yale University Press; 1953.
McKnight, G. H., With the Assistance of Bert Emsley: *Modern English in the Making*. New York and London: D. Appleton-Century Co.; 1928.
Schlauch, Margaret: *The English Language in Modern Times (Since 1400)*. Warsaw: Pánstwowe Wydawnictwo Naukowe; 1959. (In America, Oxford University Press.)
Sugden, Herbert W.: *The Grammar of Spenser's Faerie Queene*. Language Dissertations, Supplement to *Language*, 22. Philadelphia: Linguistic Society of America; 1936.

Wyld, Henry Cecil: *A History of Modern Colloquial English.* Third edition. Oxford: Basil Blackwell; 1936.

WORDS AND SEMANTICS

Bréal, Michel: *Semantics: Studies in the Science of Meaning,* trans. Mrs. Henry Cust. London: W. Heinemann; 1900.

Greenough, James Bradstreet and George Lyman Kittredge: *Words and their Ways in English Speech.* London: Macmillan and Co., Ltd.; 1902.

Ogden, Charles K. and I. A. Richards: *The Meaning of Meaning.* Third edition. New York: Harcourt, Brace and World; 1930.

Serjeantson, Mary S.: *A History of Foreign Words in English.* London: Kegan Paul, Trench, Trubner & Co., Ltd.; 1935, (reprinted, New York: Barnes and Noble; 1961).

Sheard, John A.: *The Words We Use.* London: André Deutsch; 1954.

Stern, Gustav: *Meaning and Change of Meaning, with Special Reference to the English Language.* (Göteborgs högskolas årsskrift XXXVIII). Göteburg: Elanders Boktryckeri Aktiebolag; 1931.

Ullmann, Stephen: *The Principles of Semantics,* Second edition. (Glasgow University Publications LXXXIV). Glasgow and Oxford: Glasgow University Press; 1957.

Index of Morphemes, Words, and Phrases

THE ITEMS are listed in this index when they are discussed or explained in some way, however slight in the text. When they are not so treated, they are in general omitted. Except for English, no chronological distinctions are made in the subtitles. Usually when ME items are spelled the same as in NE, they appear under NE. The order is alphabetical by word units under each sub-title. Oblique forms are only given when they are especially discussed in the text.

ENGLISH

NE

General Index

ablaut, 108, 334
abbreviation, 351-2
acronyms, 350
Addison, Joseph, 325
adjectives, Old English, 152, 157-60
affricates, 50, 53-4
affixal derivation, 338
affixes: defined, 146; inflectional, 148; derivational, 148; 167, 384
Afrikaans, 121
agreement, grammatical, 155
Albanian, 11, 90, 118, 125
allomorph, 144, 281
alphabet: defined, 30-1; origins, 34-5; Semitic, 35; Latin, 35; International Phonetic, 35, 49, 62
Altaic, 127
alveolar stop, 52
American College Dictionary, 321
American English: dialect, 184, 194-5, 349; effects on English, 363
American Indian, 363
analogy, 110
Anglo-Norman, 173-7
Anglo-Saxon, 94, 132, 133n, 137, 329
Anglian, 140, 142, 210
Angles, 134-6
"anthropological tradition," 147
apical nasal, 39
apical stop, 50
apico-dental stop, 52
Arabic, 103, 116, 363-4, 365
Arawakan, 310
Armenian, 116, 125
Art of Poesy, 305-6
articulation, points of, 49-50
artificial languages, 9
Aryan, 106n, 115
aspects, of Old English verbs, 166-7
assimilation, 57-8
aureate, 176
Austin, John, 18
Avestan, 116, 118

back formation, 337
Baltic, 116-17, 125

Balto-Slavic, 116-17, 124, 125, 126
Barnhart, Clarence L., *quoted,* 332-3
base, root, 146
Baugh, Albert Croll, 314
Beals, Ralph L., *quoted,* 3
Bede, 134-5, 136
Biographia Literaria, 312
bilabial nasal, 42
bilabial stop, 50
blends, 349
Bloomfield, Leonard, *quoted,* 105, 326
Bopp, Franz, 105
borrowing: in comparing languages, 93-7; after Norman Conquest, 178-80; interdialectical, 364; secondary, 364; international, 364; double, 364; triple, 364
Boswell, James, 317-18
bound-form, of morphemes, 146
Boxhorn, Marcus Zuerius, 103n
Breton, 119, 120
Bulgarian, 117
Burns, Robert, *quoted,* 193

cacuminal stop, 52
calques, 168-9, 175, 176n, 361
Canterbury, 142, 216
Carib, 310
Carr, Charles T., 168n, 169
Carroll, John, *quoted,* 13
Carroll, Lewis, *quoted,* 349
case: Old English nouns, 155-6; Old English adjectives, 159-60
Catalan, 98, 190-1, 196
Cawdry, William, 318
Caxton, William, *quoted,* 177, 230, 304-5
Celtic, 104, 119, 125, 126, 136, 139, 202, 365
central liquids, 44
centum languages, 118-21, 124
centum-satem, 121, 124, 126
Century Dictionary, 321
Chaucer, Geoffrey, 305, 331
Chesterfield, Lord, *quoted,* 292-3

A NOTE ON THE TYPE

THE TEXT of this book is set in CALEDONIA, a Linotype face designed by W. A. Dwiggins (1880–1956), the man responsible for so much that is good in contemporary book design and typography. Caledonia belongs to the family of printing types called "modern face" by printers—a term used to mark the change in style of type-letters that occurred about 1800. Caledonia borders on the general design of Scotch Modern but is more freely drawn than that letter.

Composed, printed, and bound by
The Haddon Craftsmen, Inc., Scranton, Pa.
Typography and binding design by
VINCENT TORRE